CONSERVATISM AMONG THE IROQUOIS
AT THE SIX NATIONS RESERVE

THE
Iroquois
AND THEIR
NEIGHBORS

LAURENCE M. HAUPTMAN, *Series Editor*

CONSERVATISM AMONG THE IROQUOIS AT THE SIX NATIONS RESERVE

••••••••••••

ANNEMARIE ANROD SHIMONY

SYRACUSE UNIVERSITY PRESS

Copyright © 1994 by Syracuse University Press, Syracuse, New York 13244-5160

Syracuse University Press Edition 1994

94 95 96 97 98 99   6 5 4 3 2 1

This book is published through arrangement with the Department of Anthropology, Yale University, and is a reprint of the Yale University Publications in Anthropology Number 65, 1961.

This book is published with the assistance of a grant from the John Ben Snow Foundation.

The paper used in this publication meets the minimum requirements of American National Standard for Information Sciences—Permanence of Paper for Printed Library Materials, ANSI Z39.48-1984. ∞™

Library of Congress Cataloging-in-Publication Data
Shimony, Annemarie Anrod.
    Conservatism among the Iroquois at the Six Nations Reserve /
Annemarie Anrod Shimony.
        p.   cm.—(The Iroquois and their neighbors)
    Includes bibliographical references (p.   ) and index.
    ISBN 0-8156-2630-4 (alk. paper)
    1. Iroquois Indians—Social life and customs.   2. Six Nations
Indian Reservations (Ont.)—Social life and customs.   I. Title.
II. Series.
E99.I7S53   1994
305.897′5—dc20   93-47512

Manufactured in the United States of America

Dedicated to the memory of Jennifer Chatfield, for her deep knowledge of the Iroquoian literature and her magnanimous assistance to scholars.

ANNEMARIE ANROD SHIMONY is professor of anthropology at Wellesley College, where she is also codirector of the Peace Studies Program. She has published many articles on the Iroquois and other anthropological topics.

CONTENTS

II. CONTENT OF THE ORTHODOX CULTURE

ILLUSTRATIONS

FIGURES

TABLES

PREFACE TO THE ORIGINAL EDITION

THIS monograph is a revision of a doctoral thesis submitted to the Department of Anthropology at Yale University in 1958. The thesis was based on field work done at Six Nations Reserve, Ohsweken, Ontario, in periods of three days to three months from the summer of 1953 to the spring of 1958. For the purpose of preparing this monograph I returned to Six Nations in the summer of 1960. My total residence on the Reserve was a little more than one year, and I was able to attend every ceremonial event in the agricultural calendar except the three-day Green Corn Ceremony. It was an advantage to be present for two winter seasons, for this allowed me to attend repeated performances of most of the curing rites, which occur mainly in winter (when the spirits of the dead cannot harm the crops).

My problem was to understand the means by which so much of Iroquois culture is preserved at Six Nations in spite of intense acculturative pressure. I found that the problem is quite complex, and in order to explain the mechanism of conservatism it was clearly necessary to give a rather comprehensive description of the structure of the society and the content of the culture. Nevertheless, this monograph is not intended to be a complete ethnography of the Iroquois at Six Nations Reserve. No systematic account is given of material culture or of economic organization, largely because these are the aspects of Iroquois life in which acculturation has proceeded farthest (though note is taken of some traditional traits in these areas of culture). There is little description of Iroquois linguistics, music, and dance, but I do not have the specialized training necessary to give these in detail. Social organization and curing rites are partially described, in sufficient detail for the purpose of the central problem, but by no means exhaustively. The recent political factionalism is discussed, and the dramatic outbreak of the revolution of March, 1959, should be understandable in terms of this discussion, but the course of the revolution itself deserves separate treatment.

The literature on the Iroquois is very rich, and I have learned much from Morgan, Hale, Parker, Beauchamp, Waugh, and Goldenweiser. However, I feel that the writings of Speck and Fenton gave me a personal introduction to Six Nations Reserve. I am very grateful to Professor Floyd Lounsbury for encouraging my research, suggesting lines of inquiry on social organization, and advising on matters of orthography. I wish to thank Dr. William N. Fenton and Dr. William C. Sturtevant for reading my thesis and making many valuable suggestions which have been incorporated into the monograph. My husband, Abner Shimony, patiently read the drafts of both the thesis and the monograph and improved the style and logic of both. My field work was a much pleasanter experience than it might have been because of the aid and hospitality of Mrs. Martha Randle. Most of all, I am grateful to my informants, who remained personally kind despite my obvious and persistent prying.

Finally, I wish to express my appreciation for the financial aid given me by the Department of Anthropology of Yale University for two seasons of field work, and a grant-in-aid-of-research from the Social Science Research Council.

Mount Holyoke College, 1961   ANNEMARIE ANROD SHIMONY

INTRODUCTION

APPROXIMATELY forty years have elapsed since the field work for the first edition of *Conservatism among the Iroquois at Six Nations Reserve* was begun. At that time the phenomenon which called for an explanation was the remarkable persistence of a traditional way of life by the Longhouse community at Six Nations.[1] Even at mid-century Canada considered Six Nations the most advanced and affluent native reserve, and many observers feared that total enfranchisement and Canadianization were just around the corner. This has not been the case, for the population has remained stable: a population that still frequents the Longhouse and believes in an ideology whose roots can be traced to reports of the earliest observers of Iroquoian culture. Consequently, an assessment is even more to the point at the end of the century than it was earlier. And, even as there was no simple explanation in the 1950s, there is none now.

In the 1950s I felt that an understanding of the viability of the conservative culture necessitated a rather descriptive inventory of the ideology and the behavior of the Longhouse community, which ultimately became the greater part of the monograph. I attempted to portray the structure and the content of the culture in as objective a manner as possible, relying to a great extent on the explanations of many of the hereditary chiefs and ritualists of that time, supplemented by my own observations at most of the Longhouse ceremonies and life cycle events.

Furthermore, I identified numerous mechanisms, on an individual level and on a collective level, which attempted to hold the membership to the orthodox standards. Preachers of the Code of Handsome Lake, expositors of the Great Law, hereditary chiefs, speakers at the Longhouse rituals, parents inculcating traditional teachings, fortunetellers instructing their clients, and herbalists curing with aboriginal knowledge were some of the most obvious individual agents of the conservative culture. But the social pressures toward mutual obligations and reciprocity also acted on a more systemic level to enforce a "take-it-or-leave-it-at-your-peril" threat. Not that these devices were entirely successful (see p. 291 *infra*), but they did at mid-century slow down acculturation for many of the participants.

Consequently, I postulated that, despite inroads from Western culture of both material and ideological kinds, there remained a conservative way of life which conveyed to the practitioner a natural consistency. Partly this coherence arose from the repetition of dominant themes reiterated in different contexts, and partly

I am grateful to Wellesley College, the National Endowment for Humanities, the Wenner Gren Foundation, and the Canadian National Museum for support of research. In particular, I wish to thank Dr. Michael Foster for his long-standing support of my Iroquoian endeavors.

[1] Unless otherwise specified, the term "Longhouse" will be used in the monograph to mean a functioning institution rather than a building.

the various contexts depended upon each other and thus reinforced the ideas and practices.

The dominant emotion of "being an Indian," regardless of acculturation or of the details of genealogy, the solidarity of the Longhouse Iroquois, which I called "collectiveness," the reciprocity and fulfillment of obligations within this group, the ordered and conventional hierarchy of peoples, offices, and forces in the universe, and a notion of the primacy of an independent mind which is clear and straight—these were the themes that seemed unifying in the Longhouse ethic.

As to the contexts which interlocked, it seemed reasonable to assert that the matrilineal clan organization, the prescriptions of the life cycle, the acceptance of the traditional peace chiefs, and the care concerning one's personal health depended upon a religious ideology and the practices disseminated within the Longhouse. To take just one example from the last domain, that of personal well-being, I argued that its routines of behavior are sanctioned by the belief in the spirit forces which render the activities efficacious, and a natural constituency within the Longhouse provides the personnel performing the required procedures.

On the other hand, I noted already in the 1950s that there existed—and it is even more pronounced today—a tolerance for inevitable changes and for substitution of traits. Naturally, each time such a modification occurs there is a sense of loss, but such losses are considered acceptable by the practitioners, since they are construed as aids in the preservation of more basic sanctions.

The critical question is, of course, how much can be substituted for, or even discarded, before the themes sound hollow and the institutions fail to support each other. What are the indispensable attributes without which the Longhouse way of life would vanish? Or, phrased differently, how much of Western culture can a Longhouse follower condone and emulate before traditional beliefs are so diluted as to engender anomie or finally passage into the white man's world.

Many devout Iroquois also pondered these questions and despaired about the survival of their traditional culture and, indeed, long ago, predicted its extinction. Already before 1912, Chief John Arthur Gibson, the Seneca Gaihwi'yo preacher and greatest ritualist in recent memory, is quoted (Goldenweiser, 1912: 692) as saying, "another generation and there will be no custom; still another generation and there will be no memory"; and Parker (1913: 5) reports that Chief Frank Logan, the Onondaga Gaihwi'yo preacher "watches the waning of his prophet's teachings with grave concern." Later, at mid-century, Chief Alexander General told me (see p. 123 *infra*), "when I am gone, and Joe Logan, and Dave Thomas (chiefs and ritualists and all now deceased), it (the hereditary council) will fold up, as the young people are not interested in old Indian ways but read comics." He felt that white civilization overwhelmed the Indian. Similarly, the followers of these concerned leaders offered predictions which were equally bleak, as Mrs. George Green's statement to me in 1953 (see p. 127 *infra*) clearly shows. "In twenty years there won't be any reserve; we'll be like white people."

Nor have the assessments by outside observers been very different, for few

anthropologists and administrators imagined that the native religion and its associated institutions would persist into the twenty-first century, given the many
conscious attempts by Canada to assimilate the Iroquois and the magnitude of
environmental changes since settlement on the Grand River.

Yet revisiting the Reserve today, one must be struck by the vitality of the four
Longhouses, the consistent attendance by an equal if not larger number of people,
and the persistence of the hereditary council of chiefs. Nor does there seem to be
an obvious diminution of the number of ritual events which are performed in order
to fulfill traditional obligations to the dead, to a medicine society, or to a charm in
the family, or for warding off and curing a physical or mental disease.

Not that it was ever possible to have hard statistics for any of these assertions,
but estimates by observers and by involved ritualists are remarkably concordant.
In the 1950s I calculated that there were approximately 1,300 to 1,400 members
out of a resident population of seven thousand, and Sally Weaver in 1978 stated
that the proportion of Longhouse members has fluctuated between 19 percent and
23 percent since 1865 (Weaver, 1978: 530). In 1992 the best estimate of knowledgeable Longhouse informants was that there might be one thousand adherents who
make the Longhouse their only religious loyalty, and probably four hundred more
who also attend the Longhouse, yet simultaneously profess some connection to
another religion as well. These are conservative figures. Since the official rolls of
the Reserve have recently been heavily augmented to sixteen thousand, to a great
extent by the addition of Bill C-31 returnees,[2] the percentage of Longhouse followers appears to have dropped dramatically. However, because only eight thousand
of these members actually lived on the Reserve in 1990 (the latest statistics available), the percentage of attenders has not diminished appreciably at the moment.
Of course, it remains to be seen whether a significant number of returnees will
also rejoin the Longhouse if they do actually take up primary residence on the
Reserve. Meanwhile, it should be noted that neither among the Longhouse nor the
Christian population is there an enthusiastic response to the readmittance of
women who had consciously given up their Indian status by marrying out, and
the Longhouse population points to Handsome Lake's supposed injunction against
marrying outside one's race.

To Longhouse attenders, on the other hand, the dominant impression is one of a
paucity of elders as they knew them, yet an increase in the number of youthful
members, creating the impression of greater attendance. Furthermore, almost
every Longhouse loyalist will assert that many Christian families are returning
to the Longhouse. That there is sentiment concerning the Longhouse religion, well
beyond any shown forty years ago, is indubitable, but that many Christian families have newly returned to the Longhouse other than for interest in their heritage

---

[2] These individuals were readmitted to band membership because of the provisions of the
amendments to the Canadian Indian Act, which permit women previously taken off the band rolls
because of marriage to a non-band member to return with their children.

is difficult to establish. When I inquired about the specific names of returning families, I elicited perhaps a single Mohawk family, and it is more reasonable to credit the observations of Longhouse adherents that a surprising number of young people participate in calendrical Longhouse events. As it was forty years ago, in my experience, the major events are very well attended, and the minor observances were then, and are now, more sparsely attended.

One factor explaining the number of youthful members may well be the realization that fluency in the indigenous languages, except for elders, is all but gone. Current parents, and adults in general, grew up at a time during which education on the Reserve and in the surrounding communities was strictly in English, and indeed many of the institutions made reversion to a native language a punishable offense. Adults today recount humiliating experiences at the Mohawk Institute, the Anglican boarding school, citing beatings and restrictions after speaking to each other in an Iroquoian language. As a consequence, by 1970 it was estimated that there were only seven hundred native speakers at all the Longhouses on the Reserve, which meant that half of the members in attendance were somewhat handicapped in their comprehension of the laws of the Confederacy and the teachings of Handsome Lake. Today, these members who were alienated from their native language and who must struggle to follow the Longhouse proceedings not only are ashamed but also do not wish their own offspring to suffer similarly. Thus, they are apt to urge attendance on their children from an early age, particularly since it is feared that the loss of understanding will inevitably herald a loss of culture, if not a disavowal of the religion. Perhaps to prevent just such an eventuality, there is currently at Six Nations a strong sentiment that English should not be spoken inside any Longhouse (see p. 132 *infra*), and even the most proficient preachers are criticized for setting a bad example if they transgress this rule. Nevertheless, the reality is most starkly demonstrated by the figures of the Sweetgrass First Nations Language Council, Inc., which were presented in June of 1992 to the Royal Commission on Aboriginal Peoples, in Toronto.

As Table 1 shows, there is already, at present, a functional total loss in the groups below forty, and Onondaga and Mohawk and even Cayuga are by the classification of the Office of the Commissioner of Official Languages, respectively *extremely endangered* and *quite endangered* on the Reserve (Foster, 1982: 8).

Of course, this compilation refers to *fluent* speakers, and it could be argued that these dire numbers slightly overstate the case because many of the fourteen hundred participants in the ceremonies still understand the gist of the observances and also speak, even if haltingly. There is no denying, however, that the current trend of language loss remains very distressing unless it is reversed.

Ominously, the community has already experienced painful demonstrations of the lack of linguistically competent speakers at both a funeral and a tenth day feast. Not long ago, a designated speaker for the bereaved moiety evidently was unable to be present, and after the clear-minded side had spoken, no one could respond for the bereaved. The head deaconess was forced to leave the ceremony

TABLE 1. FLUENT NATIVE SPEAKERS, SIX NATIONS RESERVE,
ONTARIO, CANADA, as of JUNE 24, 1992

| SIX NATIONS | AGE GROUPS | | | | | | |
	10–20	21–30	31–40	41–50	51–60	61–70	OVER
Cayuga	0	0	3	18	50	42	33
Mohawk	0	4	2	4	12	24	46
Onondaga	1	2	1	3	14	12	13
Seneca	0	0	0	0	0	0	1
Oneida	0	0	0	0	0	0	0
Tuscarora	0	0	0	0	0	0	0
Totals	1	6	6	25	76	78	93
% of Totals Reported	0.34	2.06	2.06	8.59	26.66	27.36	32.63

Source: Based on Sweetgrass First Nations Language Council Inc., presented to Royal Commission on Aboriginal Peoples, Toronto, June 1992.
Population at Six Nations as of Oct. 31, 1991: 16,443.
Number of fluent speakers at Six Nations: 285.
Percentage of population that is fluent: 1.73.

and telephone for a substitute, thus interrupting a service. The interruption was contrary to the prescription that once a funeral has left the house with a corpse, nothing may interrupt its progress because such an interruption signals another death in the family in the near future. Ritualists say that the clear-minded speaker should have been borrowed across the fire, a better solution than interruption; yet the message that funeral speeches must be taught to members of the congregation was very clear. Similarly, at a recent tenth day feast of a well respected elderly matron, a female was forced to substitute for the male officiant, since no male in attendance felt confident enough of his native language to announce the event. A change in sex roles would under any circumstances be notable, but because a death ritual is one so endowed with potentially serious consequences, the substitution caused much comment and the speaker involved felt uneasy.

Significant in both instances are two facts: the congregation did find an alternative in dealing with the crises, and the need and will for language training were reinforced. The first lesson is one already very evident in the 1950s, for a realistic flexibility concerning inevitable substitutions, given modern life, was exhibited over and over again. But the concerted effort at reintroducing native languages into the official school system is a newer development. As already mentioned, the generations now approaching parenthood and grandparenthood were taught in their youth at school to strive for English, and this emphasis held for the Longhouse as well as for Christian pupils. There was little prestige—on the contrary, there was disdain—for native speakers, and consequently these generations were discouraged from experiencing a pride in linguistic diversity. Even as late as the 1960s, fluency in a native language was not a cause for admiration, but rather an admission of a lack of sophistication in English. It was, therefore, a courageous action around 1970 that twelve Longhouse families petitioned the Christian Superintendent of Schools, J. C. Hill, to introduce the teaching of Iroquoian languages into the elementary system on the Reserve. Mr. Hill was sympathetic, and fifteen minutes of Cayuga were introduced into schools Number Eleven, Twelve, and Six (in the predominantly Longhouse "down below" area), and fifteen minutes of Mohawk into School Number One, at the upper end.

Today, primarily upon the initiative of the Longhouse population, that program has grown to a full-scale immersion language program at School Number Eleven for Cayuga and School Number One for Mohawk. In 1990, 156 children out of a total elementary school population of 1,042 were enrolled in the immersion program. Furthermore, there is now a coordinator for the Native Language Program and a Six Nations Language Research Center at School Number Five, which with the Woodland Cultural Center develop teaching materials. Classes, which currently include kindergarten through grade six, have eight to sixteen pupils, and this academic year twenty-four students are expected in the kindergarten at School Number Eleven. Since School Number Eleven includes the district closest to Lower Cayuga Longhouse, it is not surprising that it has the most developed program of native language instruction and the greatest number of students.

Six teachers, Alva Jamieson, Louise Hill, Frances Froman, Marge Henry, Geraldine Sandy, and Lottie Keye, are assisted by Janice Thomas and Jane Johnson at School Number Eleven; and Ima Johnson, Isabel Maracle, and Candy Squires teach Mohawk at School Number One. From all accounts the students compete fairly with non-bilinguals on an academic level, while parents and grandparents, placing much hope in these children to become future leaders of their culture and religion, are proud to be surpassed by their progeny.

The observed increase of younger attenders at the Longhouses is a promising sign, but whether the native languages can be saved from near extinction at so late a date as 1992 is questionable. Again, the Sweetgrass Council believes that only five to ten years remain "to curb this language loss" (1992: 3), but to expect a younger generation to revitalize a language when few mid-life adults use it in the home is optimistic.

Even though the classroom is not a sanctioned locus for proselytizing, parents do expect that their children will attend the Longhouse more willingly once they understand the proceedings, and as the Sweetgrass First Nations Language Council argues, the entire world view of First Nations depends on language retention. Certainly, native singing and dance groups have a new lease on life at Six Nations, and the younger children's singing groups from School Number Eleven are particularly popular. The Longhouse community and the Confederate Council hope that the Canadian government will continue funding for bilingual and immersion programs, and lobbying along these lines is a priority with them.

Fearing that school indoctrination or the procedures in place at the Longhouses (see p. 129 *infra*) cannot adequately preserve the necessary speeches for sacred and ritual events, several prominent Longhouse persons have also instituted private academies for ceremonial instruction. Foremost among these is Chief Jacob Thomas, who not only teaches in several of the native languages but also has demonstration recitations of the Great Law in English for the benefit of the many interested monolinguals and Christians. Because English within the Longhouse has been criticized, his recitations have lately taken place in Ohsweken at the community hall and in a tent at his homestead. Thirty years ago such events were unimaginable, yet despite some current criticism interest in the recitation is high, attendance is large, and the listeners profess to being uplifted and inspired. In many cases this is the first time that Reserve Christians have heard of the Lawgiver's (Deganawi′daʔ's) "Good Message: Power, Peace, and the Great Law," so familiar to Longhouse devotees. To insure that the narration will be available to everyone, Mr. Thomas promises to offer audiovisual tapes of his nine-day recitation this year.

Preserving Iroquoian tradition in the vernacular and in English has become an important motivation for many of the concerned Longhouse officers, for the spectacle of ever fewer ritualists is real. So many elders, who recited the set speeches and who performed the ceremonies, have died since the predominantly European educated adults have been in the ascendency, that any device for the preservation of traditions must now be exploited in spite of Handsome Lake's general prohibition against writing. Consequently, Mr. Reg Henry, who is a noted linguist, a most revered ritualist and head deacon of the Deer side at Seneca Longhouse, has also instituted a "school" in which he teaches the Cayuga language. In a trailer parked near his house and adjacent to the Onondaga Longhouse, he instructs several of the native language teachers in the linguistics of Iroquoian languages. Furthermore, he teaches to any interested person the Thanksgiving Address (see p. 134 *infra*) and the rudiments of ritual speeches for Adō′wa and Stirring Ashes Days, and for repenting and funerals. He too noted that there is a particular need to instruct people in funeral speeches to avoid precisely those episodes recounted above. Furthermore, more Christians seem to be asking for tenth day feasts, and even if these are now syncretic observances (including as one did recently, Christian-inspired eulogies to the deceased), they nevertheless call for a certain native linguistic competence.

Perpetuating First Languages has not been a contentious topic for the Longhouse community, but documenting the culture, and religious observances in particular, has created a dilemma for its proponents. They wish to utilize the most modern and efficient tools to record the traditions, yet numerous prohibitions forbid any recording other than in the memory of participants, because the Creator himself endows an individual with the ability to "pick up," to speak, and to perform (see p. 89 *infra*). Longstanding use of mnemonic canes and copies of texts taken by early ethnologists notwithstanding, many orthodox believers condemn all writing and recording equipment, particularly within a Longhouse or during an actual performance. Consequently, attempts by outsiders and by concerned Iroquois to ensure the perpetuation of their traditions by making documentary records have been criticized, and even ritualistically involved chiefs have been reprimanded by their clan mothers. Furthermore, still very much alive is the belief that whenever a desperate need for a performer arises, an individual will have learned secretly and will come forward with the proper expertise (see p. 128 *infra*). Currently, one hears rumors of individuals who are practicing to preach and speak, and who will step forward once the present ritualists retire or die. Similar predictions reported in the 1950s (see p. 128 *infra*) proved justified, and even today one may credit such reports, for there are indeed a few men in training. But reliance upon such assurances will inevitably become more hazardous as Longhouse members lose their language and become accustomed to modern habits of learning. Emphasized in the educational system today is facility with reading, audiovisual materials, and computers, and not the training of an auditory memory. It is perhaps not a coincidence that one of the most competent ritualists at Six Nations today has achieved his prominent position by dint of his uncanny memory and not of his schooling, though he is, as might be expected, among the few mid-life fluent Cayuga speakers who grew up in an observant and ritualistically active Longhouse family. But to rely on similar combinations of circumstances to bring forth future ritualists is more and more utopian, and the teachers of the native languages and the tutors of the sacred traditions are the first to make these arguments. In sum, there is a conscious effort to perpetuate the Longhouse way of life precisely by several members who are most knowledgeable, and the fact that they utilize some previously disfavored means in no way indicates any diminution of their religious convictions. To them, the means justify the ends.

Since 1961 when the first edition appeared, modernization has transformed the Reserve along so many dimensions that a returning visitor might well believe himself to be a latter day Rip Van Winkle. And, if one inquires of elderly Longhouse adherents what has changed since the 1950s, the typical answer is simply, "everything." Accounting for part of this response are rampant changes in material culture and living standards for many of the Longhouse population, whose daily life today approximates that of the Christian population even more than it did in the 1950s. Social services on the Reserve, be they universal health care, augmented pensions for the aged, educational opportunities, loan programs for housing improvements, or countless community services for special needs, have reached everyone, and the Longhouse population is no exception. And, contrary to the 1950s, it is rare today to find a Longhouse adherent who fails to own a band status card, if only to be eligible for health benefits. But notwithstanding physical, economic, and communication advances and all the accommodations that accompany these processes, the same elderly informants will declare that at the Longhouse nothing has changed. For today, in spite of obvious physical changes of material culture at the Longhouse and in the lives of the Longhouse members, the ceremonial and spiritual aspects of the religion are still perceived as having remained traditional. The Longhouse building, as at Onondaga, may be rebuilt, enlarged, electrified, and totally new, yet the most minor deviation of procedure occasions comment, if not outright disagreement.

As an example, one might cite just such a disagreement at Onondaga Longhouse, where contrary to the expectations of several members, a single set of Feather Dances rather than two sets was announced in 1985. Each of the contenders appealed to an authority for the accuracy of the number of sets, but unfortunately, both of them, Mr. Howard Skye and Mr. Roy Buck, had died in 1971 and in 1983 respectively. The issue was considered important enough to bring to the attention of the Three Brothers Wampum Keeper, who, by dint of his peace chief title, normally has the right of quieting arguments in the Confederate Council, and since this chief also happened to be the head deacon of the Deer moiety, he was considered an appropriate arbiter. (Actually, the position of wampum keeper was traditionally assigned to a Wolf title, but at Six Nations a Deer clan chief has been invested with these responsibilities.) And this head deacon now wondered which was the more appropriate aboriginal procedure and what might be the authority for the printed version (see p. 65 *infra*), which incidentally was his recollection of the program as well. Nevertheless, in fairness to a respected deceased elder of the Longhouse, and also to the plaintiffs, he was making earnest investigations. (For rather similar disagreements of procedure, as well as emotional attachment to verisimilitude of programming, see p. 184 *infra*.)

Similarly, in 1985, also at Onondaga Longhouse, several deaconesses disagreed about the appropriate foods to be served at Seed Planting. Should it more properly be sweetened flint corn as reported in the 1950s, or should the mush be flavored with the modern equivalent of the ancient wild animals believed to have been utilized long ago? And if so, should these be chicken or pork? The argument revolved about the contention that in the past it was pheasant, which is closer to chicken, and therefore the use of pork, reported for that occasion, was an unwarranted innovation. Obviously, changes along these dimensions are not going to affect the basic faith of believers, although they did seem to have embittered personal relations.

Although an observer might relegate such incidents to the sphere of normal cultural change (namely, different understandings by various persons), the protagonists do not appreciate such impersonal judgments. For concern over such details is justified by the conviction that the more accurately past practices are perpetuated, the more acceptable are the offerings to the Spirit Forces and the more authentic is their Indian character. In an atmosphere which attempts to assimilate Indians in countless insidious ways, holding faithfully to established custom validates one's Indian heritage and simultaneously demonstrates a measure of resistance to Canadian pressure. Furthermore, it is precisely such vigilance which has kept the ceremonials relatively stable, and fosters the genuine belief that nothing has changed in the Longhouse, when at a certain level change is all too evident everywhere.

A final ethnographic episode may illustrate how constant the Longhouse proceedings appear to their officers. On inquiring from a head deaconess what she felt had changed most at the Longhouse in the last forty years, she responded that it was becoming more difficult to procure the large white corn for those occasions at which it was needed. But this year her brother had grown seventeen strings and also had some further basketsful, so providentially the problem had been solved. Nothing else did she think had changed. Actually, frozen lyed white corn may today, unlike forty years ago, be bought in the stores on the Reserve, but what the deaconess may have had in mind is that contrary to religious prescriptions very few of the members now grow their own garden produce, for it is this that should be offered at the Longhouse. However, that admonition had, by the less devout, been transgressed ever since subsistence farming had declined, or women worked out and could not tend their own gardens.

To the Longhouse member then, and as far as an outsider can judge without actually attending the entire cycle of annual observances, the ceremonials are maintained as regularly today as they were forty years ago. The yearly round of events is scheduled, takes place, and speaks to the needs of the participants. To some extent the warning symptoms—a disappearing language, a decreasing number of knowledgeable ritualists, an even more materialistically oriented and acculturated congregation than before—are more threatening today than they were in the 1950s, but in response, the level of concern and the will to counteract these dangers have become more conscious and, as suggested above, are being addressed in various ways. Presently, dispiriting incidents, such as the two-hour wait endured by one congregation during a Green Bean ceremony while the Turtle head deaconess searched for a speaker, are still balanced by encouraging developments. The magnificent, newly built Onondaga Longhouse, dedicated in October 1991 (with a fire-moving ceremony), and the other well-maintained, older religious centers testify to the vitality of the community. Nor is there any denying that these very visible achievements have revitalized the morale of the Longhouse congregations, and the overflow crowd at the 1992 Green Corn ceremony at Onondaga was seen as vindication of the efforts expended to dignify the traditional religious heritage. And as long as the Longhouse religion satisfies the emotional needs of its adherents, it is in no danger of imminent decline.

Some historical reflections are to the point here. In the 1950s, generally speaking, the Longhouse community was held in low esteem. Adherents were considered socially inferior to Christians, and the religion of Handsome Lake was usually designated as a "pagan" belief—officially, and in the mind of the public. Furthermore, the stereotypical perception of Longhouse members was that they were socioeconomically inferior to the rest of the Reserve residents, although that was by no means the case in most instances. They were pictured as being superstitious, backwards, uneducated, unacculturated, and content with living conditions which the more professional and acculturated members would never accept. In short, they were perceived to be closer to the aboriginal red Indian than were their Christian brethren, and the very designation *Indian* was a pejorative term. In Brantford in the 1950s one discriminated against Indians, and the dominant attitude by most of the Whites and many of the socially prominent Christian Reserve members was one of disdain, if not outright ridicule, of the Longhouse community. Even I was always referred to by Christians as "the original Longhouse girl," and the appellation was double-edged.

Nor did some anthropologists who wished to laud the Indians and the Longhouse religion totally mask their condescension. Frank Speck, who evidently was a genuine admirer of Chief Alexander General (then the predominant ritualist at Sour Springs Longhouse), wrote in the introduction to a description of the Midwinter Rites at Sour Springs Longhouse (1949: 4), "[the Longhouse] at Sour Springs is still conspicuously free of influences of European social artifice, commercialism, and Christian sophistries. The Cayuga possess that quality which we know as the Indian heart. A delightful unsophistication redolent of an age-old atmosphere of dignified myth and 'superstition' prevails, unfolding a cooperative health-preserving ideal framed in thanksgiving and rejoicing. The Long House Cayuga devotee has somehow fortified his inner spirit against most of the cheap ideas and untried innovations of an age of perplexities and hypocrisies in religious teaching alien to his traditions."

Understandably, the community reacted defensively. Chief Alexander General composed an oration which he brought to Christian audiences in an attempt to explain the Longhouse religion. "We are Deists, not Pagans; a clearer understanding of our fundamental principles would show they are not heathenish incantations but a development of thought evolved from an age-long experience in spiritual emotion and in ethical teaching; the old faith of our forefathers is as good for them as the old of your fathers is good for whites; we denounce ridicule and adverse criticism of others' beliefs and expect that the same consideration be given to ours"[3] are literal phrases from his speech. But to the less intellectual members, a common response was to retreat into the Longhouse and find understanding among like-minded individuals. There was not only ostracism of the Longhouse community by Christians, but also a certain amount of self-segregation by the Longhouse members. The two populations did not interact prominently, and, in fact, such contacts were discouraged by both groups (see p. 130 *infra*).

How different is the climate today! Even the most cursory inventory of the Six Nations citizens, be they Christian or Longhouse, reveals a changed self-image.

---

[3] Annemarie Shimony, "Alexander General, 'Deskahe,' Cayuga-Oneida, 1889–1965," in *American Indian Intellectuals,* ed. M. Liberty (St. Paul, Minn.: West Publishing, 1978), pp. 163–64.

Both communities are proud of their heritage, but because the Longhouse adherents have retained so much more of the traditional culture and also represent the greater number of individuals who understand Iroquoian languages, even if fluency in speech has been lost, they tend to be regarded as "genuine Indians." And, instead of the previous disdain, they now garner esteem for their authenticity. The response of the younger members to the changes has been positive: the greatest difference between them and their mothers is that as *Indians* they have much more self-respect. There are no more apologies for a failure to emulate Canadians and their culture, as had been required of their parents at the missionary schools and particularly at the Mohawk Institute, the residential school which was so influential in the training of teachers for the Reserve population. Quite the contrary, pride of nation derives from membership in the community of First Nations, and among these the Iroquois consider the League to be *primus inter pares*. For unlike any of the other tribes and bands, they maintain, only the League was an ally rather than a subject of the British prior to Canada's existence, and relations were regularized by treaties as one sovereign nation to another. Furthermore, long before Canadian Confederation (in fact, before the British had arrived in the New World), the League had its own laws, which the Longhouse community has respected without interruption. Such assertions of sovereignty and independence are not new, for they had been proclaimed since Brant moved to the banks of the Grand River. But while in the 1950s these declarations were routinely discounted if not ridiculed, these statements carry weight and give hope to their advocates in the 1990s with the advent of a more sensitive and informed understanding of Amerindians in Canada and their increasing political influence.

Undoubtedly, the Six Nations population has also benefited from the ethos of the postimperialist world, in which Third World peoples have gained a position at the bargaining table. That a Eurocentric point of view is no longer viable could not have been more symbolically demonstrated than by Elijah Harper's withholding his vote on the Meech Lake Accords, as he drew spiritual strength from the eagle feather in his hands. Phil Fontaine, then Ojibwa Grand Chief of the Assembly of Manitoba Chiefs, articulated the position of the Indians very clearly when he asserted that they were not necessarily opposed to a distinct society and special status for Quebec, "But if Quebec is distinct, we are even more distinct. That's the recognition we want, and will settle for nothing less." And, as Dickason (1992, p. 409) notes, Fontaine believed recognition implies power, and power in turn would allow for self-government and the installation of a justice system more compatible with the traditions of native peoples. Surely, the Hereditary Council at Six Nations could resonate to these sentiments.

Moreover, not only is the Indian community buoyed up by the recognition of traditional political rights, but social equality also has become implicit in the disapproval of racial and ethnic hierarchy. World War II was widely perceived as a war against racism, and the establishment of the United Nations, with its doctrine of recognition of the inherent rights of all ethnic groups and all races, has helped diminish prejudiced judgments concerning Canada's Native peoples as well. Consequently, no matter what the private views of the Six Nations' neighbors may be today, or even the views of the more acculturated Christian Indians who had previously distanced themselves from the native culture, "Longhouse bashing" is most definitely "politically incorrect."

Furthermore, the burgeoning interest in Indian culture and the rediscovery by Whites of Indian art have not gone unnoticed at Six Nations. In the 1950s the public was invited to learn about Iroquoian history in the annual dramatizations of piquant moments from the past presented by the Pageant Committee, and the Six Nations Fair demonstrated current Iroquoian interests; yet, there existed no indigenous professional or permanent venue from which to educate the public about the Iroquois. And the Brantford Chamber of Commerce, which hoped to draw tourists to the area, primarily featured the homestead of the poetess Pauline Johnson as a historic site.

Today, by contrast, capitalizing on the need to satisfy curiosity about Indians, the Six Nations established the Woodland Cultural Centre out of the defunct Mohawk School. Here, with a relatively modest financial disbursement from the Canadian government, the Centre presents a diverse offering of native achievements as natives would have them be seen. It reasserts the validity of traditional knowledge, language, religion, crafts, and art, and the Centre's various organizational components—the library research department, the language section, the Class A Museum—cooperate in their public relations to further these aims. And not inconsequentially, the Centre informs some of its own people as well about native creativity and the relevance of their aboriginal culture. Similarly, it is not surprising that the various indigenous cultural enterprises have flourished in the post-1980s atmosphere. The Six Nations Women Singers, the various dance troupes, and the powwow organizations have drawn large audiences and increased their standing beyond all expectations. The thirteenth annual Grand River Champion of Champions powwow in 1992, for example, drew fifteen thousand visitors and awarded twenty-five thousand dollars in prizes. Remarkably, these entrepreneurial ventures are mainly organized, and often staffed, by traditional Longhouse adherents, who can draw upon their conservative culture to educate and entertain the audiences.

Of interest in these developments is the inevitable interaction of Longhouse followers with peoples of very different orientations, and, to a certain extent, this behavior implies an inevitable turn to greater acculturation. Gone is the previous isolation, and gone also (to a large extent) is the self-segregation in the Longhouse community. It may seem paradoxical that, just as these members agitate for a return to their native language and for the inculcation of traditional political and religious customs, they adopt more cosmopolitan attitudes and accept an increasing number of material conveniences. However, as in the 1950s, similar psychological rationalizations dispel these seeming inconsistencies, for what determines Indian status is a spiritual frame of mind rather than the rejection of modern devices or the conservation of defensive behavior engendered by a prejudiced and exclusionary White and Christian world.

Descriptions of the Reservation population have in the past dichotomized the society into Christian and Longhouse communities, although a more accurate designation might have been one of differential acculturation (see p. 14 *infra*, Weaver, 1978: 530). Yet, in the popular mind the Christians were progressive and the Longhouse members traditionalist, eschewing white, middle-class aspirations and the Protestant ethic. Although this view was overgeneralized and each of the groups had complicating subdivisions with varying attitudes about native religious and political positions, it was not a totally inaccurate assessment in the past. However, in the last forty years this characterization has become less apposite. Compulsory education and increasing participation by Longhouse personnel in the economic life of southern Ontario have combined to mitigate even such differences of progress as existed in the 1950s. Preachers and speakers may still counsel a simpler life, with "Indians in one canoe and Whites in another scow," but today, even more than previously, these admonitions are understood as an expression more of the ideal than the real culture. To the extent that the Longhouse community has profited from educational advances and the financial rewards of better jobs, its values follow those of Christians. Greater affluence allows both groups an upgrading of life-styles, private and public. Unthinkable in the 1950s, Longhouse members now take vacations on pleasure cruises to the Bahamas, own swimming pools, drive recreational vehicles, subscribe to cable T.V. and place large dish antennas in their yards, own the latest VCR, hi-fi, and computer equipment, fly to cheer their relatives across the continent in sports events, and bet at the races. And, they also save to buy or improve their houses, care about the education of their children, and hope to participate in whatever social mobility is afforded to them. Publicly, the Longhouse community supports its religious property as do the Christians, and the fact that a women's committee was able to raise one hundred thousand dollars locally in six months to pay for the building of Onondaga Longhouse is a remarkable testament to the industry and commitment of a community.

However, none of these acquisitions or attitudes indicates that the religious devotion to the Longhouse is in any doubt. And, in fact, attentive Longhouse adherents point to the very message of Handsome Lake himself, in which he permitted the imitation of white behavior—cultivation, house building, and stock keeping—as long as there is no pride by the Indian (Parker, 1913: 38). Analogously, it is argued today, accepting advanced technologies is not a sin unless accompanied by pride. It is this argument precisely which some proponents of electrification for Sour Springs Longhouse advance in order to persuade the opponents of modernization to follow the example of Onondaga and Seneca Longhouses, which are already electrified. Less legalistically, many of the Longhouse members assert again, as a response to their greater social interaction, that an inner conviction rather than incidental manifestations of life-style determine Longhouse devotion. As long as one believes in the Creator, his Spirit Forces, and the commands of the Lawgiver, one adheres to one's tradition. That the tradition still persists, despite changes, is proven by the continued observances of the annual Longhouse cycle.

As mentioned before, the ceremonials, with some obvious local variations similar to those existing in the 1950s, are still observed. The greatest deviation pointed out to me occurs in the Sun and Moon festivals at Onondaga and Seneca Longhouses, for the program given (see p. 157 *infra*) seems to have followed a reversed order from that performed today. Since the majority of the descriptions came from Sour Springs, where this observance had long been omitted, the previously described program was not one which I had attended personally. Nor have I now, but according to Reg Henry, head deacon of Seneca Longhouse, the order of events is as follows: the women set the date, and the ceremony opens in the morning with the events dedicated to the Sun, which is considered a male ceremony. The Thanksgiving Address opens the proceedings, followed by a speech indicating the day's program. This in turn is followed by the men's Adō'wa, including the use of the sun disk. Thereafter, a Skin Dance (gane'hōō) ends the program. There is no Feather Dance as had been reported. White corn mush is the distinctive food offered. After lunch the Moon ceremony opens without another Thanksgiving Address, and the program is turned over to the women for continuation, as the Moon is in the female sphere. Women sing their planting songs, followed by the Bowl Game of men against women. An old style Ska'nye (Women's Dance) and the Thanksgiving Address end the festivities, and the congregation leaves without a further distribution of foods.

Although some Longhouse followers attend several ceremonial centers, the more common practice is consistent attendance at one Longhouse (see p. 130 *infra*). And before the greatly increased mobility of today, there was a marked tendency for families to remain at the same Longhouse for several generations and thus to become familiar with the speakers and singers, many of whom were relatives. Consequently, traditions arose at each locus, to which participants related comfortably and to which they became attached. Familiar routines with familiar personnel bestowed feelings of continuity, coherence, and unity—all important values in the Longhouse ethic (see p. 130 *infra*). Local variation within a general pattern arose because each Longhouse had identifiable deacons and speakers who stamped their personalities on the particular center with which they were associated. Lower Cayuga Longhouse had in the 1950s an attitude which strongly separated the religious observances from the political considerations of the hereditary chiefs, although all the other Longhouses had incorporated the chiefs to a great extent (see p. 100 *infra*). This stance is still the case, despite several chiefs with strong Confederate convictions making Lower Cayuga their home Longhouse. Yet the Longhouse leadership there has been so stable that even today funeral speakers who deliver the obsequies and condole the bereaved in the order of the conventional social distinctions—chiefs, deacons, people, and children—are reprimanded and asked to omit the category of chiefs (see p. 244 *infra*). Inertia is a strong force at the Longhouse, but it will be interesting to see whether upon the passing of the current leadership this separation of church and state will continue. Indeed, many talk of a "pope" at Lower Cayuga Longhouse.

Yet it is not only the philosophical inclination of a Longhouse which becomes known but also the specific routines of the programming; and to the extent that the details are kept constant, participants feel "nothing has changed." As indicated above, to the extent that variation occurs, particularly within a single ceremonial center, attenders take notice and adopt factional positions. Unfortunately, as deceased deacons, speakers, singers, and performers have not been replaced by younger members, Longhouses have been forced to share specialists. Jacob Thomas, Reg Henry, Gordon Buck, Hubert Buck, Sr., and Huron Miller are just some of the current ritualists who are in constant demand. Whether their ubiquitous contributions will act as homogenizing agents at the four Longhouses or the ceremonies will be simplified and degraded remains to be seen. With smaller congregations than Onondaga and Lower Cayuga, Seneca and Sour Springs Longhouses particularly have fewer personnel from which to replace deceased ritualists, and they realize that their ceremonial observances are at a critical juncture. Perhaps symptomatic of their difficulties is the unusually long interval between the death of the Turtle moiety head deaconess in October 1989 and the appointment of her replacement, which in October of 1992 had not yet occurred. The ceremonies have proceeded in the interim because the other deaconesses substituted for the missing officer, but the predicament in which Sour Springs finds itself portends an "imperiled continuation." An even more distressing omen was the attempt, by a long-standing member of Seneca Longhouse, to preach in English at the Longhouse, but this substitution was too much for the congregation and the speaker was silenced.

Respect for elders is a recognized value of Iroquoian culture, as demonstrated by the formulaic expressions in the ritual addresses, and as the number of elders who are erudite about the traditional culture has diminished, the remaining ritualists are cherished all the more. "Learning from our elders" had always been a corollary of respect, but in today's climate that phrase has become a potent native symbol. Embedded in the expression is the notion of recapturing a more authentic native spiritual experience precisely because it derives from an older source, which not only is closer to the original but also has been transmitted by a generation antedating the corruption of a more assimilated one. More so than in the 1950s, younger members wish to learn from their elders, and the Six Nations Library instituted an oral history project in which the elderly recorded their reminiscences. The Woodland Cultural Centre, interested in aboriginal organization, taught students to collect genealogical histories in order to retain knowledge of matrilineages and clan affiliation, before these concepts, so important in the traditions, become even more neglected. The current curiosity about native roots has abetted these efforts, and a number of occupational options concerning Native Studies have provided satisfaction as well as heightened morale to the professionals from Six Nations.

Knowledgeable elders are asked to officiate at more diverse and more numerous occasions, thus accelerating the trend of concentrating traditional ceremonial expertise among fewer specialists. It is this phenomenon, I believe, which accounts for the impression, reported by every ritualist, that "doings" (ritual activity for the welfare of an individual, see p. 274 *infra*) have increased since the 1950s, not only for the Longhouse constituency but also more surprisingly for Christians and even for Whites. Furthermore, persons from other Iroquoian reservations come to Six Nations in order to pass their ritual obligations, for Six Nations yet remains a reservoir of knowledge for many of the ceremonies. But as in the case of the attendance statistics at the Longhouses, it is difficult to ascertain the relative frequency of personal curing events compared to forty years ago. During the pass dance days at the Longhouses (see p. 178 *infra*), officers in charge of arranging the events say they are very busy, and observances in private homes also continue actively. For example, the Six Nations community has several groups of performers who belong to the Pygmy Society and perform the Dark Dance for individuals in need of that rite (see p. 281 *infra*). According to the testimony of two of the women singers and cooks of one of these "gangs" (as they are termed at Six Nations), they conducted three or four ceremonies each week in the homes of patients throughout the winter of 1991 to 1992, often cooking and singing on consecutive nights. Furthermore, they knew that at least one other group ministered to patients on some of the same nights because, at times, the male speaker was in demand at both events. They claim to have performed fifty observances during that winter, which includes requests by visitors from the Wisconsin Oneida and from Akwesasne, who came to Six Nations for their pass dance. As in the 1950s, fortunetellers may have temporary preferences for certain curing rites and prescribe them more often, creating fads, which could explain the popularity of the Dark Dance last year. Even if the estimates are somewhat overstated, an astounding amount of ritual activity is indicated, for the Pygmy Society is only one of the eight societies (see p. 281 *infra*) on the Reserve. All of these observances of the 1950s seem still to be current at Six Nations.

To my knowledge five fortunetellers are frequently consulted by Six Nations clients, including a rather expensive but renowned female fortuneteller at Lewiston, who is used by Six Nations people living in Niagara Falls. And, undoubtedly, there are others who practice on a more limited basis. Interestingly, even fortune telling has been modernized, for if one is in need of a quick diagnosis, one may telephone the fortuneteller, give one's Indian name, and receive a reply without tendering the Indian tobacco or leaving some item belonging to the patient (see p. 270 *infra*). Surprising in these telephone diagnoses is that a fortuneteller has been known to prescribe a major obligation, such as a Tutelo spirit adoption ceremony, yet the patient was satisfied and planned to gather the costly necessities as soon as the appropriate season (winter) arrives.

Fortunetellers are agents simultaneously for stability and change, for on the one hand they prescribe traditional "Indian" procedures and thus keep the conservative culture going (see p. 274 *infra*), while on the other hand they initiate changes as their prescriptions permute familiar elements according to the specific circumstances of the patient and the inclination of the fortuneteller (see p. 272 *infra*). Although the general pattern of the diagnosis and treatment of ailments and ritual obligations seems to me to have remained consistent in the forty year interval, a very common complaint at Six Nations is that "we have such crazy fortunetellers now." Participants in the doings remember past instructions and do not appreciate a change of routine. For example, the gift obligations associated with the commonly utilized ritual of making friends have become more burdensome, for while in previous times friends exchanged cloths when the friendship was formed, now, at least in some instances, an additional exchange is demanded after a year (see p. 221 *infra*). Mr. Reg Henry says that the innovation was at the command of a fortuneteller. He also remembers that once it was only the supplicant to the relationship who presented the cloth, although in the 1950s, the practice of exchanging cloths was already prevalent (see p. 221 *infra*). Furthermore, officiators say that fortunetellers "come up with new rules," such as demanding that False Face maskettes be given in situations which had not called for them previously, or adding a dead feast to the Shake Pumpkin ceremony because "the Grandfathers" (spirit forces) who wish to hear the ceremony expect to be honored by being served the obligatory doughnuts.

The most frequent ritual observances in private homes today, by all accounts, are the small feasts, in part because they are appropriate responses to many situations, and in part, perhaps, because they are relatively simple observances. The only prerequisite is that the sponsor have an Indian name, but should he lack one, a name will be bestowed prior to the feast. The sponsor arranges for a male speaker and some female cooks who know how to prepare the conventionally required foods. Feasts today follow the general ideology and procedure which were common in the 1950s (see p. 274 *infra*)—a tobacco burning during which the proceedings are explained to the recipient of the ceremony, an apology for the transgression by the sponsor and a plea for forgiveness, and the offering of the tobacco and food to the recipient.

Very common today, say the speakers who officiate, are dead feasts solicited by a new constituency, namely those who failed to bury their kin in the Longhouse manner. Often when a family is disunited about funeral arrangements and the choice finally committed the loved one to a Christian service and cemetery, some of the Christian relatives begin to feel uneasy that traditional "Indian" expressions of respect for the dead were omitted, and should they dream about the dead, the usual interpretation declares that the dead are disturbed and need attention. A dead feast is the obvious response, and if a fortuneteller had been consulted, it is invariably advised. Longhouse families, who for some reason or another omitted either the tenth day or the year feast, are even more prone to sponsor dead feasts in order to satisfy the expectations, as well as the "hunger," of the dead (see p. 279 *infra*), for unsatisfied dead spirits are potentially very dangerous, causing disease, ill luck, or death. Forty years ago, Christians who had not observed Longhouse mortuary etiquette sometimes sponsored dead feasts as years later they began to reflect on their omission, but a Christian burial and a tenth day feast on the tenth day by these same Christians is an innovation. Such ecumenicism, so soon after death, would have been very unusual for a socially prominent Baptist family then; yet, today it is accepted and declared spiritually satisfying.

Evident here, I believe, is some of the same tolerance and respect for native religious belief that has animated the general reburial movement on the continent, of which Six Nations is very much a part. Ever since the exhumation of Indian remains at Middleport (a site just across the River from the Reserve), Mr. Reg Henry has been the most prominent officiator at reburial services, and today he is in demand by construction supervisors throughout Southern Ontario. Mr. Henry says that he "dons buckskin in order to show respect for the deceased," burns tobacco to transmit the message, and explains that the affront to their repose was unintentional. He asks for forgiveness for the disturbance, hopes the dead will not "bother" the living, promises a reburial, and affirms that no further discourtesy shall ever mar their reinterment.

Mr. Reg Henry, as one of the principal speakers at Six Nations, is kept inordinately busy performing small feasts of all kinds for Six Nations supplicants. He is needed many nights (and some afternoons) per week, and when I inquired about his estimate of the frequency of death feasts, he remembered that the week before he had officiated at three such events in one night—two for Longhouse members and one for a Christian family. Another speaker mentioned he owned forty shirts, each a token of gratitude for his services at a feast, which also gives an indication of both the frequency of these events and the reliance upon a single ritualist.

Six Nations families also continue to fulfill obligations owed to hunting charms (tjinhgē'da) lodged in their families, and the observances are filled with as much trepidation today as they were in the 1950s (see p. 285 *infra*).

As in the past, Indian medicine is still available from general practitioners and from well-recognized specialists (see p. 265 *infra*), who, for example, have teas for "female problems" and for depression specifically from "stress in two cultures" (an innovation), as well as for general suicidal tendencies. To my knowledge these practitioners claim to have gained their expertise from their parents or some older medical practitioner.

Thus, despite changes and despite greater incorporation of Six Nations peoples in the Canadian culture, the conservative community has retained many of its practices, and I do not foresee the sudden disappearance of their practices and folk beliefs.

If one takes the assessment of the interlocking of various aspects of culture seriously (see p. iii *supra*) and looks for institutions at Six Nations which influence each other in many complicated ways yet contribute to a general retention of an Indian culture, one must surely take account of the institution of the hereditary chiefs (who constitute the Confederate Council) and its relation to the Longhouse.

For even as the Longhouse way of life has come under pressure from the forces of modernization and acculturation, so has the Confederate Council, which has reacted with its own shifts of political tactics and ideology.

A common view of the Confederate Council has been that it represents the political position of the traditionalist Longhouse population, and while there is truth in this assumption, it is an oversimplified picture (see p. 99 *infra*). Consequently, to understand the changes which the Confederate Council has undergone since the 1950s, one must resort to a somewhat deeper historical analysis, for several of the strains which make current functioning problematic had been built into the institution from the very beginning.

One of the most fundamental of these is the ambiguity concerning the status of the Council. Is the Council merely a secular political organ for the Iroquoian League, or is it an extension of an Iroquoian sacred tradition because its definition and functioning derive from the Deganawi'da? myth? Anthropologists have debated this issue for a century (see p. 96 *infra*), and so have the Iroquois. But despite the majority opinion of observers that the condoling councils are merely civil councils, "a public installation or inauguration of chiefs," as Beauchamp (1907: 379) argued, many Iroquois deny this. At issue is the related ambiguity of the entire League Tradition, as Woodbury (1992) has termed the Deganawi'da? epic.

Some evidence that this epic and the ceremony of chiefs' installation were seen as sacred (already before the Confederate Council was replaced in 1924 and the hereditary faction perhaps had partisan motivations to style its chiefs as extraordinarily appointed) is provided by the fact that there had long existed a name taboo for the culture hero who established the league and devised the system of chieftainships. For it is the custom now, and was already part of the culture in 1900 when the chiefs codified the League Tradition, that his name could not be used except in an actual condolence ceremony or during a rehearsal or discussion of his messages (Scott, 1912: 230, Parker, 1916: 105). On all other occasions, the circumlocutions of *Lawgiver* or *Peacemaker* are the only appropriate appellations. This is not the only indication that the League Tradition is sacred. The overall messianic flavor of the narration (with the implication of "failure to follow My rules will cause Iroquoia to perish"), the prominent use of wampum as an earnest, the many supernatural incidents, and the current practice of attaching religious officials to some chiefs give the same impression. The religion of Handsome Lake, a graft after 1800 onto the older religious beliefs, has its own personnel and other functions (see p. 98 *infra*), but to many Iroquois this fact does not rule out the sacred character of the League Tradition. Also, as I pointed out before (see p. 97 *infra*), the symbolism in the Longhouse religion and in the League Tradition are similar, and therefore evoke similar emotions of awe before a superhuman power.

Had all the chiefs been Longhouse followers when they were appointed by their matrilineages at Six Nations, the dichotomy of religion and politics might never have arisen, as all the incumbents would have shared the values and emotions attached to Deganawi'da? and the League Tradition. But a problem arose because after the middle of the nineteenth century Christians outnumbered Longhouse believers, which also meant that more chiefs in the designated matrilineages were Christians, and according to Weaver (1978: 530) by 1890 over eighty percent of the chiefs were Christian. As Christians tended to have more education, they were not bound by the directives of Handsome Lake, who feared, as did his conservative Longhouse followers, that a European education would undermine the traditional religion as well as the Iroquoian culture. In general, with education came a proclivity to secularize the Confederate Council, partly due to a more acculturated understanding of the functions of the Council and partly because there was no longer a belief in the traditional aspects of the appointment of hereditary chiefs. To this faction, then, retention of the hereditary council was more a matter of Iroquoian sovereignty than a matter of an integral sacred tradition, which included a belief in the Deganawi'da? myth with all its ramifications. Consequently, before the dissolution of the Confederate Council by the Canadian government in 1924, many of the chiefs in hereditary positions who had converted to Christianity and permitted themselves to be installed by a Condolence Ceremony at the Longhouse did so without religious conviction but as a formality to fulfill the form and trappings of chieftainship. Although both factions were united in desiring Iroquoian sovereignty, there nevertheless developed an increasingly bitter split between Christian acculturated chiefs and Longhouse traditional chiefs. It should be emphasized that this was a disagreement within the Confederate Council and concerned a secular versus a sacred view of chieftainship. Simultaneously, there was a movement by individuals on the Reserve (both Longhouse and Christian, though predominantly Christian) who wished simply to have an elected council and to dispense with the Confederate Council altogether because they saw it as an antiquated and inefficient instrument.

The Confederate Council at Six Nations no longer made decisions concerning nations and tribes, for despite Iroquoian objections, the Iroquois were subject to the Indian Act and forced to accept Canadian suzerainty. Consequently, the duties of the Confederate Council resembled those of a municipal government, because the Council had to legislate, administer, and enforce local ordinances. This work had to be accomplished, and consequently the chiefs in Council came to an informal agreement that they would forget their religious differences while meeting as a governing body. However, as the rift between the factions widened, this compromise became increasingly difficult to honor.

The second strain, which was not completely unrelated to the religious differences, was the degree to which the Council chiefs tolerated Canadian hegemony. All the chiefs probably wished for sovereignty and unhampered self-government, yet varying widely were the accommodations to the Indian Act each chief was, or was not, willing to make out of conviction, necessity, or opportunism. Certainly to the more nationalistic among them, Canada was perceived as imposing a system akin to Indirect Rule on the Iroquois, as the decisions taken by the Confederate Council were ultimately subject to Canadian approval and could be reversed by the Superintendent or the Dominion government. Therefore, nationalistic factions —whether the nationalism was based on religious or secular convictions—construed any cooperation with the Canadian government as disloyal to Iroquoian sovereignty, and in fact, the very recognition of Canada was interpreted as the abdication of native sovereignty. To them, the Deganawi'da? myth gave the Iroquois their sovereignty and determined political procedures. An attitude of extreme noncooperation became very prominent in the early 1920s and had as its spokesman a charismatic Cayuga chief, Deskahe, who was able to mobilize many from both the religious Longhouse faction and the Christian nationalist faction represented by the Mohawk Workers. Since there had been decades of agitation to replace the Confederate Council, the Canadian government now felt sufficiently pressured by the progressive elements to call for an investigation. The result was an Order in Council which installed an elected body in place of the uncooperative and dysfunctional hereditary chiefs.

Nevertheless, despite de facto loss of power in 1924, many of the aggrieved hereditary chiefs believed their replacement so illegitimate that they continued to meet according to the customary procedures and to claim aboriginal sanctions for their behavior. That there existed much sentiment at Six Nations which concurred with these chiefs should be amply proven by the fact that today, almost seventy years later, the Confederate Council continues to meet and to voice the opinions of its constituency. Thus, since 1924, the Reserve has been seriously divided between followers of the Elected Council and the Hereditary Council. Religious adherents of the Christian and Longhouse faiths are also divided, so that there is not a one-on-one correlation of either faith with either council. And the same is true of families in lineages which had the rights to a chief's title. Every possible combination is present, and, to gain a total understanding, one would have to follow each of the choices made by families at Six Nations, particularly those families which were intimately involved with the Confederate Council. Because such a detailed description is beyond the scope of an introduction, I shall try to indicate the trends and alliances which seem most relevant.

An alliance which continued after the precipitous, but not totally unexpected, abrogation of the Confederate Council was the one forged by Chief Deskahe (Levy General), consisting of Mohawk Workers—who were mainly Christians, though with some Longhouse adherents—and the more nationalistic Longhouse believers. Mr. General, as did his brother Alexander, who succeeded him in the title, believed that the need for allies who would agitate for the reinstatement of the Confederate Council was so critical that the differences in religion were secondary concerns. However, partly because many of these nationalists advocated militant tactics which conflicted with the doctrine of peace and united minds so prominently displayed in the Longhouse religion, and partly because the Christians were deemed ignorant of the sanctions which linked the League Tradition to the Longhouse culture, opposition to this political coalition developed in some of the Longhouses, as well as among the more religiously oriented chiefs. (There was actually some physical violence between these factions.) At the other end of the spectrum, those Longhouse members who felt the Confederate Council had outlived its usefulness and supported the Elected Council (including an erstwhile confederate chief who was one of the first elected councilors) also objected to the coalition, though their objection was not founded on religious convictions but on their more advanced acculturation, or, in Reserve terminology, "progressiveness." Yet despite these centrifugal tendencies, in 1959 and 1970 hereditary chiefs who subordinated their religious convictions to an insistence on the reinstatement of the Confederate Council perpetuated such an alliance by cooperating willingly with energetic nationalists, termed "warriors," who attempted to regain power by forcibly ejecting the Elected Council.[4]

Perhaps because both attempts at revolution failed and their followers were disappointed, and also because some of the strong-willed chiefs who were instrumental in backing the action-prone nationalist elements had died by the beginning of the 1980s, a new leadership gained prominence in the Confederate Council which emphasized the more ritualistic and sacred aspects of the League Tradition. And it is this orientation which is prominent today. Nevertheless, the current Confederate Council is no less desirous of sovereignty for the Iroquois than were its predecessors. A position paper on self-government issued by it in February 1991 (Hodenosaunee at Grand River, 1991) unconditionally rejects all Canadian Indian legislation from the British North America Act of 1867—which was negotiated without the Six Nations at the table and obviously therefore not as allies—to the offers of self-government and devolution of the present. Every piece of legislation (including the offer of self-government, though moot since the defeat in October 1992 of the Charlottetown Accord) is seen as an attempt to reduce Indians to second class status and to assimilate them into Canadian society. The Confederate Council in this position paper gives notice that its self-government is based solely upon the Great Law, established by the Peacemaker, and dedicated to the principles of peace, power, and righteousness.

Nor does the Confederate Council wish the Great Law to be used as a model and appropriated by "some of our people in their communities," for it fears that such an adoption by communities operating under Canadian jurisdiction would endanger the Iroquoian status as allies to the Crown which they believe to have been negotiated in the Friendship Treaties and the Two Rows (or Two Paths) treaty, both documented with wampum belts. But even as the Confederate Council issues this warning to elected councils, to warriors, to chiefs' councils which are not part of the Confederacy, and to the Assembly of First Nations (although these bodies are not identified by name), it acknowledges that "new rafters need to be added to the house" and is willing to accommodate them, provided that the newcomers

[4] For a discussion of the Revolution of 1959, see Annemarie Shimony, "Conflict and Continuity: An Analysis of an Iroquois Uprising," in *Extending the Rafters: Interdisciplinary Approaches to Iroquois Studies,* ed. M. K. Foster, J. Campisi, and M. Mithun (Albany: State Univ. of New York Press, 1984), pp. 153–64.

reintegrated into the Confederacy abide by four nonnegotiable principles. The first of these demands adherence to the Great Law, with an emphasis on unanimous agreement; the second specifies that deliberations must proceed in good faith with a Good Mind and abjure weapons of war; the third insists that the sacred circle of fifty chiefs must be retained with all the laws, customs, traditions, language and beliefs of the Hodenosaunee people; and the last declares that no laws can be created which leave the Iroquois subjects of another nation. The position paper also gives notice that the Confederacy is not prepared to accept a transition of power from the Elected Council to themselves under the terms of Canadian law.

The next day an addendum was released, obviously addressed to the Elect Council, which set forth the areas in which the Confederacy must have exclusive jurisdiction. In numerical order, they are: (1) the Great Law and its laws, (2) our land, (3) our treaties, (4) international relationships in regard to war and peace, commerce, and taxation, (5) membership, (6) installation of chiefs, (7) maintenance of all of our ceremonies, and (8) justice and law. Emphasized once more is the difference between elected band councils, which work within the context of the Canadian government, and the Confederacy, which operates on a nation-to-nation basis; but should the chiefs have exclusive jurisdiction in the above mentioned areas, then they will accept every one.

The realignment of political relations from those prevailing during the tenure of the influential chiefs Deskahe, Thadoda'ho?, and Hahstawē?thrō'ntha? (Alexander General, Joseph Logan, Sr., and Joseph Logan, Jr., respectively, and all deceased by 1981) is remarkable. No longer is the Confederate Council willing to make alliances with warriors and Christian Mohawk chiefs but wishes that the circle of chiefs abide by its third principle, namely, traditional mores. And in accordance with this philosophy, the Confederate chiefs have lately endeavored to fill all empty titles with Longhouse members who actively participate in the religion of Handsome Lake and understand the full import of the League Tradition, who can understand, or better yet speak, one of the native languages, and, of course, who support the Confederacy. Since the Confederate Council has been relieved of responsibility and accountability to a cross section of Reserve inhabitants, as it was not before its ouster, ecumenical cooperative agreements are no longer a necessity, and a more homogeneous composition is possible. But this uniformity comes at a price, for it results in empty titles, and even today, when titles have been significantly reassigned, many of the monthly meetings lack a quorum, which is defined as attendance by at least one chief from each of the five tribes. Furthermore, this rather restrictive strategy risks isolating the Confederate Council from a wider constituency, which, unrepresented, finds the Council irrelevant. However, the Confederate chiefs believe that only by a sincere reversion to the traditional procedures and aims of the League—taken in a fundamentalist sense—can they earn the right to act as leaders of a self-governing Iroquoian Confederacy which does not deprive future generations of their native heritage.

Even as the chiefs mistrust the Canadian government to honor their treaties and return power to them, so are they apprehensive that warriors whom they often suspect of illegal activities, Iroquoian nationalists, and elected councils—none of whom share in the beliefs of the League Tradition—intend to use the Confederacy for their own claims to legitimacy. And, as these groups appropriate power under a feigned allegiance to the Confederacy, they might not only cede sovereignty to a foreign power but also destroy Iroquoian culture. For to the Confederate chiefs today, politics and religion are indissolubly combined. Longhouse members who believe otherwise are dismissed as "dehorners," and Christians are disqualified for being remote from the old ways.

In view of this pervasive mistrust, it is ironic that relations between the Confederacy and the Elected Council at Six Nations had never been better than during the term of the elected chief councilor, Mr. William Montour (before his resignation in 1990). He had personally attended a meeting of the chiefs in an effort by both sides to build trust and foster communication, and a gratifying sign of goodwill toward the Confederacy was his return to them of the wampum strings known as "the mace," which were displayed during council sessions before the changeover of 1924. Since that time, however, their whereabouts had been unknown, until Mr. Montour "found" them in the council safe. The occasion of the return in May 1988 coincided with a ceremony of repatriation to the Confederacy from the Heye Foundation in New York of eleven wampum belts which had been irregularly collected. But, whereas these belts were returned only under threat of litigation by the Confederacy's lawyer, the mace was unexpectedly and gratuitously restored to the community for which it was meaningful.

It is not a coincidence that the chief's position paper makes prominent mention of the Friendship and Two Rows wampum belts, as these cogent symbols of a once-powerful Confederacy have finally been reclaimed after a ninety year absence, during which the Confederacy had been subjected to much humiliation. More important than the physical repossession of these belts, their interpretation by Chief Jacob (Jake) Thomas has reinforced the political orientation that the chiefs consider appropriate. This interpretation, along with emphasis on the Great Law—of which Chief Thomas is also the foremost expositor—help to explain the revivalist sentiment of the Confederacy.

A common view of leading traditionalists who are recreating the old Confederacy, including Chief Thomas and the wampum keepers of both nation moieties, is that the reinstatement of chiefs into positions which are currently unfilled would greatly strengthen the claims of the hereditary council to be recognized as the legitimate representative of the indigenous nations. Consequently, many of these same opinion leaders feel that a single slate of fifty chiefs, rather than the duplication of League chiefs now extant in the United States and Canada, would be more authentic. In the meantime, however, the effort to install suitable candidates in the Canadian roster of chiefs has accelerated. The chiefs' conviction, strengthened by legal advice, has motivated recent intallations, and in particular, nations heretofore poorly represented in the Confederate Council (Seneca and Mohawk) were given representation. Many of these positions had become vacant due to the lack of families with eligible lineages at Six Nations, or because chiefs in these titles were unrecognized by the Confederate Council due to irregular installations. Consequently, in 1989, both the Three Brothers and the Four Brothers had Condolence ceremonies to fill positions according to the traditional protocol.

A condolence ceremony is an expensive and complex undertaking, often lasting eight hours even without the social celebration at night, and necessitates knowledge of the native language and a considerable amount of ritual expertise. That the chiefs were able to sponsor two condolences in successive weeks should substantiate the determination of both moieties to fill empty titles. Yet it is noteworthy that in 1989 certain titles and their adjunct personnel (chiefs' deputy, matron, chiefs' deacon) were borrowed from lineages not conventionally in line for some of these offices, on the ground that the incumbents must understand the traditions as well as be willing to attend meetings of the Confederate Council. As with any institution, the choice of candidates, even ones as definitively ascribed to the matrilineage as are the hereditary chiefs and their "covering" (see p. 80 *infra*), allows for some political maneuvering. And because the rules for the selection of chiefs and their entourage derive from oral tradition, with no single canonical authority, there exists sufficient uncertainty that partisanship may enter. In particular, at issue—already since the beginning of the century, and documented by the varying prescriptions of Seth Newhouse and a committee of chiefs in 1900[5]— is the degree of control granted to the matron (clan mother) as opposed to the chiefs of the moiety concerned with the appointment. Generally today, matrons claim that they are the only arbiters in the choice of chiefs, while the chiefs are convinced that they have veto power, as well as the right to locate titles into whatever lineage they choose should a title remain empty too long. Although there is nothing new about the principle of "borrowing" personnel in case the correct lineage had died out or was unable to nominate a candidate, it is nevertheless instructive to see the pattern of recent applications of this principle.

One aspect of borrowing today which gives the chiefs some latitude in appointing congenial personnel is the necessity of ignoring some of the conventionally prescribed requirements for chieftainship. Because the attributes demanded of a chief were fashioned in preindustrial times and were also amplified in folk practice, finding candidates who fulfill all the desiderata is almost impossible. Acculturation has simply advanced too far, and the assumptions of isolation, subsistence economics, clan adhesion, and a unified aboriginal culture no longer hold true. Consequently, as the chiefs forego some of the ideal qualities for chieftainship, they may ignore those which do not fit the designated individual whom a faction would like installed. It is here that political considerations may enter and that compromises must be accepted. Typical compromises today are: allowing monolingual English speakers; tolerating some Christians; appointing chiefs who do not belong to the canonical clan; choosing persons unable to satisfy the requisite moral

---

[5] For the text of both versions, see Arthur C. Parker, *Parker on the Iroquois*, ed. W. N. Fenton (Syracuse: Syracuse Univ. Press, 1975).

and behavioral standards; accommodating ambitious politicians or individuals who in their life style are deemed too acculturated; overlooking the racial strictures normally demanded; and sanctioning the errors of the current ritual specialists and the misunderstanding of the practitioners. From a strict constructionist point of view the composition of the Council, given such compromises, may be flawed, but the flaws are rationalized as unavoidable by the faction which has been able to gain moiety approval for the appointments.

Here the Confederacy is presented with a dilemma. On the one hand, its legitimacy depends upon continuing as much as possible according to tradition, and on the other hand, leaders wish to make use of the margin for action left them to further their aims. Since at present the ecclesiastical faction is in the ascendency, it has used its opportunities in order to install credibly traditional chiefs and their covering, even if, for example, the matron is the daughter of the chief. In a changing world values must be ordered, and currently the usual Iroquoian emphasis on procedural matters must be subordinated to the dominant ideological concerns.

Primary among these concerns in the 1990s is the restitution of Iroquoian sovereignty under the leadership of a hereditary Council of chiefs, who believe that their authority derives from the Deganawi'da? epic and who conceive of themselves as guardians of a sacred trust. As lineal descendants of supernaturally appointed ancestors who had entered into a covenant with Deganawi'da? to continue their chiefly functions within their matrilineages forever, these chiefs perpetuate Iroquoian policy, thereby ensuring the nations' identity and survival. Consequently, at Six Nations, participation in the Confederate Council is as much an obligation to demonstrate the continuation of a reconstructed native heritage as it is action for political purposes. Although the Confederates hope they may again govern the Reserve in the future, the pragmatic business of the Council as an instrument for local government, which was prominent prior to 1924 and which remains the focus of the Elected Council, is understandably a secondary consideration. The primary concerns at this moment are to save a culture and to be recognized as the legitimate representative of that culture, whether or not Canada truly institutes self-government.

Not surprisingly, the chiefs are apostolic about these priorities and attempt to engage as many people as possible, if not in the institution of chieftainship directly, then in the customs which anchor the institution in a traditional belief system. Obviously, their most congenial constituency is that Longhouse population which construes chiefs as integral to the religion, because the appeal to these members rests on common religious understandings. Those nationalist Longhouse members who disavow the chiefs' authority in the Longhouse itself, as is the case at Lower Cayuga, nevertheless share many of the basic mores and certainly support the Confederate Council as the authentic representative of a sovereign Confederacy. But in addition, the chiefs hope to involve a wider network of individuals who do not share either the religious or the nationalistic motivations for support of the Confederacy. The appeal to many of these is made in asking them to observe the special chief's tenth-day condolence, should a matrilineal relative of a chief die. If the kin of the deceased are already Longhouse members, such a condolence is automatic, but if, as is often the case, the relatives are agnostics or converts to Christianity, the chiefs try to persuade the surviving next of kin to sponsor the ceremony anyway, intimating that failure to do so is disrespectful to Iroquoian tradition. Wittingly or not, the sanctions which usually bring about compliance with these requests are fears concerning transgressions of traditional mortuary customs, for the dead are a source of potential danger. To the chiefs, the ostensible reason for the observance is to clear the mind of a grieving chief (see p. 260 *infra*), but the very fact that the observance takes place emphasizes the importance of the confederate institution of chiefs, and reacquaints the apostates with their heritage. The rules specifying how closely related the deceased and his chief must be to necessitate a tenth-day condolence are vague, giving leeway to the more devout chiefs to incorporate more and more mourners into the traditions of the confederate chiefs. In fact, one of the more important and frequent actions of the chiefs at Six Nations is to conduct such tenth-day observances.

But the insistence on the traditional chief's tenth-day observance is only one of the indications that the current Confederate Council is serious about reviving a culture rather than a mere political system. In the deliberations of the Council, one may observe many of the same attitudes and behaviors which characterize the Longhouse and which corroborate the claim that religion and politics cannot be dissociated. Not only are the dominant themes of identifying oneself as being Indian and respecting one's mutual obligations, of having straight and united minds, of observing the hierarchical structure of man and the spirit forces (see p. ii *supra*) taken for granted, but so are the more specific beliefs in the supplication of the supernatural powers and their consequent efficacious intervention. Thus, Indian tobacco as a messenger, an intercessor, and a facilitator is a commonly used device, and the Council is urged to burn tobacco to aid in the removal of asbestos from schools, to combat disruptive warriors on the Tuscarora Reservation, to oppose the introduction of bingo games there, to strengthen the return of the wampum strings, and to chasten chiefs who have strayed from their duties. Similarly, other feasts and False Face observances at the Longhouse are called upon to counter aggressive moves by warriors at Oka and by smugglers. Another suggestion for the social control of the more deviant forces in society is to summon the miscreants to Six Nations and to have the elders either preach to them or sponsor a recitation of the Great Law of Deganawi'daʔ, for both events are believed to have a salutary influence on the listeners. And, should the warriors repent, the chiefs are very willing to reincorporate them into Iroquoian society.

There is little doubt that the chiefs are earnest about their faith, but they are not naïve, and they simultaneously attempt to send negotiators to trouble spots (such as Oka) to help gain recognition for the Confederacy there. Unfortunately, in the past the necessity of following the procedures of intramoiety and then intermoiety agreement has made rapid action difficult. Furthermore, the chiefs are hampered by their palpable fear of committing the Confederacy to any entangling alliances, and they will not join any organization for fear of losing their sovereignty. In fact, any hint of cooperation with the Canadian government or the Elected Council has brought forth questions by the Mohawk nation, which ironically seems now most militantly conservative, whereas earlier in the century it was considered forward looking.

The recent planning for the forced devolution of education from the Department of Indian Affairs to the Six Nations provides an interesting example of the caution displayed by the Confederate Council, as well as the difficulty of fashioning unanimity within the Council. Realizing that self-administered education was inevitable, a committee, called the Community Education Project, had held wide-ranging interviews for four years, in order to plan the transfer and agree on educational goals. The Confederacy had been represented and involved, establishing a good working relationship with open communication between all the interested parties. In fact, there had been suggestions by the Confederacy that consequent to negotiations by the Elected Council, the strongest and most binding method of concluding the educational arrangements with the Canadian government would be a treaty signed by the Confederate Council, since the Elected Council was seen as a compromised administrative body only and not an independent agent. Such a signatory, according to this argument, would indicate to Canada that the Confederate Council speaks for the entire Reserve and consequently would obligate Canada to deal with it once again. Whether this strategy implies that Canada would recognize the Confederacy as the government of the Six Nations was also discussed, and it was thought that as far as education was concerned, the answer is "yes." At the same time, the Confederacy wished to make a special point of the fact that, if it were the responsible educational administrator, all constituents of the Reserve should be served democratically and that a politically neutral school board would define its relationship to both councils.

Despite a general consensus among the chiefs concerning such an eventuality, there yet were some among them who felt that even this degree of compromise with the Elected Council would jeopardize the Confederacy, and furthermore, one chief from the Four Brothers moiety opposed the education project for religious reasons. Consequently, when the interim board of governors for the postsecondary education program was constituted (since Six Nations has to administer that program from September 1, 1992 until March 1993, when further disposition will be ascertained), the two seats reserved for the Confederate Council had to remain vacant. It is hoped that, with further discussions, the Confederacy will consent to play an official role in Reserve educational policy because by September 1994 all education will have to be self-administered, and it is much to the benefit of the traditional population to have an input concerning bilingual programs and the continuation of the immersion schools.

The Community Education Project's negotiations had engendered an optimistic spirit of anticipation about conciliation between the two Councils particularly because both constituencies realized that, as First Nations who fear Canadian niggardliness in funding education, they shared common aims. Neither Council wishes a system based on taxes from the Reserve population, nor does anyone on the Reserve today desire municipal status. In fact, many non-Confederate inhabitants had looked to the Confederacy to bolster their claims to Native self-government and the benefits which might derive therefrom, and they felt disappointed that the Confederacy did not act more forcefully at a critical moment. What these impatient members perhaps did not understand was that the procedures for consent in the Confederate Council constrain the minority, who must defer to a minority of one, and precisely because the chiefs are earnest about following the traditional procedure as a hallmark of legitimacy, they are effectively barred from swift action.

Actually, the chiefs themselves, along with their renewed traditionalism, realize that some accommodations must be made to satisfy the impatience of their petitioners, and thus they established three committees, comparable to those of the Elected Council, to deal with practical problems of the environment, education, and hunting and fishing. Health and social service committees, especially concentrating on children's aid, are also under discussion. Even after committees have done their work, however, business in the Confederate Council is often held over for later meetings because of its caution about investigating each case and deliberating in the conventional manner (see p. 121 *infra*), and tabling issues has been a very frequent device.

After Tom Longboat, Jr. (son of the Olympic runner), renowned Gaihwi'yo preacher and Secretary of the Confederate Council for many years, died in March 1992, the chiefs appointed two younger knowledgeable Longhouse ritualists who understand Onondaga and Cayuga and are also conversant with English and modern parliamentary procedures. It is hoped that, without infringing unduly on traditional procedures, the importance of issues can be kept in proper perspective by working out an agenda before the monthly meetings, thereby moving business along in an expeditious manner. Consequently, many in the community who had previously paid little attention to the chiefs are hopeful that decisive action is now more likely, and that the common aims—educational funding, retention of lands without taxation, vigilance against environmentally unsound dumping on the Reserve, continuation of currently abated sales taxes, respect for native hunting and fishing rights—will be more readily recognized by Canada. Furthermore, Christian opponents of large-scale gaming are hopeful that the Confederacy, cognizant of the religious prohibition against gambling by the Longhouse community, will cooperate in blocking a positive recommendation for the establishment of gaming casinos on the Reserve.

Even so, when one sees the small number of chiefs at the monthly meetings (an average of twelve to twenty-six attenders, often counting the assistant chiefs who substitute for their titleholders, designated stand-ins, and visiting chiefs from other reservations), one must wonder why the Reserve is so relatively attentive to Confederate pronouncements, which, after all, are totally without legal force. The answer must surely be that there yet remains a sanction system largely based in the Longhouse religious community, which accepts the Council of chiefs as the legitimate locus for leadership, and that non-Longhouse individuals have gained an appreciation of and nostalgia for their traditional heritage. With native self-government a political possibility in the future, the time has come for everyone to look to the past. As in the 1950s, the chiefs do all in their power to reinforce such beliefs precisely because they see themselves, practically and symbolically, as the keepers of the culture and the uncompromised representatives of the Iroquoian nations. And in that capacity, the chiefs issue Confederate status cards to their constituents, which are honored by most merchants.

"Looking to the past" has also brought with it some unexpected problems. Today the desire for an authentic Indian name is keener than ever, but because many families had let the practice of bestowing a matrilineally same-sexed name of a deceased ancestor lapse (see p. 210 *infra*), and because mothers do not remember enough free names from their matrilineage, there is currently a true shortage of names. Furthermore, many of the "keepers of names" (see p. 212 *infra*) have died, and it is now necessary to make scholarly searches for names in anthropological and other archives. Interestingly, both secretaries of the Confederate Council are engaged in this activity, and they are much commended for their efforts. Particularly the adherents of the "down-below" Longhouses are hard pressed for names because, some time after Mr. Joseph Logan, Jr. had been borrowed to fill the Mohawk Bear clan title, Hahstawẽʔthrõ'nthaʔ (see p. 105 *infra*), he discovered that his mother was not, as had been believed, a member of the Ball clan, but that she was in fact a member of the Bear clan. Consequently, his own and his sister's clan designation would have to be changed, as well as that of his sister's offspring and her progeny through women. Many individuals are affected by this reassignment, and most known names are taken, occasioning the comment that "people are now fighting for names." That sentiment about clan-specific names is so strong, and that more and more individuals truly desire names, are further indications of revivalist tendencies. In addition, some of the descendants of this family are now concerned about a correct clan assignation, since marriage within the same clan is not favored, and some engagements are in doubt. In the 1950s, clan exogamy was also desirable, but it was honored more in the breach, and it is surprising that forty years later rules which then were fading are resurrected.

In fact, as ceremonial and political regulations have become partly forgotten or ambiguous, ritualists who fervently wish "to do the right thing," have felt more anguished. The uncertainty concerning a successor to the Thadoda'hoʔ title is a good example. Joseph Logan, Sr., titleholder of this important position from 1904 to 1961, is believed to have declared on his deathbed that no further chief should be installed in this title, and a similar understanding about Thadoda'hoʔ is current in the family of the Onondaga chief Awe'ʔkᵉhnyat. Jesse Lewis, erstwhile holder of that title (from 1922 to the late 1930s) and an acquaintance of Mr. Logan, held the same opinion. At present, there exists an American Thadoda'hoʔ titleholder, however, and it is uncertain whether the disinclination to fill the position derives from a desire to avoid duplication or a belief that the title should be absolutely vacated. Research along these lines is being undertaken by the Confederates, and they are interested in documentary evidence to settle this doctrinal point. In general, the chiefs are as earnest about following the commands of revered deceased traditionalists and of Deganawi'da? as the Longhouse congregation is intent on following its notables and Handsome Lake, and the attendant difficulties—of acculturation, of differing traditions and understandings, of reinterpreted and syncretized concepts—are identical in the political and religious domains.

What can one predict about the next forty years? I believe that the Longhouse will persist, even if more and more of the ceremonies will be forced to incorporate some English. I also believe that the Confederate Council will persist and will remain integrated into the religious and traditional culture. In fact, precisely the coupling of a forum of political activity with a traditional way of life has already been instrumental in keeping Six Nations as conservative as it is. But in the political arena, as in the religious one, there are some signs which portend crises and disillusionment.

Perhaps foremost among these is the well-entrenched position of the Elected Council, because a majority of the Reserve members are unwilling to replace this modern, complex bureaucratic institution by a Council that still operates on traditional lines, no matter how authentically Indian and how ideally legitimate. Secondly, younger "warriors," who lack the religious traditions of most of the current chiefs but consider themselves more militantly nationalistic, are willing and ready to use any means to achieve power and could once again take control. Although the chiefs are properly wary of such a danger and in their selection for office have bypassed individuals suspected of warrior sentiments, their self-imposed decency and insistence on united minds, peace, and supernatural sanction may render them politically ineffectual. Yet another worrisome fact for the Confederate traditionalists is the increasing number of interracial marriages. To counter the assimilative effect of such a liaison, the Six Nations spouse would have to convert his/her partner to the Longhouse and to a belief in the hereditary principle of office holding. Furthermore, as self-appointed guardians of traditional morality, the chiefs are also concerned about the social pathologies of the times. They hope to bring all errant individuals, but particularly the young, back to Handsome Lake's standards of morality, which certainly preclude drinking, drugs, gambling, smuggling, contraception, abuse of spouses, and rowdiness. And finally, there is the ominous possibility that Canada will decide that the Six Nations Iroquois are advanced and Canadianized to the extent that they can be subsidized at a lower level than at present (as is already feared for the educational budget) or even taxed. Forced Canadianization inevitably means greater acculturation, and that in turn threatens the retention of native institutions.

Foreboding aside, Iroquoian conservative society has been astoundingly adaptive and resilient. It has successfully constructed mechanisms that make for cohesiveness and pride of nation. And in the last forty years, pride of nation has been extensively cultivated and is likely to remain an outstanding fact for the Mohawk, Oneida, Onondaga, Cayuga, and Seneca peoples.

BIBLIOGRAPHY

DICKASON, OLIVE P.
   1992.   *Canada's First Nations: A History of Founding Peoples from Earliest Times* (Norman: The University of Oklahoma Press).
FOSTER, MICHAEL K.
   1982.   *Canada's First Languages* (Language and Society, no. 7, Office of the Commissioner of Official Languages, and insert to article, Ottawa).
HODENOSAUNEE AT GRAND RIVER
   1991.   *Position Paper on Self Government* and *Addendum* (Brantford: Woodland Cultural Centre).
SWEETGRASS FIRST NATIONS LANGUAGE COUNCIL INC.
   1992.   *The Status of Aboriginal Languages In Southern Ontario* (Sweetgrass News, issue 3, vol. 2, special edition, pp. 1–6, Brantford).
WEAVER, SALLY M.
   1978.   *Six Nations of the Grand River, Ontario* (in "Handbook of North American Indians," Bruce G. Trigger, volume editor, vol. 15, pp. 525–536, Washington: Smithsonian Institution).
WOODBURY, HANNI
   1992.   *Concerning the League: The Iroquois League Tradition as Dictated in Onondaga by John Arthur Gibson* (newly elicited, edited, and translated by Hanni Woodbury in collaboration with Reg Henry and Harry Webster on the basis of A. A. Goldenweiser's manuscript, Algonquian and Iroquoian Linguistics, Memoir no. 9, Winnipeg).

Wellesley, Massachusetts   Annemarie Anrod Shimony
January 1994

I. STRUCTURE OF THE ORTHODOX COMMUNITY

A STATEMENT OF THE PROBLEM
A SURVEY OF THE CONSERVATIVE POPULATION

IT has long been observed that the Iroquois Indian has retained an amazing number of native traits in the face of 300 years of white contact. The 7,000[1] Indians residing at Six Nations Reserve, Ohsweken, Ontario, Canada are no exception, particularly those who are still members of the four Longhouses dedicated to the religion of Handsome Lake. The exact number of members cannot be determined, since there is no formal enrollment, but a reasonable estimate is approximately thirteen hundred to fourteen hundred active members, and these are the primary carriers of the conservative tradition.

My method of estimation is as follows: On the most popular day of the ceremonial calendar, namely, the first day on which the Great Feather Dance is performed during the Midwinter Ceremony, attendance at the Longhouse is greatest. Usually, there are from 300 to 350 people, including children, at each Longhouse. Allowance for overlapping personnel (since the Longhouses do not schedule their events on identical days, so that individuals often go to two or more Longhouses for the same rite) and also for absentees would yield a conservative total of thirteen hundred to fourteen hundred. Martha C. Randle (1951: 176) gives the number of Longhouse people as 1,500; Rioux (1952: 94) estimates 1,100; and the Superintendent of the Six Nations Agency for the Dominion government estimates 1,260. On the whole, at least from recent data, the Longhouse population has been stable. Speck (1949: 174) gives attendance records at Sour Springs Longhouse for 1933, and, despite the general claim that Sour Springs "is losing fast," the attendance then was about equal to, or even less than, that of today. Of course, in view of the fact that the population as a whole is increasing rapidly (and has more than tripled since Brant settled at Grand River), there is a relative decline in the Longhouse. The exact ratio of Longhouse to non-Longhouse people over time cannot be determined, and in particular it is not known what percentage of Brant's Mohawk followers were Longhouse members, for there do not seem to be any statistical accounts of attendance earlier than Speck's. Of the four Longhouses on the Reserve today, Lower Cayuga probably has the largest congregation, but Rioux's statement (1952: 96) that half of all Longhouse members belong to Lower Cayuga is probably an overestimate.

---

[1] Fenton (1940: 215) gives the number 4,500; in 1950 Fenton (1950: 40) estimates 6,000; Rioux (1952: 94) mentions 5,500; Randle (1951: 175) gives the number 6,000. As of July, 1956, the Canadian Indian Affairs Branch, Six Nations Agency, lists the population as follows: 2,600 Mohawk, 650 Oneida, 1,450 Cayuga, 400 Onondaga, 250 Seneca, 550 Tuscarora. Also residing on the Reserve are 200 Delaware. It must be remembered, however, that the Canadian government registers nationality patrilineally, so that for social and ceremonial purposes the count might be quite different. For example, the child of a Cayuga mother and Mohawk father would be registered as Mohawk, whereas the Iroquois themselves would consider the child Cayuga. The Cayuga registration is apt to be especially inaccurate, since many residents attempt to be placed on the Cayuga list in order to collect an annual disbursement of Cayuga interest funds (approximately $2.00 to $3.00 per person per year). For such purposes the wife of a Cayuga husband is also registered as Cayuga. It must also be remembered that only about 75 per cent of the total membership reside on the Reserve at any one time, especially since many are absent for seasonal labor. Finally, it should be noted that approximately 400 Chippewa live at New Credit (or Mississauga Tract), which adjoins Six Nations. This region, together with Six Nations, is officially designated as the Grand River Reserve (see Figs. 1, 2).

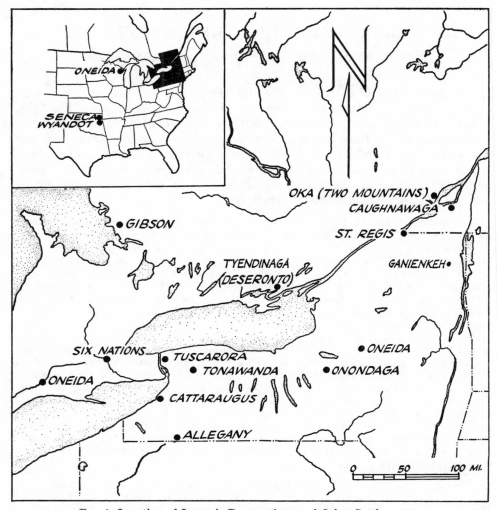

FIG. 1. Location of Iroquois Reservations and Other Settlements.

Perhaps the most striking feature of Six Nations is the factional and diverse nature of the social groupings. Groups align and realign on almost every conceivable level. Religion, political allegiance, kinship, economic status, and degree of acculturation are only some of the criteria differentiating one group from another. It is possible, however, to identify without undue arbitrariness the group which carries on the Iroquois tradition. It consists of those individuals who share allegiances and characteristics as follows: in religion they adhere to the Longhouse; in politics they uphold or advocate the hereditary chieftainships; in kinship matters they count descent matrilineally and recognize clan and moiety affiliation; they reside primarily

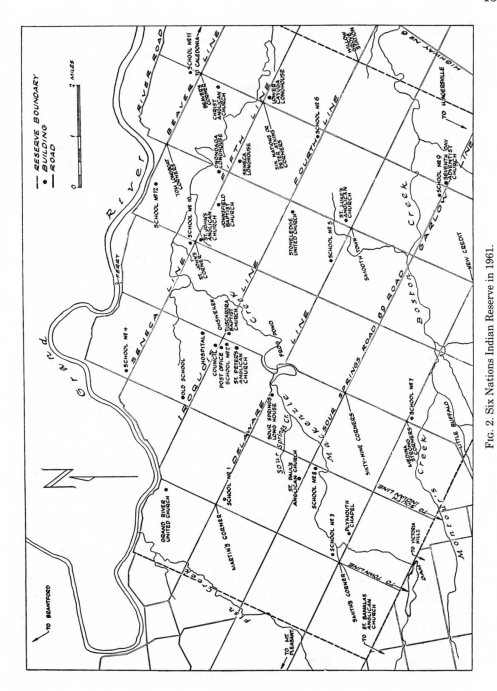

Fig. 2. Six Nations Indian Reserve in 1961.

on the Reserve; and, while willing to accept some white material traits, they are consciously opposed to acculturation in regard to their philosophy of life. This group strongly desires to remain Indian and attaches a superior value to Indian ways and mores. Their motto is: "Do not step out of the Indian canoe into the white man's scow." Economic status, while an element of differentiation, is not a satisfactory criterion for distinguishing the conservative from the nonconservative group, for many of the Longhouse people are relatively well off in comparison with some of the Christian and more acculturated groups. Nor is it possible to distinguish between the majority of the conservative group and the majority of the acculturated members in respect to living accommodations, log or clapboard house, type of car, television set, material goods in general, or occupation. Ideally, followers of Handsome Lake are enjoined to live as simply and traditionally as possible. By this, of course, the preacher interprets "traditional" in terms of his concept of "Indian living." At convention times and at the Strawberry preaching event, when the Code of Handsome Lake is recited, the preacher interpolates and extemporizes upon the standard text. He recommends that people should live in log houses, should have no electricity, should collect no material wealth, choose no occupation which requires reading, writing, or education, and preferably should farm.

Parker (1912: 38) gives a version of the Code of Handsome Lake which suggests building houses just like those of the white population; but at Six Nations, preachers definitely frown on building wooden houses. Parker presents the Code as saying that two men of each tribe should be instructed in English; yet the informants seem to agree that the elder men and preachers are opposed to sending anyone to the English schools. At present, however, all children on the Reserve go to government grade schools, where all instruction is in English and follows the standard Canadian curriculum, until age sixteen; and many Longhouse children go to the high schools in neighboring towns off the Reserve despite strong disapproval from some of their elders. Jackson (1830), quoted by Deardorff (1951), reports that Handsome Lake advised against school for children. Handsome Lake's recommendation of farming is also to be found in Parker's version of the Code.

Above all, one should not work outside the Reserve, and, if possible, not outside the Longhouse community. The preaching is a conscious attempt at isolation in the face of acculturative pressure, but it is rather flagrantly disregarded, even by some of the preachers themselves. The standard retort is, "One has to live," and this is a realistic accommodation to the present facts of life, especially since many of the members do not own enough land to make farming a worthwhile activity. As a result, Longhouse followers and Christians engage in the same economic pursuits: farming, seasonal labor on the nearby fruit and tobacco farms, unskilled labor in the neighboring communities of Brantford, Caledonia, Buffalo, and Niagara Falls, some semiskilled factory labor, some high-steel construction, and some clerical and domestic jobs. With the earnings both groups tend to buy the same material things, so that the furnishings are indicative only of the income status, and not of the cultural allegiance, of a family. Ceremonial paraphernalia, such as splint corn sieves and baskets, water drums and turtle rattles, cow-horn rattles and snow snakes, may be seen in the conservative household after some examination, but by no means are they conspicuously displayed. Especially, more "particular" instruments, such as flutes and Ohgi'we drums, are generally kept out of sight, as are most costumes and masks. The reticence about displaying one's Longhouse affiliation is an indication of the pressure to acculturate, but should not be construed as a loss of culture.

The empirical description of the conservative group given above is sufficiently discriminating that almost any member of the society could, from this description alone, be classified as an adherent to either the conservative or nonconservative culture. This distinction is easily recognizable to both an outside observer and members of the Reserve. In other words, there are practically two distinct cultures at Six Nations, and the distinction between them is clear cut and obvious.

It is also true, of course, that in a rapidly changing culture, subject to many outside pressures, the process of acculturation is not an all-or-nothing change but consists of a selective acceptance of individual and discrete traits by individual people. Consequently, one can find individuals representative of a continuum of "Indianness," or conservatism, from very orthodox to completely Canadianized.[2] Neither pole is extant today, since there is now no aboriginal Iroquois culture, nor is there an Indian on the Reserve who does not have some tinge of "Iroquoianism," if only by the fact of being a Reserve Indian. Where precisely along this continuum one says "he is Indian, and he is Canadian" is a matter of fruitless categorization. One has either to accept the statement and belief of the individual concerned or else to have a "feel" about the allegiance of the individual. As mentioned above, there are criteria definitive of the orthodox pattern—e.g., Longhouse allegiance, matrilineal descent, health attitudes—but to specify a definite set of these as necessary to classify an individual one way or another would be academic and spurious. The fine combinations of traits and values, and the degrees of tenacity with which each is held, are almost endless; nor is there a rational system for each individual.

THE PROBLEM OF CONSERVATISM

One purpose of this study is to describe and characterize the conservative culture as it exists today at Six Nations Reserve. Although one is continually reminded of the varying degrees of acculturation of individual members of the Reserve, the extent to which this culture remains intact, both in personnel and in constituent traits, is impressive. The Indians of Six Nations have been in close contact with the dominant white culture for over three hundred years, and have been subjected to political domination, the preaching of subsidized missionaries, economic controls, and the attractions of modern technology and entertainment. Understandably, the

---

[2] By this I mean indistinguishable from the surrounding Canadian farmers. It could be claimed that these farmers are somewhat acculturated to the Six Nations Indians and have accepted a few traits from them, but this is surely a minor consideration, since there is a strong prejudice against the Indians and their culture. Few Canadians, other than those who marry into the Reserve, concern themselves with the old Iroquois culture or its remaining traits. Perhaps the most acceptable traits are those concerned with medicinal curing (some of the surrounding tradespeople trying Iroquois herbs and cures) and some of the folk beliefs, such as bad luck due to owls.

conservative culture at present is neither identical with the aboriginal culture nor merely a concatenation of aboriginal traits, but rather a historical outgrowth from the aboriginal culture under acculturative pressure. An "explanation" of the conservative culture today would necessarily involve an intricate reconstruction of this historical process, which will not be undertaken here. (See Fenton, 1940 and 1949a, and Deardorff, 1951, for historical reconstructions.) However, contemporary ethnographic data on the Iroquois, together with reference to the major historical descriptions, ought to provide the basis for at least a partial understanding of the composition and viability of the conservative culture today. The second purpose of this study is to arrive at just such an understanding: specifically, to see how various elements function in the culture as a whole, to describe the devices of the society for maintaining its membership and continuing its practices under difficult circumstances, and to discern the primary motivations of the members for "keeping on."

The following four chapters are a discussion of the structure of the conservative community. Traditionally, each of the Iroquois tribes, or "nations," had a quite complex social organization, with subdivisions into moieties, clans, lineages, and families. The second chapter is concerned with the functions of these social units at present. In particular it is claimed that in many instances the distinctions between these units have become blurred, that they have lost or exchanged many of the functions historically attributed to them, and that their matrilineal character has either been modified in recent generations or was never as unequivocal as the anthropological literature asserts. It is also stated that the units of social organization have some interesting relations to the Longhouse. On the one hand, a number of the functions historically assigned to the clans are now performed by the Longhouse, thereby diminishing the importance of the clans. On the other hand, the Longhouse helps perpetuate the clan and moiety divisions by giving them roles in the Longhouse ceremonials. The Longhouse has, in fact, emerged as the central social institution of the conservative culture, and each of the four Longhouses at Six Nations functions not only as a religious organization, but as a pulpit for moral education, an irredentist society for defending Indian rights, a cooperative for mutual aid, a medical center, and a social club. The composition, organization, and leadership of the Longhouse are discussed in the third and fourth chapters. The fifth chapter is concerned with the hereditary council of "peace chiefs," who traditionally governed the Confederacy of the Iroquois nations, but whose political powers were transferred in 1924 by the Canadian Indian Office to a newly constituted elective council. The attempts of the displaced chiefs to obtain special prerogatives in the Longhouse illustrate one of the remarkable devices by which the conservative culture has survived, namely, the reshaping of an institution which is unable to maintain its original functions in the face of external pressure.

The sixth, seventh, and eighth chapters are concerned with the content of the conservative culture. Much of the ideal culture is expressed and periodically communicated to the orthodox members in various Longhouse addresses, particularly the Thanksgiving Address, the speeches at the calendric agricultural rituals, and the preaching of the Code of Handsome Lake. These addresses and the ceremonies in which they occur are described in the sixth chapter. In the seventh chapter there is a discussion of the events in the life cycle of the orthodox member, and it is stated that many of the peculiarities of these events can be traced to the themes and maxims of the ideal culture. Furthermore, the Longhouse addresses are claimed to have a general conservative effect over and above their specific recommendations, for they contain frequent exhortations to preserve "Indian ways," whatever these may be. Conversely, following the daily routine of "Indian" life induces participation in the Longhouse, for many of the secular activities, such as naming, forming a ritual friendship, and performing certain cures, must be performed in the Longhouse. Finally, in the eighth chapter, there is an examination of Iroquois medicine, which is the area of greatest elaboration and most intense interest in the culture. It is proposed that concern for personal health is the ultimate sanction for a very large part of the activity of the conservative members, including participation in the Longhouse.

The outline given above constitutes a hypothesis about the interconnections of the elements of the conservative culture at Six Nations and about the forces which tend to perpetuate it. The attempt to demonstrate this hypothesis will necessarily involve a rather comprehensive ethnological survey of the culture.

SOCIAL ORGANIZATION

RESIDENCE

WITHIN an area of approximately 72 square miles, surveyed roughly as a rectangle, 12 miles along the southern shore of the Grand River and 6 miles in average depth to the south of the river (located in Tuscarora and Onondaga Townships of Brant County, Ontario and in Oneida Township of Haldimand County, Ontario), about 80°13' to 80° longitude and 43° to 43°6' latitude, live the 7,000 Indians of the Six Nations Reserve. (There is also a small tract on the north side of the river of about 2 square miles.) This area is what remains of the land granted by the British to resettle the loyalist Iroquois led by Joseph Brant, who had fought on behalf of the Crown against the colonists and had consequently left New York State.

The original stipulation, according to Brant (quoted by Stone, 1838, 2: 239), was "six miles on each side of the river, from the mouth to its source." Unfortunately, there has been some confusion and ill feeling over the status of the reservation lands ever since. The Haldimand deed of 1784, according to some sources (Noon, 1949: 86), first gave lands "upon the Banks of the River commonly called the Ouse or Grand River, running into Lake Erie, and extending in that proportion to the Head of the same River . . .," and the Simcoe deed of 1793 gave the definition "six miles on each side." Stone implies that Brant knew of the "six-mile clause" from the beginning but thought that this territory would be encroached upon by white settlers and thus would be useless for hunting, whereas it was too large to be tilled; consequently, he began to sell some of the area. This caused dispute, and the Simcoe deed definitely forbade the sale of land to any non-Indian. It further declared the lands Crown lands, which today is considered the legal justification of the Dominion trusteeship, since the Dominion government considers itself the legitimate heir of the Crown. When land-settlement questions arise in the elected council at Six Nations, the councilors nominally pass on all claims, but in reality the final authority rests with the Indian Affairs Branch.

Except for a slight clustering at Ohsweken, the Six Nations Reserve consists of scattered homesteads in a predominantly agricultural setting. According to tradition, various bands with their leaders settled at particular locations within the Reserve, for example, the Mohawk in the western section, a band of Cayuga led by Chief Dyoōhyŏ'ngo in the central section (around Frog Pond and 69 Corners), another Cayuga band at the extreme east, the Delaware along the Smoothtown Road running from the center of the Reserve to the southeast, and so on. However, it is rather difficult today to assess the situation in these terms, since with tribal intermarriage, neolocal residence, and inheritance of land by children, wives, and friends the national populations have merged. The Canadian government lists band affiliations patrilineally, so that a tribal reconstruction with the intent of discovering a pattern of band residence would be extremely difficult. Perhaps the only large blocks of land associable with tribal groups today are the Mohawk territory in the northwestern section and the Cayuga territory in the northeastern section.

Despite the fact that the Reserve as a whole is owned by the Six Nations and presumably no part of it is alienated, ownership among the population is on an individual basis. This practically destroys the aboriginal pattern of clan owner-ship,[1] especially when combined with the Canadian emphasis on patrilineal succes-sion. Since both men and women own land, any man who dies intestate leaves his lands to his legal wife and children, or if he has several families, to the children of his first legal wife. Thus the land is often lost to his own clan. In any case the land is lost to his mother's family. At the death of a woman that part of the property given to her children remains in the clan, the remainder is, in general, alienated. When there are no nuclear-family heirs the property may be awarded at the dis-cretion of the council or revert to band land. Usually, there are a number of con-testants—siblings, nieces, nephews, the individual who cared for the deceased during the final illness, or even common-law partners who made improvements upon the land. In theory there is still a semblance of tribal control, since all transfers, in-heritances as well as sales of land, should be approved by the elected council, but in such settlements the council makes no attempt to keep family and clan hold-ings intact.

Parents who own tracts of land often express the intention, while they are alive, of dividing it among their children, and a son or daughter who marries may settle on this property. Often rent is paid to the parents, and, indeed, a number of old couples augment their income from such a source. Ideally, it is considered wrong to charge rent for land which is used by one's own children, so that, on the whole, such transactions are kept secret. Since land is usually divided among all the children who wish to remain at home, no single rule of either matrilocality or patrilocality emerges. The newly married couple usually lives wherever there is land and "a place" (i.e., a house), or, if both spouses have landholdings, where the particular situation is most gratifying. Such factors as location, fertility of the soil, amiability and health of in-laws are considered, but no rule of residence is held up as the ideal. In such cases, however, where neither partner has any landholdings or neither will live with in-laws, the Canadian idea of the prerogative of the husband prevails. In these instances the wife is expected to settle at the discretion of the husband. This is particularly applicable in neolocal residence off the Reserve. Also, when there is no land available, the couple often stays with one or the other of the in-laws,

[1] Morgan (1901, 2: 273) says: "As a member of the clan or household an individual had the right to a place in the dwelling, to a share in its food supply, and to the exclusive possession of a field. When he died or emigrated the clan was his heir, or, more accurately, his administra-tor." Also *ibid.*: 272: "The tribe had its property also—its lands, tenements, and heredita-ments . . ." For documentation on aboriginal land concepts, namely that land belonged to the nation, or tribe, *in perpetuum* and could not be personally owned, see also Snyderman (1951: 15–34). Since land went with the residential longhouse, a matrilocality was feasible. Parker (1910: 24) speaks of "communal fields" and also of certain fields reserved for food for councils and national feasts. On page 92 he mentions individual rights to fruits cultivated on clan property. Goldenweiser (1912: 467) says: ". . . in ancient times a clan owned a burial ground and possibly communal lands."

usually depending upon who has the most room, until a neolocal residence can be found.

Fenton (1951b: 43) has noticed a tendency for two or three related nuclear families to aggregate in a cluster. This is due just to the type of land inheritance explained above and to one other reason: namely, there is a concept that "homes are for old age," and, therefore, before any land is sold, siblings should be given a first lien on it.[2] Especially with the increasing emphasis on agriculture, owning land and leaving it to one's children has become a focal value, and childless farmers with large landholdings are much pitied.

Since the general pattern of land divestment outlined above has been in force for about 80 years, it may be fairly stated that residence today is determined primarily by the economic situation in each instance, and any original band settlements or concentrated holdings by one religious faction or another have been dissolved. Neighborhoods are only residential units and seldom have in-group feeling or band-type organization. Those activities which are organized by neighborhood residence, for example, the adolescent softball games, in which teams are formed according to the "line" on which members live, have very little social cohesion and break up at the end of the softball season. Furthermore, all the residents along the "line" (the roads dividing the Reserve into concessions, in the Canadian township pattern) may not even know each other.

In one sense, of course, the Reserve *in toto* represents a community, since there is a definite feeling of loyalty and identification in being a band member and living at Six Nations. However, 7,000 people cannot interact intimately or reside together in face-to-face association. The point, therefore, is not that there are no definite communities, but that these are determined by factors other than immediate residential propinquity.

THE UNITS OF SOCIAL ORGANIZATION

Traditionally, the Iroquois have been designated as *the* example of the kinship state. While such a designation would be inaccurate today, it still is true that the old social organization has, with few changes, been maintained in connection with the conservative political system and with the Longhouse organization.

The units of social organization recognized at Six Nations are as follows: (1) The NUCLEAR FAMILY (no Iroquois term). (2) The OHWACHIRA, or EXTENDED FAMILY (khwadji'ya'ã?, akhwa'dji'ya?, ohwa'dji'ya; Mohawk ohwatsi'ra?). In the literature this has always been defined as the matrilineal extended family. Today, however, according to some informants, it may be understood to include the mother's

[2] Fenton and A. F. Brown (1951b: 41) point out that at Onondaga and Tonawanda Reservations, and to a somewhat lesser extent at Allegany and Cattaraugas, the physical distance between the separate households of a mother and a daughter is not great. At Six Nations, however, distances are often 10 miles, and mobility is therefore strained, despite cars. Children may come home for special occasions, but the land dispersion definitely does work against the matrilineal household.

father and some of his kin as well. (3) The FATHER'S KINDRED (agadõniho'nõˀ). In the literature this has been interpreted as the father's matrilineage. In fact, however, the group designated by this term, as it is used at Six Nations, is the father's bilateral kindred. (4) The LINEAGE. This often coincides with the matrilineal extended family. It is not terminologically distinguished from the extended family. (5) The CLAN, i.e., MATRISIB (gasya'deˀ, or ˀoda'aˀ; Mohawk oˀta'raˀ). (6) The MOIETY, or "SIDE." There is no general term for moiety, though in ceremonial discourse they speak of the "two sides of the fire" (thodidjẽ'hõt) in referring to the moieties. In English the term "side" is used. Among the Cayuga the separate moieties are named for the leading clan in each, namely Wolf and Turtle. Among the Onondaga, as also among the Seneca, they are named the Two Fireplaces and the Four Houses (Onondaga: dehodiˀda'ãge, gaye'i hodinũs'ge), respectively. (7) The TRIBE. On political and politico-ceremonial occasions this may exhibit a phratry pattern. This is not necessarily a moiety pattern, but may be a tripartite or quadripartite organization. (8) The LEAGUE. This also has a moiety organization, being divided into the Three Brothers (Onondaga, Mohawk, and Seneca) and the Four Brothers (Cayuga, Oneida, and the adopted nations of the Tuscarora and Delaware, adding later the Saponi, Tutelo, and Nanticoke).

Whereas all eight of these kinds of units are recognized in varying degrees and believed important for certain purposes, there has developed among most of the population a general confusion as to delineation, function, and even linguistic identification. The indefiniteness of the social distinctions of the lineage, clan, phratry, and even moiety are due in part to the peculiar historical circumstances of Six Nations Reserve; in part to the particular interaction of the four Longhouses and the system of Confederate chiefs; and in part to the localization, reinterpretation, and disintegration of relevant traits of the older and more complete culture. While almost all the participants are specifically aware of the current confusion and disorganization (it is usually expressed in Reserve parlance as "we are slipping," "we are going down hill," "we're losing fast"), few find this very disturbing. The stock retort is, "It is not particular," meaning no physical harm, such as death or disease, will result from inaccurate social identification. However, this does not negate the central position of social organization, but simply implies that the sanctions for maintaining a *particular* system of clans, phratries, and moieties are either flexible or weakening. For example, enough awareness and attention yet adhere to proper clan and moiety affiliation that when an individual switches from one side of the Longhouse to the other, or consistently sits with the wrong clan, be it from ignorance or willfullness, comments are made; but the transgressor is often not even told of his error, for it is considered more unpleasant to criticize than to endure the social misdemeanor. That this rather lenient attitude has existed quite a while is indicated by Goldenweiser's (1914: 369) astonishment in 1913, when he found that "the clan and the maternal family, notwithstanding the existence of separate terms for the two kinds of social units, are constantly being confounded by even the most competent informants."

THE NUCLEAR FAMILY

CITIZENSHIP

Even though the identification of the nuclear family presents no problems, the Canadian government has, by its insistence on a patrilineal system of band enrollment, disturbed the unity and continuity of the family. Since official band enrollment is accounted patrilineally only, a Six Nations woman is denied the right to confer citizenship on a non-Six Nations man through marriage; in fact, she herself loses citizenship in the band. Consequently, any offspring of a band woman by a non-band husband is also denied citizenship in the Canadian band; nor is the individual accepted in the United States band (assuming the father was an American Indian, which is frequently the case), for here the child is enrolled in the band through the citizenship of the mother. Furthermore, should a woman later divorce or leave her non-band husband and bear children by a subsequent marriage with a band member, her children are not automatically Canadian band members, but their citizenship must first be granted by the elected council. While this lack of citizenship would not interfere in the ceremonial duties of the individual in Canada, since all Canadian government impositions of patrilineal affiliations are systematically ignored in such matters as clan affiliation and duties, chieftainship, ceremonial obligations, etc., it does interfere with the continuity of the family, for the unfortunate individual cannot inherit land or legally remain at Six Nations. In practice, the council—the elected legislative body which replaced the hereditary council in 1924—is not particularly strict about insisting on expulsion. However, the real authority resides in the Indian Affairs Branch of the Canadian government (a subdivision of the Department of Citizenship and Immigration), and a shift in its enforcement policy is always a possibility, particularly since the department may at times not be completely free from political pressure. On the whole the local branches of the Indian Office try not to exhibit their authority excessively, so that the council has at least a semblance of autonomy. Consequently, the Indian Office seldom interferes in local cases of citizenship determination. But Noon (1949: 82) cites an instance in which the council was actually overruled by the department in a citizenship case, and the knowledge of such a case fosters a certain amount of insecurity. Even when an individual appeals to the council for the purpose of obtaining citizenship, he is not always successful. Noon (1949: 76–82, 126–37) cites various cases in which contradictory verdicts were reached and citizenship was granted to one litigant and denied to a second litigant in a similar position. As in any political body, influence, local politics, and favoritism to relatives or special friends are important factors. These inevitable human phenomena are especially marked in a society in which family ties are strongly maintained and revered, and in which the government-imposed council is either not recognized as fully legitimate or is considered a means of political and personal advancement for the councilors.

LEGITIMACY

A second very prominent feature of the Grand River nuclear family is the emphasis on legitimacy. This emphasis is again imposed by the government, because in traditional Iroquois law legitimacy is of minor importance. However, today, a child may be a citizen of a band only if legitimately registered, that is, the mother must be married and claim the child by this marriage. When this is not the case, application must be made to the council for the admission of the individual. Here again, a large element of uncertainty enters as to the direction of the council's decision. No set standard of rules is followed, though it is easier to enroll an illegitimate child both of whose parents are band members than one whose one parent happens to belong to another band, or is non-Indian, or an enfranchised Indian. These provisions seem particularly unjust to the orthodox Iroquois, especially since the function of the nuclear family in these situations is a strange and new one. Band membership, or, modernly expressed, citizenship, was automatically determined by birth into the clan of the mother, and consequently was a function of the clan. The mother determined the allegiance of her offspring by virtue of her membership in the clan, not by virtue of her marriage to her husband. The consequence of the imposed new function of the nuclear family has given the family a definitely patrilineal political status which does not fit very well into the otherwise matrilineally oriented and extended Iroquoian pattern of social organization. In fact, it may be just this confusion which causes the individual cases of citizenship determination (aside from favoritism in the council) to be so arbitrarily decided.

The superimposed emphasis on legitimacy has actually been somewhat disruptive of social relations among the orthodox community, producing considerable ambivalence in various situations. Aboriginally, marriage was not an emphasized *rite de passage*, nor is the Longhouse marriage ceremony today a complicated or important ritual (much in contrast to Christian Indian marriages), but the emphasis on legitimacy now focuses much attention on marriage and mate choosing. Parents show particular concern that their daughters marry band members and that the children of any marriage be legitimately enrolled on the band lists. Should a daughter contract a relationship in such a manner as to be deprived of her band membership, her children are also automatically excluded from the band lists. If land is deeded to someone who is not officially a member of the band, it must be disposed of to a band member within three years. Longhouse families with a strong attachment to the land feel particularly aggrieved at the entire shift in emphasis in social relations, which has resulted in uniting inheritance with legitimacy of marriage and conception. Again the nuclear family is involved in a new role.

The Christian church, from Jesuit times, has also added considerable weight to an emphasis on legitimacy, and legitimacy was evidently a matter of concern during the period of Handsome Lake, the Iroquois prophet. Handsome Lake considered the subject and admonished his followers not to chastise a bastard. Section 18 of the Parker version of the Code (1913: 35) states:

Tell your people that ofttimes when a woman hears that a child is born and goes to see it, she returns and says in many houses where she stops that its mother's husband is not its father. Now we say that it is exceedingly wrong to speak such evil of children. The Creator formed the children as they are; therefore, let the people stop their evil sayings.

Also he advised each spouse to overlook the infidelities of the other (sections 11 and 12), especially if the couple had a child (section 18). The very inclusion of these topics indicates a concern therewith, and this concern has been particularly heightened at Six Nations by the patrilineal emphasis of the nuclear family and the large Christian overlay. Handsome Lake's dicta give rise to a rather ambivalent attitude: on the one hand, the Longhouse marriage is characterized as particularly binding, obeying a higher law (that of Handsome Lake and the Great Creator), and, on the other hand, the marriage is considered haphazard due to the lenient incorporation of the illegitimate child and the casualness of the ritualization of the marriage contract. To berate a bastard is a sin, according to the Code, and despite the inevitable gossip, the orthodox member accepts illegitimate children without particular prejudice. A well-known anecdote might illustrate the feelings of the Christian and the orthodox groups on this subject. A certain prominent member of the Reserve, who himself was a son and nephew of hereditary chiefs, had embraced Christianity and became much concerned with the registry and assignation of children on the tribal rolls, calling illegitimate children "bastards." In view of his conversion and prominent social position he was disliked for his pride. Later, when his own daughter bore an illegitimate child, it was rather universally agreed to be a case of direct punishment by the Creator for disobeying Gaihwi'yo and calling other people's offspring "bastards."

ADOPTION

Adoption is still another function once attributed to the extended family and the clan and now taken over by the nuclear family in all except ceremonial form. Hewitt (1920: 530, 532, 534) ascribes the right to adopt an alien through the advice of the presiding matron to the ohwachira as well as to the clan through the action of one of the constituent ohwachira. Today, however, any serious adoption, with intent to receive disbursements of funds, to be inscribed on band rolls, and to inherit land, must be made by the nuclear family on behalf of the individual to be adopted. Cases of approval by the council are rare, especially lately, since the emphasis of the government and the council is on decreasing tribal rolls if at all possible, rather than on increasing or reconstituting an extended family after a war or loss of a member as in aboriginal times. Citizenship by incorporation into the social structure was the prime mechanism of the Iroquois for population maintenance and was an effective way to deal with conquered tribes. Both individual and tribal adoptions are a familiar cultural theme, documented for at least 300 years. But even then two types of adoption were distinguishable, the adoption to replenish a deceased or lost member of the family and honorary adoption to indicate friendship and confer certain obligations and privileges (see Parker, 1916: 49–50). Beauchamp (1907: 404) takes note of this distinction and mentions that the latter type of adoption "can now be had for a consideration." Chadwick (1897: 47–8) also discusses adoption in Canada in his time, listing the various dignitaries adopted by the council, and remarks that they were expected to give small presents to the council.

Today at Six Nations three types of adoption can be recognized and distinguished.

There is the family adoption, done legally through the elected council and the Department of Indian Affairs, though prior to 1924 it was in the domain of the hereditary chiefs and the Indian Department. This type of adoption, which replaces the old system of replenishing a family, occurs mainly between related families, as when a sister or mother's sister adopts an illegitimate child as her own, and it also occurs when babies are left on doorsteps. (Foundlings do actually still appear at Six Nations. The only white male to have been adopted at the Reserve was left on the steps of a woman, who reared the child, now an integrated member of the community. There are other white males among the population, but they married in before the rules against living on the Reserve and being placed on the rolls other than through birth and adoption were as rigidly enforced as they are now.) Once legally adopted, of course, the member can also be inducted ceremonially, be given a name in the Longhouse, and enjoy all privileges of the native-born citizen. This, however, is not the case in the other two types of adoption, in which the legal and political aspects of the person have perforce become divorced from the ceremonial aspects.

A less important type of adoption, which is akin to the type purchasable in Hewitt's time, is adoption by the elected council. Here a prominent member of the government, a dignitary, or a benefactor can be named a member of the tribe, which means that he usually pays (or the tribe subsidizes from tribal funds) a sum of $75.00, for which a Plains-type headdress is purchased, and the chief of the elected council or the Superintendent of Indian Affairs confers the headdress and an Indian name, from any clan, on the individual. The clan whose name has been used has no responsibility for the individual; he is told that he belongs to that clan and may call the clan members brothers, but no one seriously recognizes any reciprocal obligations. The beneficiary of the name is tacitly expected to contribute to the Reserve in some manner, unless the entire ceremony is a publicity stunt or a patriotic and sentimental show, which is often the case, as when the commander of the warship *Iroquois* was made a member and given a name. Local officials, such as the director of the Chamber of Commerce, and local clergymen often wish to be made members in this way for reasons of their own, not realizing the very insubstantial nature of the adoption. When such adoptions coincide with the annual Six Nations Fair or the Agricultural Fair, there is little doubt that the ceremony is largely a show. Nevertheless, the very fact that such adoptions take place and have been standard for a long period indicates the prominent position which adoption must once have had, and it gives an indication of Canadian-Indian relations and interactions, if only from a romanticized viewpoint.

The third kind of adoption is midway between the two previous ones. The legal forms and acts have been omitted, but the adoptee is religiously inducted into a family at the Longhouse, given a name (which is "hung about the neck," since it is not a consanguineal adoption), and incurs all the responsibilities, obligations, and reciprocal rights of any regularly adopted member, other than those contrary to the restrictions imposed by the Canadian government acting through the elected council. Such adoptions are sponsored by a family after consultation with the matron of the ohwachira and the approval of both moieties. But since such an adoption can never be fully legal, it is quite just to infer that the primary member-replacing type of adoption has been shifted to the nuclear family, albeit by outside forces.

The historical record leaves some doubt as to whether adoption was a secular or religious rite and also, despite Hewitt's belief that it was a clan function, just how often an extended family or a clan did decide on the adoptee. The Parker version of the Constitution (1916: 49–50) implies that the matter is a secular one, in the jurisdiction of the hereditary peace chiefs ("Lords of the nation"). In Beauchamp's resumé of recorded cases one detects a mixture of secular and religious regulation, with secular and peace-chief confirmation as well as individual decisions to adopt in the earlier instances, and "prayers" and council meetings mentioned in later cases. Beauchamp (1907: 344–5) himself thought the rite mostly a secular one. He says: "Adoption and the giving of a name might take place in any civil council and was often attended with debate and ceremony. In important cases a general council might agree on the name to be bestowed. In such cases there would be a formal announcement, without the ceremonies usual at other times. In other cases a national council or a family would agree on the name. . . . Still further, any person might bestow a name, and then the ceremony would vary with his taste. All these are considered as a class here because they have no religious observances properly belonging to them, differing essentially from those festivals which embody acts of worship. They are not all strictly councils, but have somewhat their character." Poncet, Milet, and Joncaire seem to have been adopted on a secular individual basis and given the status of the names bestowed upon them, much to the benefit of the French; Kirkland seems to have understood that adoption into the Seneca would give him "professional" advantages despite the religious overtones; Colden implies he was adopted at the invitation of "Cayenderongue" of the Bear clan and took over the actual status of that warrior and "often afterwards had the kind Compliment of Brother Bear." Whenever tribes were taken into the League it seems to have been on the decision of the chiefs in council—a secular and political event.

Today at Six Nations, however, the emphasis in the Longhouse adoption is on the religious aspects. It is neither the family nor the chief who bestows the new status, but the Longhouse official (who may be a chief, but who acts in the capacity of an emissary of Handsome Lake, the Angels, or the Great Creator), nor is the Longhouse community willing to concede that this was not always the case. With the stripping of power from the hereditary peace chiefs it is interesting to note that they try to incorporate heretofore secular duties into the religious sphere, for it is in this sphere that some degree of power yet remains to them.

THE EXTENDED FAMILY, LINEAGE, AND CLAN

INTERRELATIONS BETWEEN THE EXTENDED FAMILY, LINEAGE, AND CLAN

Historically, the basic consanguineal kin group has been described as the household, comprising a matron, her daughters, and descendants through females—

"those who came out of the same house." This phrase refers to the unilocal extended matrilineal kin group once resident in a single longhouse, which was most probably exogamous, though Fenton (1951b: 46) mentions one instance in which tradition has it that a man could go out one side of the longhouse and procure a wife by entering the other side. Today the household is synonymous with the nuclear family, and the coresident matrilineally extended family does not exist (except in the fortuitous event that adjacent houses and land are divided among daughters only). The result is that the concept of "my family" may apply to a group as small as one's mother and one's siblings and, when used by a woman, simply to one's children; or it may apply to the entire lineage. The term used, "ohwachira" (Mohawk ohwatsi′ra?, Cayuga ohwa′tsi′ya?), is the same, whether applied to the household or to the lineage.

The fact that there is no separate term for the lineage probably indicates that a lineage represented merely a spilling over of the extended family into several longhouses or into multilocal residences, while still theoretically tracing descent to a common ancestor. When such a genealogical connection can no longer be remembered, a clan is defined. At present, however, the lineage is an important social unit, since a chief is chosen from a matrilineage. Consequently, there is much friction concerning which lineage truly owns a chief's title and which families are included in the lineage. Families desirous of owning a title often make false claims of lineage affiliation, with the result that controversies have been in progress on this matter as long as can be remembered. Certainly, Seth Newhouse's enumeration in 1885 of the status of the families owning chieftainship titles at Six Nations documents a concern with the problem even then (see Fenton, 1949: 150).

The lineages and clans present at any time and the number of members in them depend on local factors, such as birthrate, mobility, the degree to which the connecting links between lineages and clans are remembered, and the assertions of the members themselves about their lineage and clan affiliation. With the increasing emphasis on the nuclear family, even Longhouse participants often do not know their lineage and clan affiliation, and when asked will simply name the leading clan on their moiety side, assuming that to be their own clan. This tendency is particularly marked among the Cayuga and the attendants at the Cayuga Longhouses, where the two moieties are named "Wolf" and "Turtle" and two of the clans have the same names. Consequently, many members who may be of the Bear clan would say, when asked, that they are Turtles, and members of the Bird clans would say that they are Wolves, simply because the clans are grouped under the moiety system in this manner, i.e., Bears sit on the Turtle side and Birds on the Wolf side. The confusion indicates that there is a basic breakdown of information concerning social organization, so that children are not told accurately what their clan affiliation is. Consequently, the Longhouse ceremonials often tend to perpetuate social distinctions (for ritual purposes) more than do the social institutions themselves.

There are further factors which preclude a definite and constant lineage and clan distribution: e.g., individual lineages die out, and immigrants from the United States reservations or other Canadian reserves bring new lineages with them in their persons. A related reason for the confusion between families and clans was pointed out by Goldenweiser, namely, that with the depletion of a clan, a single maternal family and a clan may become identical. In such cases it is little wonder that the one is confused with the other, since analytically and genetically both rest on the same assumption, matrilineal descent. Conversely, a unit described as a "clan" at Six Nations may be simply a lineage segment from another reserve, which, when transplanted to Six Nations, sits in the Longhouse with those clans which are of the same moiety as its own at home and after a while claims to be a clan at Six Nations. An example is the Oneida Suckling Bear clan, which is represented by one family at Sour Springs. This was most probably a lineage which moved to Six Nations and after its arrival there lent a member to a lineage in need of a chief. But thenceforth the family asserted that it was a clan in which this title should be retained. (See p. 115 for the title of Deska'he?.) (Goldenweiser states that the subdivisions of the Oneida Bear clan had their own distinct names, and each claimed a chieftainship title.) The immigrants from another reserve may cause confusion even when they do not constitute themselves as a new clan, since a desire for the privilege of appointing a chief causes these members to claim lineage affiliation with lineages on the Reserve, even in the absence of remembered consanguineal connections. All these factors make comparison with older data and with the clans and lineages at other reserves somewhat difficult. In general, it can be seen that the supposedly consanguineal kin groups sometimes define themselves through ceremonial or political affiliation rather than through known or putative matrilineal descent.

THE CHANGING FUNCTIONS OF THE CLAN

When a culture is changing rapidly, as is the culture of Six Nations Reserve, and yet is not disintegrating, emphasis and detail are bound to be shifted from those areas in which it is impossible to retain the old organization under present pressures to those in which some semblance of the old organization may be saved. Thus, the fact that the ceremonial and political institutions make use of social forms, even if not in exactly the same way as when the Iroquois represented a fully functioning, integrated, and self-sufficient culture, helps to retain some of the differentia of the older social organization. Characteristically, members of the Reserve who belong to families and lineages owning chieftainship titles and who therefore have strong political and ceremonial interests, are more aware of the lineage and clan names and affiliations than those belonging to lineages with no hereditary office or title. However, with such a displacement of emphasis, two possibilities arise: one, that the traits, patterns, and institutions in the new form will be simplified, the other that they will be elaborated. In neither case can one reasonably assume that it is possible to shift a culture pattern, for example, the functions arising from family, lineage, and clan affiliation, from its original orbit to a new one without some change of the pattern itself. The new orientation in the organization of the culture necessitates a change in the pattern. Here is just such an instance. The matrilineal social organization and the extended family residence and cooperation patterns are under great stress, and the matrilineage and the clan can no longer perform all their traditional functions. A check of the present locus of execution of the functions attributed to the clan by various anthropologists in the past will quickly reveal the extent to which the clan has lost those functions.

According to Morgan (1877: 71) the gens (i.e., clan) "is individualized by the following rights, privileges and obligations . . .

    I. The right of electing its sachem and chiefs.

    II. The right of deposing its sachem and chiefs.

    III. The obligation not to marry in the gens.

    IV. Mutual rights of inheritance of the property of deceased members.

    V. Reciprocal obligations of help, defense, and redress of injuries.

    VI. The right of bestowing names upon its members.

    VII. The right of adopting strangers into the gens.

    VIII. Common religious rites, query [sic].

    IX. A common burial place.

    X. A council of the gens."

Goldenweiser (1914: 467) presents a similar list:

"1. Clan exogamy. (As this trait became extended so as to embrace the clans of identical name in all tribes, the clan in each tribe can no longer be regarded as an exogamous unit.)

2. Each clan has its set of names.

3. The majority of the clans claim a chief and participate in his election.

4. A clan owned a burial ground.

5. Clans may have been associated with longhouses, although probably not in the sense of one clan occupying or predominating in only one longhouse.

6. Clans may have been associated with villages.

7. Clans have the right to adopt outsiders.

8. Although the clans as such do not figure at ceremonies, they elect their own ceremonial officials."

There is an inherent difference of conception of the genesis and distribution of clans here. Morgan (1901, 1: 77) believes that clans appeared prior to tribes, so that a clan was split into five units, and a fifth of each was placed in a tribe, either at confederation or before. The like-named clans in all the tribes were brothers, bound to each other by ties of consanguinity. Goldenweiser (1914: 466), on the other hand, thinks that the exogamy provision was extended to like-named clans at a later date, the original rule of exogamy being restricted to each clan within a tribe only. He says: "Whether the clan system of the Iroquois tribes are derived from a common historical source, it is impossible to say. It cannot be doubted, however, that for a long period of time the clans, Wolf, Bear, etc., of one tribe were in no way associated with the corresponding clans of the other tribes. During the formation of the Confederacy and since, the intimacy of relations between clans of identical name but belonging to different tribes became very great. It always remained an equalization, however, not a fusion. And to this day each clan of each tribe must be regarded as the social unit. The practice of exogamy, it is true, has been extended to all clans of identical name; the clans of each tribe, on the other hand, have preserved their distinct sets of individual names." Morgan's interpretation arises out of his assumption that at one time all the clans were represented in all the tribes, and the eastern tribes which now have only three clans have presumably lost the other five. However, there seems to be no evidence that the Mohawk or Oneida did actually have more than the Bear, Wolf, and Turtle clans. Morgan arrives at his conclusion by the following reasoning: Bear, Wolf, and Turtle are all on one side of the moiety, moieties are exogamous, and therefore no Mohawk or Oneida would have been able to marry unless the other clans had been represented. Morgan's error seems to lie in not realizing that the moiety organization of the Seneca did not carry over to the Mohawk and Oneida (see Morgan, 1901, 1: 77). Goldenweiser, incidentally, agrees with Morgan that the moieties, where extant, were exogamous. In *Ancient Society*, Morgan seems to imply that a moiety (phratry) is anciently a single clan (gens) which has become subdivided, and the original restrictions with respect to the prohibition against marrying into a person's own clan had followed to its subdivisions. This conclusion is deduced from moiety exogamy. Morgan goes on, however, in a manner rather contradictory to his arguments in *The League of the Iroquois*, to state: "This restriction, viz., that marriage within the phratry is disallowed, however, was long since removed, except with respect to the gens of the individual" (Morgan, 1877: 90–1). Here Morgan (1877: 91) also speculates that clan formation comes through segmentation and local separation of members, and that clans are not indefinitely stable within moieties (phratries).

Today, of Morgan's list, only the first, second, and sixth functions still belong to the clan, and the first and second are strictly not so much clan as lineage characteristics.

The third function in Morgan's list, clan exogamy, has been retained spottily. Some of the Longhouse members think it is the "proper" procedure; others ignore it. In general, the marriage and incest rules are at present very diverse, due to the changes in social organization which have taken place and are now taking place, so that informants are confused.

In Hewitt (1944: 82), edited by Fenton, Simeon Gibson is cited as follows: "Anciently, the uterine or maternal families were units in marrying. Big Bear married Small Bear, etc. Later, people married only within the tribe, i.e., Cayugas were reluctant to marry Onondagas, etc. Now they marry between tribes. I think that after the formation of the League marriage was 'across the fire.' My father, Chief John A. Gibson [who according to Goldenweiser (1912: 692–4) and Fenton (1944: 231) was unquestionably the greatest mind of his generation among the Six Nations], said that it was preferable to marry in the opposite moiety rather than on 'the same side of the fire.' " This statement is interesting for two reasons. First, it indicates the uncertainty about marriage rules and has inherent in it historical rationalizations for either the procedure of marriage within the clan or moiety or the procedure of marriage in the opposite moiety. Second, here, as in Goldenweiser's notes (1914), there is reference to the social organization "before and after confederation" as interpreted by the informant. While interesting, this should not be taken at face value, as Goldenweiser and Hewitt seem to have done. The Gibsons seem to account for any semi-myth or for any discrepancy with modern times by simply making the distinction of pre- and post-Confederation. Goldenweiser (1912: 465), for example, lists a Seneca "Duck" clan as pre-Confederation and then accounts for its absence today by stating that it had died out after the Confederation. Actually, there seems to be no historical record of the existence of such a clan, the only reference to it being in the Deganawi'da? legend and the tradition of the Confederation.

The common opinion is that marriage is prohibited with any known relative. Thus, Mrs. George Green says: "Never marry anyone who is a cousin" or "Do not marry here [in the family] forever." When she says "here" (i.e., in the family), she means any individual to whom a direct consanguineal relationship can be traced, limited only by the memory of the family. In the definition of incest taboos, the relevant connections are not limited to the more common Iroquoian uterine, or matrilineal, relations, but also include agnatic links. Therefore, an Iroquois is forbidden to marry into his ohwachira (his matrilineage, or, as the informants say, "the main family") and into his father's kindred (agadōniho'nō?). The group of persons termed agadō'nih includes all bilateral relatives related to ego through an initial ascending agnatic link, i.e., through the father, but not the father himself; some informants also omit from this group the lineal relatives in the second and higher ascending generations, e.g., the FaMo, FaFa, etc., but this causes no confusion, since marriage with one's father is obviously forbidden, and with one's grandparents both forbidden and unlikely. The group does include siblings and cousins of lineal ancestors, therefore precluding marriage with a patrilateral uncle or aunt, and it does include all degrees of patrilateral cousins, be they parallel or cross. The group termed kheya'?dawēh includes all the bilateral relatives through an initial uterine link in the ascending or same generation, i.e., through ego's mother or ego's siblings. This of course means that the ohwachira is a subgroup of the kheya'?dawēh. To the Iroquois, however, the two groups seem quite distinct; the ohwachira is always considered more closely related and is "my own family" or "my main family." While the marriage prohibition is more stringently observed in the ohwachira, it also applies to the kheya'?dawēh. For example, a desired marriage between a girl and her MoMoMoFaBrSoSo was disallowed, not because of the generation difference (the couple were of approximately the same age), but because they were related to each other as kheya'?dawēh and agadō'nih.

As far as the marriage rules just described are concerned, considerations of clan are quite beside the point. This is why many people steadfastly maintain that "clan has nothing to do with it, it is a matter of relations." However, there are individuals, such as Mr. Alexander (Jack) General, the leader of the Turtle side at Sour Springs Longhouse, who insist on clan exogamy and moiety exogamy in addition to the marriage rules described above. The following from a letter on June 28, 1954, shows Mr. General's attitude.

Oh yes! you ask me if I know anyone that intermarried within their clan or family. Well, honestly, I can't name anyone that committed that, that is in our neighborhood, especially of the Longhouse faith. So I think we still adhere to that law. So far as I know of. I hope you do likewise.

When numerous examples of endogamy are mentioned, the informant will say: "Well, one is a Cayuga Bear, the other an Oneida Bear,[3] so that they are not

[3] According to the laws recorded in English in 1900 by Seth Newhouse of Six Nations and corrected by Albert Cusick of New York State (Parker, 1916: 42), marriage between members of the same clan is not allowed, even if the spouses are of two different nations. But the rule in itself can give no indication of the degree of actual adherence to it in 1900. Parker's version of the Constitution gives only a set of dicta; it is not an examination of practices at the time (1900), his statement on page 12 notwithstanding.

related," or "One is a Big Bear, and the other a Suckling Bear, so they are different clans,"[4] or "One is from our reserve and the other from Muncy Reserve," or even "One is from a 'down below' clan and the other from a 'Sour Springs' clan." In short, there are countless rationalizations and relaxations of the clan exogamy and moiety exogamy rules, if, indeed, moiety exogamy anciently existed. (Fenton noticed examples of intraclan marriage at Tonawanda as well, which were explained in analogous terms. The father was a Tonawanda Snipe, the mother a Buffalo Creek Snipe, etc. There, too, to marry in the same maternal household is much worse than to marry in the same clan.)

Even as there are rationalizations concerning the moiety and clan exogamy rules, so are there rationalizations for allowing marriages between relatives who call each other kheya'ʔdawēh and agadõ'nih. One does find many examples of these ideally prohibited marriages, particularly since the reservation population is relatively small and has been endogamous for a long time. However, when such a marriage has taken place there still exists a fair amount of anxiety. For example, in the case of a marriage of a girl with her MoFaMoBrSoSo, there was much apologizing and rationalizing that it was allowed only because the second link was a Fa.

There exists one further prohibition of marriage, and that is between individuals who are related through a ritual friendship. Ritual friendship establishes a marriage prohibition, since "friends" of similar age refer to each other as "brother" and "sister." Therefore, they cannot marry each other or any close relative of either. (See p. 218 *infra* for a discussion of ritual friendship.)

Today, however, the younger generation finds the Canadian idea that marriage should be with a freely chosen partner very attractive, and this is lessening the importance of the social organization as a factor in regulating marriage.

Returning to Morgan's list, it is found that the fourth function, inheritance of the property of deceased clan members, is almost entirely lost. Most of the property today is individually owned and may be bequeathed by will to persons belonging to other clans. To the extent that children now inherit their father's estate, clan inheritance is impossible, unless the parents happen to have belonged to the same clan. As explained above (p. 19), should an individual die intestate and with no nuclear-family heirs, the council decides among the various claimants and makes no effort to keep land within the clan of the deceased. Most of the personal belongings of the deceased (to which Morgan may not have been referring, since he was probably considering land property) are distributed to various helpers at the funeral preparations. To the extent that the helpers are of the moiety opposite to that of the deceased, which is correct, these belongings pass to other clans. However, this distribution of personal goods probably should not be considered a matter

---

[4] This rationalization is used even though it is questionable whether the subdivisions of the Bears into Big Bear, Little Bear, and Suckling Bear do not constitute lineages rather than clans. It is practically a matter of definition, since actual relationships are not remembered. Goldenweiser (1914: 466) notes the subdivision of the Oneida clans and points out that these have their own sets of names and chiefs.

of inheritance, but rather an acknowledgment for services at the funeral. Only at the most orthodox of the Longhouse burials, among the Lower Cayuga community, are inheritances of land announced at the tenth-day feast, which is the occasion for distributing personal belongings.

The fifth function of the clan—reciprocal obligations of help, defense, and redress of injuries—today has shifted from the clan to the Longhouse community. When a bee is to be held for agricultural chores, the Longhouse member will first call on the fellow members of his own Longhouse, and the procedure of communication is exactly the same as for any religious celebration. A man is asked to "go around," characteristically not very long in advance of the date set for the bee, and he announces the desire of the Longhouse member for a bee. The same courtesies shown to a religious message bearer must be shown to the announcer. If, for example, he appears at mealtime, he must be asked to remain to share in the food. However, no acceptance is necessary. The announcer simply states his request and leaves. This sometimes occasions difficulty, since a host may prepare an elaborate meal in the expectation of a large turnout for the bee, and only a handful may actually show up. This is more often the case in Longhouses where there are internal factions. Nevertheless, the Longhouse is the first organization to which a member in trouble appeals. Supposed injustices inflicted by the Canadian government on the orthodox population, such as, for example, the recent edict (now repealed) that marriage must be registered with a bona fide Canadian justice of peace, are first brought up in the Longhouse. There a nucleus of defense and action is formed, which often goes on to the council of hereditary chiefs. The essential point is that mutual protection, once the function of the clan, now is the function of the Longhouse community.

The sixth function in Morgan's list, the right to bestow names, may still be a clan function, but it is now floundering due to the nonremembrance of the older names. The usual procedure is to take the name of a like-sexed deceased member of one's immediate family (ohwachira). A mother choosing a name in this manner often does not realize that it is a "clan name" rather than a "lineage name," for she will have taken the name from her own matrilineage. If one asks a "keeper of names," that is, any individual who remembers a lot of old names, the assurance that the name supplied is of the proper clan is not very high today. Functionally, the clan association of a name is irrelevant, since an Indian name is important today in order to use it in connection with curing rites, not to indicate clan affiliation.

The remaining functions in Morgan's list have been lost or transferred. The right to adopt strangers, as explained above, is now a function of the nuclear family. Religious rites are not held in an assembly of a single clan, but rather are mostly a Longhouse function, and their effective locus is the Longhouse community. Burial also is now a Longhouse and not a clan function. However, individual families are associated with particular Longhouses, so that a matrilineal burial ground does tend to be maintained. As a result, husbands and wives are sometimes separated at death. However, one notices the encroachment of Christian ideals, in that most Longhouse families now bury spouses side by side. Certainly, all those nominally Christian families which are buried at Christian cemeteries on the Reserve bury spouses side by side, even though the individuals may have been attending a Longhouse as well. Finally, a council of the clan does not meet today. Meetings today are confined to the chiefs or to officers of the Longhouse, with a few observers, and appointments are not made by a democratic assembly of males and females, as Morgan (1877: 85) would have us believe.

Goldenweiser's list would meet with approximately the same analysis as Morgan's.

The result of the transfer of functions from the clan is that it has become perhaps the least important social unit. Clans never meet in a body, have no functions relegated to them alone, and are never singled out as units of action. (See Fenton, 1936: 18, for a similar situation at Coldspring.) The clan is never invited as a unit to any Longhouse event. One invites a segment of the clan, namely the matrilineage, or one invites the entire Longhouse community, or perhaps one invites all the participants in a particular rite or members of a medicine society (in which case clan and consanguineal relationships are irrelevant). There does not seem to be one ceremony, medicine society meeting, or occasion at which it would be appropriate to assemble a single clan. This must make the identification of the collection of members included in a theoretically defined "clan" a difficult matter for a member, which may be another reason for the confusion shown by informants ever since Goldenweiser's day. The important functioning units today are "my family" and "my relatives," by which one may mean any collection of relatives from the nuclear family to the bilateral kindred, and "my Longhouse."

Some attributes of the clan nevertheless remain intact, for the clans are named units, they determine the seating with the appropriate moiety, they own sets of names, and they have chiefs associated with them. Although the Longhouse has appropriated many of the functions of the clan, it is the Longhouse, by being the locus of the traditional ritual, which perpetuates the clan and moiety distinctions. The Longhouse has, however, reinterpreted the old social groupings and has used them in its frame of reference. For this reason, it will be realistic to examine the Longhouse, and then to discuss the details of lineage, clan, and moiety distribution in terms of the four Longhouses at Six Nations.

LONGHOUSE MEMBERSHIP AND ORGANIZATION
LONGHOUSE AUTONOMY

LITERALLY speaking, the Longhouse (ganŏ'hses) is the actual building which accommodates the orthodox congregation in the performance of the yearly ceremonial cycle and the various observances connected with Gaihwi'yo (The Good Message of Handsome Lake). A Longhouse is symbolized by a fire which is burning, and when a Longhouse is discontinued, one refers to the extinction of the ceremonial center by saying, "A fire is out." Each Longhouse is legitimated by owning a "Longhouse wampum," which can be interpreted as the charter of the particular congregation. The actual composition of the wampum strands is immaterial, and the strands vary from Longhouse to Longhouse as well as through time (beads are lost, given away to help another Longhouse, or added to), but the possession of some wampum to symbolize the "burning fire" is essential. For example, when the Newtown Longhouse strands were lost in a conflagration at the custodian's house, each Longhouse was asked to contribute some beads toward a new set in order to relight the Newtown fire, for without the wampum the fire is also considered extinguished.

Each of the several Longhouse groups consists of a congregation, and these congregations of believers form the most actively functioning social units at Six Nations Reserve today. Each Longhouse community is a ceremonial and jurisdictional entity conducting its rites for its own congregation and bound only by the general Iroquoian pattern and the Iroquoian institutions. Actually, the content and philosophy at the various Longhouses are the same, but the details of execution have become quite varied over time. Fenton has stressed the importance of recognizing local diversity among the Iroquois communities and of using the concept of locality as a tool in the reconstruction of Iroquois history (Fenton, 1951a: 10). At Six Nations, with four different Longhouses all within 8 miles of each other and with well-developed possibilities of communication, local diversity within a narrow geographic region reaches its height, and each congregation can be viewed as a small political, social, and ceremonial entity.

All the "fires" are equal, except that Tonawanda Longhouse in New York State is considered the "head fire" because it is from here that the circuit of conventions bringing the Good Message to participant Longhouses originates each September (see p. 192 *infra*), and it is here that an all-circuit preacher is validated. However, Tonawanda Longhouse has no jurisdiction at all over any of the other ceremonial centers once a circuit schedule has been decided upon, nor does it have the authority to commit each Longhouse to the circuit. Thus, Sour Springs Longhouse decides, independently of the September meeting at Tonawanda, whether it would like to participate in that season's convention rounds.

Exactly why Sour Springs is not tied into the Good Message circuit nobody is

35

really able to say. It is, however, an interesting example of local autonomy and procedure at one of the "home fires." Tradition has it that when the Longhouses first pledged at the main fire at Tonawanda to participate in the cycle, the representative of the Sour Springs Longhouse did not pledge to participate, but simply said that Sour Springs would take part whenever it felt able to do so. The Sour Springs community, therefore, considers itself "free" from the cycle and decides upon the need and suitability of a convention separately each year. It is always at the end of the Strawberry Festival that Sour Springs Longhouse discusses whether to pledge itself to a convention that coming fall. Other Longhouses have pledged themselves at Tonawanda the previous fall to be present at the next meeting, but also they discuss the exact arrangements at the Strawberry Festival. The reason is that Handsome Lake awoke and announced his vision on June 15, 1799 (see Deardorff, 1951: 79), and this time of year coincides with the Strawberry Festival, which takes place approximately in the middle of June, when strawberries are "coming on," i.e., ripening. (In 1956, Sour Springs celebrated the Strawberry Festival on June 22, and Onondaga Longhouse celebrated it on June 23. In 1954, Sour Springs had the Strawberry Festival around June 15.) Strawberry time is particularly associated with Handsome Lake and with his admonitions to the community to perform its duties to the Longhouse and to live a good life. The deacons of the Longhouse are particularly admonished, and the preacher tries to create a strongly emotional atmosphere by stressing the bounties of the harvest to come, the gratitude all feel at seeing each other again, and the thankfulness which should be in the hearts of everyone. Many of the congregation are moved to tears, and, consequently, when the wish for a convention is added to the general feeling of religiosity, it is hard to resist.

The practical and perhaps rationalized explanation given for the independence of Sour Springs is that "we are a small gang, and cannot afford the cost of a convention every two years." At convention time the guests and attendants must be housed and fed by the congregation, which does put a strain on the community. Great emphasis is placed on preparing ample and "Indian" meals. In 1956, at a small chiefs' convention (which is called when the chiefs of a single Longhouse believe that the congregation should have an extra session of preaching and confession or when they merely wish to give pleasure to Handsome Lake), Sour Springs Longhouse was able to provide corn soup and feast food despite anticipatory doubts, while Onondaga Longhouse, at a similar chiefs' convention, merely served a typical American dinner of bread and canned goods. The type of food served is a measure of prestige and hospitality, and the first question asked about the Onondaga convention at Sour Springs was, "What did they serve for lunch?" Sour Springs is particularly conscious about the quality of the food served its guests, perhaps because it is the Longhouse in the most acculturated area of the Reserve.

The procedure in deciding whether to participate or not in the coming season's Good Message circuit is as follows (the data are taken from the 1956 meeting at Sour Springs): Alexander General, who holds the title Deska'he? and is the leading speaker for the Turtle side at Sour Springs, rose to speak after the second Feather

Dance, while the deacons were preparing the food for distribution. He said that there would be a convention in the fall and that children should come. The last convention (held one week previously, but only a local chiefs' convention) was not adequate, he thought. After some whispered consultation a Turtle moiety deacon, Chief Hōwatshadě′hō (Big Bear clan, Oneida), was sent to seek the consent of the Turtle women by asking a Turtle deaconess.[1] The chief, Levy Jacobs, was probably sent across to the women's side because the Turtles did not at that time have a head deacon, due to the recent death of Timothy General. A Turtle deaconess, Mrs. George Green, then relayed the men's desire for a convention to the Turtle head deaconess, Esther Jamieson, who in turn consulted with the Wolf head deaconess, Maggie General. The women agreed that a convention would be desirable, and the Turtle head deaconess instructed Mrs. Green to inform Levy Jacobs that the women were in agreement. Mr. General then formally announced the decision of the women and asked the Wolf men whether they approved of the convention. Grant General, the speaker for the Wolf side, replied that the men, too, were in full accord. Then Mr. General announced that the entire house was in agreement. Grant General (Wolf moiety) then elaborated upon the topic of food at the convention, saying that at the last convention they had assumed they had no food, but finally they were "not stuck for food, and so it will be again." "Our Maker brings supplies," he added rather philosophically. Several Turtle women thought of the idea of having "tea meetings," which is the standard method of raising money for any future project. This decision was relayed by Mrs. Green to Levy Jacobs, who told Mr. General, who announced it to the congregation. The meeting was then closed. Had the women disagreed, the men would not have scheduled the convention, as there would have been no women to cook the food. However, under the circumstances of the meeting, the women felt compelled to agree to the convention unanimously. Actually, after the event, several of the deaconesses confessed that they were not enthusiastic about having another convention so soon, but that they had felt they could not disagree.

The entire topic is discussed once again at the Green Bean Festival, and the congregation evidently gets a second sobering chance to decide on a convention. Theoretically, the common people (i.e., non-deacons) are also asked to express their opinions, the Turtle side conferring among themselves and the Wolf side among themselves. No single side objects, for that is felt to be bad form, but at times both sides decide simultaneously that too many conventions are going on during that year, and therefore Sour Springs will forego participation that season. Although this is the explanation given for the deferment of a convention, a contributing factor often is the expense involved.

[1] The officers of the Longhouses have been variously identified in the literature. Morgan, Kurath, and sometimes Fenton refer to them as "faith-keepers"; others call them "deacons" or "matrons." I shall use the terms "deacon" and "deaconess" to refer to the Longhouse officers appointed to serve as religious officers, whether they are appointed for merit or by inheriting a position in their lineage. I shall use the term "matron" to refer to a woman holding the titular wampum beads of a chief. A matron is ex officio a Longhouse deaconess, see *infra*, "Longhouse Functionaries."

One may notice in the episode described above that at Sour Springs it is the chiefs who call for the convention. This is a local feature, since the chiefs do not universally have so large a role in the Longhouse (particularly not at Lower Cayuga). Other features of the procedure are universal, however, for example, the formality of reaching a decision with conventional pressure toward unanimity.

LONGHOUSE COMPOSITION
LINEAL AND RESIDENTIAL AFFILIATION

Each Longhouse is an institution with an established following, an established procedure, and a definite sense of in- and out-group feelings. On a small scale one can observe the operation of the two classic principles of solidarity, kinship and residence, for a Longhouse community depends for its composition on both of these. Membership in the Longhouse is primarily based upon the matrilineage, for one's "home" Longhouse is ordinarily the one to which one's mother and one's mother's family belonged, and where one was given a "baby name." For this reason a Longhouse represents a number of matrilineages which still reside in the same neighborhood. Since these lineages also cooperate in activities extending well beyond the range of ceremonial activities, the classic description of the older clans is in many ways applicable to the Longhouse community, with the difference that lineages from many clans act together as one unit.

Residence is the second most important consideration in choosing Longhouse affiliation. Though it may seem that 8 miles is not a great distance, especially since almost everyone has the opportunity to go by automobile, the psychological difference of going to the closest and most convenient Longhouse is out of proportion to the actual distance.

The Reserve is divided into two large sections, commonly referred to as "up above," by which one means any of the territory between Ohsweken and the western and southern boundaries of the Reserve, and "down below," meaning the territory from the eastern boundary of the Reserve to approximately one concession east of Ohsweken. (The Reserve is laid out in the Canadian township concession pattern, consisting of survey rectangles approximately one by one and a half miles.) "Up above" is the area associated with the Sour Springs Longhouse. "Down below" maintains three Longhouses: Onondaga Longhouse, one-eighth of a mile north of the intersection (sometimes called Silversmith's Corner) of Seneca Line Road with the "side road" running from Smoothtown through Tom Longboat's Corner;[2] Seneca Longhouse, about a quarter of a mile east of the same intersection on the south side of Seneca Line Road; and Lower Cayuga Longhouse, which is just east of Six Nations, or Peter Atkin's Corner, a mile and a half east of the intersection between Onondaga and Seneca Longhouses. The region east and northeast of Lower Cayuga Longhouse is often termed "way below" to distinguish it from the neighborhood around the Onondaga and Seneca Longhouses, which is approximately mid-Reserve.

[2] Unfortunately for the identification of Onondaga Longhouse, this road is usually referred to as "the Onondaga Side Road."

In general, the Longhouse families like to cluster around the Longhouse which they attend. One of the considerations in choosing a home is its location in relation to the Longhouse, especially since living in a distant section of the Reserve will very often mean being ill informed or not informed at all about either the "doings" at the Longhouse or the feasts and medicine-society meetings of the members of the home Longhouse, and this gives a person an insecure and rejected feeling. This is a feeling of not being able to participate in the most important social group to which one belongs. Thus, one of the members of the Onondaga Longhouse, who lived on the Fourth (or Iroquois) Line, moved to the Fifth (or Seneca) Line, partly because his previous neighborhood is not included in the Onondaga Longhouse rounds of the "Uncles" on Stirring Ashes Day (see p. 175 *infra*) nor of the traveling False Face Company on False Face Day in the spring (see p. 149 *infra*), and worst of all, it is often missed in the telling around of the smaller Longhouse "doings."

One of the rules of Gaihwi'yo, as preached at Six Nations today, is that a Longhouse member should not belong to any social organization, club, or association other than the Longhouse; he should be a "clear man." If this rule is obeyed—and many people do abstain from the "white-influenced" ladies'-aid societies, fraternal lodges, and the Six Nations band—social isolation follows unless one is able to participate freely in the Longhouse activities.

The band is forbidden on two counts: it has violins, which are forbidden by Handsom Lake, and it is an essentially "white" organization. The most common affiliation of Longhouse members which does not seem tabooed is membership in one of the two "burial societies" at Six Nations, called "The Benevolent Society" and "The Temperance Society." (The latter has the secondary aim, besides that of paying funeral expenses, of inducing members to abstain from liquor, and it therefore appeals to "strong" Longhouse members particularly. However, not all abide strictly by the temperance rule.) For a stipulated monthly or annual payment, usually until $100 is paid, the society member is guaranteed a "good" burial at death. The societies are nondenominational, including both Christians and Longhouse members. They do not have any other functions, such as mutual aid, which is a common feature in the more social organizations. In short, one might conclude that these societies are more or less for installment buying, made palatable and more binding by electing officers and emphasizing payments by occasional meetings.

Receiving information about the events at the Longhouse is a matter of major importance under these circumstances.

The traditional way of informing members of any activity is to send around a messenger who goes from door to door and announces the event orally. Handsome Lake did not approve of "white man's writing," and there still exists a strong feeling that imparting information by mail or leaving a note is not the "Longhouse way."[3] Writing "would have been fixed so that it were natural for the Indian to

[3] In fact, the strongest ritualists and preachers think it is wrong to use any sort of written aid in learning to preach or in learning any ritual. Some of the preachers own copies of the Parker version of the Good Message, and some of the rituals are in fact written down. Nevertheless, it is not the case at Six Nations, as it is at Coldspring (Deardorff, 1951: 79), that preachers will admit that the Parker version of the Good Message "serves as a trot for men preparing to be 'Code' preachers."

read" if it had been meant for the Longhouse. Consequently, Longhouse officials often mention that writing is not the Indian way and that it is wrong to go to school. As a result, in spite of the fact that many Longhouse members do read and write, the messengers apparently do not leave a note in the absence of the person to be informed. Since the event is usually announced by the messenger "going around" one day previous to its occurrence, or often on the very day of the ceremony, and since the messenger is usually "in a hurry" and unwilling to come a second time when there is no one at home and also unwilling to go any great distance out of his way, many people miss the Longhouse events. Often the event becomes known to the supposed participant only after its occurrence, which is disruptive both of the ritual and of the psychological well-being of the individual. All the Longhouses complain that it is hard to find men willing to spend the time to inform the constituents, so that communication between the members is often haphazard. Also, one of the most frequent excuses for not giving a scheduled medicinal feast or for postponing an Ohgi'we meeting, is that "the ladies could not find anyone to go around for them." When one resides near the Longhouse, the chances of being missed or not noticing a Longhouse event are much smaller.

The neolocal residence pattern today also interferes with Longhouse affiliation according to lineage. When a woman marries a man in a different neighborhood and moves to his neighborhood to live, she will probably attend her husband's Longhouse for the sake of convenience. If, on the other hand, the neolocal residence is in the neighborhood of the wife's Longhouse, she may be able to persuade her husband to attend her Longhouse, the more easily if she is a matron or deaconess there. There is no fixed rule of attendance nor compulsion about enrollment in any one Longhouse, nor even a tally of Longhouse membership, yet any conversant Longhouse adherent is able to say immediately with which Longhouse any particular individual is associated. Usually, there has been a weighing of factors to decide whether it is more convenient for the person to remain with the lineally affiliated Longhouse or to switch to the Longhouse closer to the new residence. Factors involved in the choice include compatibility with the new group, relative position in the Longhouse, transportation, and agreements with the spouse.

Multiple Affiliation and the "Home" Longhouse

If an individual has shifted his Longhouse, he will, if he follows the general pattern of loyalty conflict, feel most uneasy about where to attend during the more important ceremonial days, especially at Midwinter time. Often the lineally affiliated Longhouse will be attended at the Feather Dance, Adõ'wa and Skin Dance Days of Midwinter; and if a mother attends another Longhouse on account of change of residence, she may take the children back to her lineal Longhouse to be named on Adõ'wa Days (Green Corn and Midwinter time).

There are two further classes of individuals who are affiliated in one way or another with several Longhouses. In one class are those individuals who attend one Longhouse because of a chief's or matron's position there but for all practical purposes associate in their daily behavior and in their medicinal activities with another Longhouse group. The second class consists of individuals who, for social or personal reasons, consistently participate in several of the Longhouses; such instances are to be expected, since no social group is completely isolated in so small an area as Six Nations.

The Cayuga chief, Gadjiʔnõnda'whyõ, is an example of the former class. He is "supposed to be setting" (*sic*) at Lower Cayuga Longhouse, especially since it is believed that the two chiefs, Hagaʔa'ēyõnk and Gadjiʔnõnda'whyõ, founded Lower Cayuga Longhouse, and Gadjiʔnõnda'whyõ is the principal Cayuga chief as well as the leader of the Wolf moiety. Consequently, it is deemed proper, perhaps because of sentiment, that he should attend Lower Cayuga. Lower Cayuga Longhouse has a very definite community spirit, at least at present, which is strict as to ritual, conservative, and anti-chief. As a result, the current incumbent much prefers the community at Onondaga Longhouse and even the Seneca Longhouse community, and he usually attends Onondaga Longhouse. But when a planned event falls at Onondaga and at Lower Cayuga on the same day, he feels it his duty to attend Lower Cayuga. However, when his Cayuga affiliation is not important, as in the singing practices and in those rites which do not demand nation-moiety seating (Four Brothers and Three Brothers), he will often be seen with the members who band together for the Onondaga Longhouse rituals.

Mrs. Susan Johnson is a good example of the second class, which consists of individuals consistently attending more than one Longhouse. She is a matron at Sour Springs, but since her grandmother had come from "down below," she also associates with Lower Cayuga Longhouse members, and whenever the two Longhouses have rituals on separate days she can be seen at both. She plays important roles at both Longhouses, and she is one of the women most instrumental in communicating between the two ritual centers. She is an obvious link in the diffusion of traits from one Longhouse to the other.

In all cases, however, if a person is orthodox, he will try to be buried at his "home" Longhouse. Ordinarily, this is the one most closely associated with his matrilineage, but it may be one which he has adopted, if he has had a falling out with his original home Longhouse. In the final analysis the burial place is considered the most important single index of which Longhouse has been the "home" Longhouse. For example, although an elderly woman has been head deaconess of a moiety at one Longhouse for several decades, and although her husband is buried at that Longhouse, yet when she dies it is expected that she will be buried at her Longhouse of origin, with her matrilineal kin. The important concept is not that one is buried with one's family, but at the Longhouse associated with one's family. An incident may illustrate this concept. There was a regular member at Lower Cayuga whose family had traditionally attended there. One day she became angry at the Lower

Cayuga policy of not permitting whites into the Longhouse,[4] whereupon as a threat she said, "When I die, I shall not be buried at Lower Cayuga, but at Seneca Longhouse." Several people later repeated her expression to me and indicated that it must have taken great emotional stress to make one want to change one's burial location to a different Longhouse. The feeling of loyalty to the Longhouse group at least matches, if it does not exceed, the feeling for the matrilineal family, and with the decrease in the importance and functioning of the lineage, the Longhouse liaison will probably become increasingly strong.

Tribal Groups and Longhouse Affiliation

An important fact to keep in mind when considering the various Longhouses and their composition today is that no Longhouse represents a homogeneous tribal group. Thus, Cayuga Longhouse is not a Cayuga ritual center, Onondaga is not an Onondaga community, and Seneca is by no means Seneca. The strongest statement which can be corroborated today is that there is a tendency for many members at Onondaga to have some Onondaga extraction, and at the Cayuga Longhouses to have Cayuga extraction. Seneca Longhouse is not Seneca at all, and, indeed, it used to be called "the new Onondaga Longhouse." Approximately 65 years ago, it is said, Onondaga Longhouse was split in two by factional disputes over how rituals should be conducted, and, consequently, one group left to build what is now termed "Seneca Longhouse." The members of the current Seneca Longhouse are descendants of the dissatisfied group, plus the increment of members who have chosen Seneca as their social group or who live around Seneca Longhouse and go there for the sake of convenience. Evidence that Seneca Longhouse is not even organized on Seneca lines but is simply another Onondaga Longhouse is that the moiety seating follows the standard Onondaga moiety arrangement found in the United States and at Onondaga Longhouse in Canada, whereas the Seneca community in the United States has a different moiety arrangement. The Seneca moiety arrangement of the United States has never been known in Canada.

On the whole the Reserve has been an in-marrying unit for approximately 170 years, although during the early nineteenth century, when Irish and Scotch immigrants were laying railroad tracks in the vicinity, there seem to have been numerous marriages with whites. Many of the surnames left on the Reserve testify to these unions, and to speak of "full-blooded" Iroquois in a genetic sense is unrealistic. Chadwick (1897) pointed out the Dutch names among the population,

---

[4] Lower Cayuga was visited during the Midwinter Festival in 1951–52 by a reporter from a Toronto newspaper, who wrote a derogatory, sensationalistic feature story; and since then Lower Cayuga has not allowed outsiders, especially anyone who has been seen taking "notes." In 1955–56 the superintendent of the Reserve was invited, mainly to convince him that the Longhouse activities were not immoral. This invitation occasioned much criticism and debate, both at Lower Cayuga and at the other Longhouses.

for example, "Staats" and "Claus" which indicated admixture while the Iroquois were still in New York State, and these names are common at Six Nations even today. More important for present considerations, however, is the very extensive intermarriage among the different Iroquois nations. Historically, one must consider that ever since the time of Brant, the group which resettled in Canada was not composed of isolated "national" groups which had no contact with each other. It is true that Brant led mainly Mohawks into Canada, and tradition has it that the other groups arrived in small bands which first settled at Cayuga Flats, at Tutelo Heights, and at the nearby site now called "Cayuga," as well as at various other locations around the Grand River; but with the loss of land, all the groups moved into the narrow confines of the Reserve. It is difficult to conceive that there was no contact and intermarriage between the groups under these circumstances. Since marriage with one's own clan in another tribe is not forbidden (and does not violate exogamy rules as they are understood in Canada), it is reasonable to assume that intertribal marriage has been in process since the settlement of the Reserve. Also, the number of eligible spouses, if counted within the band only, would be very limited, particularly when the population of the entire Reserve numbered only 2,421 in 1858 (Chadwick, 1897: 21) and was even less prior to that. Six Nations has incorporated within it Tutelos, Saponis, Delawares, Munsees, Mahicans, Nanticokes, and Mississaugas, and the Cayuga are particularly a composite people with a long tradition and history of adopting and integrating other tribes. Fenton (1940: 224) says:

> The Cayuga have been a composite people throughout their history. Possibly themselves an early offshoot from the Seneca, in 1668 the population of the three Cayuga villages was composed partly of Huron and Andaste captives (Jesuit Relations, vol. 52, p. 179). Adding to these Tutelo and Saponi, some Delaware, Catawba, Cherokee, and odd Muskhogeans, not to mention captives from the Erie, Neutral, Algonkin, Ottawa, Miami, Illinois, and other of Central Algonquians, we see how mixed the Cayuga population was. In any one of the Iroquois nations, there were diverse opportunities for acquiring new elements of culture so that today we cannot speak of Cayuga, or even of Iroquois, culture with any degree of certainty.

Speck (1949: 1) was aware of "long association and intermarriage between these people," and there is no reason to assume that the Oneida and Mohawk did not intermarry equally freely with the Onondaga and Cayuga on the Reserve.

Pragmatically, if one asks the members of Six Nations what nationality their parents and grandparents were, one finds that almost none are unilineally Cayuga or Onondaga or Seneca. At Sour Springs, for example, Speck (1949: 185) listed the tribal identities of the parents of 21 male household heads in order to find evidence for the Cayuga predominance at Sour Springs. The list, which was compiled by Alexander General, is as follows (but should be slightly emended, since Ernest *Jimerson* should be *Jamieson*, and his mother was Cayuga, while David Jacob's mother was Chippewa-Cayuga, and William John's father was Cayuga):

Family Head	Mother's Tribal Identity	Father's Tribal Identity
Oscar Johnson	Cayuga	Cayuga-Mohawk-Tutelo
William Isaacs	Oneida	Cayuga
George Bumberry	Nanticoke	Cayuga
Ernest Jimerson	Tutelo	Cayuga-Mohawk
Norman General	Cayuga	White
Norman General	Nanticoke	Cayuga-Oneida
Jerry Aaron	Mohawk	Cayuga
James Johnson	Cayuga	Shawnee
David Jacob	Delaware-Cayuga	Cayuga
William John	White	Onondaga-Tutelo
Alec General	Cayuga-Oneida	Cayuga-Oneida
Timothy General	Cayuga-Oneida	Cayuga-Oneida
Ernest Davis	Mohawk-?	
Lawrence Davis	Mohawk-?	
John Montour	Mohawk	
Charley Davis	Oneida-White	
Reginald Martin	Mohawk-?	
Robert Henhawk	Onondaga-Mohawk	
John David	Onondaga-?	
James Henry	?	Cayuga

In none of these cases were both parents purely Cayuga, and in only two cases in the emended list were both parents at least partly Cayuga. If one considers matrilineal descent only, one finds in the emended list four Cayuga mothers, one Chippewa-Cayuga mother, and two Cayuga-Oneida mothers. In the latter two cases, those of the brothers Alec and Timothy General, the mother's mother was of Oneida extraction, whereas the mother's father was the Cayuga member. It does not seem, therefore, that this sample favors the hypothesis that Sour Springs is a ritual center of the Cayuga nation. Furthermore, when one asks the national affiliation of the deacons, officers, and speakers at the Longhouses, one finds a plethora of nationalities. Thus, at Sour Springs the head deaconess on the Turtle side today belongs to an Oneida matrilineage, and the head deaconess on the Wolf side belongs to an Onondaga or possibly Wyandot matrilineage. At Onondaga the head deaconess of the Deer side is of Tutelo extraction, the one on the Turtle side is Cayuga, and at Seneca Longhouse the male leaders of both sides are of Cayuga extraction.

In general the attempt to determine the nationality of any particular member at Six Nations is of questionable value, since the population has intermarried since the 1780's, and since it is difficult to determine what nationality allegiance is felt by children of cross-marriages. Theoretically, a child belongs to the nation of his mother, but if the father was a stronger individual the offspring might learn his father's language and identify with his father's group. This certainly happened in the case of the famous Simeon Gibson, who associated with the Onondaga group of his father, John Gibson, rather than the Cayuga group of his mother, Mary Sky.

If a child is ritually inclined, he will usually follow that parent who is also involved in ritualism, regardless of nationality.

Nor is language a legitimate index of the nationality to be associated with a Longhouse. Seneca Longhouse mainly uses the Cayuga language at present, Onondaga Longhouse uses Cayuga as freely as Onondaga, and Sour Springs tries to use Mohawk and will often translate a Cayuga speech into Mohawk for the benefit of its Mohawk contingent. The particular language used at any Longhouse at any particular time depends on what the speakers and leaders happen to use and therefore changes with changing personnel.

For all these reasons, the only characterization which can be made of the Longhouses at Six Nations is that each group has its own tradition, and that this tradition is unique to the extent that the group has had continuity and stability over time, as well as to the extent that it has been isolated and has developed individualistic traits. But to attempt a reconstruction of Cayuga or Onondaga or Seneca ritual on the basis of the ritual of the correspondingly named Longhouses, as many anthropologists working there have done, is unrealistic. It should be emphasized again that the designations "Onondaga," "Cayuga," and "Seneca" applied to the Longhouses should be construed merely as names and not as tribal identifications.

The Commitments of Longhouse Membership

It is not necessary to be a regular attendant at the Longhouse itself on the standard ceremonial dates to be accounted a functioning member of the Longhouse group. If one calls for and aids the medicinal services of a particular Longhouse, helps in the upkeep of that Longhouse, goes to the ball games and tea parties or to the burials there, then one can be counted as functioning in the community associated with that Longhouse. Almost all the social activities and needs of a person touch in some manner upon his Longhouse affiliation, and for this reason residence near the Longhouse and near the group of people who interact to form the Longhouse community facilitates participation at various times and for various purposes.

Also, the less an individual participates in the activities of the Longhouse group, the less willing the group becomes to help that individual at critical times. A case in point is that of a woman who, after marrying a nominally Christian husband, had rather neglected her connections with her Longhouse group. Since it is now hard for her, because of her age and the distance involved, to move about and attend her own Longhouse, she has become isolated and "lonely." She complains that "no one helps me to give a dance now." She had a small "dance" for which she had to hire a group from another Longhouse and pay them $3.00; had she been a regular member of that Longhouse, the home Longhouse of the performers, it would certainly have been free. At her own Longhouse, where singers are scarce and "busy," she was unable to find any to aid her.

Each Longhouse group depends on patterns of cooperation, and the idea of mutual obligations and reciprocity is of utmost importance in the preservation of the Longhouse. Deviation from this idea is curbed in many subtle ways, and since the Longhouse represents not only religion, but also social intercourse, physical well-being, and spiritual equilibrium, exclusion from the functions of the Longhouse is a serious matter. One of the theses which will be developed in this study is that the incorporation of functions from many aspects of culture into one institution, which thus presents the individual with a package arrangement of all or nothing, is an effective means for conserving much of the culture under stress. Each trait is intimately linked to another, so that the individual has less of a chance to reject one rather "unimportant" trait after another, until he is conveniently able to "pass" into the surrounding Canadian culture. With the consolidation of many traits under the sanctions of one institution, the individual would have to discard a much more integral and meaningful part of his culture than the separate traits, which would be more painful and more disruptive of his personality.

Such a consolidation seems to have occurred in the Longhouse. As pressure to acculturate built up in the various aspects of culture—in social organization, economics, politics, and government—the Longhouse began to incorporate traits from these aspects into its conventional structure. Individuals affected by the encroaching culture sought refuge in the Longhouse, and as far as possible attempted to maintain their original influence under Longhouse protection. In many cases it may not even have been a matter of retaining influence, but merely a preservation of their existence and status by banding together in the Longhouse. Thus the Longhouse became a nucleus of resistance to change and a center of conservatism not only in religion but in the entire philosophic conception of the Indian. And, as the Longhouse became a bulwark of conservatism, it also developed strong prescriptions in order to maintain itself in the new role. One of these is that frequent participation and the fulfillment of obligations concomitant with participation are necessities. Failure to comply brings punishment, as can be seen in the case mentioned above. Noticeable in this instance is that punishment did not occur in the religious sphere, but in the area of health and personal well-being, an area of great concern to the individual.

LONGHOUSE ORGANIZATION

MOIETY DIVISION

Physically, the Longhouses are approximately similar: each is a rectangular wooden hall with two fireplaces, centered, one at either end of the building (see Figs. 3–10).

The fireplaces, or "fires" (actually pot-bellied, wood-burning stoves), identify and symbolize the moieties. Each moiety "owns" one of the stoves and gives this stove its own name, i.e., Wolf or Turtle in the Cayuga Longhouses, and Two Fireplaces or Four Houses in the Onondaga and Seneca Longhouses. In the latter two Longhouses, however, the stoves are more often identified by the "leading" clan on each side of the moiety and are called the Deer stove and the Wolf stove. (See p. 56 *infra* for a discussion of what constitutes a "leading clan.") Each moiety considers that half of the Longhouse in which its stove is located as its own territory, and it offers its stove for use and service to the opposite moiety. Physically, action takes place around the stove, and figuratively the speeches bring to life the "fire" of the moiety. The room is ringed by tiers of benches, and each moiety rings its own stove on those ceremonial days when the "house" is not divided into male and female halves. The central space between the two stoves accommodates personnel from both sides (i.e., both moieties) of the house, and it is the traditional area of the singers and performers in the dances and in many of the medicine-society rites. Between the two stoves are placed movable benches, on which the singers sit facing each other inward when there are two parallel benches, or sit with their backs to their own moieties, looking toward the opposite stove when they straddle the benches, as in the Great Feather Dance performance. Most of the Longhouses (not Onondaga) also have two doors, each door similarly associated with a moiety. Property, such as rattles, paddles, drums, and insignia, may occupy the walls of the "house," and that property which belongs to each moiety is hung in its half of the Longhouse. There is no doubt whatever that the concept of duality is an important organizational theme in the Longhouse.

Aside from the spatial orientation into sides, there is the fact that anyone who enters the Longhouse associates with one moiety or the other, belongs to one, and exchanges services with the opposite moiety. There is no ranking of moieties in any way whatever. No special value is attached to the particular clans in the moieties nor to the collection of clans which compose a moiety. One moiety is complementary to the other, and all action is reciprocal.

Though the concept is the same at all the Longhouses, there is some variation among them in the execution of the reciprocal duties. At Sour Springs and Lower Cayuga the moieties take turns in all the actions during one ceremony, and they alternate between ceremonies. Thus, if a Wolf member opens the assembly, the next speech ought to be delivered by a Turtle member, then a Wolf should again be given a task, then a Turtle, etc. The closing should be entrusted to a Turtle, since a Wolf opened the meeting. The next day or the next occasion should find a Turtle member opening the meeting and a Wolf member closing it. If one Midwinter Ceremony is opened by a Turtle, the next Midwinter should be opened by a Wolf. The clan to which the speaker on either side belongs is immaterial, and the speaker himself may not know what his clan is. When medicine-society dances are held at Sour Springs, Wolf and Turtle members should alternate in holding their feasts, although often activity goes on simultaneously, the Wolves being treated by the Turtles on the Turtle side and the Turtles by the Wolves. In the Stirring Ashes Ceremony the groups alternate—Wolves, then Turtles, then Wolves again, etc., or vice versa, depending upon which side opened the day's proceedings. When food is passed to the "house," deacons from both sides pass around, usually starting their passing on the side opposite to their own as a gesture of respect to those "across the fire." At all events an effort is made to apportion obligations, duties, and privileges with scrupulous equality, and this is carried out when feasible in all Longhouse activities. Decision making, announcing, speaking, singing, dancing, leading the dancing lines, making the fire, cleaning the Longhouse, fetching wood, in short any action down to the small details, should be divided equally. In practice this does not and cannot always occur. For example, if there is an uneven number of events between the opening and closing speeches, it is impossible to have a Wolf begin and a Turtle end and at the same time maintain strictly the alternation of speaking between the two moieties; in such cases the rule of having the meeting closed by the opposite moiety from the one that opened it, overrules the strict alternation.

At Onondaga and Seneca Longhouses the two moieties alternate being leaders for one year each. The first ceremony after the Midwinter ceremony, usually the Bush Dance, is the first one to incorporate the change in moiety leadership. (This, incidentally, implies that the Midwinter rites are considered the last rites of the agricultural calendar. Thereafter the cycle begins anew for the following year.) The side which is the leader for the year initiates and closes all meetings for that year. In 1954 the Deer side led at Ononaga Longhouse, while the Wolf side was the leader at Seneca Longhouse. The side which is the ritual leader for the year is also the initiator, i.e., the leader of the dances, and it has the larger voice in date setting and organization. Duties and obligations, such as helping to cure, making the fire, and cooking, are shared by both moieties throughout the year, just as at Sour Springs and Lower Cayuga.

Often a side is unable to fulfill a particular function, due to lack of speakers or knowledgeable singers, in which case, in all of the Longhouses, the opposite moiety will perform the duty. This is not considered very "particular," and aside from comments such as "we're going down," "we're a small gang," or "the Wolves should come more and help," there is no feeling of opprobrium in receiving help from the other side. The feeling is more akin to regret that so few *cognoscenti* are left or attend. Unequal moiety participation may alter the ceremonial performance in that certain formalities may be dropped, but it has not been as destructive of native ceremonialism as Speck thought (see Fenton, 1951b: 47, footnote 9). The congregation has been flexible enough to disregard instances of moiety nonreciprocity, or it has allowed ritualists to be "borrowed" from the opposite moiety. On special occasions a side may ritually borrow a person from the other side in order to fulfill the moiety obligations, this being done particularly in the case of rituals concerning the dead. In such cases a formal request for the lending of a man or a woman is addressed "across the fire," and at the end of the performance the person is ritually returned to his side of the fire. The borrowed speaker will open his remarks by saying politely: "I've been asked to speak on behalf of my cousins ('people on the other side') on account of the fact that the speaker has not yet appeared for some reason or other. We expect he may appear later to take over." If such a borrowing has occurred for the Condolence Ceremony, and a Four Brother substitutes for a Three Brother member, then he prefaces his remarks by saying: "I've been asked to act as a 'two-faced' and to speak for the Three Brothers." Here the concept of the duality of the moieties is most specifically stated, as it is in general most emphasized in matters of death.

There is some joking in regard to moieties, for when a person is borrowed "across the fire," he is generally teased about belonging to the other side now, and there will be general merriment if he should then sit on the same side as his wife. (This may be an indication of a preference for marriage outside the moiety, since the teasing takes the form of incest insults. However, when the two spouses are naturally on the same side of the fire, and this is often the case, no one takes particular notice nor teases. Fenton, 1953: 141–2, discusses the problem of moiety exogamy and of whether the joking relationship which he recorded, namely with one's father's clansmen, could be interpreted as a piece of evidence in postulating a previous moiety exogamy. At Six Nations, however, just as at Tonawanda, this particular type of joking relationship is not known. On the other hand, Fenton does not mention the joking when spouses are ranged on the same moiety side at the borrowing of one spouse. As Fenton points out, the evidence for clan exogamy is as convincing as for moiety exogamy, and the addition of small items such as these is not conclusive. Fenton himself finally decides in favor of the theory that clans were the original exogamous units, rather than moieties, and that the individual person rather than the moiety was the unit with which one joked.) There is also a general teasing in conversation and in the Eagle Dance[5] about membership in a particular moiety and clan. The teasing usually consists of an analogy between the members of the moiety or clan and the correspondingly named animal. The Wolves taunt the Turtles with being slow, and they may taunt the Bears with being sleepy because they hibernate all year and with being overly fond of sweets and honey. (In this context "Wolves" and "Turtles" designate the members of moieties rather than of clans. For a further discussion of joking between moieties see also Speck, 1949: 27. For example: "The Wolf moiety people are accused of being greasy and tricky; the Turtle people as being 'slow, homely, humpbacked, of sitting in the sun and liking it.' ") However, joking relationships are not confined to cross-moiety situations, for any member can tease other members, including those in his own clan. New analogies are appreciated and amuse as much as the standard ones; for instance, one of the members of the Suckling Bear clan seemed vastly amused when he was presented with a pacifier to indicate the "babyhood" status of his clan eponym. No ill humor should be shown at the teasing, and, as far as could be observed, no one resented the teasing and joking.

There is no doubt that the moiety arrangement and the concept of reciprocity between two groups are important themes in Iroquois culture and that they pervade many of the beliefs and activities. However, a difficulty arises today in that in each specific case, as opposed to the general conception of dual functioning, the

[5] Fenton's (1953: 55–6, 61, 65, 72, 141–2, 150) discussion of moiety joking relationships limits such instances to the ritual connected with the Eagle Dance. At Six Nations, however, moiety joking is frequent merely as a topic of social chitchat. In the Eagle Dance at Six Nations, unlike at any American performances thereof, it is not good form to make personal jokes. The standard joke, for the purpose of encouraging the dancers to perform greater feats, is to comment on the fact that in previous times the dancers were nimbler and better. Intraclan joking is found at Six Nations, even as it is at Coldspring (*ibid.*: 141).

individual is not quite sure to which of the two moieties he belongs and how he should orient himself spatially in the various events in order to indicate his membership in one of the moieties. Partly, this is the effect of the breakdown of the clan (see pp. 27 ff. *supra*). Partly, the reason for the uncertainty is that there is now no known organizational principle which specifies unambiguously which clans are grouped together on each side of the fire. When one asks how the individual knows which side a clan should sit on, he will say that it takes its orientation from the seating of the chief who represents the clan. Thus, if a Heron chief sits on the Wolf side at the Cayuga Longhouses, then all the members of the Heron clan will follow the lead of their chief and also sit on the Wolf side. The chiefs in turn regulate their seating so that it corresponds to the relationships indicated in the Roll Call of the Chiefs as recited in the Condolence Ceremony. Two difficulties present themselves here, however: one, the Roll Call of the Chiefs and the presumed relationships between the chiefs are not unambiguous, especially since many of the chieftainship titles are now transferred to other clans, so that the original relationships do not hold (see p. 101 *infra*); and two, not all clans are represented by a chieftainship title, so that this criterion is inapplicable to the orientation of some of the clans. (The date line which defines "original" is, of course, arbitrary, since undoubtedly clan seating has changed over time (see p. 60 *infra*), new clans have splintered off from old ones, and individual variations have caused changes.)

Furthermore, the moiety division is not the same at all four Longhouses, though the two Cayuga Longhouses try to retain the same seating, and Onondaga and Seneca try to keep their seatings similar. Despite the general (but not perfect) correspondence of clan alignment between the Onondaga Longhouse in Canada and that in New York State, the details of moiety division are in the last analysis a local matter, peculiar to each Longhouse. When members of the Cayuga Longhouses attend the Onondaga and Seneca Longhouses, the local diversity in moiety seating causes added uncertainties. Should they sit as the host Longhouse sits? Where does their clan fit into the seating at the unfamiliar Longhouse? And if their clan is not represented at all, which side is the proper side to associate with? Added to this is the unfamiliarity with the general organization of the host Longhouse. Mrs. George Green (a Sour Springs member, ex-matron of the chieftainship title Hadya'?tr°hne?, active deaconess, ritualist and herbalist, and by no means representative of the average uninformed member) says, for example: "If I were to go to Lower Cayuga or the other Longhouses, I wouldn't know how the gang divides and where to go." Alexander General, the chief Deska'he?, who is sophisticated in matters of Longhouse organization, says that at one time he asked down below why Turtles and Wolves sit on one side of the fire at Onondaga and Seneca, unlike at the Cayuga Longhouses, and the response was that once the Wolves were so few that it was decided to move the Turtles in with the Wolves, but now the Deer side is small. Morgan, however, listed the Wolf and Turtle clans as being in the same moiety among the Seneca, and the Appendix to the Lloyd edition of Morgan's *League of the Iroquois* (1901) similarly groups these clans into the same moiety among the Cayuga. It is difficult to ascertain what transfers may have been made in the course of the history of the various groups. Deska'he?, when pressed further to explain the origin of the moiety seating, responded: "We always did it this way; it is a rule to go by." There is no origin legend which specifically apportions the clans into two moieties, and Hewitt's (1916: 527–45, 1944: 80–5) explanation of the origin of the duality concept of the Iroquois on the basis of the Father and Mother and the Male and Female principles is highly speculative. Neither do any rules of exogamy determine seating.

Seating at Hēna'?idos, Eagle, or any of the medicine-society rites which exhibit moiety seating are all dependent on the arrangement of the clans in the Longhouses. That is, the Longhouse moiety seating arrangement is the definitive seating arrangement followed at all other occasions on which there is grouping of clans. It can be argued that since the Longhouse seating is derivative from the Roll Call of the Chiefs, at least in part, this Roll Call is the organizing principle. But this would be meaningful only to a minute segment of the population, since only a few ritualists are familiar with the intricacies of the relationship terms of the Roll Call. Hence, for the majority of the population the principle of organization is the Longhouse seating. Uncertainty in the Longhouse seating is therefore bound to carry over into moiety division at any of the other meetings in which moiety questions are involved.

One further difficulty should be mentioned. The population and the clans represented are not identical over time. As mentioned before, persons from other reserves come to Six Nations and participate in the Longhouses, bringing with them new lineages and clan names, while some clans at Six Nations die out. The general diversity, shifting through time, adds to the difficulty of assigning clans to a definite moiety.

It is understandable, in the light of all the complications mentioned above, that often those concerned themselves have difficulty in deciding what the moiety arrangement is and to which moiety they belong. This is particularly acute when, at a curing rite, members from both the Cayuga and Onondaga Longhouses meet in a private house and have to split into two groups. Whereas in the Longhouse the rule usually followed is: "When in the host Longhouse, do as the host does" (e.g., when a Turtle clan man and a Wolf clan man from Sour Springs go to Onondaga, both will sit on the Wolf side, because this is the Onondaga seating), there is no such clear-cut rule at a private home. Various compromises are worked out. One may respect the Longhouse grouping of the sponsor, especially if he himself is "taking charge of things" and directs the activity; or one may sit according to the usual arrangement of the performing ritualists, especially if a particular group which is accustomed to perform together is called in, and follow the advice of their leader; or one may take the path of least resistance and ignore the moiety seating, particularly in the case of the nonessential participants and visitors.

One result of the indefinite knowledge of clan arrangement in the moieties and of the lack of a rule for reconciling different moiety organizations is the current attitude of laxity about moiety transgressions. The trend seems to be that, with the increasing difficulty of assignation of the individual to one moiety or the other, moiety seating is falling more and more into disuse at private occasions in people's houses, where there is no traditionally predetermined arrangement of "sides." Even in the wake game, where one would expect to find extreme moiety awareness because of the intimate association with death, moiety seating is often ignored. Nor does the omission of the moiety arrangement impair the efficacy of the ceremony. The important consideration is the fact that the feast, dance, or ceremony is held, and not which way the participants are seated or the extent to which duality is a function of moiety division. The principle of reciprocity, which is one of the organizing principles in Iroquoian culture and is closely allied to that of duality, is interpreted to apply to any two groups which aid each other, namely, the actor and the recipient. The laxity allowed in moiety reciprocity and the reinterpretation of reciprocity from that between moieties to that between an actor and a recipient are conservative of the over-all pattern and ritual. The flexibility and substitutions allowed in the curing and ceremonial meetings are certainly factors in their preservation. Were moiety affiliation an essential factor, it would not always be possible today to marshal the proper personnel at critical times, especially since there is so much uncertainty about moiety affiliation. A random division of the participants into two sections, when these are needed, as in the wake game, is then the simplest way to keep the ritual going.

CLAN INVENTORY

An index of the clans and their distribution into moieties, as they are understood by the members themselves, will give further insight into the current status of the organization of the Longhouses. The clans now represented at Six Nations, in an arbitrary order, are as follows:

Name of Clan	*Translation of Clan Name*
Turtle clans	
ganya′hdě?, also called g?ano′wa	Mud Turtle.
ganyahdě?go′wa	Snapping Turtle or Big Turtle.
g?anowaga′hea	Small Turtle or Swamp Turtle, usually described as "in the pond."
Wolf clan	
thahyǒ′ni	Wolf.
Beaver clan	
nya?ganya′?gǒ	Beaver.
Deer clans	
dewa′hǒhdes	This word for deer is used as a collective designation for all the Deer clans, particularly when the clans are enumerated prior to the Bowl

Name of Clan	*Translation of Clan Name*
	Game at Midwinter and Green Corn. It does not specify a particular Deer clan, of which there are one, two, or three, according to different informants.
thadidjiyanẽ'ʔdõʔ	Big Deer. The deer is described as living in the bush and having large hoofs on his feet. This clan is the only one which all informants agree is a Deer clan. It is described as "leader of the house," meaning that it is a clan which gives its name to a moiety at Onondaga and Seneca Longhouses.
Ball clan dewẽnhe'ga	Ball. This clan is sometimes interpreted to be a "ball-playing" clan, derived from dẽwẽnho, with the origin myth that there was a family which was always playing ball and thus gave the name to the clan. Another interpretation is that the name designates a bird which sits in a tree and looks rolled up like a ball. Speck (1949: 20) was told that it is related to a bird, possibly a martin, but received no further information. The most common explanation of the clan, and that which is universally adopted down below, is that this clan is a Deer clan; the name is supposed to designate a "rock" deer which is very small and rolls itself into a ball. The chiefs officially hold to this interpretation at the present time.
Eel clan gõnde'	Eel.
Hawk clan hodiswẽʔga'iyo	Hawk. This is a Seneca clan, represented mainly by recent immigrants from the United States, though

Name of Clan	*Translation of Clan Name*

Goldenweiser (1914: 466) listed it on information from John Gibson. He does not mention it as an extinct clan, but he gives no indication of the number of its members at that time. The name of this clan, also, is variously interpreted. In Cayuga it has a linguistic similarity to the word meaning "fine boards," and as a result several informants call it Fine Boards clan or Nice Boards clan. It is also at times confused with the Small Deer (Ball) clan and called a "rock deer."

Heron clan
    skanya?di'ga

Heron. Most informants from the Cayuga Longhouses recognize this as the name of a bird and translate it as "heron." The bird is characterized as rising with the mists and landing in the water. The standard word for "heron," however, is hega'hõ. Some informants identify this heron as "a brown bird with a long beak, green legs, 2 feet tall, which 'hollers' when it looks up into the sky!" Down below the clan name is almost unanimously supposed to designate a small "wee" wolf; for its habitat this wolf chooses the prairie, and hence it is called a "prairie wolf."

Snipe clans
    dawi'sdawi, also called dawisdawih-
      go'wa

Snipe. This bird is large and runs in the fields, and the name is variously interpreted as "snipe," "killdeer," and "plover." Another frequent translation is "jack snipe." The bird is often seen on open ground.

    dawi'sdawi hodi?nehsiyo'?dẽ, also
      called dawi'sdawi hodi?nehsi'yo?s

Small Snipe or Sandpiper. This bird is described as a "small bird standing there in the sand." It is characteristically seen running along the

Name of Clan	*Translation of Clan Name*
	water. Due to a linguistic similarity, the clan is often called Fine-Sand clan.
Bear clans	
nya'gwai	Bear or (by contrast with Big Bear) Baby Bear.
nyagwaihgo'wa	Big Bear.
oda'ʔthra	Suckling Bear.

Goldenweiser (1914: 466) found in 1912 that the Bear clan at Oneida (Muncy Reserve) had splintered into three groups named according to the size of the eponymous animal. Both the Large Bear and the Suckling Bear are Oneida lineages functioning at, and integrated into, Sour Springs Longhouse, but also represented at the lower Longhouses. Goldenweiser implies that they should be classified as distinct clans, since he found that the names he collected for each group did not overlap.

Various authors have listed several additional clans for the Iroquois in general and for Six Nations in particular. Parker (1916: 42), while working over a Six Nations manuscript during the preparation of his version of the Constitution, found such clans as Wild Potato, Opposite-Side-of-the-Hand, Great Name Bearer, and Ancient Name Bearer mentioned; all of these seem spurious, and Hewitt (1917: 429–38) upbraids him for accepting them. Goldenweiser (1914: 465) mentions a Duck clan, which, according to Simeon and John Gibson, became extinct after the Confederation (see p. 30 *supra*). Informants today have not heard of any of these clans.

The story of the origin of the clans, as told at Six Nations, is that Deganawi'daʔ named the clans in the order in which he saw wild animals during the day on which he was giving clan names and rules of organization to a group of assembled headmen and their followers. The first animal seen was a wolf, and so he made the first man and his group a Wolf clan. The second was a turtle, and he made the second man and his group a Turtle clan. Third, a deer was seen, so Deganawi'daʔ made the Deer clan. Then, standing by a tree a bear was seen, and hence the fourth group became the Bear clan. Fifth, an animal "so long was seen under water," and Deganawi'daʔ told the next headman that he should belong to the Eel clan. Next a bird was seen at the edge of the water, and so the Snipe clan was formed. "There were no domestic animals, and there should be none in the ceremonial," added the informant. (In practice, however, artifacts derived from domestic animals are constantly substituted for presumably antecedent wild objects.) It should be pointed out that Six Nations ritualists tell this origin story in various ways, omitting and including different clan animals and reciting the order of the animals differently. There is, of course, no point at all in arguing whether clans existed before Deganawi'da's efforts to form the League or whether Deganawi'daʔ instituted them coeval with his efforts on behalf of the League (see Parker, 1916: 93, footnote 1). Both are origin legends, retold innumerable times, and neither is founded on linguistic or historical evidence. Bill Thomas has yet another explanation for the naming of the clans, namely, that each clan is named for the animal which it hunted at the time that Deganawi'da? was investing the clans. In this version of the story there is no ordering of the clans.

Actually, none of the origin stories are intended to impute differences of status to the various clans. Furthermore, all the clans have equal status, regardless of their order in any ceremonial listing (see Fenton, 1953: 138–9). Fenton says that among the New York State Seneca the clans are not ordinally ranked, and enumeration starts from the speaker's clan. For example, at Sour Springs, Alexander General (Deska'he?) lists the clans in the order in which chieftainship titles appear in the Roll Call of the Chiefs, and this is the order which he uses when announcing the clans on each side to "separate the house" on Betting Day. This does not, however, constitute a ranking according to descending value, as Speck (1949: 20) thought. (The ordering which Deska'he? gave Speck, 1949: 21, does not follow the Roll Call exactly, especially not on the Turtle side.) Nor does that clan which lends its name for the identification of the moiety have any special status. The adoption of the clan name to indicate the moiety—Deer and Wolf in Onondaga and Seneca Longhouses and Turtle and Wolf in the Cayuga Longhouses—is merely a matter of convenience in identification. Even as the chiefs are "trees of all one height" and each represents "one beat of the heart," so, says Bill Thomas, Deganawi'da? made all clans of equal height. At Onondaga and Seneca Longhouses the Big Deer and the Wolf clans are termed "leaders of the house," but this means only that they are named first in the ritual order of naming the clans on the day before Betting Day during Midwinter and Green Corn.

ORGANIZATION OF THE INDIVIDUAL LONGHOUSES

Sour Springs clan and moiety organization. Theoretically, the moiety seating in the Longhouse should follow that of the chiefs in the Condolence Ceremony. When this rule is not applicable or not applied, no one is able to say "why we sit this way," except that in some cases a tradition is followed, in others the clans are integrated according to supposed interpretations of their names, and in yet others there is an attempt to follow another Longhouse in which the clan in question has an established position. These rationalizations of the moiety arrangement have been discussed in general terms above, but the best way to illustrate them is to examine the seating at each of the Six Nations Longhouses.

The moiety division at Sour Springs must be understood in terms of the clans which are represented in that community today and which today carry chieftainship titles. The usual seating at Sour Springs of all the common Six Nations clans is as follows:

Turtle side: Deer, Ball, Bear clans, Turtle clans, Beaver, Eel, Hawk.
Wolf side:　Heron, Wolf, Snipe clans.

In particular, the Cayuga clans present are:

Turtle side: Deer, Ball, Bear clans, Turtle clans.
Wolf side: Heron, Wolf, Snipe clans.

These lists may be compared with Morgan's (1901, 2: 225) inventory of the clans of the Cayuga nation, according to which Bear, Wolf, Turtle, Snipe, and Eel are on one side, and Deer, Beaver, and Hawk are on the other. The discrepancies indicate considerable historical change, and also, as previously discussed, suggest that one cannot simply associate Sour Springs Longhouse with the Cayuga nation. According to Deska'he? there are today no Cayuga Eel, Beaver, or Hawk clans in the Sour Springs or Lower Cayuga communities, though members of these clans with Onondaga and Seneca affiliation do participate intimately in the ceremonies of the Cayuga Longhouses. Also integrated into Sour Springs Longhouse are many Oneida families, who, despite the Oneida clan relationships of Wolf and Turtle versus Bears (Wolf and Turtle being considered brothers in relation to their cousins, the Bears), orient themselves in the Sour Springs Longhouse manner. The same is true of the Mohawk who have joined the Longhouse, for the Mohawk division of Wolf and Turtle reciprocating with cousin Bear is also disregarded in favor of the seating "of the house" at Sour Springs. (Besides accommodating Mohawk who have long participated in the ceremonies, Sour Springs has lately had an influx of Christian Mohawk families who have adopted the Longhouse religion as a sign of protest against the Canadian government.)

At Sour Springs, Mr. General lists the clans on each moiety side in an order corresponding to the order of Cayuga chiefship titles in the Roll Call of the Chiefs. The titles have a definite order in the Roll Call, and even though no clans are mentioned in connection with the titles, there is an association of clans with titles because each chiefship is traditionally hereditary within a definite clan. (For the titles and the clans associated with each at Six Nations see *infra*, p. 104 and Table 1). There are difficulties in this procedure, first, because not all clans are represented by a chief and, second, because in spite of tradition the clans of the chiefs sometimes vary with new incumbents (for instance, when a lineage dies out and the council of hereditary chiefs transfers a title to a lineage of another clan), with the result that the order of the clans changes. The order of the clans as given by Deska'- he? corresponds to what he claims to be the ideal assignment of clans to chiefs in the Condolence Roll Call, namely:

Wolf moiety: Heron, Wolf, Large Snipe, Small Snipe.
Turtle moiety: Large Deer, Small Deer (actually Ball, but interpreted as a Deer clan by Deska'he?), Big Bear, Small or Baby Bear, and Suckling Bear.

With two exceptions, this ideal assignment of clans to chiefs in the Condolence Roll Call is the same as the actual assignment today. The first discrepancy between the ideal arrangement and the actual clan associations is that today the first chieftainship title in the Turtle moiety is held by a Bear rather than by a Large Deer. The change took place in 1863, when Chief Abram Charles assumed

TABLE 2. THE CLAN AFFILIATION OF THE HEREDITARY CHIEFS

	Morgan[a] United States	Hale[b] Six Nations	Chadwick[c] Six Nations	Fenton[d] Composite	Present, 1954–56 Six Nations
1	Turtle	Turtle	Turtle	Turtle	Turtle
2	Turtle	Turtle	Turtle	Turtle	Turtle
3	Turtle	Turtle	Turtle	Turtle	Turtle
4	Wolf	Wolf	Wolf	Wolf	Wolf
5	Wolf	Wolf	Wolf	Wolf	Wolf
6	Wolf	Wolf	Wolf	Wolf	Wolf
7	Bear	Bear	Bear	Bear	Bear
8	Bear	Bear	Bear	Bear	Ball
9	Bear	Bear	Bear	Bear	Bear
10	Wolf	Wolf	Wolf	Wolf	Wolf
11	Wolf	Wolf	Wolf	Wolf	Wolf
12	Wolf	Wolf	Wolf	Wolf	Wolf
13	Turtle	Turtle	Turtle	Turtle	Turtle
14	Turtle	Turtle	Turtle	Turtle	Turtle
15	Turtle	Turtle	Turtle	Turtle	Turtle
16	Bear	Bear	Bear	Bear	Bear
17	Bear	Bear	Bear	Bear	Bear
18	Bear	Bear	Bear	Bear	Bear
19	Bear	Bear	Deer	Bear once, Deer now	Deer
20	Beaver	Beaver	Beaver	Beaver	Beaver
21	Bear	Beaver	Beaver	Beaver	Beaver
22	Snipe	Snipe	Snipe	Small Plover, or Snipe	Wolf
23	Turtle	Ball	Ball	Sharp-shinned hawk; Ball by error	Wolf
24	Turtle	Turtle	Turtle	Turtle	Wolf
25	Wolf	Wolf	Wolf	Wolf	Wolf
26	Deer	Deer	Deer	Deer	Deer
27	Deer	Deer	Deer	Deer	Deer
28	Turtle	Eel	Hawk	Eel	Eel
29	Bear	Eel	Eel	Eel	Eel
30	Deer	Eel	Turtle	Eel	Eel
31	Turtle	Turtle	Turtle	Turtle	Ascribed to Deer
32	Turtle	Turtle. At Oa., Ball.	Turtle	Turtle and Deer both claim	Turtle
33	Deer	Deer	Bear	Bear	Bear
34	Heron	Deer	Ball	Ball or Hawk	Ball
35	Bear	Bear	Bear	Bear	Bear
36	Bear	Bear	Bear	Bear	Bear
37	Turtle	Turtle	Turtle	Turtle	Turtle
38	Wolf	Wolf	Wolf	Wolf, now Heron	Heron
39	Turtle	Wolf	Wolf	Wolf	Wolf
40	Heron	Wolf	Snipe	Snipe, once Wolf	Snipe
41	Snipe	Snipe	Snipe	Snipe	Snipe
42	Snipe	Snipe	Bear	Bear	Suckling Bear
43	Turtle	Wolf	Turtle	Turtle	Turtle
44	Snipe	Snipe	Snipe	Snipe	Snipe
45	Hawk	Hawk	Hawk	Hawk	Snipe
46	Turtle	Turtle	Turtle	Turtle	Turtle
47	Snipe	Bear	Bear or Snipe	Snipe	Snipe
48	Bear	Snipe	Snipe	Bear	Snipe
49	Snipe	Bear	Snipe	Snipe	Snipe
50	Wolf	Wolf	Wolf	Wolf	Wolf

[a] Morgan (editor's notes in 1901 edition, reprinted 1954).

[b] Hale (1883).

[c] Chadwick (1897).

[d] Fenton (1950). Fenton compiled a composite of clans from various authors such as Chadwick, Hale, Hewitt, as well as from his field experience.

Note: All titles realigned in Fenton's order.

the title. This deviation is now mentioned at each new chief's installation and at the Condolence practice sessions, so that ritualists are well aware of the ideal order. The second discrepancy is that the eighth Cayuga chief ought to be a Large Snipe, but today the title seems to be held by a Small Snipe. Whether this is indeed a discrepancy depends on whether the two Snipe groups are separate clans or lineages of the same clan. Relationship is remembered in neither, so that technically, I presume, one would have to classify them as clans. Both of these two discrepancies can be accounted for by borrowing.

Besides these two discrepancies between the current clan affiliation of the chiefs and Deska'he's version of the ideal affiliation, one must also note that Deska'he's version is based on fairly contemporary data and differs from some of the actual assignations in the historical past. While Deska'he's version is accepted today at Sour Springs, it is impossible to say how long it has been considered the proper association of clans and chiefs, since the supposed original clan affiliations are not remembered equally long when changes have occurred. To illustrate, the change from Deer to Bear in the case of the first Cayuga title is remembered from 1863, whereas it is not remembered, or at least not officially recalled at the practice sessions, that the sixth title, Dyoōhyō'ngo, belonged to the Wolf clan both at the time of Chadwick's work (1897: 93) and at the time of Hale's work (1883: 161), but has since been transferred to the Heron clan. The transfer of the title of Dyoōhyō'-ngo changed the order of the Wolf moiety, causing the Heron clan to be the first clan mentioned, since Dyoōhyō'ngo is the first title of the Wolf moiety to appear in the Roll Call. This historical shift, incidentally, weakens Speck's (1949: 15) hypothesis that the Heron clan leads among the Sour Springs Cayuga because the Longhouse traditionally was founded by Dyoōhyō'ngo, who was of the Heron clan. Another transfer which is not officially mentioned is that of Deska'he?. The title was transferred to the Suckling Bear Clan in the time of the grandmother of the current chief, at the death of Benjamin Carpenter, who was still listed as the chief by Chadwick in 1897. Previously, it was a Snipe clan title, and it is listed thus by Morgan (1901, 2: 214) and Hale (1883: 162). The current Suckling Bear clan, though known to be of Oneida origin, is obviously so well integrated into the ceremonial and political functioning at Sour Springs that it is now one of the determinants of clan order.

Several clans are omitted in Deska'he's listing. The various Turtle clans all sit together on the Turtle side and understand their affiliation to be with the Turtles. When Eel clan members come to Sour Springs they sit on the Turtle side, as, for example, Ezekiel (Ezeker) Hill, who is a deacon on the Turtle side at Sour Springs but is of the Onondaga Eel clan. When Hawk members come to Sour Springs, they usually sit with the Deer, despite the common saying that "all birds sit together." Probably there is confusion in the interpretation of the name of the Hawk clan, for Bill Thomas says that the name designates a middle-sized deer. Beaver clan, also represented in the Sour Springs community by members of Onondaga Beaver clan parentage, sits on the Turtle side now, though recently there has been a switch.

Alexander General writes:

Now regards your question about Beaver clan of Edith Jacob. Cayugas have no Beaver clan. Edith is Onondaga; only Onondagas have that clan. Of course, her father is Cayuga, her mother is Onondaga. This may appear rather complicated for you to understand. You see Onondaga Beaver clan is Wolf clan moiety in their own Longhouse, but also the Turtles are; so when they come to the Cayuga they join with the Turtles instead of with the Wolves. Maybe they can take their choice who to sit with. Is that clear enough?

Edith Jacob, however, used to enter Sour Springs through the Wolf door and sit on the Wolf side, and, furthermore, her own mother was head deaconess at Sour Springs on the Wolf side until her death, when the present head deaconess, Maggie General, took over. This switch, therefore, occurred within the lifetime of Mr. General. Furthermore, other Beaver clan members who were accustomed to sit on the Wolf side were told by Mrs. Hannah Jacobs,[6] who was one of the powers at Sour Springs, that they must henceforth move to the Turtle side. Mrs. Robbie Isaac was one of the Beavers who thereupon switched from the Wolf to the Turtle moiety. Mrs. Jacobs gave no reason for ordering the change, nor does anyone know why the change should be made. The source of the confusion is that the Beaver clan sits on the same side as both Wolf and Turtle clans at Onondaga and Seneca Longhouses, and hence its alignment becomes arbitrary when Wolf and Turtle clans are placed in opposing moieties.

There are some individuals who change their moiety affiliation for personal reasons. Willie John is such an individual. His mother, though white, was adopted by the Turtle clan, and for a while Mr. John appeared on the Turtle side. All of a sudden, however, he decided to identify himself with his father's relatives, who were Mohawk Wolves. He then functioned prominently on the Wolf side as a deacon and as leader of the Wolf False Face Society at Sour Springs. Other members decide that they would like to change sides in order to be more closely associated with a friend (personal, not ritual, friend), who sits across the fire; such changes, however, are likely to be temporary.

Physical orientation of Sour Springs Longhouse. Sour Springs Longhouse is situated with its long side in an approximately east-west orientation, though it is actually rotated clockwise about 30 degrees, since this is how the concessions have been laid out, and the Longhouse is roughly parallel to the road (see Fig. 3). It is convenient to follow Speck and call the door on the southeast the "east door" and the door on the northwest the "west door." Some of the informants, however, insist upon calling the door in the southeast corner the "west door," because when the sun sets in the west it shines toward that door. The east door is the Turtle moiety's door, and the east side is the Turtle side; the west door and west side are the Wolf domain.

[6] Hannah Jacobs, who was over ninety when she died recently, was the mother of the present head deaconess of the Turtle side at Sour Springs. It was in reality Mrs. Jacobs who decided Turtle moiety affairs rather than her daughter. Although she did not hold the office of a deaconess, she stirred stoves with the deacons and in general enjoyed all the prerogatives of the office.

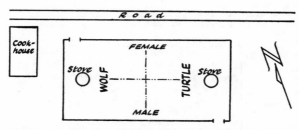

Fig. 3. Sour Springs Longhouse: Seating according to Moieties.

On those occasions when there is separation of moieties—namely, Stirring Ashes Days, society-rites' days, the Bowl Game Days of Midwinter, and the Bowl Game Days of Green Corn—the Wolf men sit along the southern wall of the west side and the Turtle men along the southern wall of the east side; the women of the respective moieties sit opposite the men on the northern wall, and the overflow of both sexes occupies the short ends of the building, the women sitting toward the north and the men toward the south (see Fig. 3). Sometimes, if there are more women than men, an entire short side may be filled with women, as in the diagram given by Speck (1949: 21); but if there should be more men, then a short side may accommodate only men.

On all other ceremonial occasions the Longhouse is divided into a male and a female half, splitting parallel to the short sides. The western half of the Longhouse becomes the female half and the eastern the male (see Fig. 4). The west door is the female door, and the east door is the male. The female door is thus associated with the Wolf side, the male door with the Turtle side. The people who shift across the house, according to the type of seating, are the Wolf men and the Turtle women; Turtle men and Wolf women never change their seating at Sour Springs. Speck (1949: 4) wonders why women at Sour Springs enter the west door, while at Lower Cayuga the women's door is the east door. Perhaps the important factor is the proximity of the door to the cookhouse, for in both cases the women enter the door closest to the cookhouse, as they do also at Seneca Longhouse, where the women's side is the west side. There seems to be no particular association of directions with male and female; the doors are simply traditionally separate for the sexes, and the choice of doors for each is merely conventional. The important consideration is that through such separation reciprocity can be vividly indicated and executed.

Lower Cayuga clan and moiety organization. The clans represented at Lower Cayuga Longhouse are the same as at Sour Springs, and the distribution of the clans into moieties is the same: Wolf, Heron, and Snipes on one side; Turtles, Bears, Deer, and Ball on the other side. Besides these Cayuga clans, all the other Six Nations clans are represented by members from the other nations. Members from the Onondaga Beaver clan sit with the Turtles; and perhaps one of the reasons why Sour Springs changed the Beaver clan from the Wolf to the Turtle side was to follow the example of Lower Cayuga (though Mrs. Jacobs and Mr. General did not give this as a reason). Eel and Hawk, so far as could be ascertained, are not

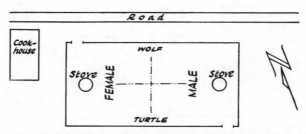

Fig. 4. Sour Springs Longhouse: Male-female Seating.

represented in the Cayuga nation, but are represented in the Cayuga Longhouse community, and they align at Lower Cayuga as at Sour Springs. There is a tendency among the population at Lower Cayuga to regard the Heron clan as a "Small Wolf" clan, as do the Onondaga and Seneca communities. The Ball clan is usually interpreted as being a Deer clan, just as Mr. General would have it.

Physical orientation of Lower Cayuga Longhouse. Lower Cayuga Longhouse is oriented in the same direction as Sour Springs, for it, too, lies parallel to the road, which runs in a generally east-west direction but rotated clockwise 30 degrees. However, the doors at Lower Cayuga are in the center of the short ends, rather than at the ends of the long sides as at Sour Springs. The western half of the Longhouse is associated with the Turtles and the males, and the eastern half with the Wolves and the females (see Figs. 5, 6). Hence, at Lower Cayuga, just as at Sour Springs, the Turtle men and the Wolf women do not change their seating positions when the division of the house changes from male-female to Wolf-Turtle.

The cookhouse at Lower Cayuga is behind the east door, which is the door closer to the women's entrance. Food is always brought in through the convenient female door, though men often carry the heavy cauldrons, usually balancing a cauldron on a stick between them. There is no apparent significance to carriers being male other than that the cauldrons are extremely hot and heavy and would be almost impossible for two women to manage.

At all the Longhouses the preparation of food, with the exception of cooking the meat at Midwinter, is the duty of the women, although men are supposed to light the fire in the cookhouse and draw the requisite water. Male-female joking arises at each Longhouse over whether each is doing the allotted work. The joking always takes a standard form; hence, they say, "The men are getting so lazy," or "The women of this Longhouse are so lazy," or "The men don't know how to cook meat any more." Again, as in the Eagle Dance joking at Six Nations, the joking is not particularly personally directed. When a deaconess is annoyed at a particular deacon for shirking his culinary duty, she may make personal comments in addition to the generalized joking. An important consideration, however, is the existence not only of clan and moiety joking but also of male-female joking of an institutionalized type within the Longhouses.

Seneca Longhouse clan and moiety organization. The moiety seating at Seneca Longhouse, as mentioned before, is not a "Seneca" seating as known at the Seneca Longhouses of New York State. At Tonawanda, Fenton (1951b: 47) finds the

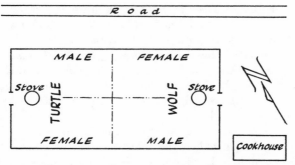

FIG. 5. Lower Cayuga Longhouse: Seating according to Moieties.

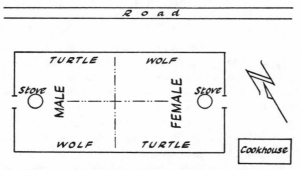

FIG. 6. Lower Cayuga Longhouse: Male-female Seating.

following arrangement: Snipe, Hawk, Deer, Heron, Eel opposed by Wolf, Turtle, Bear, and Beaver. At Coldspring (*ibid.*: 46) the alignment is Deer, Snipe, Heron, Hawk complementary to Bear, Wolf, Beaver, and Turtle. The seating at Seneca Longhouse at Six Nations is different from these. Nor is its seating identical with the Onondaga seating at Syracuse, where Fenton (1953: 71) lists Eel, Bear (now extinct), Deer, and Hawk on one side, and Turtle, Beaver, Wolf, and Snipe on the other, and Professor Floyd Lounsbury (private communication, April 4, 1955) lists Turtle, Beaver, Snipe, and Ball-play on one side, and Bear (extinct), Eel, and Deer on the other, with Wolf on both sides. The determining factors of the Seneca seating at Six Nations are apparently not known. Seating does not follow the ideal affiliation of the chiefs in the Roll Call of either the Seneca or the Onondaga chiefs. Nor can it follow the actual clan affiliations of the chiefs now installed at Six Nations in the Seneca and Onondaga titles, for the titles are held mainly by the Wolf, Deer, and Eel clans, thus leaving the seating of the other clans indeterminate.

The actual arrangement today—"because we always sit this way"—is to seat Deer, Bear, Eel, Snipe, Hawk, and Ball on one side, and Wolf, Turtle, Beaver, Heron, and Small Turtle on the other side. Hawk, which is an unfamiliar clan at

Six Nations, sits with the Deer at Seneca, because the ritual leaders of Seneca Longhouse believe it to be a medium-sized Deer clan, and all animals of a category sit together. Ball, which is believed to be the "Small Deer" clan, sits with the Deer clans for the same reason. Heron clan sits with the Wolf clan, because at Seneca the name is supposed to designate a small prairie wolf, which should therefore sit with his "brother Wolf." Both Snipe clans, the Prairie Snipe and the Sand Snipe, sit together. It is notable that the Bear clan is in the moiety opposite to the one with which it associates in the Seneca seating in the United States, and that the Snipe clan would be on the wrong moiety side if the Six Nations Seneca Longhouse were supposed to be organized in the same way as the United States Onondaga. Both Seneca and Onondaga Longhouses at Six Nations have combined and shifted the seating so that the Birds (with the exception of the Heron, which is believed to be a Wolf) sit with the Deer as at Coldspring, and the Bear clans also sit with the Deer as at Syracuse.

At Seneca Longhouse the Large Deer clan is the "leader" of its side, and the Wolf clan is the "leader" of the opposite side. As mentioned before, being the "leader" does not carry any special privilege for the clan, nor does lending the name of the clan to the moiety side have any special obligation or privilege associated with it. The "leader" is the first clan named on those occasions on which the clans are enumerated, but the order is not supposed to indicate a descending ranking. The clan order is a matter of convention and tradition, as remembered and interpreted by the particular speaker announcing the clans on the ceremonial occasion. Some hold that the leadership of the Wolf and Deer clans derives from their association with the two most influential chiefs, Honŏwiye'hdŏ of the Wolf clan and Thadoda'ho? of the Deer clan (though this title was until recently a Bear clan title). Others ascribe the first place to these clans because they were the first animals seen by Deganawi'da? as he matched each animal with a group of men and their leader (see p. 55 *supra*). Of course, the plausibility of this explanation depends in part upon using a version of the origin legend in which the first two animals seen by Deganawi'da? were the deer and the wolf.

At Seneca, as at Sour Springs, when members from clans not ordinarily represented arrive to participate, they try to be seated as the order of the house demands. Cayuga Turtles and Wolves sit together and act in one moiety complementing the Deer clans and their associates. Again this indicates that for any one person the reciprocity pattern is independent of any particular grouping of clans into moieties. Individual A may be on the same side as individual B in one event and opposed to him in another, yet in both cases the benefits of reciprocal duties and rewards are equivalent. Further proof of this is the nonchalance with which the switching of a person from one moiety to the other is tolerated, for, while it is mentioned, it is never punished in any way. Even the ritual leaders now are lax about indicating the proper seating in the Longhouse. Instead of enumerating the clans the day before Betting Day, the tendency is simply to state, "The sides will bet," which, of course, makes proper seating even more difficult because of lack of knowledge.

Physical orientation of Seneca Longhouse. Seneca Longhouse, just as the Sour Springs and Lower Cayuga Longhouses, stands parallel to the road and therefore is oriented in approximately an east-west direction but rotated about 30 degrees in accordance with the concession pattern. The doors at Seneca, as at Lower Cayuga, are in the centers of the short ends. The western door is both the Wolf and the women's door, and the eastern door is that of the Deer and the men (see Figs. 7, 8).

At Seneca on days when separation is by moiety, the Wolf women sit along the northwest wall and overflow to the door on the northwest corner. The Wolf men sit along the southwest wall, similarly moving toward the door if the crush becomes too great along the long wall. The Deer women sit along the southeast wall, and the Deer men along the northeast wall. At all other ceremonial occasions, when men sit across the fire from women, the Wolf men sit along the southeast wall and the Deer women along the southwest wall. Thus, neither the Wolf women nor the Deer men change their seating, while the Deer women and the Wolf men exchange places in the shift from male-female to Wolf-Deer separation of the house. Each stove is associated with the side on which it is located; the Wolf stove is also the female stove, and the Deer stove is also the male stove. Food is brought in by the western (female) door. This, of course, applies only to such food as is carried in from the cookhouse, for individuals also bring food with them in baskets through the doors they usually enter and give it to the deaconesses on their own sides for disposition.

Onondaga Longhouse clan and moiety organization. Onondaga Longhouse follows the same seating as Seneca Longhouse, and in fact it is the model for Seneca. However, while some informants orient the Snipe (always called "Sniper") clan with the Deer and Bear, as at Seneca, others place it with the Turtle, Wolf, and Beaver clans. This is due to the fact that one prominent Snipe family has recently changed to the latter moiety, so that Snipe sits on both sides now. Because there is no current Snipe chief among the Onondaga at Six Nations, an unambiguous guide to moiety affiliation is lacking. The fourth Onondaga chief, Honya?dadji'wak, was traditionally listed as a Snipe, and the predecessor of the present incumbent

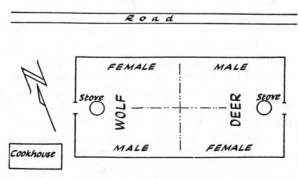

Fig. 7. Seneca Longhouse: Seating according to Moieties.

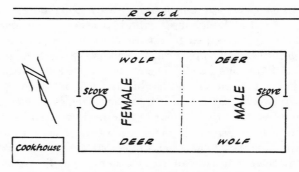

Fig. 8. Seneca Longhouse: Male-female Seating.

was a Snipe; but then the family died out, and now the title is held by a Wolf. Similarly, the fifth Onondaga chief, Awe'ʔkᵉhnyat, who should be a Snipe according to Alexander General (though the published literature does not associate a Snipe with this title), is currently a member of the Wolf clan. Despite the recollection that Snipe should be in a phratry with Beaver (as indicated at Condolence practice sessions), the absence of a Snipe chief leaves the Snipe members without a tangible example. The "ordinary people" sit as do the chiefs, and if there is no chief and also no instruction before Betting Day, confusion results. In general, the seating at Onondaga Longhouse is Deer, Eel, Bear, Large Snipe, and Small Snipe (the affiliation of which is somewhat confused, as mentioned above), Ball (which is believed to be a Deer clan), and Hawk on one side; and on the other side, Wolf, Turtle, Small Turtle, Beaver, and Heron (whose name is sometimes taken to mean a small wolf just as at Seneca). The Heron clan members are mainly Cayuga, and even though they do not identify themselves as belonging to a kind of Wolf clan, they sit on the same side as the Wolf clan at Onondaga and Seneca Longhouses because in the Cayuga Longhouses the Herons sit with the Wolves. In this case, for lack of directions at the host Longhouse, the guests sit in the most convenient imitation of their home seating. Deer and Wolf are "leaders" at Onondaga, and for the same reason and with the same force as at Seneca.

Physical orientation of Onondaga Longhouse. Onondaga Longhouse is notable at Six Nations because it has only one door and because it is situated in an approximately north-south direction. It faces the road, and the door is in the center of the house on the east side. (The Onondaga Longhouse Road intersects Seneca Line (the Fifth Line) at right angles, so that this road does not run in an exact north-south direction, but slants in a northeast-southwest direction. The Longhouse, being parallel to the road, also slants in this direction.) Men and women, Wolves and Deer, all enter through the door in any order with no distinctions or ritual. When one asks why Onondaga has only one door, the answer invariably is: "It's always been this way." The arrangement is considered completely unimportant. The south side of the house is the Wolves' and women's side, and the north side is that of the men and the Deer (see Figs. 9, 10). The cookhouse is located north of the north side of the Longhouse.

On those days on which moiety seating is observed, Wolf women sit along the southeastern wall and Wolf men along the southwestern wall; Deer women sit along the northeastern wall and Deer men along the northwestern wall. In all cases, the overflow sits along the short sides, dividing in the center of the wall under the windows. On male-female division days the Deer women take the place vacated by the Wolf men, the Wolf men move to the northwest wall, and the Deer men who used to sit at the northwest now move to the north wall. (This seems to be the preferred seating of the Deer men, rather than the northeast wall, which holds the male Deer overflow on male-female division days.) Thus, at Onondaga three parties are involved in the shift, but again the Wolf women do not move. In none of the four Longhouses do the Wolf women ever change their seating.

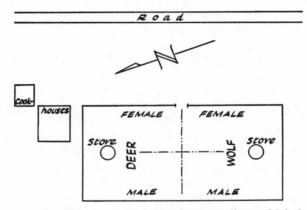

Fig. 9. Onondaga Longhouse: Seating according to Moieties.

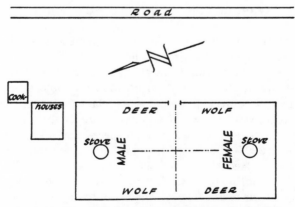

Fig. 10. Onondaga Longhouse: Male-female Seating.

No particular significance is attached to this, except that it serves as an organizational signpost when members try to orient themselves in the various Longhouses or to describe the various seating arrangements. "No Wolf women move" and "The Wolf side is always the women's side" are two generalizations applicable to all the Longhouses, and almost every informant is aware of them. (Wm. C. Sturtevant points out in a private communication that at Newtown, Wolf women do move.)

RELATIONSHIP AS A PRINCIPLE OF ORGANIZATION

At one time there must have been strong in-group feelings among the members of a clan. In the literature of the Colonial period it is often mentioned that clan members are supposed to be particularly helpful to one another, so that, for example, a person visiting a strange community was to be housed by members of his own clan. Until recently, when a stranger met a member of the community, his first words were to ask the member's clan (nesẽ?da'o?dẽ?, "your clan?"); the member would then tell his clan (typical replies being genya'hdẽ? nõngi?da'o?dẽ?, "I am Mud Turtle," or ganya'hdẽ? nõngese'edẽ?, "I belong to the Turtle clan."), and then the stranger would divulge his own clan. This procedure is not followed today, particularly since so many people would be embarrassed to answer that they do not know their clans. (However, if one does ascertain that a stranger belongs to one's own clan, there is a spark of camaraderie.) As discussed previously, the importance of the clan in the life of the individual has greatly diminished. Clan and moiety distinctions, though they have been emphasized in the literature, are not vital and basic to the functioning of that part of the old culture which remains at Six Nations. They are still important, however, but their importance now lies in their serving as an organizational mechanism. The existence of clans and moieties is useful in the ceremonials, especially by facilitating reciprocal action. But clans and moieties themselves do not enter the "charter" (Malinowski, 1944) of the society as imperative values, so that if division along clan and moiety lines is not easily obtainable, any organization which fulfills the ideal of reciprocity is satisfactory.

It seems reasonable, furthermore, from the frequent shifting of clans within the phratries of chiefs, that clan substitution has been permissible over a fairly long period of time, certainly from Handsome Lake's day on, for he was borrowed for a chieftainship (Deardorff, 1951: 79). Two possibilities could account for the loose integration of clan and phratry divisions: either clans are not a very old and therefore not a very integrated element of Iroquois culture, or there has arisen a modern leniency in order to conserve those basic aspects and values of culture which constitute the "charter." The latter possibility is connected with the fact that insistence on details of execution, when such details are impossible to fulfill, would be destructive of the entire pattern. A combination of both of these possibilities could be feasible, and one might suspect this to be the case. (There has, incidentally, been much argument and speculation about the phratric divisions among the

Iroquois; see Hewitt, 1944: 81, with comment by Fenton on Hewitt's criticism of Lowie. Lowie conceived of Iroquois councils as tripartite, Hewitt as dual. Fenton himself, 1950: 54, emphasizes the "two and three" pattern of organization.)

At Six Nations quite strong in-group feelings have developed at each Longhouse. These feelings are in no way based upon the older kin and tribal groupings, since the Longhouse membership cuts across clan and tribal lines. However, it is interesting that kinship terminology is used between members of a Longhouse, which indicates that kinship serves as an ideal principle of organization in any situation in which a feeling of community exists. Thus, at Sour Springs, one usually refers to a member of the opposite moiety as "cousin" within the Longhouse, whereas one might greet such a member as "brother" if he were met in a different social context. This terminology is not an expression of consanguineal relationship either between or within the moieties. Nor do the appellatives "cousin" and "brother" as used in these contexts carry any implication of a rule of exogamy. "Brother" is used only in order to show the closest ideal relationship, and it should evoke feelings of friendship and mutual aid. When members of Sour Springs, even though of opposite moieties, call each other brothers, it is to indicate their feelings of fraternity to any outsider.

LONGHOUSE FUNCTIONARIES
DEACONS

INTRODUCTION

THE affairs of the Longhouse are regulated by an indefinite and shifting number of male and female officers, who are appointed in the Longhouse or who hold positions in the Longhouse through being associated with one of the hereditary chiefs. Morgan (1877: 82) referred to these officers as "Keepers of the Faith" and asserted that they were advanced to this office by each gens as evidence of the fidelity of the gens to the religion. Morgan's description (*ibid.*) is a good starting point for examining the differences between the functions of the faith-keepers at his time and today, for these differences reflect the shift of power from the clans to the Longhouse and the integration of the chiefs into the Longhouse.

The Keepers of the Faith were about as numerous as the chiefs, and they were selected by the wise men and matrons of each clan (gens). After their selection they were raised up by a council of the tribe with ceremonies adapted to the occasion. Their names were taken away, and new ones belonging to this class bestowed in their place. Men and women in about equal numbers were chosen. They were censors of the people, with power to report the evil deeds of persons to the council. It was the duty of individuals selected to accept the office; but after a reasonable service each might relinquish it, which was done by dropping his name as a Keeper of the Faith and resuming his former name.

Morgan (1901, 1: 177–91) further ascertained that, despite the duties of the faith-keepers and the right of reprimanding and accusing wavering members of the group, the faith-keepers did not qualify to be described as either a religious order or a priesthood. They were distinguished by no special emblem, costume, or privilege. They were common people, and their office was one of necessity, without reward and without particular honor to the individual. "Under the League itself no sacerdotal office was recognized. . . . No religious dignitaries were ever raised up by the council of sachems to fill any priestly station" (*ibid.*). (See Fenton, 1941: 158, for a discussion of the source of Morgan's account, namely information given by E. S. Parker of Tonawanda.)

Fenton (1936: 6), in his description of the ceremonial complex at Coldspring, finds that at Coldspring:

The administration of the longhouse festivals rests with a body of officers, elected equally from each of the eight clans, to hold office for life. . . . The office was instituted by Handsome Lake out of something similar that had preceded him. Theoretically, each clan should have two representatives, a man (hodi'·ǫt) and a woman (godi'·ǫt).

At Coldspring an officer is raised simultaneously with a member of the moiety opposite to his, and in the investiture the two officers "stood opposite" each other (*ibid.*). Head faith-keepers at Coldspring are also reported to be hereditary within maternal families of particular clans. Fenton (*ibid.*) then goes on to quote Goldenweiser's unpublished field notes from Six Nations, in which Goldenweiser maintains that each Longhouse at Six Nations had three male and three female officers in each clan.

At Six Nations this office is commonly known as belonging to the "deacon," though the term "faith-keeper" is known, and I have been asked on occasion why anthropologists call deacons "faith-keepers."[1] In Cayuga a male deacon is called hodri'hŏnt (pl., hona'thriŏnt), a female deacon or deaconess is godri'hŏnt (pl., gona'thriŏnt), the head deacon is hodrihŏntgo'wa, and the head deaconess is godrihŏntgo'wa. Each Longhouse has one male and one female head deacon per moiety, and these have the final authority in the Longhouse functions and direct the ordinary deacons on their respective sides and transmit information to them.

FUNCTIONS OF THE DEACONS

Social and psychological functions. The primary functions of the deacons are to arrange, direct, and administer all Longhouse activities. Today they also perform additional services for the Longhouse community. With the disappearance of integrated clans and of strong matrilineal families having head women, the deacons function more and more in the capacity of advisers outside the Longhouse as well as within. Thus, when a family has any problem, must make a ritual decision, wishes to "pass a dance" for the health of the family, or has a grievance against the elected council or the Canadian government and wishes assistance from the Longhouse group, the deacon is the logical person to be consulted. In all such cases in which, according to the older literature, the clan head, family head, or even the chief in a clan would have had jurisdiction, the deacon now is the most available and convenient adviser.

In general, female members ask assistance from female deacons, and male members from male deacons. A deacon will then relay the message to a deacon of the opposite sex if the question cannot be handled by the initially consulted deacon or if a group decision is necessary. There is a very strong feeling that it does not accord with propriety for a woman to ask a male deacon for any official assistance or for a man to ask a deaconess, although, when a female deacon asks a male deacon, or vice

[1] People at Six Nations have had long and varied experience with a multitude of anthropologists and are quite sophisticated about answering questions. It is not at all uncommon to be asked whether one wishes the answer in terms of Parker's, Hale's, Hewitt's, or Fenton's description. More unnerving yet is to be asked whether one has read the Johnson Papers in the original at the British Museum, as have several of the residents of the Reserve while on a trip to the Royal House of England and to the old League of Nations to persuade them that the Canadian government should have no jurisdiction over the Six Nations Reserve. (The delegation very independently wrote out its own passports, "good anywhere in the world," making typescript copies for each member. No interview was granted either with the King or with the British and Canadian representatives, for the verdict in England and Geneva was that the government in Ottawa had jurisdiction; but Alexander General proudly reports that when the delegation managed to see an official at the League, he said: "It is the best passport I've ever seen.") Mr. Merle H. Deardorff notes the presence of equally sophisticated individuals at Coldspring and Tonawanda (private communication, April, 1955).

versa, the act is approved. There are exceptions to the general practice of asking a deacon of one's own sex to act for one. For instance, it is traditionally decreed that "a man should go around" to announce a feast for a family and that a man should announce an impending Ohgi'we feast, and if an ordinary woman is making the arrangements, she may hire the messenger directly. Ordinarily, it is less embarrassing to seek the service of a deacon to communicate with the opposite sex. In the Longhouse an ordinary woman would be much embarrassed to have to cross over to the men's side, but such crossing by female or male deacons is proper. Deacons, therefore, often constitute the communicating link between the sexes in a situation where a kind of sex taboo prevails. The expression of this taboo is usually phrased in the form, "I'm shy to cross over to the other side" or "I don't want to go by myself."

The office of deacon today is thus not merely an organizational device for allowing the Longhouse activities to function smoothly. True, the deacons organize and administer the Longhouse rites, seeing to the food, the necessary artifacts, and the order of events; but more important, the deacons actually share the responsibility of action with each of the members who seeks their aid. Inherent in each application to the deacon is the idea that the deacon will lend his advice and judgment to the act, or at least impart authority and respectability. Transacting rituals through the deacons buoys up the confidence of a member, for he does not have to stand before the congregation alone. Even though an individual may be intent on "putting the thing through" (i.e., "passing" his dance or feast), he will seldom do this on his own initiative, but will consult with the appropriate deacon at the time of performance. When at Midwinter time, for example, a woman wishes a False Face Dance performed, she will bring the requisite food to the Longhouse herself and, when she has mustered her courage, will tell her desire to a deaconess or perhaps even to the head deaconess of her moiety. This deaconess has had no prior notice that the False Face Dance was to be performed, and no formal arrangement to provide for masks has been made. However, since the False Face Dance is a standard dance, it is hoped that some of the male members will have brought their "faces." Should the deaconess consider the dance to be inappropriate, she has the power to dissuade the supplicant from "passing" the dance. This seldom happens, however, and in general the consent of the deacon is only a formality. If the deaconess approves, she will inform the head deaconess on the opposite side of the desire on her side to have a False Face Dance. The head deaconess then must see to it, either herself or through a deacon on her own side, that some men are asked to perform the dance and that the dance is announced by the speaker. All the people consulted and involved are acting in order "to help," for the group action is pleasing to the supernaturals and also is "part of the medicine." Deacons are particularly "helpful" to all members in the Longhouse, and they derive their reward from the knowledge that they have acted in accordance with the demands of the Great Spirit and of Handsome Lake for the good of their fellow congregants.

When in the Longhouse, the members feel that there is a definite hierarchy of material, human, and spiritual things; and the people, the deacons, and the higher officials (which includes head deacons, chiefs, and speakers) are ordered into this hierarchy (see p. 195 *infra*). Each level must be treated with the respect due it, and each higher level must be accorded the due amount of increased respect. If one is an ordinary member, one must not presume to be on an equal footing with the officials, or the representatives of the Great Creator and the reciters of the Code of Handsome Lake. Even if one of the officials happens to be the husband, close relative, or friend of a common member, the common member would rather act through a deacon than confer directly with the official when he is acting in his ritual capacity. Morgan is correct in saying that there are no emblems or symbols of a separate class for the officials of the Longhouse and that it would be difficult to define a priestly order; the officials are ordinary people outside the Longhouse, engaging in the same economic pursuits as all the rest of the members. Nevertheless, while in the Longhouse, feelings of respect toward the hierarchy cause the speakers and chiefs and ritualists to be removed from the populace and seem awesome. Deacons, therefore, provide the link between the common member and the higher officials. The status of the deacons as a somewhat more elevated group than the common members is constantly mentioned in the ritual speeches, and they are allowed certain privileges in the Longhouse ceremonies which indicate their "higher" position. They help stir ashes before the turn of the common people, they go out to the cookhouse to burn tobacco with the speakers and chiefs at Green Corn time, they are outside the Longhouse dousing the dancers with water during the Thunder rites, they often lead the dances, and in general they are always conspicuous over and above the congregation by sitting in the front benches and leading the rituals. However, when food is distributed, the female deacons should eat last. When male deacons pass food to the congregation,[2] they are usually handed their baskets by the female deacons, who take out one piece which they hand to the male passer before he goes on the rounds of the Longhouse with the basket. Thus, the men are assured a share of each item. The head deaconess is sometimes neglected, though the deacon should hand her a share. The elevation of the deacons requires an added amount of responsibility, righteousness, goodness, and obedience to the Gaihwi'yo. Morally and ethically the deacons are expected to be superior to the common worshiper, and they are also supposed to be more religious and diligent in their attitude toward the Longhouse. The ideas of helpfulness and reciprocity are definitely involved in the office of deacon. That in fact some deacons may not always conform to these ideals, but may on occasion drink, neglect their duty, or be no more religious than any other member, is, perhaps, to be expected, but it does not vitiate the office itself so long as there remains a corps of deacons who fulfill their roles sufficiently well to satisfy the members and not disillusion them.

There are several other respects in which the functions of the deacons are related

[2] A head deaconess collects food from her own moiety and sends deacons from her side to serve people on the other side. However, when in the rush of distribution there are already several deacons passing in one section of the Longhouse, the deacons may start on their own side. Fair distribution is watched more carefully than strict moiety distribution.

to general traits of Iroquois culture. For example, the mores of the Longhouse and of Iroquois culture in general indicate that a member ought to be "shy" and reticent, not only toward members of the other sex but toward the public in general. If an individual is not so by temperament, it is incumbent on him to affect a certain amount of reticence. Consequently, it would be considered out of place to institute any action without a deacon. Volunteering or giving indication of being able to perform songs and rituals without being asked or coaxed by the congregation through the deacons would be considered boasting, and boasting is one of the traits most criticized. Also, secrecy is dreaded, and the relaying of information through the deacons, who are officially instituted channels of communication, rules out any chance of treachery or witchcraft, which, despite being outlawed by the Longhouse, is feared at all times.

Routine and physical functions. The more routine duties of the deacons are well known. They must set the dates for the ceremonial cycle, they must arrange to have men "go around" to inform the congregation, they must arrive early at the Longhouse on the day of the ceremony and make the fires in the stoves and in the cookhouse. They must assemble and prepare the food, and they must clean the Longhouse after the ceremony is over. During the ceremonial they assist the speakers and ritualists in various ways (and, in fact, the deacons are sometimes called "prompters," because they remind the speakers of what should be said in case of lapses). It is interesting to see how the deacons themselves conceive of their duty. Esther Jamieson, who is a head deaconess at Sour Springs, said: "I just cook, clean up, fix dates, and give names." It seemed that her greatest pride came in the cookhouse, where she was diligent about arriving early, having pounded the corn before coming to the Longhouse.

The duties are apportioned between the male and female deacons, but the Longhouses follow slightly differing patterns. Date setting, for example, falls to the women at Sour Springs much of the time, while at Onondaga and Seneca Longhouses the men are usually in charge. At Sour Springs the two head deaconesses together set the time for the following ceremonies: Bush Dance after Midwinter, Maple (when held, for it is not usual now at Sour Springs), Seed Planting Festival, Strawberry, Raspberry, Green Bean, Corn Testing, Bush Dance after the large Green Corn Ceremony, and Harvest (Thanksgiving) Ceremony. The male head deacons arrange the dates of the large Green Corn Dance, Midwinter, and Moon, Sun, and Thunder Ceremonies (when these last three are held, for they are now infrequent at Sour Springs). The date of False Face Day is not set by either the male deacons or the deaconesses, but by the head False Face Society men of both moieties. When the male head deacons set dates, the speakers are often consulted. At Onondaga and Seneca Longhouses the women help set the dates for the two Bush Dances, which usually occur one week after the end of the Bowl Games at Midwinter and at the large Green Corn Dance; but all the remaining dates are determined by the men. In food preparation the men are enjoined to help with meat preparation, but in fact the women often get the men to do the more difficult chores of cooking, such as lifting the heavy pots, fetching the wood, starting the fires in the Longhouses and the cookhouse, and fetching the water from the river (especially if the river is frozen over and must be chopped to obtain water).[3] On "Scrub Day," which is usually the fourth day in the Midwinter Festival, on which day no ceremonial activity occurs in the Longhouse, men are also supposed to help fetch water in order to clean the Longhouse. Women, however, do the heavy work of scrubbing the floors and benches, which on a cold winter's day with inadequate heating (usually only one stove being lighted) is indeed an onerous task.

Deacons must also hold meetings to discuss Longhouse finances and maintenance, and, in short, such matters as are normal in the administration of a congregation. When the beams at Sour Springs, for example, needed repair, long and elaborate meetings of the deacons took place, in which estimates of repair costs were obtained from builders, material was examined, and arguments over the design of the building were settled. Final decisions should all be unanimous, but as is only natural, even when everyone agrees in the end, there may still remain dissatisfactions. Disagreements do not reveal any pattern of moiety competition, for deacons may on such occasions find fault with their colleagues of their own moiety side as readily as with those "across the fire."

The deacons may also decide which people should be selected to serve as their colleagues. Some deaconships are hereditary within particular families, and in such cases the families concerned have a choice, but if the other deacons disagree with a choice, the family should search for a more suitable candidate. However, the non-hereditary deaconships, which are unlimited in number, are usually filled on the recommendation of the deacons. They will "reward" a deserving and diligent member by naming him or her a deacon, or they may wish the services of a particular person and for that reason appoint him a deacon.

Deacons also supervise the burial grounds associated with each Longhouse, for today the graveyards are really extensions of the Longhouses (in contrast to previous times, when the literature attributed the graveyards to clans). When the Longhouse community has its annual Ohgi'we Ceremony, or even when a particular family sponsors a dead feast, tradition demands that the graveyard be cleaned and burned to eliminate weeds. The whole community should turn out, but deacons are expected to participate particularly prominently and to organize the work parties. The congregation works as if it were a bee, bringing lunches and warming food; and, despite the solemnity of a cemetery, the attitude is one of taking care of and helping deceased members of the congregation, who are still as much a part of the community as the living. Since deacons should minister to the congregation as a whole, they are automatically obligated to help those who "have passed beyond."

A final notable activity of the deacons is to initiate and supervise the recreational activities and "tea meetings" so prominent at Six Nations. Sunday afternoon

[3] The well-known trait of scooping water as it flows downstream, as is done, for example, in collecting water for the Little Water Medicine, is not exemplified in fetching Longhouse water. The pails are merely dipped into the hole in the fastest and most convenient fashion.

raffles for Plains type Indian headdresses, various grocery goods, lacrosse implements, and quilts are among the most popular Longhouse activities. Onondaga Longhouse, through the energetic showmanship of Howard Skye, is noted for its suspenseful raffles and luridly designed headdresses. The method of the Sunday afternoon social is to drive up to the Longhouse and buy a 25-cent chance at the gate. No admission charge is asked, but the presence of the chancesellers is quite obvious. There usually is a softball game, either by boys' or girls' teams, and on special occasions there may even be a lacrosse game. Refreshments are served, which have been prepared by the deacons and from which they hope to net a profit. At the end of the game the raffle takes place, followed by social dancing in the Longhouse. Before the dancing begins, the speaker offers the Thanksgiving Address, which is characteristic of all meetings and social affairs, but usually the Longhouse is scarcely occupied until the actual dancing begins. Dances begin about 8:00 P.M. and may last until midnight. The other typical tea meeting, which is more popular at Sour Springs Longhouse, since it has no organized ball game nor an adequate field at present, merely consists of an afternoon meal, in which various foods are sold, especially corn soup, if it has been prepared by a member. For the tea meetings the members of the congregation donate the food and the time of preparation (which is done at their own homes). Indian cookies, cakes, and pies are also favorite items. The proceeds, as from the raffles, are used to finance the Longhouse.

Outside the Longhouse the routine duties of the deacons include such matters as advice on the naming of children—for deaconesses ought to know many names—aid to elderly Longhouse members, assistance in finding rides to the Longhouse, and general community-minded acts. The speakers of the Longhouse, who might be compared to the ministers of a church, should be free of such duties, even though they also, being on a high level in the hierarchy, ought to be particularly selfless.

Once again it is important to stress the "shyness" of the members, since in a sense the authority of the deacons is in direct proportion to the unwillingness of the members to undertake matters on their own. For example, when in the winter of 1955 some deer were shot by some boys, the carcasses were offered to Sour Springs Longhouse for the Midwinter Festival at an attractively low price, much less than the price of beef at the butcher shop. At that particular time, however, the deacons of Sour Springs (male deacons, who decide such matters) were not around to be consulted, and no one else wanted to assume the responsibility. Consequently, the meat was not bought, despite the fact that the congregation would have enjoyed real venison very much in preference to domestic beef. Perhaps it should be mentioned that the deacons' status is indicated by one of the names given them, for the most common reference to a deacon is "the push" at such and such Longhouse, while a head deacon is referred to as "the head push."

SELECTION OF DEACONS

Hereditary deaconships. Essentially there are three types of deacons at the Longhouses at Six Nations: those who are deacons due to descent of the office in the matrilineal family, those who are deacons because they are good workers in the community and have been appointed in acknowledgment of their services, and those who are deacons because they are affiliated with a hereditary chief. There are male and female deacons in all three categories.

Despite Goldenweiser's impression that each clan has three officers of each sex in each Longhouse (see *supra*, p. 71), there is no indication of any such arrangement today. In the first place, it is difficult to determine which clans are represented by deacons at any Longhouse, and, secondly, clans which have recently been incorporated into the Longhouse may be represented by no deacons at all. There are, however, many deacons who were appointed because the deaconship had been held previously by members in their matrilineal families.

Hereditary deacons ought to be invested with a name which accompanies the office, but today most of these names have been forgotten, and the deacon assumes office with his "baby name." Appropriate times for deciding who from the family and from the Longhouse community should be a deacon are Strawberry, Midwinter, and Green Corn times, but the investiture itself takes place only at Midwinter and Green Corn, on the days on which names are bestowed. This is the day on which the Adŏ'wa rite and the Skin Dance take place; and because the two other sacred rites, the Bowl Game and the Feather Dance, are also performed at Midwinter and at Green Corn, the saying has arisen that deacons may be invested only "when four sacred things are passed." At one time, it seems likely, the deacons were invested on this particular day because they were given names, and this is the day on which names are bestowed. Now, however, when very few of the offices have a name any longer, either because the names have been forgotten or because families retain deaconships at the death of a deacon who had been appointed for merit and thus had no name, the main association of making deacons is with the four most sacred rituals. The analogy of "high" rituals with "high" people is invoked. Further, informants claim that the speech of investiture demands that deacons be installed coincident with the four sacred rites, but this is a very loose interpretation of the words ". . . it has been conferred upon me to speak on behalf of the chiefs and the officers regarding the duty of him who is appointed to be one of the attendants at the ceremonials which the Great Spirit has laid down for us to perform . . ." (Alexander General's text).

When a hereditary deaconship falls vacant and the family decides to install a new member, it announces this decision to the head deaconess of its own moiety. She, in turn, asks the head deaconess on the opposite side for approval, and then the speaker will be told to announce the new deacon at the appropriate time in the ritual. Actually, only the head deaconess from the moiety investing the deacon has jurisdiction over his acceptability; the other head deaconess is consulted but can be overruled. Also, in theory, there can be objections to the new candidate from the congregation, which the speakers report to the house; but these are very rare, and furthermore, at least in the case of a woman candidate, the men are powerless to overrule the decision of the head deaconess.

The number of reputedly hereditary deaconships at Six Nations is quite large, with some families claiming as many as three or four offices.

An example of three sisters and a brother all being deacons is that of the Hess children. Ida, Maggie, and Betsy Hess all claim hereditary positions which belonged to their grandmother's family (MoMo, MoMoSi, and another MoMoSi). Their mother held a deaconship, and now three of the four daughters have positions. A brother, Jake, also is a deacon, but I do not know through whom he claims his position. All the three female positions are stated to have been originally at Seneca Longhouse, though the mother of the Hess children (nee Mary Styres) was a deaconess at Lower Cayuga. Two of the deaconesses today do not know of a name which accompanies their office, but Betsy says that she was given a name with the position (Ganŏ'ksgwa, the name of the previous holder of the title). Maggie and Ida are deaconesses at Sour Springs, though due to their mother's affiliation with Lower Cayuga, both profess really to belong down below, and both intend to be buried there.

This alone vitiates Goldenweiser's rule of "three per clan." One of the most common causes for the multiplication of deacons in the family is that deacons are installed not only for the deceased great-grandmother, for example, but, if a certain amount of time has elapsed, simultaneously for the great-grandmother and the grandmother who had inherited the office. It is forgotten that the office should be filled consecutively and not simultaneously. Another cause is that deaconships created for merit, which ought to "die" with the death of the incumbent, are maintained in the family and passed on. Nor is this increase judiciously balanced by the lapsing of offices in those families which do not have a suitable heir to fill the position. In such cases a deacon can be "borrowed," just as a chief may be "borrowed," to fill the vacancy.

A typical case of borrowing a deacon is that of Carrie Logan Hill, (Mrs. Scotty Hill, the daughter of Joe Logan, Thadoda'ho?). Her mother, Mrs. Logan, came from St. Regis, and at the time of Mrs. Logan's emigration, St. Regis was a Catholic community which had no Longhouse and where clan organization had lapsed. Mrs. Logan, on her arrival at Six Nations, was adopted by the Ball clan, despite the fact that she is Mohawk. This is an example of how clans and nationality do not necessarily follow the classic pattern, since it would have been unthinkable to Morgan to have had a Mohawk Ball clan. Since Mrs. Logan had no previous clan and lineage·affiliation, there were no deaconships in her family. After her marriage to Mr. Logan, it was decided that Mr. Logan's family could borrow from Mrs. Logan's family (her children), because there were no eligible individuals to choose from in Mr. Logan's matrilineal family. Consequently, Carrie Logan Hill was borrowed, and it is generally agreed that the office will pass on in her family, since there still is no one in her father's family to take over at her death. Incidentally, Carrie Logan Hill was similarly borrowed to be one of the officers of the Ohgi'we Society. It is almost inevitable that a person active in the Longhouse will be given an office.

It commonly happens that a borrowed position is claimed by the family which was "borrowed in," rather than relinquished at the death of the individual who substituted for a rightful heir. Even if the family does not immediately claim the title, it sometimes happens that 50 years later an ambitious member remembers that the position was once occupied by her grandmother, but does not remember that the grandmother was merely "borrowed for her lifetime." The resurrection of offices and positions also frequently occurs on account of the influence of fortunetellers. Very often, when a family experiences bad luck or disease, a fortuneteller will be consulted, and a common diagnosis is that some ritual office has been neglected. The clairvoyant will remember a relative who had a certain position (not necessarily a deaconship but possibly an office in some medicine society or a custodianship of some ritual artifact), and the neglect of this position by the family will presumably have caused "trouble." The position must then be immediately filled by the family. In this way the fortuneteller has a conservative influence on the culture, for he (or she) is apt to keep the older functions in mind and reprimand the client for neglecting his duty. In general, the multiplication of deaconships is sanctioned, because being a deacon is presumed to stimulate interest in the Longhouse, and for this reason it is desirable to disseminate responsibilities and prestige among as many individuals as possible.

Some difficulty arises at Six Nations in deciding whether the deaconships, and in particular the hereditary ones, are Longhouse offices, Reserve-wide offices, nation-wide offices, or religious offices throughout all of Iroquoia. In general, the attitude is that a deacon has particular regulatory functions only at the Longhouse at which he was invested and where his services are most immediately needed.

Sometimes a person may be borrowed to fill a position belonging to a family which attends a different Longhouse from that of his own mother and his own affiliation. This happened in the case of Roy Buck, who had attended Onondaga Longhouse but was borrowed by Nellie Jamieson to fill a deaconship which her family owned and which was attached to Seneca Long-house. He was invested at Seneca and serves as a deacon there. His father, who was an Onon-daga chief and a staunch member of Onondaga Longhouse, was disturbed that his son allowed himself to be made a deacon at Seneca. Actually, his father had no jurisdiction in this matter, but since he was an influential ritualist, he felt entitled to direct the spiritual life of his cere-monially minded son. This feeling was also an indication of how in the minds of Longhouse adherents the office of deacon is associated with a particular Longhouse community. The Longhouses have a lien on the ritual life of their members, and they do not like to share an active member with another community more than is necessary.

The administration of a Longhouse—decisions as to finances, setting the dates of ceremonies, election of extra deacons on the basis of merit, etc.—are not shared on an inter-Longhouse basis, and advice on such matters from a deacon associated with another Longhouse would definitely be considered interference. Head deaconships are even more restricted to a single Longhouse, and a head deacon at one Longhouse can at most fulfill the role of an ordinary deacon at another Longhouse. On the other hand, certain functions of the deaconship, such as stirring ashes before the common people do, leading in dances, and sitting on the front benches—in short, all the honorific activities—may be exercised by all deacons, and it is considered good taste to invite visiting deacons to partake in particularly prominent actions.

It is certain that the hereditary deaconships are so definitely associated with Longhouses today that the average Longhouse member thinks of each position primarily in connection with a Longhouse and only secondarily in connection with a family. One indication of this is the rapid and progressive lapsing of the rule that a name should be passed on with a hereditary deaconship, for naming depends on lineage and clan cognizance. There is, in fact, a widespread feeling that it is wrong to "put one's old name in a box" (relinquish one's baby name) and assume a name for the deaconship, for everybody has come to know a person by his baby name, and anyone who needs help will call upon him formally by his baby name. Changing one's baby name, therefore, would be confusing in a time of crisis. Mrs. George Green says: "If he is lucky and grows up and is useful in the world, he can be asked to do work for one by using his Indian name. Therefore, the name should not be changed." Authority for this belief is the speech given at the time of naming a child.[4] One way of coping with this sentiment is to retain one's baby name and also to accept a name for the deaconship. This has been done recently.

Meritorious deaconships. Deacons of the second class, those who are appointed for merit, are indistinguishable from the hereditary deacons in their duties and in all aspects, except that they do not have a name associated with their office and that the office should "die" with the occupant. They are invested on the same day, preached to in a similar manner (although no Adŏ'wa is sung, since no name is assumed with the office), and they assume all the functions of the hereditary deacons. They can be selected for the office of head deacon, and they sometimes are. Deacons for merit are proposed by the community of deacons at the Longhouse. When they see a person "working hard for the Longhouse," they may recommend that he be made a deacon. Male candidates are recommended by the male deacons, and female candidates by the deaconesses. Again, only the moiety of which the candidate will become an officer must approve, and there is no way for the opposite moiety to veto a selection. In the appointment of meritorious deacons no attention is paid to the clan of the appointees, and there is no effort to have each clan represented.

Deacons associated with chiefs. The final class of deacons are those who hold their positions in the Longhouse because they are assistants to the hereditary chiefs. It is here that there is a direct and close interrelationship between the political and religious systems. When a chief is installed, he should be surrounded by an entourage, which is referred to symbolically as the "covering" for the "tree" (the term used for the covering being "deyoʔnhowe'kdŏ"). The chief is represented as a tree, and the attached personnel are the smaller branches which surround the main growth. The officers of the entourage are considered to be symbolically related to the chief. The chief's deacon and his deputy (among those nations in which there is a deputy) are called "nephews of the chief," and the matron and the chief's deaconess (the latter office existing only among the Cayuga) are the "chief's nieces." All the officers in the entourage of a chief are hereditary in the same way as the chief himself is, that is, the successor to a deceased officer is supposed to be selected by the chief's matron from among the chief's matrilineage. The matrons claim that they should have a string of wampum to signify and legitimate each of the officers of the "covering," just as for the chief himself. Any of the "covering" officers may be borrowed from

---

[4] The speeches used in the rituals and in the Longhouse are very literally interpreted and provide the justification for action and belief in many areas of life. The fact that the speeches are not numerous and not very varied adds to their individual importance, and they are scanned for meaning and guidance.

another lineage or even a different clan, if no suitable individual in the family of the chief is available. Usually the borrowing does not cross moiety lines, however. If an individual has been borrowed for the office, this fact is mentioned at the time of investiture, the expression being "agadōngwe?dani'hē?" ("she borrows a person").

Among the different nations the personnel associated with a chief varies today. In the case of the Onondaga and Seneca chiefs' titles (regardless of what the nationality of the incumbent actually is), the only officers attendant upon a chief are a matron and a deacon. The matron is the titleholder and the custodian of the wampum strings which legitimate the title of the chief, and she is also the individual who selects and appoints the deacon. This deacon is a man, called "hodri'hōnt" as are all other male deacons, and he assumes his duties in the Longhouse to which the chief is attached. Here again is a shift of association from a secular context to a definite Longhouse affiliation. A chief is personally rather than officially attached to a Longhouse, and because of this personal affiliation his deacon must be functional at that Longhouse. At one time the deacon was only supposed to attend to the ritual affairs of his chief, but now the deacon who is appointed for and with the chief is as important at the Longhouse as any of the hereditary or meritorious deacons. In fact, many of the members now believe that the deacons should, if "things went right," all be of the type attached to a chief.

One head deaconess who was consulted thought it an innovation established by the chiefs that anyone who is "smart" (which means helpful and quick) could be appointed to a deacon's position. She believes that originally the only deacons were the actual assistants of the chiefs. These alone, she says, should have any role in the Longhouse. Her view may perhaps be influenced by her adherence to the Mohawk Workers and the Indian Defense League, both of which actively advocate the importance and return to power of the hereditary chiefs. These organizations hope to attract any of the groups which have a vested interest in the hereditary chiefs by enlarging the roles of the chief and his personnel. This deaconess is of the opinion that a Longhouse could not and should not function without the chiefs and their aides, and consequently she has given special emphasis to their roles.

Not only has the chief recently become identified with the organization of the Longhouse, but so have his officers. Deacons of this kind may also be chosen as head deacons if they are assiduous. It is hard to think of duties which the chief's deacon could perform in the service of his chief, outside of preparing the food at the death feast of the chief and of helping prepare the installation feast for the new chief-elect. He does have one important function which is in some sense in the service of the chief, namely, to approach the chief, along with the matron, in order to reprimand him if he has been negligent. In general, since the chief has few ritual functions, the deacons naturally are thought of as primarily functioning in the Longhouse.

The Mohawk, Oneida, and Cayuga appoint not only a deacon, who attends to the chief's Longhouse duties, but also a deputy chief, or "second," who is to help the chief and, according to Morgan (1901, 1: 64), is supposed to stand behind the chief on important occasions and to run his errands. Actually, according to Morgan, the chiefs of all the nations had these deputies, or "runners" (so-called because they are the people who "run with the wampum string" to the opposite nation moiety to announce the death of the chief), and Chadwick (1897: 89–90) does list some of the Onondaga and Seneca chiefs as having them; but today the Onondaga and the Seneca do not install the deputies. The Mohawk, Cayuga, and Oneida still attempt to find a suitable member of the lineage to be the deputy to a chief, but he does not have an official standing in the Longhouse in the way that the chief's deacon has.

The matron of a Cayuga chief not only appoints a deacon and a deputy along with the chief, but she also appoints a woman to be a deaconess in the Longhouse (called "godri'hŏnt" as are the other female deacons) and to cook for the chief and attend to any of his ritual needs which might fall into the female realm. Again, there is very little that this deaconess can now do for a chief outside the Longhouse, and, consequently, this deaconess is firmly integrated into the Longhouse. In fact, even though the chief's deacon is at times invested along with the chief, the chief's deaconess is always invested in the Longhouse on the regular Adŏ'wa Day, when the hereditary and meritorious deacons are installed; the only difference in the ceremony is that the speaker mentions that she is one of the "covering for the chief" or is "the niece of the chief." The process by which a matron appoints a deaconess who attends a chief is exactly like the process of appointing a hereditary deacon, for the office of chief's deaconess is considered hereditary in the same way as any deaconship to which a name is attached. It is agreed that names should exist associated with the position of the chief's deacon and deaconess, but almost no names seem to be remembered. (An exception is Oscar Johnson, who received the name Gŏngyeda'ses, a Heron clan name, for being hodri'hŏnt to Chief Dyoŏhyŏ'ngo. He also retains his baby name.) When a matron wishes to install the deaconess to accompany a chief, she simply chooses a candidate and tells the head deaconess on her own moiety side to mention the selection to the speaker of her moiety. The information is communicated on the appropriate day of the Midwinter or Green Corn Festivals without prior warning. Only the head deaconess of the moiety involved need approve the selection, while the speaker and the chiefs and the men must accept it. The matron of the chief's title takes the candidate, leads her to the speaker, and stands beside her and the speaker while the investment is in process. This is the same pattern as in the investiture of a chief.

The matrons themselves, who guard the wampum strings, are ex officio deaconesses in the Longhouse. They have so integrated themselves into the Longhouse organization that they tend to be considered slightly "higher" than the ordinary deacons or deaconesses in the Longhouse. They function as deaconesses without any special installation in that office, for a matron is "spoken to" ceremonially only when she is installed in the office of matron. Special respect should be shown to a matron, and she is expected to be particularly active in Longhouse affairs. When a new matron is sought, the family will usually look for a person active in the Longhouse.

At Six Nations the interconnections between the Longhouse and the chiefs has become extended more and more since the chiefs have lost power in the civil sphere.

By analogy and extension, the same applies to the personnel associated with a chief. In all cases, however, it must be remembered that often positions are not filled, and a chief may even be "all alone" (which is considered very sad) if his matrons and "covers" have died and no one has been found to take their places.

Installation and Deposition of Deacons

The installation of the deacons is performed by the moiety of which the deacon is a member in all the Longhouses except Onondaga, where the candidate is preached to by the opposite moiety. The candidate is led over to the speaker by a matron or by a head deacon or head deaconess, and he stands next to the speaker during the "charge." If the candidate to the deaconship is one of a chief's entourage, this fact is mentioned along with his or her name and clan. "Being spoken to" and having one's name announced as deacon are legitimating actions and make the candidate an officer of the Longhouse.

A typical speech charging the officer with his forthcoming duties is the following (Alexander General's version):

So-and-so (name of appointing woman or deacon) has confidence in . . . (name and clan of appointee) to take the place of the deceased officer. This appointed officer will terminate when he (she) is deceased. This office will be for the natural life of the individual and will terminate when he (she) is deceased.

It has been conferred upon me to speak on behalf of the chiefs and the officers regarding the duty of him (her) who is appointed to be one of the attendants at the ceremonials which the Great Spirit has laid down for us to perform. At first I would direct your mind to the fact that your duty is very solemn. As you are working you will serve the Great Spirit. Therefore, you are to be faithful, and you must cooperate with the rest of the officers to carry out the duty of all officers. You must be united in mind and in the work that you have to do at all times. Should you come at any time to where we gather, you are not to wait for anyone to prepare what may be needed for the ceremonials. And I also direct your mind to the fact that you must be patient in doing your duty, and you are to refrain from all evil according to the commands of the Great Spirit, of which you are aware for we have heard the words time and again at the reciting of the words of the Great Spirit. There may be such a time that some of the persons may find fault in your doing your duty, but you are to forbear taking too seriously what they say to you. This duty that you are now appointed to, you are to serve your time as long as you are able, and as long as you can do your duty on earth. We understand according to the words of the Great Spirit that the officers are on a very high standing, which means that he who is faithful complies with the commandments of the Great Spirit. I hope that this will adhere to your minds hereafter. This is the number of words I have spoken on behalf of the chiefs of this gathering.

These charges to the deacons, like those to the chief at a chief's installation and to the populace when the Code is recited and at various other times, are among the most influential factors in molding popular opinion. For example, when explaining the role of the deacons, Mrs. George Green said:

They must do good work, not just be a deacon. They must always be kind to one another. They are high up. Higher than just common people. All kind words, no arguments should occur between them. When they go to the Longhouse they should thank Our Maker that they were able to come, and not blame other deacons for being late.

It is easy to see where she derives her conception of the duties and ethics and social position of the deacons. It is also interesting to note that the general population actually does conceive of the deacons as "higher" (closer to the Great Spirit), and that special respect should therefore be shown them. Again, it should be emphasized how frequently the same general pattern is utilized to accomplish various purposes. The constant repetition of a few traits seems to make any procedure familiar and impressive, which helps to ensure its continued existence. Installing a person in an office, whether a chieftainship or a deaconship, is always done by standing beside him and speaking to him, and the mere listening is considered highly important. The process is so simple and so little in need of artifacts that it is easily followed in almost any situation.

Once a deacon, no matter of what type, has been installed, he is a deacon for his entire life. A deaconship cannot be relinquished simply by announcing that one's old name is reassumed, as Morgan found among the New York State Seneca. Even if a deacon is later installed as a chief, he still retains his office as deacon. In general, should a deacon who has a name connected with his office later be given another office which carries with it a name, both names are kept. A deacon can vacate his office during his lifetime only by being deposed for unsatisfactory conduct. The rules for deposing chiefs have been extended to apply to the deacons, so that if a deacon does not do his duty, he is "talked to" by the speaker who originally installed him and also, in the case where the deaconship is a hereditary one, by the matron who suggested him. The matron may reprimand her deacon privately, but the second warning is usually in the company of the speaker who invested the deacon or of some other official in a "higher" position than a mere deacon. The deposition of a deacon or deaconess is a rare occurrence, though at Sour Springs it apparently did happen in one case. A hereditary deaconship does not end when the incumbent is deposed, but it passes to some other member of the family, just as in the case of a chieftainship.

It is hard to know to what extent the rules governing the chiefs are extended to apply to the deacons. Knowing the tendency to analogize at every possible occasion, one suspects that the extension is considerable. For example, would the office pass to another lineage in the clan if a deacon committed murder, just as a chieftainship is transferred on account of murder? A reasonable guess is that the same rule would be followed as for chiefs.

When a chief is deposed, none of the officers of his "covering" suffer the same fate, and all continue in office. When a chief dies, the deputy chief, among those nations in which the office exists, loses his office; and it is said that "the branches of the tree die with the death of the main tree." In spite of this dictum, the deacon and the deaconess associated with the chief (and of course the matron) do not "die" with the chief but automatically pass on to be attached to the new chief who assumes the title. Thus, the investitures of a chief and of his "nephews" and "nieces" do not usually coincide. A chief may be installed and inherit both a deacon and a deaconess (the latter, of course, only among the Cayuga). If the deaconess of a Cayuga chief dies during the incumbency of the chief, a new candidate is simply installed on the

Midwinter or Green Corn naming day. If the male deacon of a chief dies, a new candidate may be installed on one of the naming days, or the position may be left open until the chief himself dies and then filled at the time of installation of the new chief. The most striking point, however, is the difference between the rule governing the office of the deputy chief, who is not a Longhouse official, and the rules governing the chief's deacon and deaconess, who are Longhouse officials. The fact that the deacon and deaconess of the chief do not "die" with the chief is a further indication of the extent to which these offices have been incorporated into the Longhouse. At the installation of both of these officers, service to the Longhouse is emphasized far more than service to the chief.

Selection of Head Deacons

Almost all informants today say that head deaconships are not hereditary, and that the head deacons are selected by the other deacons in the Longhouse, the male deacons of a moiety choosing a male head deacon for that moiety and the female deacons choosing a female head deacon. In several cases a female head deaconship has passed from a mother to her daughter or granddaughter, but it is stated that these cases were coincidences and that actually the succession was due to "merit."

It might be useful to indicate who occupies the current head deaconships at each of the Longhouses, and to give the succession of head deacons at one Longhouse as a case study. The head deaconesses are as follows:

Onondaga Longhouse
    Wolf moiety   Mrs. Patterson Davis (nee Mary Bomberry). Her mother and
                                 great-grandmother had the position earlier. Nevertheless,
                                 the informants insist that the position is not hereditary, but
                                 that these members deserved the office.
    Deer moiety   Minnie Fish. She took the position after her grandmother.
Seneca Longhouse
    Wolf moiety   Mrs. Fred Jamieson.
    Deer moiety   Nellie Smoke.
Lower Cayuga
    Wolf moiety   Lucinda John (nee Bomberry).
    Turtle moiety   Lilly Nanticoke (Mrs. Williams).
Sour Springs
    Wolf moiety   Maggie General.
    Turtle moiety   Esther Jamieson.

The head deacons are as follows:

Onondaga Longhouse
    Wolf moiety   Bill Jacobs.
    Deer moiety   Joe Logan.
Seneca Longhouse
    Wolf moiety   Enis Williams.
    Deer moiety   Walter Crawford.
Lower Cayuga
    Wolf moiety   Freeman Jacobs.
    Turtle moiety   Pat (Sandy) Crawford.

Sour Springs
 Wolf moiety   Norman General (called "Trump" or "Sixty-Nine Norman,"
                to distinguish him from another Norman General, the chief
                Dyoŏhyŏ'ngo).
 Turtle moiety   Levy Jacobs (who is also the chief Hŏwatshadē'hŏ).

The Sour Springs Longhouse, since its removal to the present Reserve site, first on ground south of its present position and then at its present location, has had the following head deacons:

Wolf moiety (male)

1. A man remembered now only as Thahgo'wes. The Longhouse was situated on land belonging to an old woman in his family, perhaps his mother, called Gaŏhya'khwaˀ (Picking-up-the-Sky), who turned to the Baptist Church, and with her conversion demanded that the Longhouse be moved. This was done, and the Longhouse was built on its present site sometime before 1870 (about 1855, according to Speck). Thahgo'wes then "gave up." I am not sure whether he resigned, which would be unusual, was ousted, or died.
2. George Aaron, Djigra'gŏ, assumed the head deaconship. He was not related to Thahgo'wes.
3. Norman (Trump) General, Thohwēˀga'hgwē (Picking-up-Rails), was chosen. Again he was not related to the previous head deacon. He had married the previous head deacon's daughter's daughter, but this does not constitute grounds for automatic succession. It indicates, perhaps, that influence with the family which last held the position, whether through relationship or otherwise, is a major determinant of the succession. At Sour Springs head deaconships are filled for "merit," yet if there is a meritorious person related to, or in some way close to, a previous head deacon, there is some sentiment in favor of choosing that person.

Turtle moiety (male)

1. Joseph Isaac. Mr. Isaac died at the age of ninety-seven in 1920, having held the head deaconship from the inception of the Longhouse on the Reserve until his death.
2. Timothy General. He was not related to Mr. Isaac (except distantly through marriage) and was chosen strictly for his good character and assiduity.
3. Levy Jacobs. He is not related to Timothy General (except distantly through marriage) and was similarly chosen for his faithfulness to his Longhouse. He is also a chief.

Wolf moiety (female)

1. Mrs. Aaron, the mother of the head deacon George Aaron.
2. Mrs. Joe Jacobs, Agogwani'yŏ, mother of Edith Jacobs (who is present titleholder of the chieftainship Tha'tkᵃhdŏs). Mrs. Jacobs was of the Onondaga Beaver clan. It is noteworthy that she was head deaconess of the Wolf moiety, whereas today the Beaver clan sits with the Turtle moiety (see p. 119 *infra* for the recent change of sides). Mrs. Jacobs was not related to Mrs. Aaron, who was of the Heron clan.
3. Maggie General (nee Hess), who is of the Heron clan and

not related to Mrs. Jacobs. In this case it is not true that there was no one suitable in the matrilineal family of the previous incumbent to succeed to the position, since Mrs. Jacobs' daughter is very active in the rituals of the Longhouse.

Turtle moiety (female)
1. Wally (Mary) Isaac of the Oneida Big Bear clan.
2. Esther Jamieson (nee Jacobs), the "granddaughter" of Mrs. Isaac (sister's daughter's daughter), assumed the position upon the death of Mrs. Isaac.

FIRE-KEEPERS

The fire-keeper of a Longhouse is the individual who guards the wampum (otgo'?a?) which legitimates the Longhouse. Neither clan nor moiety affiliation is considered in the choice of a fire-keeper. The main requisite is that the individual be trustworthy, in the sense that he strongly believes in the Longhouse system and is opposed to granting any jurisdiction to the Canadian government, as there is a strong fear that the government is constantly in search of the "wampums." This arises partly from the fact that the Longhouse members view the wampum as the embodiment of the Longhouse, and they attribute to the Canadian government the belief that if it could obtain this wampum it would thereby destroy the Longhouse. Partly, this fear arises from the earlier reliance on wampum to legitimate any treaty. In addition, the wampum itself is considered sacrosanct, and it is scarce today. (The current value of a wampum bead at Six Nations is about 15 cents; the attitude toward each bead is one of great reverence.) The sale or "treacherous" disposal of wampum is always feared and is a common theme, and indeed the transfer of any wampum for almost any reason is viewed with suspicion. The Longhouse wampum itself is not often in evidence. It is displayed only during the recitation of the Code of Handsome Lake and during confession, and occasionally at important conventions, when there is a "wampum reading" for revivalistic purposes.

There are other and perhaps more real dangers than the government to the integrity of the wampum. With the advent of energetic collectors, the pressure to sell wampum "to preserve it in museums" and to hand over other ritual objects for "safe-keeping" or "perpetual remembrance" has been very strong. There is a current belief that a former chief who held the Cayuga nation Condolence wampum sold the set to J. N. B. Hewitt, of the Smithsonian Institution, in 1919. Fenton (private communication) says, however, that this belief is erroneous and that the chief in question only helped Hewitt make a model of the strings for purposes of study. Another set of Condolence strings is alleged to have been sold to the Royal Ontario Museum in Toronto. It is said that the guilt felt over this sale brought about the illness and ruin of the seller.

The replacement of missing wampum by a copy is allowed, for as long as the beads are genuine shell there is no resistance to using newly constructed sets. A copy of the missing Cayuga Condolence wampum has been made in order to complete the set turned over to the contemporary keeper of the Four Brothers Condolence strings. Another copy of the Cayuga Condolence wampum has been made from a picture in the *Journal of the Washington Academy of Sciences* (1944: 78). This copy is not of shell and is not for official use. The individual beads are made quite realistically of rubber tubing. The set is not used at actual ceremonies but only for practice.

There seems to be some uncertainty or disagreement as to the legal ownership of the various strings of Condolence wampum. There is a question as to whether they properly belong to the Longhouses, to the individual nations, or to the nation moieties, or whether they may even become the property of the appointed keepers. In one case, the view is that a particular Condolence string belongs to one of the Longhouses and is borrowed by the Four Brothers moiety for all Condolences. This seems to indicate some ambiguity as to the sphere into which the Condolence should fit. Does it have primarily a secular and political function, or a religious function? The Condolences arise from the political confederation and are part of the Deganawi'da? cycle; yet today they are looked upon as religious ceremonies. The fact that the personnel executing the Condolences are the same as those active in the Longhouse strengthens the religious flavor.

There is some conflict of opinion as to whether the fire-keeper should be a chief. Those who are in favor of perpetuating the power of the chiefs insist that the Longhouse wampum should be kept by a chief. Others think that any responsible person who will not deliver the wampum to the Indian Office of the Canadian government is acceptable. Actually, there is no reason why the fire-keeper of a Longhouse should be a chief, other than an analogy to the political system, in which the fire-keepers of each nation and of the Three Brothers and the Four Brothers are hereditary chiefs.

At Sour Springs the chief Dyoŏhyŏ'ngo is the fire-keeper, but this position is given to him more as an honor than as a hereditary office associated with the chiefly title. Dyoŏhyŏ'ngo supposedly was the founder of the Longhouse, and for this reason he may keep the wampum as a sign of respect. The present incumbent of this title actually does not keep all of the wampum which belongs to the Longhouse. For example, that wampum which is sent to the various Longhouses to announce any meeting or convention at Sour Springs is currently being kept by the head deaconness of the Wolf moiety. Some opinion favors keeping all of the wampum together, but the arrangement just described now prevails at this Longhouse.

At Lower Cayuga the chiefs Haga?a'ēyōnk and Gadji?nōnda'whyŏ should, in the opinion of those who would have the chiefs take an uppermost part in Longhouse rituals, be fire-keepers, because they are the fire-keepers of the Cayuga nation and also because they traditionally helped found Lower Cayuga Longhouse. The Lower Cayuga community at present feels, however, that chiefs should be subordinate in the Longhouse, and, consequently, neither of these hereditary chiefs actually keeps the wampum today. Upon the death of the chief who allegedly sold a set of the Condolence wampum to Hewitt in 1919 (see above), the Lower Cayuga wampum passed into the hands of the then head deacon of the Wolf moiety, who was not a chief. At a later time the strings were entrusted to the holder of the chiefly title Hadya'?tr°hne, but they have now been entrusted to other hands.

The present wampumkeeper at Seneca Longhouse refused to accept a position as a chief, because he preferred his duties as keeper of the wampum. His mother's sister holds the titular wampum for the chieftainship, but she "borrowed" a man when her sister's son could not accept the title because of his office of fire-keeper. The latter explained that "he couldn't be two persons."

At Onondaga Longhouse the chief Thadoda'ho? is the fire-keeper. He was probably given the Longhouse wampum because he already kept the wampum of the Three Brothers (*ex officio*) and because he is one of the most active and respected of the ritual leaders.

It is perhaps appropriate to mention here also an office which is not traditional but has recently, come into being, namely the office of the treasurer of the Longhouse. He is simply the keeper of the money which has been collected from several sources for the Longhouse.

SPEAKERS

The individuals who deliver the traditional and the extemporaneous addresses at the Longhouse are referred to simply as "speakers." They have a somewhat anomalous status, since they are neither "officials" in a strict sense, nor are they classed as "ordinary people" in the Longhouse community. Speakers are not elected, appointed, or invested, nor are they obliged to perform definite administrative duties at the Longhouse; yet they are recognized as occupying a "higher" position in the hierarchy of people, and it is universally acknowledged that they perform invaluable service to the community. Speakers are to be differentiated from "preachers," which is the modern term for those individuals who restrict themselves to the recitation of the Code of Handsome Lake. It may happen that a preacher also speaks at a Longhouse, as, for example, David Thomas, who is both a "circuit Gaihwi'yo preacher" and a principal speaker at Onondaga Longhouse. Most of the speakers, however, are not able to "preach Gaihwi'yo."

"The ability to speak" is considered preordained, a gift to the individual from the Great Creator, and therefore any talented individual may become a speaker. There are no requisites other than that the individual be a male and that he be able to deliver the addresses to the satisfaction of the community. Actually, there seems to be no "rule" which forbids a woman to speak in the Longhouse, although no examples occur at Six Nations nor are any recorded in the literature. Women often do know the ritual speeches and addresses, including at times the Roll Call of the Chiefs, but they never perform in public. However, women may make short announcements in the Longhouse, and they address the Eagle Dancers just as do the men. In practice each Longhouse community tacitly recognizes one or more persons who habitually speak on a moiety side, and these people become identified as the speakers for their side at their home Longhouse. Thus, were an outsider to inquire about speakers at a Longhouse, definite persons could be pointed out on each side. All the Longhouses try to encourage more than one individual in each moiety to learn to speak, so that embarrassing occasions of having to borrow speakers from the opposite moiety or from other Longhouses can be held to a minimum, and also so that the congregation will not have to forego the performance of a rite for lack of a knowledgeable speaker. All aspiring speakers ought to be given opportunities to perform and should be encouraged by their elders. Ideally, the altruistic aim of service to the community—the sharing of one's preordained talent—should be sufficient to motivate the expositor. However, a speaker is much admired; there is therefore an additional satisfaction to be derived from taking up this service.

There are two distinct types of speeches in the Longhouse (aside from the recitation of the Code): the recitation from memory of traditional addresses and the extemporaneous but patterned moral exhortations. At times one individual is known to excel at both, but usually the talents of a person are limited to one or the other of these two modes of expression. Only the recitation of traditional addresses, however, is the duty of a speaker representing a moiety. The exhortations, which approach "preaching" much more than ceremonial, have no association with moiety division. Certain individuals at Six Nations have a reputation for impassioned Longhouse speaking of the revivalist kind, and they are invariably asked to address the "house" for inspiration when they visit a Longhouse other than their home Longhouse. In general, the ceremonial speeches of each Longhouse are recited by speakers who belong to the Longhouse. This is a stabilizing influence, since it not only attaches certain regular personnel to a Longhouse, but it also makes for a familiarity of expression by minimizing personal variation. On the other hand, the custom of having an individual speak at one Longhouse, and only one, for perhaps 30 years produces at each Longhouse a local version of the ritual, and it eventually results in the type of local diversity seen at Six Nations. This is particularly evident when the speakers "do not get around much" and never attend another Longhouse on those ceremonial days on which the standard addresses are recited. Alexander General, for example, who speaks for the Turtle moiety at Sour Springs, has not been to any other Longhouse for many of the agricultural events nor even for some of the Midwinter rites. His speeches are derivative almost entirely from his immediate teachers, Jacob Isaac, and the speakers at Sour Springs of a generation ago, and, consequently, Sour Springs has a very definite local tradition.

Speakers often acquire considerable political power within the Longhouse and the community, and, despite the fact that no administrative duties are officially assigned to them, they often control the dating of events and the operation of the Longhouse. In fact, in all the Longhouses the speakers are among the most powerful and influential individuals, and, in recognition of this fact, they (together with the deacons) are called the "pushes" of the Longhouse.

THE HEREDITARY CHIEFS
RECENT POLITICAL HISTORY

AT Six Nations today there is a wide range of opinion on the religious functions of the hereditary chiefs, extending from the view that a Longhouse is unable to function without active control by the chiefs to the view that chiefs can be dispensed with entirely. The diversity of opinion reflects the turmoil and the uncertainty regarding the position of the chiefs which resulted from the political deposition in 1924 of the council of hereditary chiefs (also called the Confederate Council) by the Canadian government. A digression into the politics of the 1920's will be useful, because that forms much of the background of the present status of the chiefs, and, indeed, of the life of the Longhouse members today, for feelings which erupted then into active hostility still smolder.

The transition from a hereditary council to an elective one, though violent when it occurred, was not unexpected. There had long been a struggle between the hereditary, or "peace," chiefs and the "warriors" (then in the guise of World War I veterans and other acculturated personnel on the Reserve, who wished the Reserve to be as similar to the surrounding Canadian townships as possible). There had been a steady stream of altercations between the two groups, with action committees attempting to influence the population, and the factions had bitterly accused each other and had disrupted community activities. The provincial and Dominion governments had also for a long time been interested in enfranchising the Indians, thus reducing the official Indian census. When the Indian Department perceived that there was local unrest and an indigenous desire to abolish the system of chiefs (who had in general followed a policy of noncooperation with the Department), it is not beyond suspicion that the government, or at least the local representative, the superintendent of the Six Nations Reserve, thought that an auspicious time for action had arrived and that such action would not be unilaterally an imposition of the Canadian government. The chiefs also felt the pressure and had tried to consolidate their position by obligating as many people as possible and administering the Reserve in favor of those who made application to them. The method of initiating action in the council was to "counsel" with the chiefs, which meant that the interested party discussed his business with a chief, and the chief would then attempt to obtain favorable action on the request in the council. After some time, charges of bribery became common, and it was alleged that only by a payment to the chiefs could any action be terminated favorably. (For example, one of the most devout Longhouse followers said: "I am for progress. The old council was so reckless and careless. They put themselves out. The old council wanted you to pay $10.00 to help you in your case.")

The council, furthermore, was divided into factions. There were both Christians and Longhouse adherents in the council, for religious belief and inheritance of a chieftainship were independent of each other, but there were conflicts between the Christian and Longhouse elements. The Christian chiefs felt superior to their "pagan" colleagues, while the Longhouse members avowed that no chief could function unless "raised" in the Longhouse and installed "with an ox." This expression refers to the Condolence Ceremony (see Fenton, 1950), the traditional ritual for the installation and validation of a chief. Since it is one of the most complicated native ceremonial activities and requires a considerable amount of specialized traditional knowledge, it is, in the mind of the Six Nations community, an eminently "Indian" occasion. "Indian" traits are primarily perpetuated in the religious complex, and for this reason (among others) the ceremony for the installation of chiefs had come to be interpreted as a religious rather than a secular rite. And for similar reasons, a chief had also come to be associated with the Longhouse religion. Any chief who did not sponsor the expensive installation ceremony because he did not believe in its necessity or because he was not an adherent of the Longhouse religion was considered to be unfit and ineligible for service. To mitigate feelings on this subject, a saying had developed at Six Nations that before the chiefs entered the council "they exchanged their suits for buckskins." This metaphor means that a contract was agreed upon by the chiefs in council at Ohsweken, namely, that all chiefs would work together as one Indian group regardless of their faith. However, the extreme conservative faction never accepted this compromise and steadfastly insisted upon full allegiance to the Iroquoian religion in order to qualify for the office of peace chief.

The council was also divided politically, into a liberal faction, which would have cooperated to some degree with the Canadian government, and an extremely conservative and revivalist faction, which completely disregarded and disavowed any government jurisdiction. The latter faction, aside from having the usual grievances of loss of land, loss of game, loss of timber, etc., specifically complained that the government had defrauded the Indians of tribal funds by refusing payment for the Grand River Navigation Claim and the New England Company Claim.[1] These

[1] The Grand River Navigation Claim arose from the following circumstances. A company in the 1840's had been formed to dredge the Grand River in order to construct a canal, but with the advent of railroads this company faced bankruptcy. In order to save the company's investment, the Colonial Office was persuaded to invest some of the tribal funds, which of course were lost when bankruptcy ensued. Since then there has been steady agitation for the return of the money invested in the stock, plus all the interest which would have accrued had the money been invested wisely from approximately 1840 to the present. It is claimed that the investment was not made according to the dictates of the tribal council at Ohsweken and therefore is invalid. There evidently was some inclination to return the principal, but the council and especially the conservative elements would settle for nothing short of the principal plus interest. This is still the theme today.

The New England Company Claim is a claim which the council has against the Dominion government because one-sixth of the lots on the Reserve had formerly been granted to the New England Company in return for proselytizing and for keeping the Mohawk Institute and the Anglican churches. The lots were finally returned to band lands, but the council now claims revenue on these lots for those years in which they were alienated. The council again claims that the land alienation occurred without its consent. The Dominion government actually construes all land to be Dominion land, and, consequently, does not recognize the claim.

two claims have been the focal points of dissatisfaction and have rallied many people into the conservative camp. The vision of large amounts of money accruing to the tribes has given an entirely unrealistic ardor to those who hope for payment of the claims. Nor are these issues any less acute today than in 1900 or in 1924. Funds are constantly being solicited to hire lawyers to represent the Iroquois nation, and various unscrupulous outsiders have appeared with promises to settle the matter favorably for a certain down payment.[2] In any case, in 1924, with the aid of these grievances, the conservative faction was able to carry through its program of complete nonrecognition of the Indian Department and of absolute non-co-operation. This sparked the final decision to abolish the hereditary council.

In 1924 the Canadian government was petitioned by the "warriors" to institute an elective council, and a commission was sent to investigate general Reserve sentiment toward such a move. Since the faction counseling nonrecognition of the government was in power in the Confederate Council, the hereditary chiefs as a body refused to give the commission their side of the argument, and only those members of the Reserve favoring an elective council appeared to defend their views. Thereupon, the Canadian government decided that an elective council should be instituted. Finally, during a session of the Confederate Council in 1924, the hereditary chiefs reputedly denied the request of the Superintendent of Indian Affairs at Brantford to preside over the council in place of the secretary of the council. During luncheon recess the Canadian Mounted Police closed the council house, and thereafter an elective council was decreed.

The chiefs bitterly resented being locked out of their own council house, as well as the interference of the Mounted Police, against whom they were powerless. But most bitterly of all, the chiefs resented the action of the "warrior" group, which gave the Canadian government an excuse to depose the chiefs with the sanction of at least part of the population. Even today there is strong animosity toward this group on the part of those who are in favor of the hereditary council, and they are variously termed "traitors," "dehorners" (because they wished to "take the horns of office," which symbolizes a chief, from the crown of the chief), and "loyalists" (because they were loyal to the Canadian government).

Complete disregard for the Canadian government is still the attitude of the conservative faction, because any recognition whatever would make it appear that the Iroquois accept the right of the government to adjudicate in Indian affairs. This attitude is exhibited in all sorts of boycotts, for example, refusing baby allowances, refusing old-age pensions, and not voting for candidates to the elective council. Furthermore, hostility is directed toward any individual who accepts some or all of the services of the Canadian government. However, the nonrecognition of

[2] It is against Canadian law to solicit funds on the Reserve for "foreign" purposes or to be on the Reserve for any unauthorized reason. Consequently, one of the solicitors was arrested while collecting funds at Sour Springs. Unfortunately, these lawyers find a fertile field among the Longhouse group and among the Mohawk Workers. Two of the lawyers who have "worked" on the Indian claims for many years will occasionally invite certain of the less acculturated Indians to their offices and show them the "pile of books" they have to work on the "Indian case." This is usually followed by a demand for money.

the government is never a consistent all-or-nothing attitude. This means that there is probably no one today who categorically refuses all the services of the government and disobeys all the by-laws of the elective council or is able to disregard the present elective council completely. Everyone who is opposed to the current political arrangement and who wishes either the return of the hereditary council or the establishment of the Six Nations as a sovereign state shows his resentment and contempt of the government by flaunting some of the by-laws or refusing some of the services, but rationalizes the acceptance of others. The range of combinations of acceptance and rejection is wide and varied; one criticizes the next person for accepting some particular service which he himself happens to reject, and thus a multitude of factions are formed. These feelings carry over into the Longhouse, into the medicine societies, and into almost every cooperative venture. The lives of most of the hereditary chiefs who still believe in the "old council" and who carry on the old tradition are thoroughly embittered by their antagonism toward the government and toward the "traitors."

Sour Springs Longhouse in particular was split by the change of the council, since their then most influential chief was one of the most ardent of the conservatives. He counseled against every measure which the Canadian government tried to impose, including rationing during World War I; he advised his followers not to accept ration cards, with the result that several families were unable to obtain food. He also agitated in the United States for aid for the Six Nations in obtaining sovereignty, and he made a trip to the League of Nations and to "the Queen."[3] His family, who dominate Sour Springs Longhouse, supported him, but a large part of the Longhouse opposed him. For approximately 20 years cooperative bees at this Longhouse were unsuccessful, because neither of the factions would help the other, and all Longhouse business involved some question of the loyalty of members to one or the other of the factions. Even today, this chief is blamed by all but the most conservative for his implacable non-cooperation, for it is now maintained by the more liberal Longhouse members that, had the chiefs presented their side of the argument, the government would not have been able to impose its decree so easily. Since a chief "should care for his people," personal blame for the change, probably more than is justified, is laid upon the action of the chief. However, the conservative chiefs and the Mohawk Workers have not profited from this example of extreme isolation, for they still counsel the same nonparticipation. The successor to this chief perpetuates and amplifies the policy. He will not vote, for this would acknowledge the legitimacy of the elective council, and he will not attempt to have the system changed through parliamentary measures, for this also would be a recognition that there is some legitimacy in Canada's control of Indian affairs.

[3] Even though the reigning monarch of Great Britain at the time of this mission was King George V, it was always said that he went to see "the Queen." Undoubtedly, the British monarchy is associated with Queen Victoria, in whose honor pieces of wool broadcloth were distributed to the Indians, and whose birthday was "Bread and Cheese Day," for bread and cheese were given to the members of the Reserve not only while she was alive but even today.

In general all the Longhouses are exhorted against voting for the elective council, and those members who do vote are labeled as traitors by the majority. Of the current population (7,000) only approximately 600 votes are cast at each election, which indicates the controversial character of the entire problem of chiefs and elected councilors, for it is definitely not merely a matter of apathy. Even at the first election in 1924, only about 10 per cent of the eligible voters cast ballots, which indicates that the "warriors" were not nearly so strong as the Canadian government had believed. The council of hereditary chiefs continues to hold monthly meetings, and all the traditional procedures are followed (see *infra*, p. 121). Although it has no political power, the hereditary council is still important as a kind of standing committee for airing grievances and organizing resistance against Canadian regulation.

CHIEFS AND THE LONGHOUSE

With each passing year the probability that the hereditary council will be reinstated becomes more remote. The elective council has become firmly entrenched, and enough vested interest rests in it so that it would be hard to effect a change without a great struggle, especially since the Canadian government favors the elective council. Consequently, many of the Christian families have lost interest in installing new members in chieftainship positions, since for them it would mean only an expense. Before 1924, being a chief involved prestige, power to a certain extent, and "board money" (money paid to the chief to reimburse him for the time spent in counseling and in the council), but after 1924 being a chief had, from a purely political standpoint, no meaning whatever. Nor is there much of an ideological incentive for Christian families, since they have very little contact with any of the legends and rituals related to the chieftainships.

In those families which belong to the Longhouse, however, the fact that their chiefs have lost political power is vividly remembered, for not only does the Longhouse tend to be conservative of tradition, but it also keeps any grievances in the limelight. The character of the speeches in the Longhouse is definitely "Low Church," and despite the formality of procedure the exhortations to the congregation may cover any topic which the speaker feels important. The form of expression is traditional, and therefore the content is accepted as perfectly suitable. In this manner, the question of chiefs and their power is constantly brought before the congregation. Not only is the topic discussed at the Longhouse, but at a Chief's Condolence, for example, the speaker may end by making an appeal for action to reinstitute the chiefs or to protest to the Canadian government about some new rule, as, for instance, the recent ruling that marriages had to be legitimated by a Canadian justice of the peace.[4] Also at the end of curing sessions, singing-society meetings,

---

[4] One of the functions of the chiefs had been to perform marriage ceremonies, which were then considered legal and binding. (For a discussion of these ceremonies, see pp. 226–7 *infra*.) But in 1955 the Indian Department in Brantford decided to enforce the rule that couples could be married only by authorized persons, which did not include the hereditary chiefs. When Clara Hill tried to have her marriage registered with the Indian Office, she was informed that it was

social dances, bees, tea meetings, ball games, or any other activity in which the Longhouse group comes together, it is considered appropriate to remind the community that there should be continued agitation to reinstate the hereditary chiefs. Those chiefs who have always been Longhouse members, and who before 1924 had already insisted that chiefs "ought to be made in the Longhouse and not in the council," are particularly vocal about their "rights" and attempt to rally a faction around them. The constant agitation and constant jockeying to attract members into the factions which wish the return of the chiefs to political power, or wish the dominance of the chiefs in the Longhouse, or wish the leadership of the chiefs in both areas or in neither, cause a very strained atmosphere even within the Longhouse.

The majority of the chiefs who are Longhouse members claim today that chiefs should administer to the population in all affairs and that a chief is essential for leadership not only in the political sphere but in the religious and ethical sphere as well. The question arises whether politics and religion were linked in the hereditary chiefly office prior to the forced Europeanization of the political system at Six Nations. Morgan did not seem to think that the chiefs had any religious office or that the political system was in any way tied to the Longhouse cycle. On the contrary, he (Morgan, 1901, 1: 118–9) makes the distinctions of civil, mourning, and religious councils, which, incidentally, Beauchamp (1907) follows. The civil councils were concerned with the internal and external affairs of the nation, the mourning councils "raised up chiefs," and the religious councils were concerned with the religious life of the nation. Morgan sees these as three separate institutions, though of the mourning councils he says:

... the mourning council was always made an occasion for religious and moral instruction Many of its exercises were of a strictly religious character, and it would be more proper to designate it as a religious council, than by any other name, but for the circumstance that its object was to raise up rulers, and its ceremonies were entirely distinct from those at the religious festivals.

---

not legal until a Canadian justice of the peace performed the ceremony. Clara Hill is a member of Onondaga Longhouse, and the entire community was upset. Several meetings of the chiefs were called, including joint councils with the American chiefs. Since Canadian law says that marriage according to native custom is legal, the chiefs were able to have the Indian Office rescind the ruling in 1957. Here is the incident in the words of a leading chief: "We have overcome the controversy of Longhouse marriage, by a good fortune that some white people helped us out, who happen to be a lawyer from Toronto who offered his services without remuneration. The provincial government had to repeal the act as they had no jurisdiction to pass an act on us. The lawyer was ready to make a test case in court. The Indian Department officials were very much upset, including the councilors. The Lower Cayuga accepted the provincial marriage law; they had appointed Patrick Longboat to register as a priest marriage officiator under the provincial law. So they also felt cheap. We have another test case pending against the elective councilors, who are everlasting surrendering our Indian lands in Brantford, which will come before the Supreme Court sometime in September" (letter, August 24, 1957).

This passage indicates that Morgan did not consider the chiefs to be connected with the religious ceremonies, and the fact that civil installations had religious overtones does not necessarily indicate that the same personnel functioned in both institutions.

Hewitt (1920: 543) was of the opinion that aboriginally civil and religious affairs were not united. He says:

In Iroquois policy there was definite separation of purely civil from strictly religious affairs. So the office of civil chief was clearly marked off from that of prophet or priest. . . . The civil assembly, or the council of chiefs and elders or senators, was in no sense a religious gathering, notwithstanding the custom of opening it with a thanksgiving prayer in recognition of the Master of Life—a strictly religious act. The officers of the religious societies and assemblies were not the same as those who presided over the councils of chiefs.

There was, to be sure, a common symbolism, for the term "Longhouse," which aboriginally referred to a residential structure, was applied to the body politic, the religious community, and the residential community. However, the use of common symbolism in various institutions and various aspects of culture seems to have been an old Iroquoian trait, which can be documented from the speeches of early warriors. This by no means indicates that the same personnel functioned in these institutions or that the institutions were "interlocking" ones, as the following statement by Noon (1949: 46) would have us believe.

Our discussion of the conflict between the Christian and Longhouse chiefs in Council paved the way for an understanding that government and religion were probably interlocking institutions in pre-contact society.

In view of the fact that the political system of the Iroquois was complex and well-developed by 1650, it is particularly unjust to characterize it as part of the religious system, the more so if any comparison with the surrounding tribes is made. On the other hand, it is unrealistic to think of any two areas of the culture as thoroughly unrelated, for that would merely indicate the disintegration and spuriousness of the culture.

Rioux (1952: 98) applied himself to the problem also, criticizing Noon for drawing conclusions as to the linkage of religion and politics from modern data only; but then he himself decides, on the basis of an examination of Onondaga and Lower Cayuga Longhouses today (finding in the former a close interrelation between church and government and in the latter very little interrelation), that "in pre-contact society it would appear that church and government were interlocking to a certain extent, not so much as the Onondaga longhouse would like them to be, but more than the Cayugas think they ought to be." Rioux implies that the relation between the two complexes, religion and politics, has not changed very much, although he thinks that the entire religious complex has changed and has taken on focal importance since the advent of Handsome Lake. He says (1952: 98):

If we compare what we know about the ancient religion with the Code of Handsome Lake, which is actually practised on modern reservations, we arrive at the conclusion that we are dealing with nearly two different religions.

Not only the forms, but the functions, uses, and meanings of the religious complex have changed, according to Rioux. Actually, one may strongly doubt this. Handsome Lake merely incorporated some Quaker doctrine (see Deardorff, 1951) and some Christian concepts into the older agricultural cycle. Very little seems to have been changed, except that the Strawberry Festival became more prominent after 1800. Even the curing societies outlawed by Handsome Lake are now integrated into the Longhouse again. Fenton suggests that even such seemingly Christian concepts as confession were aboriginal rather than borrowed. Furthermore, in his study of Longhouse behavior, Rioux decides that the Onondaga are, in Voget's (1953) terminology (with his own modification), "consciously native," while the Cayuga are "traditionally native," in regard to whether chiefs should or should not function in the Longhouse. Thus, he tacitly assumes that chiefs at one time were not part of the Longhouse, for "native" means that the "basic orientations of the individuals are in terms of the unmodified aboriginal past."

The present writer's belief is that before the change of the council and in the more distant past the religious offices and those of the council were separate, and that the personnel of the two were not necessarily identical. To the extent that the chiefs did belong to the Longhouse there must have been a random amount of overlapping of personnel. One can think of the example of Handsome Lake himself, who held the hereditary title of Skanyada'iyo and later became the foremost ritualist in the new Longhouse religion. At Six Nations there have been influential chiefs, such as Abram Charles and Levy General, who at the same time were leading members of the Longhouse and took an active part in the Longhouse ceremonials. But these are cases of individual personalities and not of rules of the system. The Longhouse has its own complement of officers, and it is only lately that the chiefs have claimed that no Longhouse can possibly operate without the services of the chiefs. People at Sour Springs can remember when the Longhouse operated without chiefs in attendance, but the consensus of opinion is that "it is nicer to have chiefs setting there." In all the Longhouse ceremonies there is only one situation in which a chief is definitely specified for an action, and that is in the Bowl Game, where the last throw on the losing side should be executed by a chief "because he is peaceful, and no fights will start." It is true that moiety orientation follows the seating of the chiefs (see p. 50 *supra*), but the whole seating problem is very indefinite today, and "following the chief's example" is merely an expedient in the face of not knowing where to sit. If there were a close connection between the political system and the Longhouse, one would expect the pattern of consultation when questions are being discussed to be similar in the two cases. This is not so, however, for within a tribe in the council the consultation is between phratries (see p. 122 *infra*), whereas within a moiety in the Longhouse the men and the women consult with each other. In the Longhouse, furthermore, action is through the deacons, and a chief cannot overrule them merely because he has the title of "chief." Finally, the fact that relationship terms are used both in the civil and religious councils does not indicate that the two are connected, for the Iroquois terms are commonly extended in metaphorical senses.

The current emphasis that chiefs are to be installed in the Longhouse and "should come out of the Longhouse" seems to be more an indication of the conflict between the Longhouse religion and the Christian religion than a question of whether chiefs have always played a prominent role in the Longhouse. The more acculturated Longhouse members and those who are not so personally involved in nominating a chief in their own family see no conflict between an elected council and a smoothly functioning Longhouse, although they would like the added power and prestige of having some of their fellow adherents hold administrative positions. Lately, none of the elected councilors have been Longhouse members, which means that the interests of a large group of the Reserve are not represented as well as they might be or as they were before 1924, when approximately one half of the council belonged to the Longhouse. Under such circumstances one would expect the Longhouse to be dissatisfied, to be wary of discrimination, and to intimate that "if things were right" the Reserve would be administered at least in part by Longhouse members. The Longhouse member feels hurt that his chief has no more power, and this grievance is kept alive. An eminent matron says: "It is not much use putting in a chief. When they ask me to put in a chief, I say nothing. I just look at them. Never put in a chief unless we kill the ox.[5] No matter how much he'll spend, it won't help. He just wanders around and nothing happens. It was different when there was a whole house. It was nice. I don't know why they [those who agitate for the reinstatement of the hereditary chiefs] are stubborn. I couldn't tell why they don't quit, why they don't realize." She further says: "We can never go backwards, but we get lonely for the old ways—we're getting civilized." As a consolation she suggests that the chiefs "should look after the Longhouse, keep people kind to each other, be friendly, have good words, smooth off anything that pops up."

It seems to the writer that the matron has indicated the crux of the problem. Chiefs are not essential to the Longhouse, nor were they ever; but since their political functions in the council have been usurped, they have turned to the Longhouse in order to preserve at least some of their influence. As Christian chiefs have died and their families have not renewed the personnel in vacant positions, the Longhouse chiefs have taken it upon themselves to transfer the title, if possible, to families which will maintain interest in the positions. Even when the unfilled positions belong to Longhouse families which happen to have no suitable candidates, the chiefs have tried to transfer these titles to families which are eager to install members for the honor of having a chief. In this fashion a worthy man is often rewarded by the chiefs by being made one of their number, and thus there has come about a concentration of titles among the more devout and active Longhouse families.

In three of the Longhouses at Six Nations, and particularly at Sour Springs and Onondaga, chiefs who have ability actually do play prominent roles. Seneca Longhouse, while it respects the status of a chief, does not happen to have many especially

[5] The saying today among the Longhouse adherents about chiefs who did not have the formal Condolence Ceremony, with the requisite feast pattern, is: "He didn't go in with an ox, but as a kick went in with eggs."

active chiefs among its regular members. Lower Cayuga differs from the other Longhouses mainly in the current attitude of the deacons, who do not admit that the chiefs have a "higher" station in the hierarchy of people. Justification for their position is taken from an interpretation of the Code of Handsome Lake, as improvised and extemporized by current preachers. When the names of Red Jacket and Cornplanter are mentioned during the recitation, the appellation used is "hadigowanēs" (big man), which is interpreted by the deacons of Lower Cayuga Longhouse to mean that the two were chiefs. Both of these leaders are condemned in the Code, in the formal as well as in the apocryphal texts. By extension—because these men were chiefs and because they sold land and were "bad"—chiefs ought not to be leaders in the Longhouse ceremonies. When a chief enters a Longhouse, say the deacons of Lower Cayuga, he catches his antlers on the lintel of the doorway, and they fall off, thus symbolically divesting the chief of his special status. This divestment is supposed to occur especially at Midwinter and Green Corn times. Opponents of this interpretation, which include the leaders of the other three Longhouses and all the hereditary chiefs, argue that whether or not the land was sold, hereditary chiefs were not involved. Neither Cornplanter nor Red Jacket were peace chiefs, for neither held one of the 50 hereditary titles during his lifetime. Consequently, nothing in the Code can be interpreted to condemn the chiefs, nor did a chief sell land. The reason that the word "hadigowañes" was applied to the two leaders is that the white men of the time called them this on account of their influence with the Indian population, and Handsome Lake simply used the same term when referring to these two "instigators."

The difference among the Longhouses in regard to the chiefs is mainly in dominant attitude, for even at Lower Cayuga Longhouse the procedures of installation, of mourning for chiefs, of seating, and of granting the last throw in the Bowl Game to the chiefs are the same as at the other Longhouses. Furthermore, at Lower Cayuga, as on the Reserve in general, the chiefs agitate for their rights in both the political and religious domains, for they do not acquiesce to the deacon's interpretation of the Code. When the chiefs, including those who belong to Lower Cayuga Longhouse, speak about the question of the religious function of the chiefs, they claim that Lower Cayuga "lost its faith," "got wrong ideas," and showed the white man's influence in depriving the chiefs of authority. In a way, the strategy of the chiefs, whether conscious or unconscious, is to represent the retention of the culture as an all-or-nothing proposition, and in this way to integrate the political and religious institutions; for if this is not done, runs the argument, then the Longhouse will be destroyed even as the hereditary council was destroyed. In general, it is true that interlocking sanctions affect all those institutions which are in any way connected with these sanctions, and that a smoothly running culture is an amalgam of many institutions which are made meaningful to the individual through a few ultimate values, for the sake of which he acts and through which the culture "makes satisfying sense." Nevertheless, in the Iroquoian culture there are no sanctions which so link the religious complex with the governmental one that the destruction of one automatically destroys the other. The Longhouse has functioned without chiefs, and there was political organization without the Longhouse. Some of the Reserves which send chiefs to the hereditary council at Six Nations have at times been without an actively functioning Longhouse; at Oneidatown (Muncy), for example, the Longhouse has sometimes consisted of an extremely limited group of a few families, and St. Regis and Caughnawaga acquired Longhouses only recently. Furthermore, the Longhouse, in order to forestall the loss of the religious complex, has long been using other sanctions, which affect a much wider segment of the population than those families interested in the maintenance of the hereditary chiefs. These sanctions are concerned with the health and death problems of the individual members, for neglect of the Longhouse and neglect of the medicine societies will bring personal disaster. Despite Handsome Lake's attempt to restrict the medicinal and magical elements in the Longhouse ritual, it is precisely these which make the Longhouse most necessary to the individual. The type of government can be substituted, but the aid of the supernaturals, whose manipulation is known only by those members who keep the knowledge alive in the Longhouse, cannot be substituted.

THE CHIEFS AT SIX NATIONS TODAY

RECORDS OF THE ROLL CALL

In view of the rather complicated status of the chiefs at Six Nations, it will be useful to comment briefly on each title in the Roll Call of the Chiefs, and to indicate the grouping of chiefs into phratries. Politically, the phratries are the committees of chiefs which confer in council discussions (see p. 121 *infra* for the actual procedure in the council). Knowledge of the phratries is perpetuated in the practice session for the Condolence Ceremony, where kernels of corn are laid out and arranged to designate the chiefs and their relationships and groupings. The relationships are supposed to be derived from the Roll Call of the Chiefs, but because chiefs are "borrowed," there are changes in the clan affiliations of the chieftainships, so that the ideal and actual relationships do not always coincide. During the practice sessions such discrepancies should be mentioned, discussed, and pointed out to novices attending, so that the phratries will not become permanently skewed. In some cases, however, the fact that a change of clan affiliation has occurred is forgotten. Various changes will be evident in a survey of the individual chieftainships, and it will also appear that there has been considerable flexibility in the institution of the chiefs, which permitted the retention of many traits under strained circumstances.

Fenton (1950) has given an account of some of the relationships between the chiefs, in terms of their phratry and moiety arrangements, as seen from a Condolence cane found at Six Nations. This cane gives a mnemonic picture list of the meanings of the 50 chieftainship titles, and it indicates, by the arrangement of pegs on the cane, the groupings of the titles. The listing on the cane was found to coincide with the listing of chiefs in the text of the Condolence Ceremony as re-

102

Fig. 11. Mnemonics of Iroquois Chiefs' Titles as found in the Notebook of Ernest Jamieson.

corded by Newhouse, and with the listing in the notebook of Abram Charles, who was a chief associated with Lower Cayuga Longhouse. The cane, which Fenton describes, was in the possession of Andrew Spragg, and directly or indirectly it was used to teach ritualists at Sour Springs Longhouse as well as at Lower Cayuga, for Robbie Isaac at Sour Springs is reputed to have had a cane which he copied or borrowed from Spragg, which was then handed to Jake Isaac, who in turn gave it to Alexander General. Mr. General says that the cane which came into his hands was Spragg's own cane, but it may have been a copy, since the cane described by Fenton was collected in 1920. Today, Jack General has a copy of the Spragg cane which he made himself after seeing Fenton's blueprints of the cane. Many of the ritualists utilize Fenton's publication to help them learn the order of the chiefs. But even before the appearance of Fenton's work, Six Nations ritualists used several notebooks with mnemonic pictures to aid in the recital of the chiefs. I found the accompanying set of mnemonic pictures (Fig. 11), which are the same as those on the cane discussed by Fenton except for a few differences in the Seneca roster, at the home of the mother-in-law of Ernest Jamieson (whose personal Indian name was Thoihwa'ẽndõ, Leading-off-the-Word), who had been the Cayuga chief, Dyaõ-whe'thõ. He died in 1939 and therefore could not have made use of Fenton's reconstruction. Also, the cane from which the pictures in Jamieson's notebook were copied cannot have been Spragg's own, for other material in the notebook, e.g., treasurer's reports and notes on lacrosse teams, indicates that the copying was done between 1930 and 1933. It is said that Chief Jamieson was taught by Jake Isaac, Chauncey Isaac, and Jack General.

Learning the Roll Call is an arduous process, even with the help of devices like the cane, for the mnemonic pictures are actually of little help today. Through time the pictures and the meanings of the titles have drifted apart, so that the pictures do not now represent the meanings of the titles. In fact, the ritualist not only must learn the order of names, but also must learn the pictures which go with the names. Consequently, knowledge of the chiefs is highly specialized, and it is difficult, with no official records of the chiefs, to discover exactly who holds which position. The following pages list the positions and their occupants as well as could be determined in 1958. There are also some comments on each, especially in order to relate the present clan affiliations of the titles to those mentioned in the literature.

It will be noticed that some of the chieftainships are filled by members of Canadian reserves other than Six Nations. None of the chiefs, however, are members of the Iroquois reservations in the United States (with the possible exception of the last Seneca chief), and, in fact, there is a duplicate council of 50 chiefs with the same titles in the United States. The protocol between the two councils has not been worked out completely or to the satisfaction of everyone. The Iroquois chiefs in Canada recognize the status of their counterparts in the United States, but they resent the fact that their tolerance is not reciprocated, for the council in the United States claims that the chiefs from Canada "lose their horns" when they cross the border.

THE MOHAWK TITLES[6]

The Mohawk titles are apportioned among three clans, Turtles and Wolves being cousins to the Bears. All authors agreed on the clan distribution, and there has been little confusion.

1. *Dega'iho'gē*. This title is said to have the meaning "his mind was divided," with the implication that "if a man has some doubts, yet there might be something in it." (Fenton, 1950: 59, lists various related meanings.)

The current holder of this title is Jim "Chief" Martin, who has Longhouse affiliation and comes to the hereditary council meetings at Onondaga Longhouse. He is reputed to have a matron. The previous holders of the title were Eli Burning and Elias Lewis. The title should be in the Lewis family, according to Alexander General, but they are "not interested." The incumbent belongs to the Turtle clan.

2. *Hayŏ'hwatha*?. The meaning ascribed to this name is "he was awake," because "the chief supposedly got a message and didn't sleep over it, but was awake all the time thinking about it." He was the first person approached by Deganawi'da? at the founding of the League. Actually, the Deganawi'da? legend related that neither the title of Deganawi'da? nor that of Hayŏ'hwatha? should, in honor of the two most influential founders of the League, be perpetuated. In the case of Deganawi'da? this was followed, but ritualists do not know why this was disregarded in the case of Hayŏ'hwatha?. Roy Buck said that he had asked Joe Logan, Six Nations' Thadoda'ho?, who is reputed to be best informed, but he could not answer this question either. Evidently, the question is frequently raised at the Condolence practice sessions. Henry K. Powless, a Christian, had the position last. He was installed, however, in the Longhouse, and his matron was Mrs. Peter Garlow. Both the chief and the matron are dead now, and the position has not been filled. Powless was of the Turtle clan and still attended councils after 1924.

3. *Sha?dega'ihwade*?. The meaning is "things of equal height." No one seems to know the present holder of the title, but he should also be a Turtle chief.

4. *Shaĕho'wa*. This is the first of the Wolf clan chiefs, who are addressed as brothers by the Turtle chiefs. However, as I have mentioned before, when Mohawks attend the Cayuga Longhouses, and many of them go to Sour Springs since it is located nearest to the Mohawk neighborhood, Turtle and Wolf chiefs sit on opposite sides of the fire. This indicates a difference between the political and religious divisions. William Loft used to have this position at Six Nations, for even though his mother was reputedly a Muskhogee, the family claimed a chief's title. After that the title was held by Pat Martin, who is also dead. Now the chair is empty.

5. *Deyŏ'nhehgwē*. The name sounds similar to Dyŏnhe'hgŏ and is often called just that, consequently it is interpreted as "our life" (see p. 136 *infra*). This title was held by George Johnson, son of John Smoke Johnson, who was Hale's informant. George Johnson was the interpreter for the Reserve in the Indian Office, and he belonged to a Christian family. Today no one knows who holds this title. It is supposed to be a Wolf clan title.

6. *Aowĕhe?go'wa*. Mr. General interprets this to mean "eagle-head headdress," and Roy Buck says it means "big eagle." The title is currently held by James Squire Hill, and his aunt, Mrs. Sarah Green, holds the wampum for the title. Mr. Hill was installed at Onondaga Longhouse, and though he is not a regular member of either the church or the Longhouse, he occasionally attends the Longhouse. Mrs. Green is a church member. Mr. Hill is of the Wolf clan. The previous holder of the title was Isaac Doxstater.

---

[6] The language used here in listing the titles is Cayuga, as pronounced by Alexander General. Also, unless otherwise stated, he is the one from whom the meanings of the names were obtained. Fenton (1950) has a compilation of meanings as given by Hale, Chadwick, and various Six Nations residents (notably Howard Skye and Simeon Gibson, but Mr. General also supplied him with some of the meanings). See also Hewitt (1944, edited by Fenton) for further interpretations of the names.

7. *Thana?ga'ine*. This is the first of the titles of the Bears, cousins to the above. Job Martin was the last incumbent, but he died before 1924. No one has held the position since. Job Martin was a church member.

8. *Hahstawĕ?thrõ'ntha?*. The meaning has consistently been reported as "he puts a rattle on." Charles Silversmith had this title, but he died about five years ago. Nellie Smoke is the matron, and she is also the head deaconess of her side at Seneca Longhouse. Mr. General says that since Mr. Silversmith's death the title has been empty, evidently not recognizing that Mrs. Smoke has "borrowed" Josie Logan, a Small Deer clan member (which is usually identified as a Ball clan, see p. 53 *infra*), to fill the position. Mr. Logan is a devout attender at Onondaga Longhouse. During the last chief-making, April, 1954, there was discussion about this title, for the Upper Mohawk claim the title. However, Charles Silversmith was not an Upper Mohawk either. Simon Bomberry held the title previous to Mr. Silversmith.

9. *Shoskoha'owa*. The meaning is "large branch." No one holds this title at present.

The Oneida Titles

The Oneida titles are also apportioned among the three clans, Turtle, Wolf, and Bear, but the order of naming is Wolf, Turtle, Bear. Again the Bear clan members are the cousins, the Wolf and Turtle brothers. Very little is known of the Oneida titles at Six Nations, since most of them are held by members of the Oneida Reserve at Oneidatown (Muncy). The only Oneida chief at Six Nations today is Hõwatshadẽ'hõ.

10. *Hoda'tshehde*. This title is held by Amos Elijah of Oneidatown. It is a Wolf clan title.

11. *Ganõhgw?ẽyo'dõ?*. The title is held by William Day of Oneidatown.

12. *Thaõgwẽ'nde?*. This title was held by David Hill, who seems to have been a friend of Levy General, even though he was associated with the church and not the Longhouse. He did not come from a family which owned a title, but through Levy General's recommendation was made a chief. Actually he turned out to be a "dehorner" working to end the Confederate Council. He was thereupon "cut off" (deposed), and the position has been empty ever since.

13. *Shonõ'hses*. This is the first of the Turtle titles. It is held by Joe Cornelius of Oneidatown, who is a Baptist and goes to church.

14. *Thona'ogẽ?*. This title also belongs to a family at Oneidatown, but at Six Nations it was not known who was the chief, nor did Sandy Elijah know when asked at Oneidatown.

15. *Hadya?donẽ'htha?*. The title is held by Nicholas Elm of Oneidatown. Jacket Hill of Six Nations held the title prior to Elm. The meaning is said to be "he swallows the body."

16. *Thathaõhde'nyõ?*. The meaning of this title is said to be "moving ears." Robert Freeman was the last chief, but the position seems empty now. This is the first chief of the Bears, the cousins of the Wolves and Turtles.

17. *Honya?tᵃhsha'yõ*. No one holds this title at Six Nations.

18. *Hõwatshadẽ'hõ*. The meaning of this title is given as "he was damp, foggy." Hale and Speck give the translation "somebody burying him" (see Fenton, 1950: 61, Speck, 1949: 183). Sometimes it is also translated as "fog" or "mist." The current holder of the title is Levy Jacobs (whose personal Indian name is Thod?agro'dõ?, Snowbank), who is attached to Sour Springs Longhouse, but who works about 50 miles from Six Nations. His matron, Esther Jamieson, is the head deaconess of the Turtle moiety at Sour Springs, and strongly believes that chiefs "should be sitting" in the Longhouse. Ceremonies are frequently timed to coincide with the days on which Mr. Jacobs is able to come "home." This was done particularly when Alexander General, the chief Deska'he?, was in the hospital. Levy Jacobs is Esther Jamieson's brother; he is of Oneida origin and belongs to the Big Bear clan. Mr. Jacobs' cousin (MoSiSo), Scott Isaac Hill, is his runner, or second, and he now attends Onondaga Longhouse, having switched because he married down below and his wife belongs to the Onondaga Longhouse.

Levy Jacobs took over after the death of his uncle (MoBr), Jacob (Jake) Isaac, who acquired

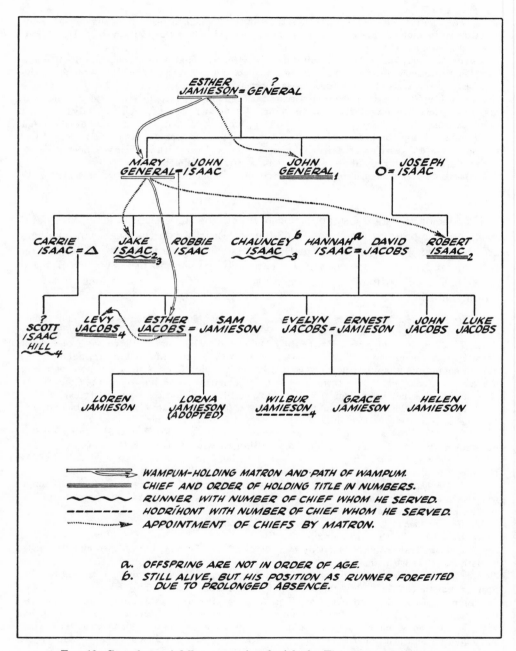

FIG. 12. Genealogy of Officers associated with the Title Hŏwatshadē'hŏ (18).

the chieftainship after the death of his cousin (MoSiSo), Robert Isaac (it is coincidental that both are called Isaac, the sisters having married men who were brothers), for whom he had been the runner. The chief prior to this had been Robert Isaac's uncle (MoBr), whose name was John General (Ska'ŏhyadi). This succession of chiefs has been very regular, without any borrowing outside of the family. The wampum has also been passed regularly to a matron who was either a daughter or granddaughter, and Mrs. Esther Jamieson has a white and a purple strand today. Since this is such a typical and regular succession of chiefs, a genealogy ıs given for illustrative purposes (Fig. 12).

THE ONONDAGA TITLES

In the practice sessions for the Condolence, which at Six Nations are now the official occasions for deciding the order of the chiefs, the kernels of corn which indicate the relationships among the chiefs are laid for the Onondaga chiefs as in Figure 13.[7]

The Onondaga positions at Six Nations are filled as follows:

19. *Thadoda'ho?*. The name is interpreted as meaning "he blocks the path" or "entwined." This interpretation comes from the Deganawi'da? legend, in which the head of Thadoda'ho? is entangled with snakes, which must be combed out. Thadoda'ho? was one of the most influential chiefs, despite the fact that "all the trees are of the same height." He is second in power only to Honŏwiye'hdŏ, who is able to break tie votes in the council. At Six Nations, however, due to the strong personality of the current Thadoda'ho?, Joseph (Joe) Logan, there is no doubt that he is the most respected and most influential chief. All questions of procedure and substance are ultimately referred to him, and his word is law among the chiefs. He is of the Deer clan (Big Deer). His matron (Ann Buck General, MoSi) is dead now. When a matron dies, the chiefs are supposed to be informed of the new holder of the wampum, but in reality this is very seldom done. Consequently, the general public does not know where the wampum resides until a new chief is installed in the position, and the title-holding matron appears in the Longhouse. If a matron dies suddenly without leaving any instructions as to the disposition of the wampum, the chief himself may at times actually hold his own wampum, and decide to whom it should pass. Joe Logan attends all the Confederate Chiefs' council meetings at Onondaga Longhouse and is active in almost every ritual activity in the Onondaga neighborhood. The position has been reported in the earlier literature as belonging to the Bear clan. Bear and Deer are in the same moiety, so that the transfer did not influence the Longhouse arrangement.

20. *Hone'hthrē*. This is translated "central lawn," and used to be a Beaver clan title, but, as there was no suitable heir available, the title was given to a "borrowed" person, Freeman Green, who is of the Wolf clan. The matron, Flora Gibson, now has a son who could be eligible, so that the title may eventually revert to the Beaver clan. Wolf and Beaver sit on the same side at Onondaga Longhouse, so that the substitution causes no difficulty in the Onondaga and Seneca seatings, though, from the Sour Springs point of view, where Beaver has lately begun to sit with Turtle, which is opposite to Wolf, it seems that the title has been "handed across the fire." With the appointment of the present incumbent, four chieftainship titles have become concentrated in one family (Fig. 14). Ideally, no family should have more than

---

[7] Roy Buck laid out the kernels in the session which Fenton witnessed and describes (Fenton, 1950: 24, 44–5). Figure 13 is also based on a demonstration by Mr. Buck, but in this instance he did not leave a larger space between the third and fourth kernel as Fenton's diagram indicates. Consequently, he did not separate the third through sixth Onondaga chiefs. Hale (1883) thought that the first six chiefs had once constituted a single phratry. Incidentally, women can be asked to the practice sessions.

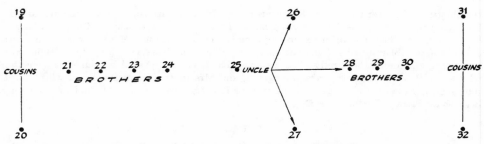

FIG. 13. The Relationships among the Onondaga Chiefs.

one title, but with the frequent borrowing of chiefs, titles easily move to the ritually more active families. Mr. Green regularly attends the Longhouse and the council of hereditary chiefs. Hone'hthrĕ is ceremonially a "cousin" to the first Onondaga chief, since he is of the opposite moiety. The kernels of corn are laid so as to indicate a grouping of the first two chiefs, and the fact that they are "cousins" is mentioned.

21. *Tha'tkᵃhdõs.* The meaning of this title is given as "looks both ways." Beaver clan holds the title, and the incumbent is Eli Yellow. His matron is Edith Jacobs, the cousin (MoSiDa) of the chief. She is a member of Sour Springs Longhouse, and accordingly now sits with the Turtle moiety. Mr. Yellow was installed in the Longhouse and is a Longhouse adherent. Before his illness he attended the chiefs' council meetings as well. The previous titleholder was Richard Harris, the matron's mother's brother.

22. *Honyaꜣdadji'wak.* At practice sessions it is always explained now that this title used to be in a family belonging to Dawi'sdawi Hodiꜣnehsi'yoꜣs, the Small Snipe (Sandpiper) clan, but that family, last represented by Chief John Hill, "cooled down their fire," i.e., died out. The chiefs then decided to transfer the title to the family of David John. Currently the title is in the family of Mrs. Sam Green†, who, as matron installed Thomas Miller and, at his death, Bill White, who, like his matron, is of the Wolf clan. When a title dies out in a family, the chiefs in council have the option of assigning the title to a new family. Some difficulty arises here about moiety affiliation (see p. 65 *supra*). This chief should be a brother to the preceding chief and consequently should be of the same moiety. Snipe members at present sit mostly on the Deer side, which, assuming they follow the lead of the chief, puts this chief in the moiety opposite to that of his "brethren." In the United States, however, the Onondaga Snipes sit with the Wolf and Turtle clans. Here again is a case of non-concomitance of chiefs' phratries and clan seating as it is practiced in the Longhouse. Again it seems that the two institutions should be kept separate, and both should be separated from kinship associations, since the designation of "cousin" and "brother" for the opposite and for one's own moiety respectively has no functional meaning as far as genealogical connections or marriage rules are concerned.

23. *Awe'ꜣkᵉhnyat.* The interpretation of this name is currently "something upright." Alexander General thought that this title should belong to the Snipe clan, but the literature has rather consistently ascribed it to Ball, and it has been in a Wolf family at Six Nations for at least two generations. Peter Thomas, a Wolf, is the current titleholder, and his mother, Mrs. Violet Thomas, is his matron. She was made the matron after the death of her mother's sister, who had in turn been designated matron on the death of her mother's sister. However, when Mrs. Violet Thomas took over the matronship, all the wampum had been lost, so that she had to buy new beads, one or two at a time, until she finally had a string ten beads long, which is considered sufficient. New wampum sets to indicate the "horns of office" are assembled at Six Nations, especially when a title is transferred from one family to another, or when the beads are dissipated. One way of obtaining beads is to buy them from the chiefs who retain the beads sent "across the fire" by a matron who is installing a chief. These are the beads which are

"dropped into their ears" (hēnahōhda'gō'hēwa'ʔsēʔ onaʔgaaʔ, "in-their-ears to-drop antlers") by the matron. Usually, five white beads (at times it has been only four), which symbolize the "white antlers of the chief," are "dropped into the ears" of the opposite moiety. Some chiefs intimate that matrons should drop ten beads. Dropping five is favored because it is then said that each bead symbolizes a nation, though dropping four fulfills the pattern number. Other methods of bead collection are to buy them from the caller of the Tutelo adoption ceremony, who receives a ring of wampum as a reward for his services at the ceremony, and to buy them from the moiety which wins the Bowl Game, for at the Bowl Game each side supplies four pieces of wampum which are hung up and matched to each other, so that the winner receives both sets (see p. 170 *infra*). Actually, there is quite a lively trade in wampum, but it is all kept extremely secret and surrounded by suspicion. Wampum pieces are revered, but they can also be dangerous, due to the possibility of witching, and each piece is carefully scrutinized and its history is desired before it will be accepted freely.

Previous holders of this title were Jesse Lewis and Joseph Sky.

24. *Thayaʔtgwaʔe?*. The meaning, says Alexander General, is "broad body." Sam Green of the Wolf clan is the titleholder, and his sister, Annie Key, is the matron. (The literature consistently ascribes this title to the Turtle clan.) The title is held in that family (an Iroquois Saxe-Coburg!), which has four chiefs, as shown in Figure 14.

The three sisters in the second generation indicated are of the same mother but of different fathers. All the members of this family are ritualists and Longhouse attenders, and the four chiefs all attend the council of hereditary chiefs. Peter Thomas and William White usually attend Seneca Longhouse, mainly because they live near there. Peter Thomas works out, and therefore he does not attend the chiefs' council as much as he would were he on the Reserve most of the time. Being "home" is a major consideration, both ideally and actually. Ideally, a chief should not work out among the whites, should be on the Reserve all day so that he can be of service at any time, and should attend all the meetings. However, economically this is not feasible any more. Still, choice of a chief depends to a large degree on whether he will be present at the Reserve. Working among the whites often makes an individual feel unable or unsuited or uncomfortable in the position of chief and is a common reason for refusing to accept this office.

The first six Onondaga chiefs, 19 through 24, were the firekeepers of the Onondaga nation. Hale thought they may all have been of one clan at one time (see Fenton,

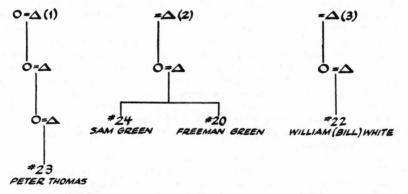

FIG. 14. The Relationships among the Holders of the Titles Hone'hthrē (20), Honyaʔdadji΄- wak (22), Awe'ʔkᵉhnyat (23), and Thayʔatgwa'eʔ (24).

1950: 62). The Sour Springs ritualists seem to invert the order of titles 22, 23, and 24. The order in which Alexander General enumerates these three chiefs is 24, 22, 23. When he recites the Roll Call, even when he uses the cane which he constructed from Fenton's diagram, he recites in the inverted order. This indicates that at most the cane is an occasional reminder, but that on the whole the list of chiefs is now memorized and recited by rote.

25. *Honōwiye'hdō*. This title is said to mean "he has sunk it." William Jacobs of the Wolf clan currently holds the title, but his matron is dead. This is the chief who has the greatest authority of all the chiefs of the Six Nations, for he has the deciding vote among the Onondaga, who themselves in the council of nations have the deciding voice. He is the chief who "quiets all argument" and "cools down the council," and may return a decision to the parties for further consultation or adjudication. It is he who "directs the minds of all other nations." Also, this chief should be the wampum-keeper for the Six Nations. David Skye once held this title, and he is still remembered as a most powerful chief. The importance of this chief, the Great Wolf, is indicated at condolence practice sessions by placing the kernel of corn indicative of the title by itself, separated by a small space from the preceding and following titles. It is the only "phratry" consisting of a single chief. According to Roy Buck, the Eulogy (Roll Call) indicates that this chief "has two uncles [on father's side] and two clans [or fireplaces]," (dekhni' thodōni'hshē?, degē?da'ak^ehne?), the two Deer chiefs following being one uncle, and the three Eel chiefs being the other uncle. This is a somewhat different interpretation from that usually found in the literature, in which it is indicated that the two chiefs of the Deer clan who follow are the two uncles. Hale, however, thought that the five chiefs who follow this title, all of the opposite moiety, had a special political relationship to Honōwiye'hdō.

26. *Gawēnē?shē'ndō*. This is a Deer clan title. The present chief is Peter Sky, and his matron is Nellie Harris. Peter Sky was adopted by Nellie's mother's sister's daughter. The previous holder of this title had been Peter Buck. This chief and the next are indicated by lateral kernels of corn and constitute an uncle (paternal) to "the Great Wolf, *Honōwiye'hdō*."

27. *Hahi'yō*. The title means "one of fifty," according to Mr. General. It used to be in the family of George Davis, but the family died out, and it fell upon the chiefs to reassign the title. They decided to give it to Daisy Thomas, who installed her brother, David Thomas, as the chief. The title is to stay in that family. Mr. Thomas is of the Deer clan. He is one of the most important ritualists at Six Nations, despite his progressing blindness. According to Parker (1961: 36), a chief who is blind should have a deputy appointed to act for him, for this defect makes him ineligible to sit in council. However, like the famous John Gibson, Mr. Thomas has not given up his duty on account of his infirmity. David Thomas opens almost every council and is also the principal speaker at Onondaga Longhouse. He is a preacher of the Code and has been legitimated at Tonawanda. Mr. Thomas started out as a church member but married into a family which was extremely ritualistic. Some time after his marriage his small daughter became extremely ill and seemed near death. Mr. Thomas then dreamed that he saw his small girl with a sand pail come and pick cookies. She said: "Four days from today I'll eat." He prepared a "feast" four days after his dream, and, indeed, the child became well. Mr. Thomas then considered himself converted to the Longhouse and has been one of the most forceful conservative leaders. This is one of the few instances in which a husband has followed his wife into the Longhouse.

28. *Hōwayōnyē'ni*. Bob Henhawk is the current chief, but his matron is unknown. Mr. Henhawk attends the council of hereditary chiefs. This title is owned by the Eel clan. It is the first of the three Eel chieftainships, whose kernels are laid horizontally and form a phratry.

29. *Hogwa'sē?*. This title also belongs currently to an Eel clan family, and Robert Mt. Pleasant is the chief. However, he goes to church and in addition tried to be elected to the elective council at one time. Also, he does not attend the hereditary council meetings, which

prompts the Onondaga to proclaim that "he is dead, because he is not working [i.e., for the hereditary council]." The Onondaga chiefs would like to take the title away from the family of Mr. Mt. Pleasant, but so far they have not mustered up the courage to do so. The transfer may await vacancy of the title.

30. *Shago'khee?*. "He sees them." Jack Kick is the present titleholder. His matron is unknown, but the title has legitimately come to him from his maternal family. Again it is an Eel clan title.

31. *Ho?draha'hō.*

32. *Skanawa'di?*. This means "on the other side of the swamp." The status of these titles determines whether there are 49 or 50 chiefs, and whether the Onondaga are entitled to 13 or 14 offices. There has long been a question whether the titles Ho?draha'hō and Skanawa'di? are two names of one chief, or whether they represent two chiefs. Some have contended that each title represents a phase of one chief, a war-chief phase and a peace-chief phase. Others claim that Ho?draha'hō is a title, and that the last chief in the Onondaga list, Skanawa'di?, simply has a dual character of peace chief and of warrior. Hale (1883: 159) believed the latter explanation, saying: "He [Skanawa'di?] had the peculiar distinction of holding two offices, which were rarely combined. He was both a high chief, or 'Lord of the Council,' and a 'Great Warrior.' " Actually, it is strange that a peace chief, who is specifically enjoined not to engage in any battle and who is disqualified if he should shed any blood is also a war chief. However, as Fenton (1950: 64) remarks, this dual character is not unusual in Iroquois culture. Roy Buck's explanation is that Skanawa'di? was a great war chief and that "they put a chief on him so he'll quit war." All the Onondaga at Six Nations believe that the titles should be assigned to two chiefs, but the Cayuga state that the titles are two names for one chief. There has been discussion in the chiefs' council over this for many years, and the title of Ho?draha'hō has been "left empty" by the chiefs. There is no living matron, and, as long as Roy Buck remembers, the position has been empty. Chadwick (1897) lists the position as "extinct in Canada." The title of Skanawa'di? is currently filled by Oliver Jacobs. His mother, Elsie Jacobs, is the matron. The first title is ascribed by the Onondaga at Six Nations today to the Deer clan (though in the literature it has always been assigned to Turtle); the latter is ascribed to the Turtle clan. Mr. Jacobs is a Turtle clan member. Skanawa'di? is another of the chiefs who is traditionally considered a powerful personality in the League.

The Cayuga Titles

The Cayuga chiefs are grouped into four phratries, each a committee with particular functions in the council of the Cayuga. The kernels of corn at the practice sessions exhibit the committees by their arrangement. They are laid out as in Figure 15. The first two chiefs are the fire-keepers, the last two chiefs the door-keepers.

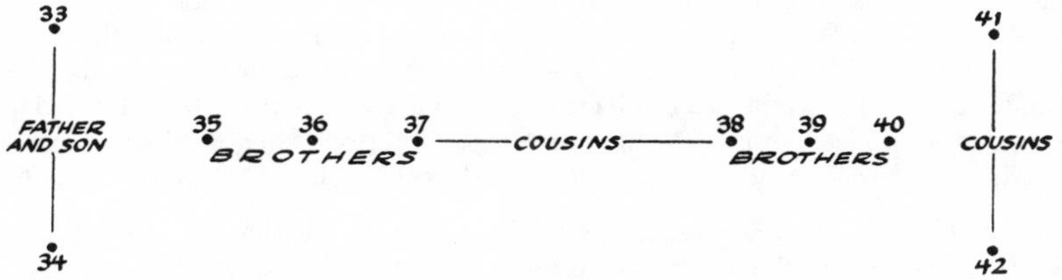

Fig. 15. The Relationships among the Cayuga Chiefs.

33. *Haga?a'ēyōnk*. The origin of this name is currently derived from the Deganawi'da? legend. Deganawi'da? came in turn to various settlements proselytizing for his League. He came upon leaders of bands in characteristic occupations and labeled them with a name accordingly. The story for this title is the following: "A man from the north [i.e., Deganawi'da?][8] came to this particular settlement and came across the leader. He invited him to come to a conference to set up their chiefs. The leader replied, 'I will consider your invitation.' The-Man-from-the-North then went back and had all the other leaders assembled, but waited for this last leader whom he had invited for the conference. He didn't appear, and so a messenger was sent after him. When the messenger got to the settlement, there was no one. All had disappeared. Again a messenger was sent to follow the leader and find him, which was done. When the leader was brought back to the assembly, he was asked why it was that he didn't appear on the day he agreed to meet. 'Well, I've been thinking about it, I considered.' Therefore he was called Haga?a'ēyōnk." Alexander General says, "It is an old word for 'I consider.'"

This title used to be held in the Deer clan, but when Abram Charles took the position it changed from the Deer to the Bear clan. His half sister, Mary Skye, was originally his matron, and at her death the wampum was passed to her daughter, Jemima Gibson. In 1945, Jemima Gibson installed her brother, Hardy Gibson. Jemima herself died later in 1945. According to Alexander General, "When Hardy Gibson was installed, it was mentioned that the titleholder was of the Deer clan, but by consideration of the people of the Bear clan, this title was transferred to the Bear clan. The Deer clan titleholders, the family of Eva Harris, are still surviving, but for some reasons have not reclaimed the title." There was much discussion, says Mr. General, and if the shift of clan had not been explained, the Three Brothers "might be suspicious and refuse to accept the nominee." The literature (see Fenton, 1950: 65) usually reports that this chief and the next (33 and 34) are "co-sons" or "sons of each other," but the relationship is actually one of father and son (Hewitt, 1945: 312). These two chiefs are not of opposite moieties, as was reported to Fenton (1950: 65), nor have they lately been. Neither Deer and Deer (Hale, 1883: 161), nor Bear and Ball (Chadwick, 1897: 92), nor even Bear and Hawk (Fenton, 1950: 65) are of opposite moieties to each other (and Hawk is not a Cayuga clan at Six Nations today). Only the assignation by Morgan (1901, 2: 214) of these titles to Deer and Heron placed them in opposite moieties. The kernels of corn designating these two titles are laid laterally, but this does not have to mean that opposite moieties, addressing each other as "cousin," must be involved (Fenton, 1950: 65). A counter-example is provided by titles 26 and 27 (both Onondaga), which are designated by two lateral kernels but which have always been reported as two Deer clan titles. The particular arrangement of the kernels remains problematical, but again it appears that the Condolence Ceremony is more of a political ritual than a ritual which indicates social relationships. The appellatives "cousin" and "brother" seem to be a manner of ritual speech rather than a reflection of actual relationships, and the groupings of chiefs seem to reflect political alignment and procedural devices rather than religious and social relationships.

34. *Gadji?nōnda'whyō*. This chief also derives his name from the Deganawi'da? legend. "When The-Man-from-the-North came to the settlement of this leader, he saw a man squatting by a stream, and he watched him and saw what he was doing. He was catching water bugs and seeing the things afloat. When asked what he was doing, the man replied, 'Oh, I am enjoying seeing bugs float.' Then The-Man-from-the-North declared, 'I now proclaim you shall be called Gadji?nōnda'whyō; you shall be the leader.'" This was once a Deer clan title, and Hale (1883: 161) listed it as Deer, but it has been in the Ball clan as long as Alexander General can remember. Mrs. Charles Bomberry is the matron. However, the only candidate in her family,

---

[8] Among the Onondaga and Seneca at Six Nations, mention of the name "Deganawi'da?" is tabooed at all times except at the actual Condolence Ceremony. At the practice sessions and in ordinary life, circumlocutions such as "The-Man-from-the-North" or "He-who-founded-the-League" should be used.

Bill Thomas, was already the Seneca Longhouse wampum-keeper, and he decided he could not be "two people" (see p. 89 *supra*). Consequently, Mrs. Bomberry "borrowed" William (Albert) Johnson (Nawha'hes) to fill the position. At his death the title should revert to Mrs. Bomberry's family, though there still is no heir (Bill Thomas and Mrs. Bomberry being the only two survivors in that particular Ball clan family). This chief, according to tradition, is supposed to be the most powerful of the Cayuga chiefs and should have "the most to say" about Cayuga affairs, though whether or not this actually is the case varies with the personality of the incumbent. The first two Cayuga chiefs are the Cayuga nation fire-keepers, and at Six Nations they are also the fire-keepers of Lower Cayuga Longhouse, for tradition relates that these two chiefs founded Lower Cayuga Longhouse. In theory, Gadji?nŏnda'whyŏ should be more prominent than Haga?a'ēyŏnk. These first two chiefs are also often depicted as competing with each other, especially at lacross games.

35. *Gada?gwa'sē?*. The meaning of this title is "something bruised it." Nellie (or "Bessie") Davis is the matron of the title, and she inherited her position from her mother, Khaŏwa'tha (Cayuga) or Gahŏwa'tha (Mohawk). Nellie Davis is a Longhouse member, but she has not installed a chief since the death of her uncle (MoBr), John Jamieson, who had been the chief. Mr. General says that since it is a Longhouse family, the chiefs "can only urge and encourage her to install a chief, but there is nothing one can do if they don't put one in." This is a different attitude from that which is assumed when a Christian family neglects to install a chief, in which case there is an instant clamor to transfer the title to an active Longhouse family, which would install a chief. The title belongs to the Bear clan, and the matron is a Bear member.

36. *Shoyŏ'wes*. The title is said to mean "long intestine." Forty years ago the title belonged to a family of the Big Bear clan, of which Austin Bill was the last chief. Annie Bill (his mother or sister?) was the matron, but after Austin Bill's death no chief was installed by this family. This matter was brought before the chiefs, who transferred the matronship to Mrs. Elizabeth Hill of the Suckling Bear clan. This was approved by the Cayuga chiefs, thus providing an instance in which transferring titles was considered a prerogative only of the nation concerned rather than of the council of chiefs. Sam General, who also belonged to the Suckling Bear clan, was borrowed for the title, but he died in 1945. Previously, Mrs. Elizabeth Hill had died, and the matron's office was passed to her daughter; however, as she wanted nothing to do with it, the wampum was given to Sam General. At his death the wampum was given to his brother, Timothy General, who was at that time head deacon at Sour Springs but not a chief. Timothy died in 1955, and the wampum is presumably still in the family of Timothy General. No chief has been installed since the death of Sam General.

37. *Hadya'?tr°hne?* (also *Hagya'?tr°hne?*). This title is interpreted by Mrs. George Green, who at one time was the matron for the title, as "you are meeting somebody." (She pronounces the title Hadra'tr°hne). The clan is Mud Turtle. This chieftainship is one which lately was transferred to a different family, because the hereditary chiefs were dissatisfied with the allegiance of the matron. Mrs. Green was the matron until 1925. She had been given the title by Peter Jamieson (Bidedrĕnda?, Fly), who was the chief until 1925, when he died. He had succeeded his mother's brother, Jacob Jamieson, and had received his wampum from his matron, Esther Jamieson, who also was his mother. Peter used his mother's maiden name. After 1924, when the hereditary council was abolished, Peter Jamieson ran for office in the elective council, and in 1925 he actually was elected to serve. This seems to have offended the conservative chiefs, and they neglected to ask the matron to fill the title at Mr. Jamieson's death. The chiefs now claim that she should have filled it herself immediately, but Mrs. Green claims that the chiefs should have approached her and mentioned that she should install a successor, which she says she would have been very willing to do (see p. 99 *supra*). The chiefs then handed the matronship for the title of Hadya'?tr°hne? to Eunice Davie, a distant relative of Mrs. Green, and they declared that Mrs. Green would, thenceforth, no longer be the matron. The new matron (now deceased) installed her brother, Alex Nanticoke (Haihwēs, Knocking-the-Words),

as chief. She also collected a new set of wampum to legitimate the title, as Mrs. Green would not give up her set. There has been friction over this title ever since. The title had long been held by individuals associated with the Sour Springs community, and Hadyaʔ'trᵒhneʔ was, in fact, considered the leading chief of the Sour Springs Turtle moiety. Mr. Nanticoke, however, belongs to Lower Cayuga Longhouse. The original matron, Mrs. Green, believes that since she has the wampum for the chief and since she is a devoted Longhouse member and ritualist herself, she ought to be allowed to install a chief. She feels that she should not have been deprived of her right merely because of her belief that the elective council is an inevitable step in the acculturation of the Six Nations. This episode, occurring about 1927, was a major factor in the split at the Sour Springs Longhouse.

The last three chiefs, all of the Turtle moiety, form one phratry.

38. *Dyoōhyŏ'ngo*. Alexander General interprets the title as meaning "hitting the sky" or "piercing the sky." At Sour Springs Longhouse, this chief is the leader of the Wolf moiety, and he is considered one of the founders of the Longhouse. It was he who brought a group to Canada and established the current Longhouse. Also, it is now related that he was responsible for introducing the Heron clan into the Six Nations, for this was a Wyandot clan, and the Wyandot were adopted by Chief Dyoōhyŏ'ngo. The present titleholder, Norman General, (Thonhaen, He-is-standing-watching) is of the Heron clan, though Morgan (1901, 2: 214), Chadwick (1897: 93), and Hale (1893: 161) all ascribed the title to the Wolf clan. Among the Cayuga of Sour Springs there is considerable pride in the career of this chief. At the time of the founding of the League, Dyoōhyŏ'ngo is supposed to have been the leader of the Cayuga nation, and the Cayuga are depicted as already organized in a fashion similar to the aspirations of Deganawi'daʔ for the League. Both Dyoōhyŏ'ngo and Hadyaʔ'trᵒhneʔ are depicted as "having smokes going up to heaven and their fires made." This is to indicate that they had a stable settlement and government prior to the League. Alexander General tells the story as follows: "When Deganawi'daʔ was organizing the League, Thadoda'hoʔ was most obstinate and would not accept it. He named the Onondaga, Oneida, Mohawk, and Seneca and said he was not satisfied. Then Hayŏ'hwathaʔ said to look for another fire, and he found the Cayuga. Thadoda'hoʔ already knew that the Cayuga had set up a system, and that is what he admired. The Cayuga were found and invited to the convention to hear the 'Good Tidings of Peace.' The Cayuga agreed and arrived at the council, chanting, on the way, the chant of the chief's installation. Thadoda'hoʔ lay on the ground and listened, and said, 'My cousins [kheya'ʔdawĕh, see p. 31 *supra* for a definition] are now coming.' [Kheya'ʔdawĕh is the conventional term applied to the Four Brother nations (of which the Cayuga are a member) by the Three Brother nations.] When they arrived, Thadoda'hoʔ asked Dyoōhyŏ'ngo, as their spokesman, to accept the 'Tidings of Peace.' He accepted the mission and set up for the League the same system as that already practiced by the Cayuga." This unusual version of the Deganawi'daʔ legend might well have been constructed from the current arrangement of the committees of chiefs of the Cayuga. The Cayuga have a fire-keeper committee, a doorkeeper committee, and two sides which consult with each other. The analogy to the League in general is quite simple, and analogy is a favorite and ever recurring explanatory device among the Iroquois.

The present holder of the title Dyoōhyŏ'ngo is Norman General, a member of the Sour Springs community. He was installed by Elizabeth (Lucy) Hill Johnson (Aaron), (Kha'eñes), the cousin of his grandmother (MoMoMoSiDa). At her death the wampum for the title was given to Norman General's mother, Mrs. Levy General, who holds it now.

39. *Deyothowe'hgō*. The meaning of this name is derived from the Deganawi'daʔ legend of the forming of the League. When this particular leader was asked who he was, he replied, "I'm the one that came from the north." Then Deganawi'daʔ said, "You shall be called Deyothowe'hgō, Cold-on-both-Sides (also Double Cold)." This title was held until his death in 1955 by Sam Jamieson, who had been borrowed by the matron, Lucy Walker Hill, because she had no willing "warriors" (eligible candidates) in her own family. The title is a

Wolf title, and the matron did belong to the Wolf clan, but the chief borrowed belonged to the Heron clan. When Lucy Hill died, Lena Sky became the matron, and she currently holds the wampum. She has "borrowed" Cleveland General of the Heron clan to be the new chief.

40. *Deyōhwe'thō*. Mr. General gives "propped up" as the meaning for this title. The title is currently held by Gus Williams of the Snipe clan. His sister, Mrs. Alex Nanticoke, is matron, and she inherited her position from her mother. The previous chief was Ernest Jamieson, half brother of Mrs. Nanticoke (same mother). The last three chiefs (38, 39, and 40) comprise a phratry and consult together as a committee. They all belong to the Wolf moiety.

41. *Hadōnda'heha?*. The meaning is derived as follows: "A man came from the north, and while he was traveling through the Cayuga settlement, it was his mission to establish people who would hold the responsibility for their group. He came to a lake and saw a man with a canoe bobbing up and down on the waves. He waited till the man came back to shore and asked him what he was doing. The man in the canoe said, 'I take pleasure in riding the waves.' Then The-Man-from-the-North said, 'Since you enjoy riding the waves, you shall be called Hadōnda'heha?.' " It is also translated "he shoulders a log." At Six Nations this position is currently empty. The last matron was Mary MacDougall, but she died, and the family is Christian and uninterested in installing a chief. The chiefs would very much like to transfer the title to another family, but so far have not done this. The last chief to hold this title, John E. Henry, was deposed. No one knows where the wampum for this title is. This chief and the next one are the doorkeepers of the Cayuga. The clan to which Hadōnda'heha? belongs is Snipe, of the Wolf moiety.

42. *Deska'he?*. Deska'he? is said to mean "more than eleven." The original Deska'he? is said to have received his name in the following manner: "He was a leader of a group which was set off by itself from the other groups who trapped fish. But the next morning the traps would be empty, and the fish caught during the night would have been stolen. Finally, the several trapping groups decided to stand guard all night, and the group of warriors under the leadership of Deska'he? were caught. They were brought to the chief and asked what they were doing and where the rest of the group was. Deska'he? told where they were and when asked how many there were, he could only answer, 'More than eleven.' That is how he was subjugated and captured, for he had been caught doing wrong and had to submit." The title at one time was a Snipe clan title but was transferred to the Suckling Bear clan, which, incidentally, is a transfer to the opposite moiety. The present Bear clan family was "borrowed" into the position at the time of the grandmother of the incumbent, and from all appearances the title will remain in the Bear clan family. The transfer is explained by the contention that if there is no candidate in the original family, the title may be given to any family which is friendly with the title-owning family and which has a good character. This is an instance of a change of the clan holding a title, and even a change of moiety, due to the retention of a title in the family of the borrowed chief.

The title is currently held by Alexander (Jack) General (Shaōhyo'wa, Great Sky) at Six Nations. He assumed office when his brother Levy died in 1925. The titular wampum was handed to his grandmother, who passed it to his mother, Liddia General, who then passed it to her half sister (same mother), Louise Miller. She is dead now, and the present holder is not known to the writer. Dave Jamieson held the title as chief prior to Levy General, but his matron (Alexander General's mother) is said to have deposed him and his "runner" (her son Dave). Benjamin Carpenter, uncle of Liddia General, held the title prior to that. Alexander General is the leading chief at Sour Springs Longhouse and probably the most forceful Cayuga chief. He is a strong believer in the hereditary council and attempts to integrate the chiefs into the Longhouse at every opportunity. His conception of chieftainship is that it is "God-given" and that a chief must lead the Longhouse congregation. He has devoted his entire life to the fight between the elected and hereditary councils.

There have been various reports as to whether the last two Cayuga chieftains are related ceremonially as brothers or cousins. Hewitt's notes say "brothers"; the Condolence text says

116

"cousins." Both were correct at times, depending on which chiefs held the titles. Again, it seems reasonable to interpret the social designation as a ritual or political device, since the actual moiety affiliations of the chiefs change, and since moiety affiliation is not a definitive index of whether a person is related as a brother or a cousin.

THE SENECA TITLES

The Seneca chiefs are depicted in the practice sessions by four pairs of lateral kernels, with the last two laid at some distance from the others, since they represent two chiefs which were presumably added at a later date. Deganawi'da? is said to have come to a new country after the initial investiture of chiefs and to have found another group of Seneca, and he decided to add two more chiefs. The Condolence mentions this addition of two doorkeepers, although the entire Seneca nation is styled as "doorkeeper" (Fig. 16). The councilors of each pair are usually of opposite moieties and address each other as cousin.

43. *Skanyada'iyo*. The meaning is "beautiful lake," but because the Prophet held this title, it is usually translated "handsome lake." The Turtle clan has this office, though at Six Nations two families contend they have a right to the title, and, consequently, the position is empty. John Arthur Gibson was Six Nations' most famous Skanyada'iyo, and Mrs. Patterson Davis, his niece, was the title-holding matron. At Mr. Gibson's death the only candidate in the family was Mrs. Davis' brother, but he was disqualified as he had served as a soldier during the war. Then a chief was borrowed, and his family now claims the title. So far there has been no settlement, and none seems in sight.

44. *Sha?dega'ōhyes*. "Skies of equal length" is the meaning of this title. The present chief is Adam Burning of the Snipe clan. His first cousin, Mrs. Nora Hill, is his matron.

45. *Shogē?djo'wa*. This is said to mean "great forehead." It is ascribed to the Snipe clan at Six Nations, but no chief currently holds the position. Even a title-holding family seems to be missing. Chadwick (1897: 95) listed the position as belonging to the Hawk clan and as unfilled in Canada in 1897. Hawk clan members at Six Nations all seem to have come lately from the United States, and it is not considered a Canadian clan.

46. *G?ano'gai*. This is a Turtle clan title, currently held by Stanley Buck. His mother, Hannah Buck, is the matron. He is a Longhouse attender, as is his matron.

47. *Nishaye'nōs*. No one at Six Nations holds this title. Fenton (1950: 67) ascribes it to the Snipe clan. Chadwick (1897: 95) also listed it as extinct in Canada.

48. *Shadye'nōwat*. This position is also empty at Six Nations. It is attributed to the Snipe clan. Chadwick (1897: 94) lists it as Snipe and as unfilled in 1897.

49. *Ganōhgi'?dawi*. This title is also attributed to the Snipe clan. Jim David Silversmith was the chief until his recent death. He was installed by order of the chiefs and had no matron.

50. *Deyoninhoga'wē*. This is a Wolf clan title. Simon Burnhouse, the last titleholder, died at Tonawanda about seven years ago.

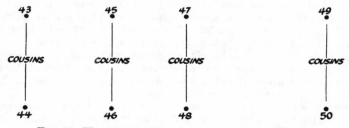

FIG. 16. The Relationships among the Seneca Chiefs.

The census lists only 250 Seneca at Six Nations at present, and, even though this is not an accurate count for purposes of ritual, since the government lists by patrilineal affiliation, it gives some indication that the Seneca are numerically few. The Seneca offices and the Oneida offices are the least filled, and there is less action to replace vacancies than with the Mohawk, Onondaga, and Cayuga offices.

MOIETY DIVISION OF THE LEAGUE

When the hereditary chiefs of the five Iroquois nations sit in council, they separate into moieties, with the Mohawk, Seneca, and Onondaga chiefs on one side, and the Oneida and Cayuga chiefs on the other. The former side is called "The Three Brothers" or "Uncles" (literally, "paternal uncles," or simply "paternal kin"); and the latter is called "The Four Brothers" or "Nephews" (literally, "fraternal offspring"). The appellation "Four Brothers" indicates the adoption of the Tuscarora and the Delaware by the Cayuga nation, but fails to take into account the fact that the Cayuga nation presumably also adopted the Nanticoke, Tutelo, and Wyandot. When the two groups address each other, The Three Brothers designate the Four Brothers as kheya'ꞌdawĕh, and the Four Brothers designate the Three Brothers as agadŏ'nih (see p. 31 *supra* for a discussion of these reciprocal kinship terms). Another common pair of designations for the two sides is "Elder Brother" for the Three Brothers and "Younger Brother" for the Four Brothers. The complete arrangement of the League, including both the division into the two moieties and the phratry divisions of each of the five nations, is exhibited at the Condolence practice sessions by laying out kernels of corn (Fig. 17).

Hewitt (1945: 306 and *passim*) liked to think of the two sides as embodying the male and female, or father and mother, principles, the Three Brothers representing the paternal and the Four Brothers the maternal. His general theme is as follows (1945: 303):

. . . the principles of blood kindred, duality (with mutual service between reciprocating units of society), relative age, and sex, as they operated in society as it was lived by the village band, were projected beyond the local group to the level of the tribe, and from the tribe to the confederacy. Tribes apply kinship terms to other tribes: they are related as mothers or little mothers (i.e., mother's sister), daughters and sons, . . .

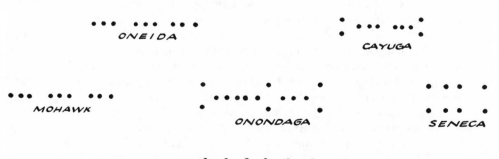

FIG. 17. The Arrangement of the League.

Specifically, he interprets the Three Brothers as father's kinsmen (agadŏ′nih) and the Four Brothers as mother's kinsmen (ohwachira). This would seem to assume a fixed vantage point from the side of the Four Brothers. Viewed from the other side, the latter would be fraternal offspring (kheya′ʔdawĕh).

Furthermore, the relationship terminology applied to the phratries within a tribe is to be construed symbolically, indicating neither actual consanguineal relationships nor the ritual relationships among clans seated in the Longhouse. It is true, as has been discussed in the chapter entitled "Longhouse Membership and Organization," that the seating of a chief in the Longhouse is often used by members of the chief's clan as a guide to their own seating. However, the limitations of this rule were also pointed out. Furthermore, there are instances of noncorrespondence between the relationship terminology employed in the Longhouse and that which is applied in the Condolence Chant to the chiefs (the Roll Call). Thus, chiefs 47 and 48 (both Seneca) are called "cousins" in the Condolence chant, yet at Six Nations both chiefs are supposed to belong to the Snipe clan (an ideal attribution, since both positions are empty at present) and hence would be "brothers" on the same moiety side in the Longhouse. Even if the clan affiliations of chiefs 47 and 48 are Snipe and Bear, as Fenton (1950: 65) lists, they still would be "brothers" at Onondaga and Seneca Longhouses, where Bear and Snipe sit on the same moiety side. (See Table 3 for a summary of the moiety divisions at the Six Nations Longhouses and at some of the Longhouses in the United States, and the chapter on Longhouse membership for a more detailed discussion.) Since the moiety arrangements at the various Longhouses differ, the correspondence between kinship terminology as applied to the chiefs and kinship terminology applied to the members of clans in the Longhouse is a local matter. In so far as relationship terms in the Condolence Chant have been handed down accurately, they may reflect an earlier organization, but it is likely that the organization reflected would be political rather than social or religious. Even if the relationship terminology of the chiefs coincides with an erstwhile moiety affiliation, either the titles have been shifted to other clans (see Table 2) or the moiety composition has changed to such a degree that today it is fruitless to attempt to match the relationship terminology in the political sphere with that in the social and religious organization.

Speck (1949: 20) seems to agree when he describes the moiety system of the Cayuga as ". . . used to designate social and ceremonial grouping rather than grouping based upon consanguineous relationship or exogamic ruling." However, one should add that the moiety and phratry divisions in the political sphere have the same type of function as in the Longhouse—namely, organizational and ritual reciprocity. It is true that a culture need not always give the same interpretation to a particular pattern in different institutions, yet it is in accord with the "feel" of the Iroquoian culture to interpret the moieties and phratries as committees which interact and have reciprocal functions. Reciprocity and organizational definiteness are two of the most widespread themes occurring again and again.

Table 3. Moiety Affiliation of Clans at Various Longhouses

NEW YORK STATE

Tonawanda Longhouse (Seneca)[a]		Coldspring (Allegany Reservation, Seneca)[b]	
Wolf	Snipe	Wolf	Snipe
Turtle	Hawk	Turtle	Hawk
Bear	Deer	Bear	Deer
Beaver	Heron	Beaver	Heron
	Eel		

Syracuse (Onondaga)—Fenton[c]		Syracuse (Onondaga)—Lounsbury[d]	
Wolf	Bear (extinct)	Wolf	Wolf[e]
Turtle	Hawk	Turtle	Bear (extinct)
Snipe	Deer	Snipe	Deer
Beaver	Eel	Beaver	Eel
		Ball-play	

SIX NATIONS RESERVE

Onondaga Longhouse		Seneca Longhouse	
Wolf	Deer	Wolf	Deer
Turtle	Eel	Turtle	Eel
Beaver	Bear	Beaver	Bear
Small Turtle	Snipe, large and	Small Turtle	Snipe, large and small
Heron	small[f]	Heron	Ball
(Snipe)[f]	Ball		Hawk
	Hawk		

Sour Springs Longhouse		Lower Cayuga Longhouse	
Wolf	Turtle (all sizes)	Wolf	Turtle (all sizes)
Heron	Deer	Heron	Deer
Snipe, large and	Ball	Snipe	Bear (all sizes)
small	Bear (all sizes)		Ball
Beaver[g]	Beaver[g]		Beaver
Hawk[h]	Eel		Eel
	Hawk[h]		Hawk

[a] Fenton (1950b: 47).

[b] *Ibid.*, 46.

[c] Fenton (1953: 71).

[d] Private communication.

[e] Some Wolf clan members sit with one moiety, some with the other.

[f] Snipe members usually sit on the Deer side, but there is some confusion, and a few Snipe members sit on the Wolf side.

[g] Beaver members sat until recently on the Wolf side at Sour Springs, but now they are asked to enter with the Turtles.

[h] Since the Hawk clan is not a Cayuga clan, there is confusion, and Hawk members are said to sit on both sides.

INSTALLATION AND MEETINGS OF THE CHIEFS

Before 1924 chiefs were invested in either of two ways: in the council, by those families which were Christian, and in the Longhouse by those families which could afford and which believed in the Condolence ritual for the installation of chiefs. However, even before 1924 some Longhouse families named chiefs without sponsoring the expensive Condolence. Today, hereditary chiefs can no longer be installed in the council house, since the elected council holds sway there, but a chief can be announced at the meetings of the hereditary council of chiefs, which still take place once a month at Onondaga Longhouse. The Condolence Ceremony is expensive, costing around $100 and it also requires large numbers of participants; consequently, families owning chieftainship titles are reluctant to sponsor such installations today, especially since there is no material benefit in "raising a chief." Only the most ardent conservatives are willing to bear the burden, and even some of them must be "coaxed" to hold the ceremony. It is often put off for several years, until the sponsor feels that he is "ready."[9] Fenton (1946) has given an excellent account of a Condolence installation at Six Nations, and therefore a description need not be given here.

The actual political functions of the chiefs today are confined to meetings held once a month at Onondaga Longhouse, with an average of ten chiefs in attendance representing the Five Nations. The procedure for discussion is still the same as before 1924. The Onondaga, who are the fire-keepers, open the meeting by reciting the Thanksgiving Address while holding the wampum which symbolizes the "fire" (i.e., the existence and life) of the League.

It is asserted that in 1924, when the Indian Department confiscated the wampum from the Onondaga fire-keeper, it was given a counterfeit set, and that the Onondaga still own the "real" set, which presumably is the set used at the openings of the council. The chiefs are very literal about construing the validity of the council in terms of holding and displaying the wampum. Since the Canadian government did not obtain the wampum, say the chiefs, the council fire has as much life as it ever did, although it is clearly understood by all that they have no power other than as a resistance committee with hopes of reinstatement. In 1924, Colonel Morgan, who was the superintendent of the Reserve, said that the chiefs could retrieve the wampum at any time, but it was withheld when they actually called for it. This incident is partly responsible for the idea, so prevalent among the conservative population, that the Canadian government is constantly foraging for the "real wampum." Actually, the government is convinced that the "real wampum" was obtained in 1924, and it has never again concerned itself with the question, especially since the elected council functions adequately as an administrative and political instrument.

As far as the writer could see, the wampum consisted of five white and one brown (purplish) string of beads attached at the top to a semilunar felt or leather head (Fig. 18). Each of the strings is approximately the length of a leg. Hahi'yõ usually opens the meeting, not because this particular chief should do so, but because the

---

[9] Incidentally, "feeling ready" can be a rationalization of behavior whenever an individual is supposed to "put up" a ceremony. When a large expenditure is involved for ritual or medicinal purposes, the sponsor may delay his fulfillment of the obligation by declaring that he is "not ready." If the delay is too long the sponsor usually experiences guilt feelings which manifest themselves in bad luck or in disease. He then quickly acts to "pass" the ceremony, or he may give a token ceremony in an abridged form until he can really afford the prescribed ritual. Condolences, due to their cost, take a long time to get ready.

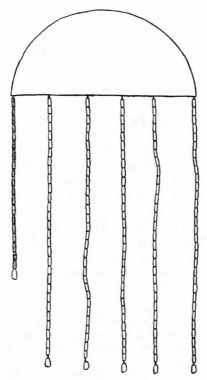

FIG. 18. The Wampum of the League.

present incumbent has a commanding personality and is one of the most revered preachers of the Code. Then the wampum is laid across a table in front of the Onondaga and remains there throughout the meeting.

The seating at the Longhouse places the Onondaga against the northern wall, "alone and right in the middle of things because they are the fire-keepers," the Mohawk and Seneca along the western wall, and the Oneida and Cayuga along the eastern wall, opposite the Mohawk and Seneca (Fig. 19). Women can also attend and are seated in the south half of the Longhouse, which is the women's half at Onondaga. Occasionally, some of the Christian women of the Mohawk Workers are seen on the men's side.

Topics for discussion are relayed by the fire-keepers (either by Thadoda'ho? or Honōwiye'hdō) to the Seneca and Mohawk, who discuss the topic and announce their decision to the Four Brothers. (Dega'iho'gẽ should announce it across the fire.) They in turn deliberate and announce their decision to the Mohawk and Seneca, who give the combined verdict to the Onondaga once more. If the Mohawk and Seneca and the Oneida and Cayuga agree, then the fire-keepers usually agree as well. Otherwise, the topic is "returned to the main door," that is, referred back

FIG. 19. Seating of the Council of Hereditary Chiefs.

to the Seneca and Mohawk for further deliberation. Each of the three groups, Onondaga, Mohawk-Seneca, Oneida-Cayuga, deliberate among themselves in whispers, or at least inaudibly to the other groups, but whenever an announcement is made to any of the other groups, as when the Four Brothers announce their decision to the Mohawk and Seneca, or the Onondaga to "the house," then a speaker rises and addresses the group in question so that all can hear. The direction of the remark is indicated by the terms of address used. The Four Brothers address the Three Brothers as "agadŏni'hshŏ?," the Three Brothers address the Four Brothers as "gakhey?ada'wheshŏ? (Onondaga goyenahda'hgŏ), and the fire-keeper is addressed as "djadjista'ne." Within each tribe there is also a special order of conference, particularly when a tribe holds a council discussing tribal matters alone, although in fact this seldom occurs today.

The Cayuga nation, when counseling among itself, follows a pattern very similar to the League in general. When a question is to be introduced, the last two Cayuga chiefs (41 and 42), the doorkeepers, announce the topic to the assembly. They have the power to decide whether a subject is fit for discussion. The two phratries of three chiefs each, "the two sides" (35–37 and 38–40), then discuss the subject in their respective committees and announce their decision to the fire-keepers, the first two Cayuga chiefs (33 and 34). The latter usually agree if the decision is concurred with by both committees; otherwise they refer it back for further discussion. Decisions become final when acted upon by the fire-keepers. The arrangement of the committees is as follows:

Gada?gwa'sē? (35)	Dyoŏhyŏ'ngo (38)—leader
Shoyŏ'wes (36)	Deyothowe'hgŏ (39)
Hadya'?trohne? (37)—leader	Deyŏhwe'thŏ (40)
Haga?a'ĕyŏnk (33)	Hadŏnda'heha? (41)
Gadji?nŏnda'whyŏ (34)	Deska'he? (42)

Hewitt (1944, 1945) gives his opinion of how the Mohawk and Oneida counseled.

Even at the full hereditary council meetings, the order of discussion is much abbreviated, because so many of the chiefs' chairs "are standing cold" (empty). Usually the few men in each group consult together and then announce their decision.

The pattern of a speaker arising and simply stating his announcement is a very common one, repeated in the Longhouse and in any of the supplicative rituals. The act of rising and speaking out gives importance to the statement, but men usually do not like the task, as they feel great responsibility and some embarrassment at the public notice directed toward them while standing. Good speakers are much admired, both for the content of the speech and the boldness of demeanor.

Since the Canadian government does not recognize any decision or act which the hereditary chiefs might proclaim, very few of the members of the Reserve bring their problems to the hereditary council today. Therefore, the meetings are devoted mainly to hearing grievances by various action groups, such as the Mohawk Workers and the Indian Defense League, to discussions among the chiefs themselves concerning measures to regain their previous position, to the formulation and execution of protest measures, and to the planning of meetings with groups from the United States and other reserves. Often, too, the chiefs concern themselves with decisions by the elected council and try to countermand them or at least to criticize them. Very little time is now spent in counseling the population and in solving individual problems. Since there is no possibility for the chiefs to lead the population through the action of the council, it seems quite natural to them to shift this aspect of their duty to the Longhouse and to claim that chiefs should "do the Longhouse speaking and exhort the people." For all practical purposes the current sessions of the hereditary council are displays of protest and delaying tactics against an inevitable encroachment of Canadian political methods. Alexander General himself laments: "When I am gone, and Joe Logan, and Dave Thomas, it [the hereditary council] will all fold up, as the young people are not interested in old Indian ways but read comics. We blame the white man; white civilization is getting the better of the Indian." He also admits that no one listens to the hereditary council, and he himself has to go to the elected council when he wishes land deeds transferred, etc. Nevertheless, the fact that the chiefs do not despair after 33 years of ineffectual monthly meetings, and still assemble in council, is some indication of the depth of feeling and the persistence of a pattern. This feeling is particularly strong among the older chiefs, who believe that their position was predestined and did not depend on their own willingness. Accepting a chieftainship is an onerous duty for which one has been designated by the Great Creator. Mr. General explained: "Chief installation is God-given." Deganawi'da? himself acted as he did through predestination, and his success was prophesied to his mother in a dream. Again, one notes a religious tone in speaking of the office, but in this case it is probably rather an old trait, since the theme of predestination for a position is very widespread in Iroquoian culture. The onerousness of leadership is also felt by the more responsible of the elected councilors, one of whom told me: "They twist you in knots in the council, no matter how good and true; it was a thankful day when I got out; I didn't know whom to face."

II. CONTENT OF THE ORTHODOX CULTURE

LONGHOUSE CEREMONIALS
THE LONGHOUSE AS A CONSERVATIVE INSTITUTION

SURVIVAL OF THE RITUALS

SIX Nations is not an isolated reserve, nor do the conservative members live in a section by themselves, but rather they are in continuous, first-hand contact with the carriers of the Canadian culture. Consequently, they have ample opportunity to observe countless Canadian artifacts and to be persuaded of Canadian values. The government also tries to have representatives visit each house to indoctrinate the inhabitants in the use of the Canadian hospital, sanitation, education, and financial aid. No description of the current culture at Six Nations would be accurate without including the contacts with and borrowings from the surrounding culture. The list of borrowed items, both ideological and material, which have been incorporated even into the Longhouse ritual and into the Longhouse complex is very long. A few examples in material culture are the use of lard for sunflower oil to anoint the masks, beef to replace deer meat, pork to replace bear meat, canned salmon and "store" bread to replace fish and Indian corn bread, nail polish as a reddening agent for red False Face masks, commercial varnish which makes a snow snake go much faster than does beeswax, and $500 steel caskets to replace the wooden burial boxes (which is especially revolutionary, since steel presumably weighs down the soul, and the corpse does not even wear a bobby pin, for the steel in the pin would impede his entry into the beyond and would weigh the soul to such a degree that it could not leave the body). In general, almost any modern artifact can be incorporated into the rituals without harmful effect to the ritual.

Every member at Six Nations realizes that the acculturative process is proceeding among them at a rapid rate, and they express this by phrases like "we are changing fast," "it is being modern that does it," "we are becoming like the whites," "we are going downhill," "it is going that way," and "we are getting poor" (meaning fewer people participate). A devout Longhouse follower says about the loss of the "Indian way of life": "When it's rotten and decayed and just ashes there, you can't do anything. You can't bring anything back that's decayed. In 20 years there won't be any reserve; we'll be like white people." But with this recognition there is a renewed effort to rationalize one's Longhouse position and to resist too radical an innovation even while incorporating unavoidable changes. The Longhouse leadership is not naive or unrealistic, for it realizes that the attraction of much of the white culture is irresistible, particularly in the material and economic sphere. Consequently, it emphasizes the ethical and philosophic aspects of "Indian ways." In the face of two ways of life, the Longhouse member is urged to keep "his way of life." He is reminded of the tradition each time he comes to the Longhouse or "carries out the appointed tasks." Ideologically, the incorporation of the new material artifacts does not affect the efficacy or the purpose of the ceremonials, and at the Longhouse the preachers and speakers explain what may and what may not be done. Thus, in the uneven and, to the outsider, irrational selectivity in borrowing and rejection of traits, the basic underlying pattern of the Longhouse ceremonials and of the Iroquoian world view is still maintained, at least in the eyes of the participants. They do, indeed, see themselves "slipping" and "losing," but still each group claims it "carries on" as best it can and perpetuates the old ways.

Looking at the phenomenon of the surviving Longhouse tradition from the outside, one cannot but agree with the verdict of the members that they do in fact "carry on in the old ways" despite the many changes which one can readily point out. Parker (1913: 15) already wondered about the apparent contradiction of the white social and economic order coupled with the Handsome Lake religion. The answer he received was in the same type of idealistic terms as the answers at Six Nations:

> Of these things we know nothing; we know only that the Great Ruler will care for us as long as we are faithful. . . . All these things (clothes, house, Longhouse) may be made of the white man's material but they are outside things. Our religion is not one of paint or feathers; it is a thing of the heart.

But both Parker (1913: 5) and Beauchamp (1907: 412) thought that the religion was fast dying out, and when one sees perhaps 10 or 12 people congregate for some agricultural rite, one wonders why, indeed, the pattern persists so long.

Particular curiosity has been expressed concerning the process of indoctrinating the younger members, since one can never perceive who is learning the ritual. This, more than the poor attendance (for at the Midwinter Ceremonies it is common to see 350 people assemble at each Longhouse at Six Nations, and the attendance figures today match those of Speck in 1933), has caused various observers to predict the end of the ceremonials. However, such pessimism is not quite justified, because usually several people have been in training all along, though they do not like to disclose this for fear they might be thought bold. There is a definite assumption that one is predestined to be able to memorize and understand the chants or to learn the songs, and boasting about such ability would offend those forces which endowed one. If one has the "gift of learning," then it is one's duty to exercise it, but modesty is at all times to be assumed. Clandestine acquisition of knowledge is a recognized pattern among the Iroquois, although this does not preclude being taught by "an old man" or going to singing-society meetings. Secret learning is related to the belief that learning should occur while listening to the elders or observing the performers, and in part it reflects patterns of respect for the elder ritualists and old men. Dave Thomas and Alexander General both claimed that they learned by sitting in the Longhouse and then practiced speaking each morning at sunrise, alone at home. If one has, indeed, learned a new set of songs or how to speak in the Longhouse, one must wait to be asked or coaxed. Volunteering is bad form and impudent. It is an honor to be asked, and at the first performance the individual is usually nervous and ill at ease.[1] These traits provide a partial explanation for the unobtrusiveness of the fledgling ritualists who will preserve the ceremonials for another generation. Although the elders are concerned with the waning interest of the younger members (whom they characterize as being interested only in "comicky books"), they make no systematic effort to recruit some of them to study the ritual. The younger members should "pick up," and when some speakers discuss the topic, they say, "Well, I had a rough time to 'pick up' what I know, and they must also struggle." However, the speakers often do exhort the congregation "to pay attention to pick up" and to go home and practice first thing in the morning. Regular speakers should take care to share the duties of speaking and performing (playing instruments and singing) with anyone whom they suspect of training. At any rate, in spite of the unsystematic character of the process of indoctrination, speakers and ritualists have usually been found in time of need, and both the recitation of the Code and the performance of the ceremonials have continued. Therefore, the observer should not be too surprised if there seems to be only one performer at some ceremony, and yet, after his death, the ceremony carries on as before. At Six Nations, for example, Bill Buck was the only singer able to perform the entire Gaihŏnda'dŏ cycle, although there were women singers to "absorb" the latter part of each phrase. (Women end the song which men begin.) But probably now that Mr. Buck has died, someone else will admit that he, too, can perform the songs. The Condolence Ceremony also seems forever on the verge of losing its last performer, but so far, one "last" ritualist has always appeared. Ernie Jamieson, for example, who was learning the Roll Call at his death, did so in secret, and his mother-in-law even kept his notebooks in secret.

THE LONGHOUSE IN THE LIFE OF THE INDIVIDUAL

So long as the culture survives in its present form, the life of the conservative member is tied into the Longhouse community. Aside from his economic pursuit, for almost no one receives enough remuneration from any religious or ritual activity to sustain a family,[2] the culture of the conservative member is influenced,

---

[1] For example, Bill Buck, who was one of the most accomplished singers of all Iroquoia, with a repertoire of thousands of songs, was extremely nervous and self-conscious at a Tutelo spirit-adoption ceremony in which he was the "helper" for the first time. He was not sure he would execute it without a mistake or without ridicule from the audience. A mistake at the Tutelo adoption ceremony is particularly dangerous to one's health.

[2] A very few ritualists, such as the singer Joshua (Bill) Buck, were able to subsist, more or less, from their ritual activity. Bill would be "kept" by various families, because it was realized that he was ritually invaluable. Ritualists are not usually paid, and their only remuneration is in the form of cloth, tobacco, wampum beads, and the food which is distributed at the end of feasts and ceremonies. Only lately some "gangs" of singers have started charging for their services. This mercenary attitude is condemned, since one should charge only the "whites" but not one's own people. In the case of Mr. Buck (who never was known to charge anyone), the family who "kept" him would have him do small errands, such as fetching water, looking after the house and chickens, and helping around the farm and kitchen. However,

if not dictated, by the Longhouse community, and particularly by the "home" Longhouse. From conception to death, the Longhouse prescribes religious, ethical, and philosophic rules. (The word "Longhouse" will sometimes be used to designate the building in which the rituals take place, but more often to designate a *functioning institution*. The latter sense is similar to the use of "the university" in a phrase like "the university has a policy. . . ." The informants themselves use both senses of the word "Longhouse," and the intended sense is always clear from the context.)

The calendric ceremonials of supplication and thanksgiving provide a periodic renewal of traditional activity, and the actual meetings to celebrate the agricultural festivities and obligations bring about a gathering of the conservative community. In this sense, the ceremonials provide a nucleus for the perpetuation of the old culture, for like-minded individuals come together as regularly as the seasons. They perform the customary routines requisite to the occasion, in which they either induce the crops to continue in their accustomed course or are thankful that their supplication has once again been heeded and all the powers have fulfilled their duties and have produced an ample harvest. Each item in the universe is carefully categorized, ordered, and mentioned; and an omission would certainly "hurt the feelings" of the neglected spirit force and bring recrimination in some undesirable, if not dangerous, form. Thus the very nature of the ceremonial has an element of stability, of continuity, and of preservation.

However, it is not only the nature of the ceremony which makes for a retention of the older culture, but also the fact that the performers meet together, discuss their ideas both about life at Six Nations in general and the particular ritual at hand, and feel drawn to each other in the carrying out of a venerable pattern among uncertain conditions and outside pressures. An in-group feeling is engendered, a feeling of "I am doing the right thing and pleasing the Great Creator no matter how much I am ridiculed by the rest of the Reserve." The Longhouse population feels particularly sensitive about any characterization of their religion as "pagan," which until recently was the standard designation by the census and the government. This the community perceives as an attitude repressive of their faith, and they are all the more spurred to consolidate their group and defy acculturative pressures.

Another factor in the retention of the ritual and the concomitant beliefs is that each ceremonial occasion is a proper and appropriate time to remind the population of their grievances and to urge them to hold to the old ways in spite of the encroaching civilization about them. Speakers exhort the congregation at great length on a multitude of practical subjects, ranging from appeals to the younger members to learn the ritual, so that it may neither change nor be lost, to claims that the

---

even he found it necessary to "work out" some summer months, in order to earn some cash with which to buy clothes, bus tickets, etc.

Preachers of the Code, when invited by a single Longhouse for a revival, are paid as a token, but the amount is only what can be collected by "passing the hat" at the end of a convention, which at Sour Springs in 1956, after three days, amounted to $17.00.

way to follow the teachings of Handsome Lake and of the Great Creator is to oppose the acquisition of television sets. For example, at a Midwinter closing meeting in 1955–56, when work things and playthings were returned to the congregation for use and enjoyment after the period of religious abstinence during the New Year proceedings, the speaker of the Wolf moiety, Grant General, added to the traditional speech:

> We Indians have just so much power, and we should be kind and love one another; and so, if you are able, fix up your home like your brother white man because your children will like it. But, I cannot say whether radio and television are good, because the Great Creator did not give these. "I cannot step over" [i.e., he, Grant General, did not have the authority to say whether these artifacts were good]. But if you can make your house as good as a white man's house it is good, and also be kind to your cattle.

Such speeches are considered "kind talk," as opposed to "talking rough," in which case the exhortations include commands to the younger members not to use lipstick, powder, high heels, bobbed hair, metal bobby pins, curls, or low-cut dresses; not to chew gum in the Longhouse (though tobacco chewing is permissible for both men and women); not to wear jeans in the Longhouse; not to dance, drink, or date in cars; not to use electricity, the radio, or television; and not to go to the surrounding high schools or work outside the Reserve. This complex of prohibitions is labeled by the more liberal members as "being strong Longhouse" and in general gives to some of the speakers a more "fundamentalist" flavor than one finds in the community as a whole. However, be the exhortation phrased mildly or positively, the ultimate purpose is the same, namely, to guard against the ever-present white influence and to hold the congregation as much as possible to the "old" way of life. How deeply the prohibitions against certain modern influences have penetrated is shown by one man's account of the painful death of his half sister. She saw men laughing at the window, and they said they were going to take her. Thereupon she said, "I'm going to leave you." The men said, "Take off your hair, take off your mouth." They were the devil. She tried to wipe her mouth and pull her hair, though she had neither lipstick nor curls. She evidently felt very guilty about having used both "instruments of the devil" during her lifetime. "Dying hard" due to guilt feelings about forbidden activity seems a standard pattern. At Six Nations many of the informants have said that their fathers or their mothers "raved" on their deathbeds and resisted dying, due to guilt about having used forbidden agents during their lifetime.

For the serious Longhouse member, who follows the precepts of the speakers and actually does not engage in any extra-Longhouse activity, the Longhouse also provides all the social entertainment he enjoys. Since association with outside clubs is forbidden, the tea meetings, the ball games, and the social dances at the Longhouse are the main sources of social satisfaction. Here the member meets similarly oriented comrades, and it is easy enough to see how the conversation would turn on subjects of the Longhouse.

Also, a most important feature of this in-group is the preservation of the Iroquois languages. English is almost never used in any official capacity in the Longhouse; the younger members will converse with each other in English, but even this is discouraged. Several languages are spoken at the various Longhouses, depending on the members and speakers, but Cayuga, Onondaga, and Seneca are by far the most common. Oneida is used only by a few Six Nations members, primarily immigrants from the Muncy reserve, and by visitors from Muncy. Mohawk is associated with the Christian element on the Reserve and, despite the fact that it is a going language on the Reserve as a whole, is not much represented in the Longhouse. At Sour Springs, however, where Mohawks have lately joined, speeches are often translated from Cayuga into Mohawk, for the benefit of those who do not understand Cayuga. Among the older Sour Springs members, however, there is a feeling of appropriateness about using Cayuga. As a result, one man, who is fluent only in Mohawk, refused a position as head deacon because, he said, "How would it look in the Longhouse if I spoke Mohawk?" Such inhibitions, however, do not affect singers, for songs may be sung in any language the singers feel proficient in.

Not only does the Longhouse provide religious and social satisfaction, but also the ethical and moral system of Handsome Lake has been intimately incorporated into the Longhouse calendar. At Green Corn, Midwinter, and Strawberry times especially, the teaching of the Code of Handsome Lake is a foremost aspect of the ritual. Code reciters are entertained and housed by the Longhouse community, and in general the same members follow the circuit of preaching as are interested in the older agricultural calendric rites. The two complexes are fused today, although the fusion is not a harmonious one. Many personal feasts, rites, and medicinal activities which were expressly forbidden by Handsome Lake are nevertheless performed both in the Longhouse itself and in the homes of the Longhouse members by the most devout of the Gaihwi'yo followers. Handsome Lake's prohibition is considered inoperative, for when he bade his followers to give up the medicine societies, no Indian tobacco was burned, which made the ritual act of "giving up" the society invalid. By virtue of this rationalization, the medicine societies are today a regular part of the Longhouse ceremonials despite Handsome Lake's injunction.

It is precisely in this realm of medicine societies and personal feasts that many of the ultimate sanctions supporting Longhouse attendance and culture retention are located. The most pressing fears of many of the orthodox community, and even of the more acculturated groups of the Reserve, are that one will be visited by "bad lucks," become ill, or even die on account of the neglect of, or insult to, the institutionally recognized supernatural forces. One must at all times guard oneself against such occurrences by taking active measures, which also are institutionalized, and which can be executed only with the help of specialists. Often the specialization is of a low degree, such as knowing how to cook corn soup, how to throw tobacco in a stove, or even just knowing of a fortuneteller who might be able to give the proper suggestions; but many of the members of the Reserve nevertheless feel that they themselves are unqualified to perform these tasks. Also, the person who needs the remedy should not, in general, apply it himself, but should "have it done."

Since these specialists are usually orthodox Longhouse members—if only because the cures make use of concepts, activities, and accoutrements which are linked with Longhouse ceremonials—the individual who shares these fears is dependent on the Longhouse. Thus, to many members of the Reserve the most important aspect of the Longhouse is that there exists a society in which the techniques and the knowledge of curative and prophylactic rites are still retained. Dependence on Longhouse personnel and ritual for the well-being of the individual stimulates attendance and interest in the Longhouse, and, simultaneously, through the retention of the Longhouse the medicinal and curative rites are preserved. Thus, each of these two aspects of the culture reinforces and helps maintain the other.

Since a conservative individual adopts so much from the ceremonials and the mores of the Longhouse for his daily behavior, and since most of the themes of life owe their conception to the Longhouse, it will be valuable to give a survey of the Longhouse calendar and activity, not so much with the intent of describing the rituals in their detail but to point out the over-all pattern of thought.

THE THANKSGIVING ADDRESS

The activities within the Longhouse belong essentially to three complexes: (1) the ethical, moral, and cosmological considerations embodied in the Code of Handsome Lake and in the apocryphal addenda recited simultaneously with the Code; (2) the supplication of, and thanksgiving to, the graded spirit forces; and (3) the activities concerning the health and well-being of the individual himself. This classification, while perhaps not so definitely formalized, is nevertheless recognized by the practicing member himself. As one member put it, he goes to the Longhouse because "it is our main body, our main meeting house. If I do what's right, it will take me to heaven when I die. It's really my church." But he also goes to the Longhouse "to pass the dances for the things that grow" and "to pass my dance."

There are some occasions which are specifically dedicated to the teachings of Handsome Lake and the moral and ethical concepts associated therewith, such as the Code recitals in the fall of the year or the small conventions of individual Longhouses held most commonly at Strawberry time or occasionally before the Midwinter Ceremony. There are other occasions dedicated primarily to one of the spirit forces, such as Green Corn, Bush Dance, and the Thunder Ceremony. There are still other occasions reserved for the welfare of the Longhouse member himself, at which the spirit forces minister especially to the human member, such as the days set aside at Midwinter on which the "pass dances" are performed. However, the majority of the ceremonies combine some aspects from all three of the complexes. There is no hard and fast line between attention to the Great Creator and attention to Handsome Lake, or even to the individual who is performing, although there is a recognition of the grading and ordering of these entities.

One must carefully distinguish, however, between Handsome Lake as the prophet and teacher of Gaihwi'yo, the moral and ethical mentor revered at the "conventions," and Handsome Lake as incorporated into the hierarchy of the spirit forces and existing as one of the spirits of the Upper Pantheon.[3] When Handsome Lake is referred to in the Thanksgiving Address, for example, he is not to be thought of as the prophet of the Code (although the Code is mentioned), but as one of the spirits. The same kind of distinction applies to human beings, for in one sense they are considered separately from the hierarchy of spirit forces and are the object of a separate complex of ceremonials, yet in other contexts man is simply one of the spirit forces on earth. The participant finds no inconsistency in the two treatments of Handsome Lake or in the two views of human beings. Every entity has its assignation and rank in the over-all ordering of the universe, and each also has its special sphere of action and attention.

Perhaps the best way to indicate the Iroquoian concept of the spirit forces is to examine the content of the Thanksgiving Address, which is the opening speech at almost any of the Longhouse meetings and at all of the religious gatherings. This address illustrates better than any other the organization of the Iroquoian world, as well as the relationships between the groups in the hierarchy. It is the repetition of this ordering, together with the "forewords" addressed to the gathering of human beings, which over and over again focuses the world for the listener. Many of the Longhouse speeches and tobacco-burning rites and medicine rites, as well as song cycles (e.g., the Great Feather Dance) are derivative from, or patterned after, the Thanksgiving Address.

The opening of the address concerns the uniting of many minds, or many people, in order to work together, and the thankfulness which attends such a gathering. This concept has become of paramount importance, for no amount of worship by the individual alone can be as effective as worship in which many people participate and help. Admonitions of "working together," "getting together," "helping" (by which is meant participating) are repeated at the beginning of almost every Longhouse speech. All society dances in the Longhouse and all dances to the Great Creator, the Four Angels, Handsome Lake, the Sky Pantheon, or the earthly sphere are considered more effective and more pleasing to the spirit forces when done by a large group rather than by a few people. Almost no curing ceremony, no cooperative bee, no singing society, no gathering of any kind, including social dances, at which the Longhouse membership is involved starts or ends without the invocation to "togetherness," and an exhortation to take part in the event. The introductory section of the Thanksgiving Address thanks the Creator for permitting the gathering, even as the people had gathered previously, without a loss to the nation, and it thanks the people for their participation. A synopsis[4] of Alexander General's version (according to his own translation) is as follows:

[3] Speck (1949: 29–33) has subdivided the hierarchy into three categories: the Upper Pantheon, the Lower Pantheon, and the Spirit Forces on Earth, of which mankind is a division. This is a convenient classification, which also is fairly explicit in the Iroquoian conception.

[4] Dr. Wallace Chafe has a literal translation of a Seneca version in press at the present time, which will add much valuable information to this sketch.

My relatives have conferred it upon me that I should speak some forewords to you. I am to speak on behalf of you people who have now gathered at this time of day, for which our Creator has given us this rule to express our thanks. First, we ourselves feel that we are all well and contented, and we have not heard of any sad incident to our people in this neighborhood. Therefore, we will greet each other that we are fortunate and everyone is well and contented, and we now unite our minds to greet each other that we have come together at this time of day.

The main body of the Address is the enumeration and invocation of the entities of the universe, beginning with the youngest and lowliest and proceeding to the oldest and most powerful and most respected. There is a standard pattern which limits the range and detail of the items mentioned, but the Address is flexible, and a good speaker will introduce as many specific themes or familiar traits as he can, or as he thinks the congregation will tolerate. Variations occur mainly after the "forewords," in the sections dealing with the earthly and heavenly spirits. A speaker may wish to impress the congregation with a particular series of spirits on particular occasions. For example, at agricultural ceremonies he may enumerate at length and in detail the various plants, foods, and perhaps water. Or a speaker may "take out certain words," which means that he may make use of a specific section of the Address out of context in order to make a point about the spirit forces involved. Mr. General thinks that "the higher up one goes in the Address, the more there is to do," that is, the more words should be addressed to the spirit forces; but this is more of an idealization than actual practice. The entire recitation usually takes approximately 25 minutes, but each speaker can vary the length according to his desire. Mr. General says that he always speaks the Address "fast," because "people get bored," but Bill Thomas, the speaker at Seneca Longhouse, says that he always uses the long version, "so that people will learn." When the Address is repeated at the end of the day's events, it is likely to be shortened drastically, and, in fact, usually consists merely of a short resumé in which each of the major categories of the hierarchy is briefly mentioned; even in this version the people are always thanked for their participation.

The first category enumerated consists of the things on earth.

Now we refer to our Mother Earth. He that created the universe, his wish was that the people that he created are to dwell on earth. His intention was that the people will enjoy it on earth.

Speakers then dwell on those things which grow or are found on earth (omitting human beings, however, even though they fit in the earthly sphere, because they have already been mentioned separately in the introduction). Special attention is given to such items as strawberries, maple trees, hickory trees, and medicinal plants, which play special roles in the Iroquoian culture. In Alexander General's version, the enumeration in this category begins with "grasses."

First, there were grasses of various kinds he has planted on earth. Some are to bear fruit which the people will benefit from. [Here are inserted references to strawberries, raspberries, etc., depending on the occasion.]

The grasses which bear fruit are already considered in a higher class than those which do not. Medicines, conceived as herbal and bush medicines, are mentioned next:

We now refer to another which he has planted on earth, the bushes that are growing. There are some of the bushes that also bear [fruit] for the people to benefit from. He has planted many bushes, some of which contain a medicinal. His intention when he planted these is that they help the people to regain their health. Should illness affect the people on earth, they shall use this medicinal for the purpose of regaining their health. It is thankful that his creation is still continuing to this day.

Mr. General then continues by describing the trees and forests:

And we also refer to the forest. There are many kinds of trees growing. There is one tree that has sap flowing from it, and we call it maple. His intention was that whenever the wind changes this tree will flow sap, and that the people will benefit in consuming this substance. [Hickory trees are also mentioned here, especially during the False Face ceremonial, for the hickory is the special familiar of the False Faces, and both the cane and the "face" itself are often fashioned from hickory. Fruit-bearing trees may also be mentioned here.]

Animals, especially wild and food-bearing animals, are enumerated next :

We now refer to the animals which he created. They are to roam on earth. Some of the animals would be for the purpose of sustenance for the people. From small animal to large animal, the purpose is that people benefit from them. It is thankful that we still see the animals roaming on earth for our benefit. We are thankful that his creation still continues.

Food is the next to be mentioned:

We now refer to our food, which he has planted on earth for our benefit. It was his intention when he gave his food, that the people will be responsible when they plant the seed. When it grows they shall attend to it, and when it comes into the ripe stage they will gather it and put it away for their sustenance when the weather is changed. It is thankful that this food has been planted for our benefit, and that his creation still continues to this day. [Particular foods will be mentioned here, according to the occasion. For instance, corn, beans, and squash—called the "Three Sisters" and also Dyõnhe'hgõ ("Our Life Supporters" or "Our Sustenance")—are all three mentioned at the ceremonies dedicated to the growth and testing of any one of them.]

Water on earth next holds the attention of the speaker:

We now refer to the water which the Great Spirit created when he created the earth. The earth should contain water for the benefit of the people. He made springs and streams and also the large bodies of water for the sole purpose that the people will benefit therefrom. So we now unite our minds to combine with the whole creation of the universe of our Mother Earth. We give thanks that all his creations still continue to this time. That is the number of words toward our Mother Earth. [At times fish may be inserted in the water section and mentioned as "traveling under the water," though Speck (1949: 30) lists fish before the forest. Speck also lists fire above water in the hierarchy, though Mr. General usually seems to omit fire, unless a very long version of the Address is given.]

Hereafter, the speaker turns his attention to the spirit forces above the earth. The Thunders are mentioned first and are designated as "Our Grandfathers" (ethi'hsot hadiwĕno′dagye?s). They are the heavenly counterparts of "Our Grandfathers," the False Faces (ethi′hsot hĕna′d?ui), who are relegated to the earthly sphere. Probably because many of the same traits are associated with the Thunderers and with the False Face Spirits, the two are viewed as manifestations, each in their respective realm, of identical spirits. One informant explained: "Our Maker has Thunder working, and Thunder never comes down to the people; while on earth, for the people, the False Face is working, and the False Face never goes up to heaven." Some of the identical traits of the Thunderers and the False Faces are that both are offered tobacco, both control windstorms, both are pictured as "old men" and are addressed as "Our Grandfathers," and both may cause disease and are the recipients of feasts. When one hears a clap of thunder, one should drop a pinch of Indian tobacco into the fire, to thank the Thunderers that they are heard once again traveling through the country. The tobacco helps send the human voice to the Thunderers, and is also pleasing as a gift. In summertime, when it is inconvenient to build a fire, the tobacco may be put on a stump outside. The invocation to Thunder is as follows:

We now refer to the spirit of Thunder, which the Great Spirit had ordained. He [Great spirit] has four appointees for the purpose of enforcing his duty to the creations of the universe. The duty of the Thunderers is to bring water to moisten the earth so all his plantations will grow. Even as the water refreshens we realize at this time, since the change in the weather, that they [Thunderers] still are continuing in their duty. It is thankful that their duty is still being continued to this day. We now unite our minds to thank the spirit of Thunder.[5]

Then other spirit forces of the Lower Pantheon are enumerated:

We now refer to Our Grandmother, the Moon. When he appointed her, he gave her the power to travel above where people could see her when there is darkness upon the earth. It was his intention when he appointed her that the people on earth would regulate their minds to know the number of days of the season, and also he has given her power to help force the growth of his plantation on earth. He has also given her power to control the birth of our children. So we realize, we see that she is still carrying on her duty to this day. We now unite our minds to give thanks to Our Grandmother, the Moon. [A reference to the stars may be combined with the section on the moon, though Mr. General usually gives a short version of this section which does not mention the stars. Speck (1949: 30) lists stars immediately below Thunder in the hierarchy.]

We now refer to our Great Brother, the Sun, who is our eldest brother. He was appointed to give light on earth. He (the Great Spirit) also gave him the power to warm the earth, so

---

[5] Another duty ascribed to the Thunderers, but not mentioned in the Thanksgiving Address, is to keep both the mythical and the real animals within their appointed realms, either above the sky or below the earth. The mythical animal kept above the sky is the "thunder bird," which builds its nest on the highest rocky mountain and which has "too much power" to land on earth. Were it ever to do so, it would injure the people. Below the ground, the Thunderers control magic snakes and the giant lizard. The natural animals which are controlled by the Thunderers are worms under the earth, wood ticks, mosquitoes, and injurious bugs. Were these not adequately controlled by the Thunderers, they would emerge to devour the population. [Interestingly, many of these mythical animals are identical with those mentioned in the songs which maintain the efficacy of the Little Water Medicine (see p. 285 *infra*).]

that his plantation will germinate. We see that he is doing his duty to this day, so we now unite our minds to express thanks to Our Brother, the Sun, that he is still carrying out his duty according to what he was appointed for by the Great Spirit.

Mr. General now turns to the Upper Pantheon, which consists of the supernatural and cosmological forces of the heavenly sphere. This section shows Christian influence more than any of the others, partly due to the Christian orientation of Handsome Lake and the Code, and partly due to the idiosyncrasies of the Sour Springs community, which attributes to Handsome Lake a particularly Christian origin. The first spirits mentioned are the Four Angels, or Dwellers of Heaven, appointed by the Great Creator to regulate the force of the winds. Speck (1949: 30–1) actually identifies them as Winds, but I could not corroborate this interpretation. Informants insist that "Angels are just like persons according to Handsome Lake," and they have no other connection with the wind than that they regulate the wind's velocity. However, this does not preclude a different, pre-Handsome Lake interpretation of them as Wind Spirits, particularly since four is the pattern number, and the wind is much feared in many contexts. Some informants also feel that the Angels should be mentioned above Handsome Lake, "good as he was," because they are not really people, as Handsome Lake explained, but stronger powers, and higher than Handsome Lake. Mr. General's version of this section of the Address is the following:

We now refer to his appointees, the Four People, who are Dwellers of Heaven. He has appointed them for the purpose of guarding the people on earth. As we realize that we are subject to being overtaken by misfortune at any moment, it is their duty to safeguard us in our everyday life. We also understand according to the message that we have received that they are within hearing of what we say. [The belief is that "the Four Angels watch all the time, and hear if one talks and whispers, every hour, minute, and second."] He [the Great Creator] has also given them power to regulate the current of wind to prevent causing injury to the people on earth. If the wind becomes too strong, the people on earth will suffer an injury, so it is their place to safeguard the current of wind. So we now unite our minds to give thanks to his appointees, the Four Dwellers of Heaven. So this will be in our minds, all those that are now present.

Handsome Lake is introduced next and is described in terms which show the influence of Christianity. [6]

[6] The Sour Springs Cayuga relate an origin legend about Handsome Lake which is obviously a composite of the Deganawi'da? legend, the gods, and Christian doctrine. Twelve children were born, and at the same time one was born of a virgin, and this child was called "He-Who-has-no-Father." This child taught all the others the four sacred rites (the Feather Dance, Skin Dance, Adō'wa, and Bowl Game) of the ceremonials. (Mr. General, in telling this story, says that this child was the same spirit as that one called Christ, whom he characterizes as "going toward the sunrise to preach to other people.") This was the first dispensation from the Great Creator, but after a while the people forgot these teachings, and therefore Deganawi'da? was sent to revive the teachings of the Great Spirit among the Iroquois. The teachings were obeyed until the people from overseas brought with them many evil things, and the people on this side of the water did not realize they were committing sins against the Great Spirit. Handsome Lake then received the message that they should repent of firewater (liquor), witchcraft, contraception, and social dancing.

We now refer to what has happened in later days. One of our own kind, Handsome Lake, was given the duty to preach to his people the wishes of the Great Spirit, which the angels had delivered to him. These are the words of the Great Spirit as to how the people should care for themselves. We understand that he had fulfilled these wishes during the time he preached to the people of the Longhouses, and we understand according to the Message of the Great Spirit delivered by him that those who will fulfill their duty shall receive a reward from the Great Spirit. When they depart from this world, they shall enter a place in heaven where the immortal souls will enjoy the hereafter. We now unite our minds to give thanks for the Message we have heard from his preaching, and we have no doubt that he has entered into heaven. Let this be in our minds, those that are now present.

Finally, the Great Creator is addressed, as the most revered, oldest, and most powerful of spirits, and again the influence of Christianity is evident. Mr. General says he never heard anyone explain the essence or substance of the Great Spirit. "We are the image of the Great Spirit, says Handsome Lake. I don't know why, it is too deep. We think of him as of parents; that's all there is to it." Another informant says: "Long ago people got help from Our Maker by supernatural powers, but because we don't trust and believe Our Maker we lose the power. We are also losing the power because we don't believe Handsome Lake as they used to. We read the Bible, which is an 'earthly' thing, and not from the Great Creator straight." One notices an amalgamation of ideas: the very Iroquoian ideas of "receiving power" from the spirit forces, including even the Great Creator, and of the hierarchal spheres; and the Christian concept of having "faith." Mr. General's invocation is as follows:

We now refer to the Creator of the universe, who has given us the mercy (hodēnida'ōnthraʔ) where the immortal soul will rest and enjoy hereafter, provided that we abide by his commandments. We now give thanks to the Great Spirit, that he has spared us to this day. Let this be in our minds, those that are now present.

One must not underestimate the importance of this Address, for the form and content are repeated by the speakers with near monotony. Each of the items is a familiar entity of the culture, which has been anthropomorphized and which demands respectful and "appropriate" conduct from the speaker. Furthermore, the Address is interpreted very literally, so that any query concerning the items mentioned will be answered by quoting the text of the Address. Conversely, any trait which occurs in the culture and is mentioned in the text, is justified from this text. Thus, for example, children are conceived in relation to the moon, "because it says so in the Thanksgiving Address and Our Maker made it so."

Furthermore, the formula used in the Thanksgiving Address, namely, mention of the item, note of its duty, recognition that the duty is still being performed, thanks for the fulfillment of this obligation by the item, and indication that some reciprocal action and recognition has been extended and will be extended, is also applied to countless cultural items not customarily included in the Thanksgiving Address. Thus, tobacco, wampum, the False Faces, and the animals of the animal societies are invoked and addressed in the same manner. Analogizing from one situation to another is a basic cultural mechanism among the Iroquois. When in doubt about the handling of any situation, one should always copy an analogous one and explain this to the spirit involved. Since each natural phenomenon is anthropomorphized and pictured as being created by the Creator with a certain duty and usefulness to man (if man only knew how to employ the item, or if man could only remember how to use the item beneficially), it is appropriate to use the same forms of supplication to all of them. The only crucial difference between phenomena is that some are more "particular," i.e., more dangerous and powerful, than others, and therefore must be accorded especially careful and respectful attention. As long as one renders unto the False Faces the things which are the False Faces' and to each spirit force the things which are his, man can live in harmony with the universe. Man cannot really control any of the spirit forces, but if they are acknowledged and thanked and treated with respect, even as the Thanksgiving Address indicates, then man need not fear, but can be assured of their assistance. The Great Creator is conceived of as especially benevolent, for the Thanksgiving Address repeatedly mentions that many of his creations are expressly intended to help mankind. In all relations with the universe, there is the element of mutual obligation and assistance between man and the Creator and the things which were made by the Creator, even as there is between moieties, between ritual friends, and among members of a family.

RITUALS OF THE AGRICULTURAL CALENDAR
The General Conception of the Calendric Rituals

In the main the calendric rites of the Longhouse are observed in order to recognize the spirit forces, to thank them for their activity on behalf of the human community, and to perform the ceremonies pleasing to them. In return the spirit forces will continue their duties for the benefit of mankind. Essentially, all spirit forces are viewed in the same way, and therefore the general conception of serving them is the same for all of them. Each spirit force recognized and celebrated at a ceremony has, indeed, a traditional set of rites which are appropriate—namely, specific dances, songs, and speeches—but the motivation for their execution and the expectation after their execution are common to all of them. For example, the only essential difference between the Green Bean and the Raspberry events at the Longhouse is that each is addressed to its respective spirit force. When a spirit force is addressed, the congregation partakes of the bounty of that force at the close of the ceremony. Consequently, at the end of the Raspberry Ceremony, raspberry juice is served; and at the end of the Green Bean Ceremony, green beans are served. The principle, however, is the same at both of these, as it is at all the other agricultural events, for in every case the food associated with the featured spirit force is served. For Corn Ceremonies corn is served, for Strawberry, strawberries, for False Face Day, False Face food, etc. The repetition of ideas and forms is an important factor in allowing the participant to become well acquainted with his culture. Since he may apply the same ideas and patterns in many contexts he remembers them, learns them, consolidates them, and finds the universe a coherent system. This is definitely a factor which aids the conservation of the Iroquoian culture and which ought not be underestimated.

It is true that many of the long song cycles and the long speeches depend on specialists for their performance, but if a specialist is not available at the time that the ritual is needed, then any substitute is acceptable. The efficacy of the ritual is in no way decreased by an abbreviated version of the ritual. On the contrary, the performer is admired for doing his best ("he's good stuff for trying") under difficult circumstances, and there is never any suspicion that the spirit force invoked might be "hurt," as long as a sincere effort has been made. There may be regret that "we're poor" (we do not know the ritual well), but there is no doubt that attention has been paid and the human part of the contract fulfilled. Most of the spirit forces are conceived of as being understanding and tolerant if conditions are explained to them in a respectful manner and if, out of inability or lack of knowledge, a performer is not as competent as he might be under ideal circumstances. Mistakes and omissions can be dangerous if they are not explained to a spirit force, but if some tobacco is offered after a mistake and an explanation is tendered, no ritualist need fear. This applies to the most competent as well as to the novice. There are degrees of care and respect which are due to various spirit forces, but in general the spirit forces of the agricultural cycle are not "dangerous" or "particular" in the way that those involved in curing, witching, and hunting magic are. One exception occurs in the Large Dead Feast, at which a slipping or falling of a participant is extremely serious and indicative of "bad luck" and disease. No antidote is known, and the misfortune is considered to be of the nature of an accident rather than to be a disregard of the spirit of the dead.

It has been pointed out earlier that flexibility in various institutions—in social structure, in the functions of the Longhouse officials, in moiety seating, and in the institution of the hereditary chiefs—has aided in the conservation of important parts of the aboriginal culture. The flexibility and range of allowable variation in the rituals are likewise essentially conservative in their effect. Within the general pattern of the ceremony there is a feeling of freedom of execution in which details may be changed, artifacts substituted, and personnel switched. There is an informality about all the Longhouse ceremonials which is describable as a "Low Church" feeling. Despite the organizational pattern of relaying messages to deacons, who in turn inform speakers, who in turn announce to the opposite moiety, there is much whispering, discussing, and adjudication during the performance. Rules are not rigid, and the minor details of the ritual—the positions of the speakers and performers, the order of dances, choice of songs, seating of participants, etc.—are constantly changing. Furthermore, since the idealistic content of any of the agricultural festivals is more important than the details of execution, the participant does not feel any great disappointment at a small turnout or an imperfect performance. It is better to perform at least part of the ritual than none at all, which would often be the case if perfection of execution were essential.

This informality and flexibility must be kept in mind when one reads the following description of the ceremonials, for there is always a range of allowable variation, even when it is not explicitly discussed. Unless otherwise specified, the descriptions are of the ceremonies at Sour Springs Longhouse.

Bush Dance

In the minds of the participants the first ceremony of the new ceremonial year is the Bush Dance (Dehadŏ′ni or ʔodehadŏ′ni, "Trees Standing"). It is celebrated either immediately following the Bowl Game at Midwinter time, if the game ended unusually quickly the morning of the first day of its performance, or within six to ten days following the completion of the Bowl Game. The usual occurrence today is that a week elapses between the Bowl Game and the Bush Dance, but in the not too distant past Sour Springs liked to perform the Bush Dance immediately after the Bowl Game (even if the Bowl Game lasted several days), because the congregation feared that a death might occur while awaiting the performance of the Bush Dance. In that case the event would have to be postponed for ten additional days, since no Longhouse events, other than the Midwinter Ceremony, may be scheduled until after the tenth-day feast of any deceased member of the Longhouse community. However, the rule now accepted is that the event may take place despite the death of a member of the congregation if the event had already been scheduled and announced. Thus, the Bush Dance is announced immediately after the Bowl Game and is held approximately one week later. At the Cayuga Longhouses women set this date; at Onondaga and Seneca Longhouses the men decide the exact day for the ceremony, though women are consulted.

In the literature, it has usually been supposed that the ceremonial year begins with the Midwinter Ceremony. This, however, is not accurate at Six Nations, where the participants look upon the Midwinter Ceremony as "winding up the year." Evidence for this attitude at Onondaga and Seneca is that the ritually responsible moiety ends its obligations at the end of the Midwinter Ceremony and transfers the initiative for action to the opposite moiety (see *supra*, p. 48). The Bush Dance, therefore, is the first event of the new season and is presided over by the moiety which will be the "leader" for that year, terminating its duties in turn with the completion of the Bowl Game and final Feather Dance at the next Midwinter Ceremony.

The primary purpose of this ceremony is to recognize the spirit forces connected with bushes and with trees, thank them for the latter's growth and aid to man, and express the wish that they may continue growing. The program and thoughts of the congregation are therefore directed to all those things which are connected with spirits of the "bush" and which would be both appropriate and pleasing to them. The items mentioned are those which are thought of as belonging to that complex which encompasses wood. Naturally, ashes and False Faces immediately come to mind and, indeed, are an integral part of the ritual. Balanced against this rather masculine interpretation of the event—the "bush" and False Faces usually being interpreted as falling into the male sphere—there is a secondary interpretation of the ceremony, namely, that it represents a food spirit celebration. Consequently, some informants designate the ceremony as Dyŏnhe′hgŏ ("Our Life Supporters" or "Our Sustenance"). Although the primary food spirits, the Three Sisters—corn, beans, and squash—are not specifically singled out for thanksgiving, some of the rituals performed at the Bush Dance are prominently associated with those occasions which are dedicated to the food spirits. The Husk Face rite, the Standing Quiver Dance (gʔadaʹthrot), and the Women's Dance (skaʹnye) at Sour Springs, and the Bowl Game at Onondaga and Seneca, are particularly notable for their agricultural associations. Also the fact that after Midwinter the Bush Dance is the first event scheduled and controlled by women adds to the identification of the event as a "food celebration," since "Our Life Supporters" are definitely in the realm of the women.

The ceremony opens with the Thanksgiving Address, and the speaker emphasizes bushes and trees of all kinds, mentioning some of them—especially hickory, maple, and poplar—by name, and giving thanks for the rising sap, the fruit, the medicine from the bushes, and even for the heat obtained from their growth (as firewood). Then the speaker from the opposite moiety explains to the congregation the reason for assembling, voices his thanks to the bushes and trees and their products, and announces the first event peculiar to the day. This is usually a Stirring Ashes song (ganahaʹowi), performed by one man who circles counterclockwise between the two stoves. The Stirring Ashes songs have "two different tunes," which means there are two variations of the basic pattern. There is the song which is reserved for the Great Creator and sung only as the last Stirring Ashes song at Midwinter, while the deacons stir, and which represents the "pass dance" of the Great Creator as he himself sings it; and there is the set of songs (approximately 30) which are sung by the "Uncles" and the people at the Stirring Ashes ritual at Midwinter. It is this last type which is employed here, and the singer may choose any one of this set which he knows. (At Sour Springs the singer is usually of the moiety opposite to the moiety of the speaker who announced the event; at Onondaga and Seneca Longhouses he is from the moiety which is ritually responsible during the new year.) The performance is not accompanied by any physical stirring of the ashes as at Midwinter. Since ashes are derivative from wood (and all ritual ashes are strictly wood ashes), the Stirring Ashes song is a particularly appropriate "pass dance" for the bushes. No speech accompanies the singing.

The Feather Dance (ohstowaʔgoʹwa or staʹoʔs) is performed next, and now all the congregation joins in "pleasing" the bushes. The songs for the dance should be chosen from that group of Feather Dance songs[7] which mentions the earth, bushes,

[7] Each performer "has" his own set of songs, and there is considerable variation between the sets. The following is the Feather Dance set as learned and performed by the late Joshua (Bill) Buck, who was one of the most noted Iroquoian singers both in the United States and in Canada. This particular set is in Seneca and was reported by Bill Buck in 1953. Each number represents one song; those with no title consist of burden syllables. A slow beat starts the series:

(1–4) Four songs with burden syllables. The fast beat begins. (5–14) Ten songs with burden syllables. (15) Earth. (16) Thanks for nice day. (17) Grass grows. (18) Medicine grows. (19) Food. (20) Birds. (21) Deer. (22) Wind. (23) Flowers. (24) Forests. (25) Slow beat, burden syllables only. (26) Bushes. (27) Creeks. (28) Large bodies of water. (29) Maple trees. (30) Sap. (31) Maple sugar. (32) Strawberries. (33) Raspberries. (34) Cherries. (35) Blackberries. (36) Peaches. (37) Slow beat, burden syllables only. (38–52) Fifteen songs with burden syllables

trees, medicines, sap, etc., that is, from the earthly set of songs. In the Feather Dance, one performer from each moiety takes his seat in the center of the house, straddling a bench which is equipped with added boards as reinforcement for absorbing the shock of the turtle rattle. The performers take turns choosing and initiating the songs, and they can control the speed and length of the set. Usually, the first few songs are slow, and as the congregation gains momentum and gaiety, the rhythms are speeded up. The speakers always announce both the musicians and the leading person of the dancers before each event. This is a standard rule. (For a description of this dance, as well as of most of the common Longhouse dances, see Kurath, 1951, and Fenton, 1942; for a description of the singing tools see Conklin, H. C., and W. C. Sturtevant, 1953.) After approximately 20 minutes of dancing, the speaker announces the dyōhsiʔdahdi′has songs. These are the same songs as the False Face songs (though some informants at Sour Springs claim that when they sing dyōhsiʔdahdi′has, they change the four songs slightly) but sung "dry pole," which means that the performers are not masked, that no False Face food (corn mush) is served to them, and that the instrument used to accompany the singer need not be a large turtle rattle but merely a piece of wood. Anyone, male or female, may perform, but the single singer and the leading dancer ought to be members of the False Face Society. After four songs the event is over, and the appropriate speaker announces the Standing Quiver (gʔada′throt) cycle, which is the "dry-pole" dance of the Husk Face Society; as Husk Faces are intimately associated with False Faces, the sequence is very logical. In most ceremonies in which masks are worn, a Husk Face immediately precedes the False Faces and announces them, but here in the unmasked performance in which the Husk Face does

---

only. (53) Song from Heaven. (54) Song from Heaven: Feather Dance going on now. (55) Deacons arriving now. (56) Deacons working now for the Great Creator. (57) Deacons are dancing now. (58) Everybody gathering now for the ceremony. (59) Everybody dancing now. (60) Children are coming. (61) Children dancing now. (62) Children who have names. (63) Slow beat, song has burden syllables only. (64) Everybody is running now. (65) We two are sitting at the middle bench singing. (66) Slow beat, with song meaning that our songs came from heaven. Fast beat again. (67) Great Creator taught us the songs. (68) Great Creator gave us the ceremony. (69) We must do it. (70) Thunder. (71) Sun. (72) Moon. (73) Stars. (74) Four Messengers. (75) Handsome Lake. (76) Handsome Lake gone back to heaven. (77) We must follow his tracks. (78) Flowers on the pathway to heaven. (79) To resting place. (80) Pretty place to the well. (81) That is where you see all your relatives. (82) You will see your father in heaven. (83) You will see your mother in heaven. (84) You will see your brother in heaven. (85) You will see your sister in heaven. (86) Those who repent, shall see my home. (87) Those who didn't repent, I feel sorry [for]. (88) So I shall hold my arms out. (89) Then I'll think they are following me. (90–92) Mr. Buck combines these last three songs into one long song. The translations are: "Rising water coming from under the earth. She is running in the middle of the house and doesn't know where to go. She is not laughing and she goes out."

There are further burden syllable songs, so that Mr. Buck's complete set consists of 155 songs, although he did not indicate where the remaining songs are fitted into the set. One can see the similarity to the Thanksgiving Address, for the Feather Dance set incorporates the same hierarchy with only minor changes of order. It also incorporates many ideas from the Code of Handsome Lake.

not precede the False Faces, the Husk Face Spirit is recognized only after its more powerful companion, the False Face. The performance is "dry-pole," which again means that no masks are employed, no corn paddles are carried, and no food is served to the performers. The Standing Quiver Dance is a round dance, having a leader who accompanies the singing with a cow-horn rattle and who initiates the songs, to be answered by the chorus of followers.

Then Sour Springs and Lower Cayuga perform the Eagle Dance (though this is omitted at Onondaga and Seneca). But this time the performance is not "dry-pole," for the Eagle dancers are rewarded with the traditional foods: maple sugar bits, apple bits, doughnuts, and sugar cookies. The latter are simple cookies made of wheat flour, eggs, lard, milk, sugar, baking powder, and salt. The Eagle Dance is danced for the poplar trees (onrahdōnda'hsra), for "the poplar leaves are always shaking," even as the eagle is never at rest in the Eagle Dance. Again the program is rationalized and explained by an analogy; an explanation is important, since many members are skeptical of the inclusion of the Eagle Dance, which in an unfamiliar situation is often associated with tjinhgē'da (the hunting and witching patterns). At Lower Cayuga, Onondaga, and Seneca there is a short Bowl Game, using 15 to 25 beans and performed by male versus female contestants, even as in the Corn Planting Ceremony. At Sour Springs the Women's Dance finishes the events. The speaker then repeats the Thanksgiving Address.

Even as the speaker is "finishing up," the deacons divide the food and bring in the hot cauldron of roasted corn mush. The food appropriate to the occasion is the False Face mush,[8] cookies (both traditional and modern), bread, apples, and the usual "feast foods" of doughnuts, corn bread, scones, etc. After the distribution of food, speakers may make any announcements they wish, and then the congregation goes home, leaving a few deacons to clean up.

The provision of individual items is never assigned to individual people, since there is a feeling that "the Great Creator will see to it that all will be provided," and also that the congregation knows its duties and the deaconesses will think of the necessary ingredients. Despite the Iroquoian reputation for "organization," I find this fluidity and indefiniteness very characteristic of Six Nations behavior.

The Bush Dance is definitely one of the ceremonies which concerns itself with

[8] False Face mush is made of roasted white-corn flour. One takes large white corn, roasts it in the oven till brown, and then takes it out to be pounded in the large wooden mortar (colloquially called pound-block) with the characteristic Iroquoian double-ended pestles. At Six Nations the preferred materials for the mortar are beech, oak, and maple; and for the pestle, beech and soft maple. After pounding, the mixture is sifted, and then pounded and sifted repeatedly, using a fine wire sieve (though a fine black-oak basket was once used), until there is only flour. Some women now use modern meat grinders, thus saving time, but then they feel slightly guilty at not having made "real Indian" mush. The flour is then taken to the Longhouse, where it is added to boiling water, and lard and brown sugar are added. The proportions are a little less than one-half pound of flour to two quarts of water, though the deaconesses do not measure but taste and judge as they go along. Several pounds of lard are used for a large cauldron of mush at Sour Springs. At one time maple-sugar shavings were used instead of commercial sugar, and leavings from meat and bacon were added to the mush.

"passing" the dances for the spirit forces, and it is not considered appropriate either to pass any curing dances for the people or to preach any of Gaihwi'yo. The mood of the congregation is mainly one of thankfulness rather than of supplication, although the wish that the trees continue to grow is uttered. Incidentally, it is believed that when the people dance on earth for the spirit forces, the spirit forces dance with them in their own realm, usually conceived of as "heaven."

MAPLE DANCE

Since maple trees are always "covered" in the Bush Dance, and since very few families on the upper Reserve collect maple sap today, Sour Springs Longhouse does not now celebrate the running of the maple sap, nor has it done so for many years. At Onondaga and Seneca, however, the first running of the maple sap is always celebrated in the Longhouse, and at times there is a second ceremony at the end of the maple sugar making. The first event is entitled Hadičhistŏ'ndas, which is sometimes interpreted as "putting syrup in" and sometimes as "time to tap." Its date may vary from mid-March to mid-April; at Onondaga, in 1954, for example, it occurred on April 4. The congregation is informed of the date by messengers from each moiety, who "go around." The second ceremony, called Hadiyŏnda'thahtha? ("drying of the logs"), takes place at the end of the sap-running period. The False Face Ceremony may at times intervene between the two Maple Ceremonies.

The purpose of the Maple Ceremonies is to give thanks for the recurrence of the sap runs and to ask for their continuation. Also, other trees and bushes are mentioned with thanks once again for their usefulness to man. It is of course the spirit force of the trees, and not the actual trees, which is addressed.

The program once practiced at Sour Springs, before the ceremony became obsolete, is said to have included a tobacco-burning invocation to the tree spirits at the men's stove and two sets of the Feather Dance (most probably those relative to the Earth Pantheon and to bushes in particular), with a passing of maple sap to the individual members of the congregation between these two sets of the Feather Dance. The procedure of this event was that two male deacons, one from each moiety, circled the Longhouse (the Wolf deacon on the Turtle side and the Turtle deacon on the Wolf side) in a counterclockwise direction, dipping some maple sap with a dipper from a pail which they carried and handing it to the members. Before taking a drink, each person addressed himself softly to the sap in the dipper and thanked the Great Creator and the Maple Tree Spirit that once again he may taste the sap. The member then drank the contents of the dipper, and the deacon passed on to the next member, until each had paid his personal tribute. The deacons who passed the sap took their turns after having performed their duty. The sap itself was not considered to be sanctified or sacramental, but merely was a first-fruits symbol of the recurrent rising of the sap, and it made concrete to the worshiper the object of worship. This is a standard pattern, for a similar ceremony occurs at the Raspberry and Strawberry Festivals, where a water and fruit-juice drink is passed in the same manner. At Sour Springs there is continual discussion about whether the deacons ought to hand the members the dipper filled with sap or whether the member should dip into the pail himself. The same discussion occurs in regard to the passing of food in the Longhouse. No agreement is ever reached, and both methods are employed. The significance of taking the food oneself is that it is then considered to have come straight from the Great Creator (and one never gives thanks for food in the Longhouse by saying the otherwise customary "nya'wĕh"); whereas, if the food is handed by the deacon to the recipient, there is an implication that the deacon, or the "sponsor" of the ceremony, gives the food. The latter procedure is customary at curing feasts held by families, where the food is handed to the participants by the individual responsible for running the affair. After the sap was tasted the dyŏhsi?dahdi'has set was sung, this time because it honors "hickory"—and the stick of the False Face men, which are associated with this set of songs, is made of hickory. Then the Standing Quiver Dance was performed, and finally the speaker ended the meeting with the Thanksgiving Address, paying particular attention once more to the maple and the other trees and bushes. The food served was flint-corn[9] soup sweetened with maple syrup rather than sugar. One informant thought that at Sour Springs the appropriate dish had been roasted white-corn soup sweetened with maple syrup, but the majority believed that the appropriate food was sweetened cracked-blue-flint-corn soup, as is the case at Onondaga and Seneca today.

At Onondaga and Seneca much the same program is followed today, except that a short Bowl Game is included, as at the Bush Dance. At the second Maple celebration the program is repeated, except that no sap is passed, and the members used to bring lumps of maple sugar.[10] The usual Longhouse feast foods are also contributed—cookies, scones, doughnuts, white bread, corn bread, etc.

The character of the Maple Ceremony is again one of thanksgiving to a food

[9] The method of preparing flint corn is as follows: Take shelled flint corn and place in lukewarm water for a few minutes. Take it to the pound-block and pound for a few minutes. Place it in a basket sieve (with apertures about one-eighth to one-fourth inch) and sift. Repound what is left in the sieve, and repeat about three or four times. When all material has passed through the basket sieve, sift through a fine metal sieve (once a fine basket) to take out the flour. Place the remainder in a dish and shake with a slight rotary motion to fluff off the hulls. (Feed the hulls to pigs or chickens.) If one would like to make flint-corn soup with a modern food chopper, the procedure is to boil the corn in wood ashes and water until the hulls come off; then the corn is taken to the creek in the corn basket, or else simply washed and drained and placed in the chopper. The flour and cracked corn are taken to the Longhouse unmixed, where the corn is placed in boiling water and allowed to cook until almost done, at which point the flour is added as thickening, and then the maple syrup is added as sweetening. Red beans may also be added at times.

[10] The procedure of making maple sugar is as follows: At one time, at Six Nations, the spiles hammered into the maple trees were birch and basswood wedges. A cut above the wedge allowed the sap to flow into wooden troughs. Today commercial metal spiles are inserted, and a jar or pail is hung on them. The collected sap is boiled until it forms syrup, but to render sugar some fat pork is usually added, which supposedly takes the bitterness out. When the boiling is finished, the meat is taken out and the gritty syrup is poured into a greased pan. The next morning one has sugar blocks, which are cut into pieces and taken to the Longhouse.

spirit, coupled with a supplication for the continuation of the food. Personal curing is not usual, nor is the preaching of the Gaihwi'yo.

FALSE FACE CEREMONY

The False Face Ceremony, which occurs next on the calendar, is called ?ethi'hsot hēna'd?ui ?athēnada'wēnye? ("grandfathers hunchback they travel," or in the colloquial English of the Reserve, "the False Faces are traveling").

The scheduling of this event is assigned to the two False Face Society leaders of the Longhouse, one from each moiety. The Canadian False Face Societies, unlike those at the Seneca reservations in the United States, are headed at present by men. The leaders in the False Face Society at Sour Springs in 1958 were Ernie Davis for the Turtle moiety and Willie John for the Wolf moiety. They were appointed by the men of the Longhouse, and neither inherited the position from a member of his family. The moiety division of the False Face Society is often questioned, and there is some confusion as to its propriety. The traveling bands of False Faces at Onondaga and Seneca and the company at Sour Springs Longhouse are not divided according to a moiety arrangement, nor is there moiety division in the False Face Day curing ceremony or in the private curing ceremonies at Six Nations. Informants claim, "The False Faces have no clans." Nevertheless, there is a Turtle and a Wolf False Face "headman," and at the Midwinter curing the patient is treated by False Faces belonging to the opposite moiety.

Tradition dictates that the event should occur when the ground is dry in early spring, and consequently at Sour Springs it is in the latter part of April. The rationalization which is now adduced to explain why the ground should be dry is that the False Faces should "roll" into the Longhouse on the ground, since they are the earthly counterpart of the Thunder Spirit which "rolls" in heaven; and since the False Faces are thus forced to move on the ground, they should not have to do so on wet ground. Again one notices the tendency to analogize on any level, as well as the search for rationalization and explanation. At Seneca and Onondaga, however, the False Face Ceremony usually takes place at the end of March, before most of the men leave for spring seasonal work, and often the False Faces "go around" when the ground is wet with mud and snow.

The two False Face leaders should "go around" and inform the members of their Longhouse of the date of the False Face event. At Sour Springs the messenger will be given some Indian tobacco "for the False Faces" at each household, and it is this tobacco which is burned at the Longhouse at the tobacco invocation. Today, no False Faces "travel" at the upper end, which means that the band of masked society members does not visit the houses of the Longhouse members in order to chase away disease from the house, and the False Faces visit only the Longhouse itself during the day of the ceremony. The reason for neglecting the "traveling rite" is that too many Christians live interspersed among the Sour Springs community, and the company would have to visit widely scattered farmsteads, most of whose owners would be away working. Therefore, at Sour Springs, the Longhouse is considered the "home" of each member at this event, so that symbolically the home of each one has been cleansed of disease as surely as if the False Faces had visited the actual house. At the three Longhouse communities down below, however, the traveling rite still persists, and the tobacco, instead of being given to the messenger as at Sour Springs, is given to the leader of the traveling "gang" when the False Faces purify the house. The Longhouse ceremony takes place in the afternoon, usually around 4:00 P.M., although it should really occur around noon. The "traveling rite" usually starts around 2:00 P.M., and the False Faces will often go from house to house by car. The rite of the "traveling" is traditional. For example, at Onondaga Longhouse in 1955, one band of False Faces "went around." Bill Sherry (actually a member of Seneca Longhouse) was the leader, and the tour started at his house on the River Road. The band then came westward on the River Road to Tom Longboat's Corner, up the Onondaga Longhouse side road to the Seneca Line, where they visited Mrs. Smoke and Betsy Sky, and then up to Violet and Bill Thomas and from there into the Longhouse. Members living farther away than the points on this route were missed. A typical False Face visit at a home begins with the entrance of an unmasked leader of the group, carrying a staff (the symbol of the False Faces), preferably made of hickory, and a corn-bread paddle (the symbol of the Husk Faces). Immediately following this leader, several Husk Faces (gadji'hsa?) tumble in, dancing about and hopping from toe to toe. They carry sticks and branches and corn-bread paddles and perform their characteristic dance, as the leader sings for them briefly. Then the four False Face songs are sung, and the False Faces roll in on the floor, dancing and mimicking and rubbing their rattles along the furnishings of the house. (The center of the room has been cleared to permit the dancing of the visitors.) Much of the dance and the antics are left to spontaneous action, and there is much personal variation in the performance of the False Face dancers. At the end of the purification of the house, the leader is handed a package of Indian tobacco, usually wrapped in brown paper. The False Faces emit joyous grunts of satisfaction, and gesticulating wildly, they leave the house.

The primary purposes of the False Face Ceremony are to pay respects to the False Face Spirits (which are the earthly counterpart of the Thunder Spirit), to placate them with tobacco, and to ask that they in return disperse all diseases for the coming season and control the whirlwinds and other crop-destroying winds. The chasing of disease applies not only to illness of the human body but also to the diseases which attack livestock, plants, and foods. Thus, the False Face Ceremony combines personal curing, agricultural prophylaxis, and spirit supplication.

The program at Sour Springs Longhouse begins with the Thanksgiving Address, after which there usually is an anxious, hushed waiting period, while the maskers finish dressing in the cookhouse. The masks to be used have been rubbed with lard (in lieu of the traditional sunflower seed oil) in order to have them look shiny and new (to "brighten them up"), and also to indicate to the False Face that "it is being taken care of." Rubbing with lard is partly an aesthetic and secular act, done to clean the mask and "make it look good." It also indicates that the owner is careful of, and respectful to, the mask. Since neglect of the act would "hurt the feelings" of the "Face," and in revenge the "Face" would make the owner ill, it could be termed a prophylactic medicinal action. The rubber, however, thinks of the lard as a beautifying agent. The fear of disease is the almost subconscious sanction which underlies not only the attentions to the mask, but most of the ritual.

Suddenly the door opens, and a Husk Face (male or female) runs through the house, entering at the women's door and exiting at the men's, sometimes re-entering at the men's door and exiting then at the women's door. The Husk Face is masked and dressed so as to hide the identity of the performer. The Husk Faces are dumb, and therefore they say nothing, but they must never keep still, and consequently they "wiggle" as they rush through "the house." After an appropriate pause, the gutteral whinnies of the False Face language will be heard outside the women's door, and the unmasked leader of the False Face group (False Faces from both moieties being combined into one group) pushes open the door with his hickory staff and sings the entering song of the False Faces, which belongs to the Stirring Ashes genre and is almost identical to the Stirring Ashes Song sung for the Great Creator at the beginning of the Midwinter Stirring Ashes Ceremony. The masked False Faces, always males, covered over with burlap sacking and carrying large turtle rattles, roll and tumble into the house over the sill of the women's door, go around the house counterclockwise, and lie down beside the men's stove. A considerable amount of clowning, gesticulating, rattle shaking, grunting, ash rubbing, and handling of hot coals from the stove precedes the settling down of the "Faces." Whereas an air of gaiety prevails at all the Longhouses, the False Face antics at Sour Springs seem much more solemn than at Onondaga, nor do the False Faces distract attention from the tobacco-burning invocation as they do at Onondaga, where they continue to clown throughout the invocation. At Sour Springs any False Face mask may be worn, and the distinctions of "doorkeeper" and "common" and "beggar" masks are not known. (Only one mask was recently forbidden—"taken off"—at Sour Springs, because it looked like the work of the devil and was evil and "made fun of the Longhouse." This was a mask carved by a church member, and it displayed two horns.) There is no doorkeeper at Sour Springs as there is among the New York Seneca (Fenton, 1940: 420, 427, and Parker, 1913: 127), for none of the Longhouses at Six Nations has an indigenous doorkeeper concept. However, at Onondaga, in 1955, a member who had originally come to Six Nations from Tonawanda appointed himself "doorkeeper." The doorkeeper is supposed to prevent any member from leaving the Longhouse during the tobacco invocation and the purification of the Longhouse and people. He also rubs the door with his rattle each time a latecomer opens it to enter the Longhouse, as if to disinfect it again after allowing some disease agent to enter through the opened door.

Any able speaker may perform the tobacco-burning rite, and the designated person, who is announced to the congregation, is handed the tobacco collected by the False Face leaders on their rounds to the houses. The speaker steps to the men's stove and recites the speech in which tobacco is offered to all those items in any way connected with the False Faces. The speaker reminds the False Faces of their promise to the Great Creator to protect the people, to drive away disease, and to control high winds. He offers tobacco for each attribute and asks that the spirits should still continue to fulfill their promise. Tobacco is offered also so that thunder and lightning may not strike and that the wild beasts above the clouds and the snakes and vermin below the ground will continue to be controlled. Then the speaker offers tobacco to the bush, to the trees (usually hickory) from which the staff of the False Face is cut, to the living trees which provide the material for the Faces, to the turtle rattles which are the property of the False Face men, to the tobacco which is the favorite of the False Faces, to the mush which is the food of the False Faces, to the fire and ashes which help cure, and to the Husk Face which is the messenger of the False Faces. As each item is mentioned, a pinch of tobacco is thrown into the fire. Also, at the mention of the rattles, hickory, and tobacco, the masked impersonators respond by rubbing their rattles on the ground, talking False Face language, and in general showing their pleasure at the gift of tobacco by "getting mad" (which means becoming joyously agitated). Those sections of the recitation which pertain to the False Faces themselves and the accoutrements of the False Faces are recited twice, once for the Black False Faces and then for the Red False Faces. The two categories of Faces are seen as separate groups of personalities. At the end of the invocation a pinch of tobacco is handed to each of the maskers. They smell it, blow it as in curings, rub it between their hands, place some in their pipes if they happen to be carrying them, snuff it, and throw it into the stove. The speaker finishes by burning the remainder of the tobacco and its container, usually a brown paper bag.

Two men then take their seats in the center of the house and play the four False Face tunes, to which the False Faces execute their characteristic dance. This set is played with a large turtle rattle, though not as large as those carried by the maskers. At Sour Springs the set is then repeated using only a wooden beater. (This seems to occur only at Sour Springs Longhouse. George Green made the wooden beater, which most probably is a corn-bread paddle used only for this occasion and stored in the Longhouse.)[11] Thereafter a single man sings for the Husk Faces' dance, using a corn paddle or wooden stick, and the Husk Faces perform their antics. The set of False Face dry-pole songs (dyōhsiʔdahdi'has) is sung, again, according to my informants at Sour Springs, using the wooden beater. The False Faces now rush around the inside of the house counterclockwise, chasing all the participants off their seats, touching and rubbing the benches, appurtenances, corners, and floor with their rattles, for this symbolizes the "chasing of the disease." In their act of purification the False Faces may take liberties—jostling the girls, poking the matrons, uttering False Face cries close to the more nervous of the congregation, and in general "making an impression" on the population. The "proper" attitude toward

[11] Dr. Wm. C. Sturtevant has reported that at Newtown a special wooden beater is kept at the Longhouse, which is restricted to use in False Face Society dances.

the False Faces in the Longhouse is to be frightened, and even if one is not actually frightened, one must pretend to be afraid and mention that one finds the False Faces fierce looking and "scary." (Fenton, 1940: 428–9, cites an instance encountered by Margaret Mead, in which a sophisticated woman of Shawnee-Cayuga parentage, now residing among the Omaha, remembers with dread the False Face experiences of her early childhood.) Most of the children at Six Nations will state their fear of the False Faces, although they will sing the songs and play with the masks when given a chance. Whereas one must at all times display respect for the masks, in Canada they need not be hung facing the wall or covered with a cloth. "Faces" are personified, and individuals, despite their fear, become as much attached to their masks as to friends.

The entire membership is forced to participate in the round dance around the two stoves, which consists merely of walking around the two stoves in single file, men preceding women, in a counterclockwise direction. Then the False Faces run out, using both doors. Ideally, the maskers should remain anonymous and unrecognized, but in fact everyone tries to figure out "who is dancing." The masks are recognized and discussion as to who looks "funny" in whose borrowed mask is one of the gaieties of the ceremony. It will be discussed for days, as will the general antics of the performers. False Face Day is perhaps the favorite ceremony of the general population; it certainly is the most exciting visually and the gayest, and consequently is most prominently recommended to the visitor.

Should any individual wish a cure of some specific illness or prophylaxis against future illness or a renewal of a cure, the False Faces are called back into the Longhouse for special ministration. All the cures must be accompanied by separate offerings of roasted mush and cookies to the False Faces; and corn bread, sugared grease bread, cookies, and unroasted mush to the Husk Faces, if they are asked to perform. These foods must have been prepared or secured by the patient over and above the share which is brought to the Longhouse for the general distribution of food. The offering is given to the performers immediately after their efforts at the personal cure, and is shared only by the patient and not by the rest of the congregation. This food represents not only the "payment" and the symbol of attention to the False Face Spirit, but is also "part of the medicine." No dry-pole curing may be held at the False Face Ceremony.

Finally, the communal food is distributed—False Face mush (the same roasted-white-corn mush as at the Bush Dance), cookies, scones, corn bread, bread, etc. The passing of cleansing medicinal drinks, as in the United States, is not known at Six Nations. The usual procedure of distribution is followed, and the False Face impersonators receive a share along with the rest of the congregation, for they have unmasked in the meantime and have mingled with the congregation.

At Sour Springs the False Face Ceremony is thus a mixture of general dispersion of disease, supplication of the False Face Spirits, supplication for a propitious growing season unharmed by winds, and curing of the individual himself. At Onondaga and Seneca the personal curing does not occur in the Longhouse, but those who are found unwell at their homes can be treated there.

A brief summary of the ritual at Onondaga—which is slightly different from the ceremony at Sour Springs—is as follows (data from March 29, 1955): Josie Logan announced the program to the congregation. Roy Buck gave a short version of the Thanksgiving Address. The False Faces peeked in the door and closed it again. Finally, after the Address was finished, the leader, Bill Sherry, entered followed by the Husk Faces and the False Faces. He walked toward the right singing the Stirring Ashes-type False Face song, and then seated himself in the center of the house on the players' bench and sang the Husk Face songs, accompanying himself with a corn-bread paddle. The Husk Faces danced, and were followed by the dance of the False Faces, whose song was also sung by Bill Sherry, again using the corn-bread paddle. Josie Logan then announced that Roy Buck would give the tobacco invocation, which he delivered at the men's stove. (At Onondaga, as at Sour Springs, moiety considerations do not determine roles during False Face Day.) The tobacco invocation lasted 20 minutes, during which time the False Faces continued clowning. Bill Buck's mask was conspicuous for its large nose, which was repeatedly blown with a remarkably white handkerchief. The Husk Faces flitted around fighting with the False Faces and teasing and poking them. The False Faces wiped their metal eyes, pulled their hair, brushed their teeth, teased the populace, puffed on pipes, and indicated pleasure at each offering of tobacco to them and to their accoutrements. At the end of the invocation, Bill Sherry gave each masker some tobacco, distributing it counterclockwise, which the pipe-smoking False Faces smoked and the rest burned in the stove (only the men's stove was lit). Jake Henry then sat at the center bench, facing the women, and with a corn-bread paddle sang first the Husk Face songs, to which the Husk Faces danced, and then the False Face songs. Both sets of maskers danced counterclockwise around the stoves and, at the repetition of the songs, chased the populace from the benches to participate in the dance. Bill Sherry led, followed by Roy Buck, and then by Josie Logan. The False Faces continued to "rub down" the building with their rattles and to finish the purification. Then they ran out to change. Roy Buck "finished up" with a one- to two-minute version of the Thanksgiving Address. Food was brought in by Albert and Gilbert Thomas and set at the women's stove. Sam Silversmith ladled it into pails, which were also placed at the women's stove. No cookies were passed. Time: 4:00–5:30 P.M. Attendance: 30 unmasked males, 50 females, 15 masked men.

Of the 13 False Face masks employed, one was a red wolf's head with grinning silvered teeth (not cut through), fur trim, and no hair; one was yellowish-white with a hare-lipped mouth; eight were red; the remainder black. One masker appeared in a black fur-seal coat, with a fur hat and fur tacked to his red mask. Those masks lacking hair had fur, and one black mask had bags of tobacco suspended all around the outlines of the face. Some cornhusk braids were worn as neck wreaths.

SEED PLANTING CEREMONY

The Seed Planting Ceremony is identified by referring either to the Bowl Game played at that time or to the women's planting song which is the characteristic event of the ritual. Thus, one may term the event Ganēha'õngwē dēdwa'yē? ("our seeds we bet") or Gaothõwi's?atha?. The event is also called Thõwi'sas, which was the name of the formal society of women dedicated to the planting song and planting-song rattle, but such a society does not exist now at Six Nations. Parker (1913: 126) and Waugh (1916: 12–4) both mention Thõwi'sas Societies, which also had curing functions. At Tonawanda the ceremony is called Wainõ?noēgwa?šo·? ("they the seeds soak")—(see Fenton, 1941: 159)—but there is no formal "seed-soaking" at the Six Nations Longhouses. However, some ritualists still do soak their corn in a "medicine," the contents of which are now considered private knowledge. Parker, in the translation of the Code (1913: 54), calls this medicine "ohsagan'da?" and "ohsdis'dani." Waugh (1916: 18), working at Six Nations, identifies the decoction as submerged rootstocks of *Phragmites communis* (osa'?gehẽnda?) and *Hystrix patula*, or bottle-brush grass (gu'sdistah). No corn "medicines" are brought to the Longhouse today, as was the case earlier according to Waugh.

Women set the date at Sour Springs, which means that the two head deaconesses decide and send a messenger to the members, who reminds them to bring along their packages of seeds for betting. The end of April till the middle of May is the usual time for the ceremony. (In 1954, Onondaga Longhouse held the Seed Planting Ceremony on April 30.)

The purposes of the ceremony are to inform the women that the time to plant has come once again and to explain to them how to plant the crops; to express thankfulness for the growing season in general; to ask for the help of the food spirits and rain for the oncoming season; and to this end, to "entertain" the food spirits, particularly the Three Sisters—corn, beans, and squash.

At one time this ceremony was performed in the fields before the spring planting by the cooperative group of women. Mrs. George Green relates the ritual as it used to be, as told to her by "old people."

> When everyone was still moving and therefore there were no Longhouses yet (for Longhouses started after we stopped moving), there were two women who went to one another and said, "It is time to plant. It is time to pick up our planting and take our seed which we are going to plant." They told all the women living in a group and went to the fields taking sunflower oil. But first they stood in a circle at the end of the field, and everybody oiled her hair and sang a planting song, gaõthõwi'sas. Every woman had a song, passed down from her mother or grandmother. They never ploughed but just pulled out stock.

At Sour Springs the program opens with the customary Thanksgiving Address, with particular stress on the food spirits. Then the speaker explains the purpose of the event to the congregation and delivers an explanatory lecture to the women on planting. Spring planting, hoeing, and tending the garden is the duty of all present, the speaker affirms; and he further gives practical instructions about planting with the full moon, placing seeds of the Three Sisters in one "hill," keeping the garden hoed and weeded, and so forth.[12]

[12] Although planting at full moon may have been a European notion, it is today believed to be very "Indian." The moon regulates all growing things, and those seeds planted at full moon are believed to grow most successfully, unmolested by borers and worms. Interestingly enough, many of the women do still plant the traditional women's crops—corn, beans, and squash—at full moon; but the moon is ignored completely when the men's crops—oats, wheat, and hay, which were not aboriginal—are planted. The admonitions in the Longhouse are confined to the women's crops only. If the garden crops fail, one claims that they were planted at the wrong time of the moon.

Since "Our Life Supporters" are always conceived in terms of the Three Sisters, these three should be treated as closely related and therefore planted together. Traditionally they were united, so that the beans could climb up the cornstalks. However, modern gardeners object to the squash in this combination, for it tends to overrun the corn, and they now omit it from the "hill," for today the seeds are no longer hilled up. The method of garden cultivation followed by most women today is as follows: Get a man to plough the plot in fall, although there is general agreement that in "olden times" the method of planting was to pull out the

Next, a Feather Dance set is performed, and then the Bowl Game is announced. The seating for the Planting Ceremony, as for all the ceremonies so far described, is along sex lines. The seed-betting Bowl Game, unlike the Bowl Games at Green Corn and Midwinter, is between the sexes and not between moieties. A deaconess collects the seed packages of corn, beans, squash, and pumpkins from the women, and a deacon collects the packages from the men. Packages are then paired by the deacons, and each pair constitutes a prize for the winning side. The Bowl Game is played exactly as it is at Midwinter and Green Corn (for a description of the rules see p. 171 *infra*), except that it is a shortened version, utilizing only 12 to 20 white beans as counters, instead of the 101 used in the long version. Also, no wampum is hung above the players as the "bet of the side," as is the rule at the longer games. The bowl is placed approximately at the imaginary line which divides the women's side from the men's, and the respective sexes bet from their own side. Women, represented by a head deaconess, always begin the game; nor need this person have been the last player in the previous Bowl Game, as in the regular Midwinter and Green Corn Bowl Games. When all the beans are won by one side, the prizes are awarded to that side, the winner receiving its own seeds plus those of the vanquished opposite sex. Much friendly sex rivalry is displayed throughout the game, and the result is discussed the entire year. Women claim that if men win, they should cultivate the gardens that season, although it also indicates that the gardens will be weedy. Men claim that if the women win there will be no corn that season, since the women won't plant any. However, the belief that if men win, crops will be poor, and if women win, crops will be good is also held by the men. It may reflect the feeling that the cultivation of the traditional Iroquoian foods belongs to the sphere of women's duties, and even today, it is often the women who plant the gardens in which the ceremonial food crops grow. When men farm, it usually is the larger-scale wheat cultivation which has been adopted as a whole complex from the neighboring farmers. When the seeds won at the Longhouse are planted, they are said, invariably, to produce the healthiest, most fruitful, and most luxuriant crops of the season.

The women's planting song is performed next. At one time a box-turtle rattle without handles was used to accompany the women singers and was said to have

---

old cornstalks and plant the new corn in the holes in spring. (Ploughing was not known, and the only cultivation was hoeing. However, there is no taboo against ploughing at Six Nations today, and there is great interest in the local ploughing contests, in which Longhouse members and Christians alike participate.) Then, in spring, plough the bed once again, "disk harrow" it, and roll it. For the sake of appearance make strings to indicate straight lines of planting, 3.5 feet apart each way. Planting used to be done closer, but it has been found that the plants do not thrive as well planted closely. Around May 24, dig a hole 2 inches deep with a hoe and drop in three, four, or five corn kernels. (White and blue flint corn are planted with a hoe by women, whereas the yellow corn, which is not considered "Indian" corn, is planted with a corn planter by men.) Also plant three beans per "hill." When the seeds are 3 inches high, thin them, leaving at most three cornstalks per hill, and hoe them. At one time a ditch was hoed around the plants, but now one leaves them level. Repeat hoeing and weeding until harvest time. The squash, which is now planted separately, is also planted with three to four seeds per "hill."

been part of the paraphernalia of the Thõwi'sas Society. (Speck, 1949: Pl. 14, gives a picture of such a rattle. This particular artifact, ascribed to Sour Springs Longhouse, is not now in evidence, and no box-turtle rattles of this type are currently being made. However, Mrs. Joe Logan, keeper of the Onondaga Longhouse rattle, is said to possess a similar rattle, the underside and edge of which is painted red.) At Sour Springs, today, a small snapping-turtle rattle is used, which is kept by Esther Jamieson, the Turtle head deaconess. Mrs. Jamieson says that the rattle was made for her grandmother, and therefore that it is now her own personal property. The Wolf head deaconess holds the rattle first, and softly, but audibly, she recites a prayer saying that she "has in mind" to pray for good crops and that she begs the Great Creator and the food spirits to give her the power that the "stuff" will grow. She then sings a planting song, which may have been passed on to her by her maternal family, or which she may have learned from hearing someone else sing. Each woman "has" one or more planting songs, and the congregation can identify a song as "belonging" to a particular woman. However, several women may "have" the same song at the same time, as possession of such a song is neither esoteric nor exclusive. The attitude toward the ownership of these songs is similar to that which is taken toward the Adõ'wa songs of the men (see p. 168 *infra*). Some of the songs have meaningful words, such as "my children and I, we went into the planting" (Mrs. Hannah Jacobs' song), but most of them consist of burden syllables, for example, "wa'ho ho'i ye na" repeated six times (another of Mrs. Jacobs' songs). Women stand north facing south as they sing, men stand south and face north as they sing. After the Wolf head deaconess has sung her song, the Turtle head deaconess must sing next; then the rattle is passed counterclockwise from female to female, each of whom first addresses herself to the Great Creator and the crop spirits in prayer and then sings her planting song. After all the women have had a turn, the men are handed the rattle, and each may sing either a women's planting song or his own Adõ'wa song. The Wolf head deaconess, Maggie General, then leads the women followed by the men counterclockwise around the two stoves, walking to the accompaniment of the women singing Maggie General's planting song, which consists of the burden syllables: "yowhigẽ'ne he hegẽ'ne he hegẽ'ne he he he." Men may help the women sing. On the whole the women are shy about speaking and singing, and planting prayers and songs are very simple. The tone of delivery, however, is reverent and solemn.

The set of Our Life Supporters dances—consisting of the Women's Dance, Standing Quiver Dance, Corn Dance, Bean Dance, and Pumpkin (Bottle), or Squash, Dance—ends the program. This set of dances is associated with all the women's food festivals, and although the order of execution may differ from festival to festival, the composition is the same. (For descriptions of the food-spirit dances see Kurath, 1951: 126–9, Fenton, 1942: 32–3, and Speck, 1949: 148, 150, 152.) At the three Longhouses down below, but never at Sour Springs, the Tutelo harvest songs, called Four Nights' Dance (ge'i niwahsõnda'ge), are substituted for the Pumpkin, or Squash, Dance whenever dancers and singers who are familiar with the songs are present. This set of songs is appropriate at any of the food-spirit ceremonies through-out the year. A water drum and several horn rattles are utilized with these songs, and they are of the type in which men begin the song and women finish ("absorb") the latter part. Few singers at Six Nations are able to perform the series any more. Roy Buck, Bill (Joshua) Buck (now deceased), and Bob Johnson are the most notable performers. (For a description of the series, see Kurath, 1953a: 153–62. Kurath witnessed the performance at an Onondaga "Green Corn" Festival, August 16, 1949. This was probably the "Green Corn Testing" Festival at which the series of food-spirit dances are appropriate, and that therefore the Tutelo harvest set was included. Also the early date indicates that it was the "Testing" Ceremony.)

The roles of singer, leader of the dance line, announcer, and performer are care-fully divided between the two moieties, alternating as evenly as possible. The more people participate, the more pleased the food spirits will be, and the more efficacious the event.

The Thanksgiving Address again ends the ceremony. The food appropriate to the occasion is sweetened cracked-blue-flint-corn soup, cookies, cakes and bread. The cookies, etc., are passed around, but the corn soup is ladled into the pails which members bring along, and these are taken home. Only those people who forgot to bring their pails are handed a plate of the corn soup to eat in the Longhouse.

MOON AND SUN CEREMONY

The Moon (ahsŏ'he?khaa?) and Sun (ēnde'khaa?) festivals are in the domain of the men, and at Sour Springs should be scheduled after seed planting and before seed sprouting in order to appeal to the Sun and Moon to continue their good offices toward a satisfactory planting season. However, it is said that "the men are slow," and the festivals are therefore never held any more, unless weather conditions are abnormally unfavorable. (It has been 20 years since the last celebration of the festivals.) The three Longhouses down below combine to perform this ceremony at Onondaga Longhouse. There the festival as a whole is directed more toward the moon than the sun, and consequently it occurs before the Seed Planting Ceremony, in order to ask "Our Grandmother, the Moon" to help in the planting and to pro-vide good crops, and then to ask "Our Elder Brother, the Sun" to provide the warmth for their growth. At one time the Moon Dance was held the night before the Sun Dance and lasted from moonrise to moonset, but now the Moon Dance is always scheduled for the morning and the Sun Dance for that same afternoon. Both ceremonies are short now.

The program of the Moon Ceremony consists of the customary Thanksgiving Address; the women's planting song; a Bowl Game using 21 to 26 beans, played with men opposing women as at Seed Planting; and most probably the Feather Dance. It ends with the Thanksgiving Address and should be completed before noon.

The populace then goes home for lunch and comes back in the afternoon around two o'clock to celebrate the Sun Dance. This again opens with the Thanksgiving

Address, followed by a set of the Feather Dance in honor of the Sun, and then followed by the Adŏ'wa chants of the individual men (see p. 168 *infra*, for a description of the personal chant), each of whom holds a feather wand symbolizing the sun as he sings. (See Speck, 1949: Pl. 12, for a picture of the sun-disk feather wand. Lately, Edric General has copied this to make one for Sour Springs.) The Skin Dance (gane'hŏŏ) and the closing Thanksgiving Address end the program. Sweetened corn soup made from cracked blue flint corn is served after the Sun Ceremony.

CORN SPROUTING CEREMONY

This ceremony, called Gothĕndisʔa'hgŏ, should take place three to four weeks after the Corn Planting Ceremony, at the time when the young shoots first show above the ground. This is around the end of May. At Sour Springs, however, this ceremony is not now performed. Below, at Onondaga and Seneca (for Seneca patterns itself on Onondaga Longhouse), this event is another food-spirit supplication. The food spirits are "entertained" in order that they may continue to help the crops mature into a good harvest.

The program is a repetition of the set of food-spirit dances, preceded by a set of Feather Dances. The food appropriate to the occasion is sweetened cracked-flint-corn soup, cookies, and bread.

STRAWBERRY CEREMONY

The Strawberry Ceremony, Hĕnatᵃhya'ohes Djihsŏ'ndak, was at one time scheduled five days after the "berry moon," but today it is simply scheduled "when the strawberries are on." (Dating a festival five days past the new moon is explained as a device to allow women to pass their menstrual period and attend the ceremony. This device was used in dating the Strawberry Festival as well as the Midwinter Ceremony, although the Strawberry dating now disregards the berry moon; [see p. 216 *infra* for menstrual taboos].) At Sour Springs women determine the date, and it usually occurs around the end of June. Ideally, the ceremony should be held during the morning and terminate at noon, particularly since the Strawberry Festival today is intimately linked with Handsome Lake and Gaihwi'yo, but actually the ceremony usually lasts from around 11:00 A.M. till 3:00 P.M.

The Strawberry Ceremony at Six Nations is often preceded by a chiefs' convention, which is a local recitation of the "Good Message," sponsored by a single Longhouse. (See pp. 194-9 *infra* for a description of the conventions and confession.) All the Reserve is invited to a local convention, and each year at least one Longhouse is likely to have a pre-Strawberry confession. This allows all the Longhouse members to purify themselves before the Strawberry Festival begins, even if the home Longhouse is not sponsoring a convention that year. The convention preaching is always accompanied by confession, and at Sour Springs the belief exists that this confession is even more important than the confession at the regular Six Nations conventions or the one before the Midwinter Ceremony, since the Strawberry-time confession is a spiritual cleansing commensurate with the physical purging which should take place in the spring. "Everything is coming on" now, and the individual should be ritually clean and free of sins in order to receive the fruits of the harvest. The purposes of the Strawberry Festival are to give thanks for the first fruits of the new season, to give thanks for life and togetherness, to remind each other of the duties incumbent on the followers of Handsome Lake, and, finally, to entertain the food spirits so that they will continue to favor mankind with the harvest. Strawberry, today, combines a first-fruits, spring-renewal festival with a moralistic, didactic ceremony. The dances to the food spirits, which are usually performed with reverent gaiety, are overshadowed by the religious solemnity associated with the Gaihwi'yo ceremony. The individual should not only be thankful to the Strawberry Spirit, but should have in mind the Great Creator, Handsome Lake, and the privilege of Life itself. Thus, Strawberry is among those agricultural events most influenced and changed by the Good Message and by Christianity. It is at the Strawberry Festival that preachers like to give sermons resembling the revivalist Christian harangues and concerning the behavior of the individual, rather than the traditional expressions of thankfulness and supplication to the food spirits.

The Strawberry Ceremony opens with the Thanksgiving Address, with emphasis on the food spirits and the highest pantheon. Then a speaker from the opposite moiety explains why the ceremony is being held and announces the passing of a dipper of strawberry juice, so that all may give a prayer of thanks to the Great Creator that the strawberries are seen once again and that everyone present is still on earth, well, happy, and able to taste the strawberries. If one is not able to express oneself to this effect, the speaker says, one may simply think so, "have it in mind." Then the speaker mentions the menstrual and pregnancy taboos, that if any woman happens to be present who is "in a family way" or menstruating, she should bring her own cup, "because there are children around," which is a euphemistic substitution for the reputed consequences of broken menstrual taboos (see pp. 216–7 *infra*). Two deacons, one from each moiety, thereupon take up pails of strawberry juice— crushed strawberries and sugar in water—and moving counterclockwise hand the dipper from person to person. (Whenever distributing food, the passer begins with the chiefs—either Turtle or Wolf—and then goes strictly counterclockwise. Should the supply be exhausted and the deacon have to return to the matron to have the pail or basket refilled, he will continue from the last person served.) As the strawberry juice is passed, each person contemplates the filled dipper, recites his prayer in a hushed voice, often choked with emotion and tears, and then takes a draught, emptying the dipper. The deacon finally places the pail in the center of the house on the singers' benches and utters a short audible prayer, to which the men answer "nyeeh!" at the end of each verse. (This is merely a patterned act of politeness extended to the reciter in order to assure him that one approves and is in sympathy with his thoughts.) Then the deacon drinks his dipperful.

After this the Feather Dance is announced, and the set performed is of the earthly series. Strawberry time is one of the occasions at which the traditional "Indian" dress is supposed to be worn, and those who are "dressed" should lead the Feather

Dance. "Indian" dress for the men includes any buckskin ensemble, preferably with fringes, bead or shell necklaces, bead or embroidery decoration on the shirt or trousers, armlets, deer-hoof anklets, and moccasins; Plains-type or roach-type feather headdress; colorful shirts, sashes, or trousers; and any combinations of these. Buckskin pants with no upper garment at all is a perfectly acceptable "Indian" costume. There is no standardization of the "Indian" dress for a man, and there is a wide range of variation. Some men have two red spots painted on the cheekbones, or at times a stripe, for the Midwinter Feather Dance. This costuming must not, however, be confused with the "dead clothes" (see p. 235 *infra*). Women are dressed more uniformly. "Indian" dress for them consists of navy-blue or black broadcloth leggings; a broadcloth petticoat of the same material trimmed with ribbon or braid; a cotton print (preferably a small over-all pattern of flowers) overdress with long sleeves, also trimmed with ribbon; a ribbon sash; and a neck scarf. Beads and pins are optional. The hair should be tied in back, left unadorned and in a single braid with ribbons. Theoretically, the leader of the Feather Dance should always be in Indian dress, but only at Strawberry, Green Corn, and Midwinter is Indian dress essential. Indian dress is a way of showing respect, and since on those three occasions the Great Feather Dance is particularly directed toward the Great Creator, a maximum of respect is required. The first set of Feather Dances is directed, however, to the earthly food spirits. Three songs, which are only instrumental, introduce the set, and with the change of rhythm at the fourth song, the dancers enter. The first two dancers should be of opposite moiety, but thereafter any order is permissible. After the men have danced to one song, women also enter the line. Between each song the leader of the dance line shouts "yoah, yi" and is answered by the dancers "yoah, yoah," and the singers then sing the next song. Singers and dancers may refresh themselves with strawberry juice at any time. The first set of Feather Dances usually lasts 20 minutes.

Next the preacher or speaker delivers a sermon urging the people not to forget the Great Creator and to have faith in him every day of their lives. "Never forget him, he's the only help you have. You cannot grow anything alone," Alexander General admonishes. Then he admonishes the deacons to behave well to one another, to act as if they were one person, to be kind, to be instructive to the people, and to do their duty. There follows a description of the advent of the Good Message through the offices of Handsome Lake. A speaker may embellish these sermons as much as he wishes, and personal variation is evident.

A second set of Feather Dances is now performed, this time directed to the Great Creator. The songs should therefore be chosen from those concerning the highest pantheon. Again, the average time for the set is 20 minutes.

While the deacons divide the food, speakers at Sour Springs make a traditional inquiry whether the congregation wishes to participate in the Six Nations convention for the coming fall. (See pp. 35–7 *supra* for a discussion of Sour Springs' procedure concerning participation in the biennial circuit of Gaihwi'yo.) At the other Longhouses on the Reserve, which are tied into the Gaihwi'yo circuit, there is no discussion of participation, but there is discussion concerning the contributions of the Longhouse to the circuit. The beneficial effects of the recitation of the Code are discussed, as well as the spiritual disposition of the community. Pledges to support the Good Message and thankfulness for the receipt of the Good Tidings are uttered at this time.

The deacons continue distributing the food. When a person brings an entire shopping basket of some item, the head deaconess and her assistants usually fill the basket with a variety of cookies, breads, and other ceremonial foods before returning the basket to the owner. Baskets and pails are often marked by tying a towel or a ribbon around the handle, so that the owner can claim his own. The larger part of the feast foods, that which is not divided among the baskets, is passed by the deacons to the congregation. Each person should help himself to one item as the basket is held to him. The sweetened cracked-flint-corn soup with red beans and strawberries, which is appropriate to this occasion, is ladled into the jars and pails around the women's stove, and at Sour Springs, the empty cauldron is traditionally placed before the Turtle chiefs to scrape out. The remainder of the strawberry juice is also passed around. At all Longhouse ceremonies all the food is distributed, and nothing is ever left.

Raspberry Ceremony

The Raspberry Ceremony, Hēnatᵃhya'ohes Djŏnda'iya, is scheduled by the women for the time when the raspberries ripen, usually around the twentieth of July. It is one of the food-spirit ceremonies and is designed to give thanks for the recurrence of the raspberry season and to supplicate the food spirits to continue their good offices.

The program for the Raspberry Ceremony is a typical food-spirit program, following closely that of the Dyŏnhe'hgŏ observances. The Thanksgiving Address opens the meeting, followed by a personal statement of thankfulness by each participant as he tastes again the fruits of the raspberry. Raspberry juice—mashed raspberries, sugar, and water—is passed to each individual as on Strawberry Day and Maple Day. (The same menstrual taboos apply at this ceremony as at Strawberry and Maple.) A single set of the Feather Dance follows, addressed to earthly spirits. Then the complex of food dances are performed: Women's Dance, Standing Quiver Dance, Corn Dance, Pumpkin Dance, and Bean Dance (also called "Shaking-Bottle Dance"—this dance is often omitted). The Thanksgiving Address closes the ceremony. The appropriate food is sweetened cracked-flint-corn soup with raspberries. Feast foods are also passed.

The Raspberry Ceremony is a relatively minor event. It occurs at a time when many of the Six Nations residents are away from the Reserve for seasonal employment and is not considered important enough to warrant a return to the Reserve. Attendance at this ceremony ranges from 20 to 50 people, depending on the Longhouse and the amount of advance notice.

Green Bean Ceremony

The Green Bean Ceremony, Hĕnadesa'he?da'ohes, is still another food-spirit ceremony. It is directed to the Bean Spirit and other plant spirits in order to thank them for their past bounty and to entertain the spirits so that they may continue to bear fruit. The dating, arranged by women at the Cayuga and by men at the Seneca and Onondaga Longhouses (see p. 74 *supra*), coincides with the ripening of the green beans at the beginning of August. The program is identical with that of the other food-spirit ceremonies, except that no personal prayers are given, since no bean food is passed during the ceremony. A Feather Dance set and the Our Life Supporters Dances make up the program. The appropriate food is a green-bean soup[13] and cookies, breads, etc. Again, this is not a very important ceremony, and attendance tends to be limited.

Thunder Ceremony

The Thunder Ceremony (ethi'hsot hadiwĕno'dagye?s, "grandfathers sounding their voices"), is usually considered a male ceremony, and consequently ought to be scheduled by the men. However, at Sour Springs where today the rite is rarely performed (reportedly having lapsed for about 15 years, before a recent revival of the rite) it is said to have been scheduled by women during some years. The exact timing depended on weather conditions, for it could be scheduled at any time when rain was lacking. Thus it is remembered as having taken place at Sour Springs as early as May and as late as September. At present, the three Longhouses down below combine for the Thunder Ceremony at Onondaga Longhouse, and it is usually scheduled after the Maple Ceremony as well as during dry summers when rain is needed.

The Thunderers are envisaged as seven old men with vast supernatural powers. They are the heavenly analogue of the earthly False Face Men, "working for 'Our Maker' as the False Faces work for man." Despite the fact that the Thanksgiving Address mentions four "appointees of Thunder," four being the most common Iroquois pattern number, most of the thunder origin myths mention seven "Thunder Men" (see p. 137 *supra*). (Five and seven are also prominent numbers in ritual and mythology.) Of the seven Thunderers one is believed to have been a mortal. The origin myth current at Sour Springs relates that at one time a particularly harmful snake roamed the Alleghany region. This snake could not be killed by man, nor had the Thunderers, who ordinarily control snakes, been able to kill it either. The Thunderers therefore enlisted the aid of a mortal called Hawĕna'gis (His-Voice-Amongst-Them), who was instructed to shoot with a bow and arrow at the red spot near the ear of the snake. He shot 12 red-willow arrows, killed the snake, and was taken by the Thunderers to be one of their number. He alone has a name, because

---

[13] Fresh green beans are cut into thin diagonal strips as when making Frenched beans. These are placed in boiling water over the wood fire in the cookhouse. Butter and corn flour are added as thickening (though store wheat flour may be used), as well as some salt. The whole is cooked till soft.

he came from the earth, and he is the one whose sharp crack one hears. (See Morgan, 1901, 1: 150–1, for another common story involving the Thunder-serpent motif.)

The Thunderers control the vermin below the ground, the dangerous beasts above the earth, the rain, the wind, and many diseases. Great respect is due the Thunderers, both for their power and for their status as "old men." But with respect there is fear, for the magnitude of their power can be turned against man as well as used for the benefit of man. Thunder is a rather "particular" spirit force, and one must be "careful" when talking of Our Grandfathers, the Thunderers, and when performing for them. Whenever one hears the Thunderers go by—and they always are characterized as coming from a westward (sundown) direction, hega′ahgwĕs—one should, out of respect and thankfulness, drop some Indian tobacco into the fire.

The purpose of the Thunder Ceremony is to implore the Thunderers to travel through the country, watering the fields as they go, to control windstorms, and to continue their duties of restraining pestilential animals, both natural and supernatural. Thunder-caused diseases may also be cured at this time by playing the medicinal lacrosse game for individual members of the congregation.

The program as it used to be performed at Sour Springs opened with the Thanksgiving Address, and then the congregation followed the speaker outside to witness a tobacco invocation to the Thunderers at a small fire built near the cookhouse. (Esther Jamieson says that sometimes the tobacco was burned at the Wolf [men's] stove within the Longhouse, but that the most common procedure was to build a fire outside.) Various members had brought Indian tobacco to the Longhouse, and the women had woven seven or eight small cornhusk baskets (see Speck, 1949: Pl. 12, for a photograph of a typical cornhusk basket) which formed receptacles for the tobacco, "the pouches of the Thunderers." As the invocation progressed, the baskets and their contents were committed to the fire. Lately, however, during the final Sour Springs performances and today at Onondaga, the tobacco has been kept merely in a paper bag, and the bag is burned. However, one can still obtain small cornhusk baskets at Six Nations (not recently made), which indicates that they were not all burned. Alexander General, who often gave the tobacco invocation, denies that he ever burned any of the small baskets. The invocation thanked the Great Creator for the services of the Thunderers and implored the Thunderers to continue shedding rain so that the crops might not wither. For this service the tobacco was freely given, for the Thunderers not only heard the invocation through the medium of the tobacco, but being "old grandfathers" they are particularly fond of it for its own sake. The continued control of evil spirits and beasts was also asked.

A lacrosse game for the Thunderers followed, for lacrosse is the characteristic "pass dance" of the Thunderers. In this game any number of men could participate, and the teams were arranged according to moiety affiliation. The players brought their own lacrosse sticks, and a ball was borrowed from a member who owned one as a result of having had the game performed previously as a "pass dance." The rules followed were those of the old field lacrosse (as opposed to the modern box lacrosse), and the players were told before they started the number of goals required to complete the game. Usually, either three or seven goals for a team ended the game. The speaker explained the occasion and purpose of the game to the players and finally, before tossing up the ball, admonished them to play fairly and without malice. (Indeed such an admonition was apropos, for lacrosse traditionally was, and is, an emotionally charged game, in which high feelings and witchcraft play a prominent role.) Naturally, malicious sentiments are out of place when performing the game as the supernaturals' "pass dance." No emetics were taken for the medicinal, or devotional, lacrosse games, nor did competition run as high as in the sport. Medicinally it was completely unimportant which side won the game.

Immediately after the completion of the game, the players, as well as any of the men who so desired, danced the War Dance (wasa·se), moving toward the Longhouse and finally entering through the women's door. (See Morgan, 1901, 1: 257–68, for a description of the War Dance and the striking-stick and speech-making attributes. At one time the War Dance was a boasting occasion before and after military exploits.) During this dance, the Turtle and Wolf head deaconesses sprinkled the men with water from pails which they held, symbolizing the oncoming rain. Informants usually claim that "as soon as the lacrosse game is over, rain comes, even if there have been no previous signs of a rainstorm." The men would be costumed in short pants and have a handkerchief tied about their heads, but otherwise they would be unclad. After the men were inside the Longhouse, the "striking-stick" part of the War Dance was carried on. In order to show particular attention, respect, and devotion various members had prepared cookies or had brought tobacco, which the two head deaconesses distributed in two baskets. These were handed to designated deacons, one of each moiety, and they handed the baskets with the offerings to members of the congregation who desired to "encourage" the dancers. Such a member would hold the basket and "hammer," that is, strike the floor with a stick. All dancing immediately ceased, and the hammerer would give a patterned speech giving thanks for the thunder, the rain, and the dancers, and hoping that the dancers would dance well and vigorously, even as in olden times. Here, as in the Eagle Dance, mild joking was permitted, which usually was in the form of noting that previous dancers were more expert or that the dancers were eager merely for their portion of cookies. The speaker would then remove some cookies from the basket and hand them to the deacon, who transferred them to an empty basket standing in the center of the house. This procedure was repeated until all who desired to "hammer" had done so, and all the cookies had been transferred to the central baskets. The dancers then ended their dance and received the cookies as a reward, as well as pails of False Face mush (sweetened mush made from roasted white-corn flour).

This concluded the "pass dance" for Thunder; but personal "pass dances" could then be performed if members needed a "thunder dance" (either lacrosse or the War Dance) for curing purposes. The Thanksgiving Address closed the meeting, and the deacons passed the food, consisting of sweetened cracked-flint-corn soup and feast cookies.

At Onondaga Longhouse, where the ceremony is still performed, the program is very similar. A fire is built outside, and the speaker, surrounded by the singers (with horn rattle and water drum) and dancers, offers up the tobacco invocation to the Thunderers and asks for rain. No baskets are made to contain the tobacco, and a simple paper bag substitutes for the "pouch." The dancers dance the War Dance (here considered a "rain dance") into the Longhouse, where the striking-stick speeches are directed toward the Thunderers. The Thunderers are thanked for their performance, and it is hoped they will hear the current prayers and receive the food offering. Here, too, the food is placed in a special pile, which afterward is taken out of the Longhouse again and distributed to the dancers. No lacrosse game seems to be played, and no personal cures are effected.

Corn Testing Ceremony

The Corn Testing Ceremony, or the small Green Corn Dance, Hĕnadekhwa′ohes Niga′khwa′a?, is scheduled by the women for the time when the corn is not yet quite ripe. Consequently, it is observed in the early part of September, or possibly late August if the seasons have progressed rapidly that year.

The object of the meeting is to see "how our crops are coming along" and to encourage the food spirits to continue to fulfill their duties in the final ripening stage. ("We entertain them, to encourage them.")

The program is again a typical "Dyŏnhe′hgŏ" demonstration, to give pleasure to the food spirits by dancing "their" dances. After the Thanksgiving Address, the speaker announces that he is grateful to see the corn "coming right along" and mentions that people are testing it now. Then a Feather Dance set of the earthly series is danced, followed by the Women's Dance, Standing Quiver Dance, Corn, Bean, and Squash Dances. (The exact order in which these dances are performed is immaterial. The Women's Dance always precedes the others, but the latter dances are performed in the order in which the particular speaker happens to announce them.) After the dances, the ceremonial obligations are officially transferred from women to men in anticipation of the major Green Corn Festival. The men are instructed "to hunt" (hĕnadowa′tha?) for meat for the Green Corn Dance, which at one time meant to procure deer or possibly bear meat for the festival. Today, however, "hunting" or "looking for good water for soup for themselves" are euphemisms for going out to solicit odd jobs in order to donate the proceeds therefrom to the Longhouse. This money helps defray the cost of the side of beef from the Caledonia butcher. The most common institutionalized method of procuring this money is to cut a cord of wood for a Reserve member (Christian or Longhouse) for $1.00 instead of the regular $2.00 fee. In this way both the Longhouse and the person in need of wood benefit. The Thanksgiving Address ends the ceremonies. The food appropriate for this occasion is a mush made of the slightly unripe green corn with red beans[14] and the usual feast cookies.

[14] The recipe for this dish is as follows: Scrape the ears of unripe large white or yellow corn with a ten-cent-store grater, a deer or pig jaw, or the back of a knife. (At Six Nations a gadget

Green Corn Dance

The Green Corn Ceremony, Hĕnadekhwa'ohes Gagowa'nĕ (literally, "they-gather-over-there large"), is sometimes referred to by the Onondaga as The Four Ceremonials, Ge'i niihwa'ge (Onondaga gaye'i niyoihwa'ge). It is second in importance only to Midwinter, and the observance lasts three days. Men arrange the date of this ceremony, which means that the two head deacons determine the exact day and send around the messengers. (At Onondaga the date setters need not be head deacons.)

This ceremony is a three-fold one, dedicated to the food spirits, the Great Creator, and the people; and it differs from Midwinter only in that no personal "pass dances" are performed and that the Stirring Ashes ritual is omitted. The ceremonies are intended to thank the food spirits for producing the harvest which now is ready, and to thank the Great Creator for making the harvest possible and allowing the community to witness the completion of another season of growth. The Green Corn Ceremony is mostly one of thanksgiving (as opposed to supplication), and in return for the privilege of life and sustenance the four sacred rituals, which properly "belong" to the Great Creator, are performed. Although the four sacred rituals (the Feather Dance, Adŏ'wa, Skin Dance, and the Bowl Game) are usually believed to have been transmitted to the Iroquois by the Great Creator when he made the earth and the people, Alexander General has a highly acculturated version of an origin tale of the rituals, according to which they were brought by Christ.

Long ago there were 12 children born, one of whom had no father and was delivered by a virgin. They called him He-who-had-no-Father. This one taught the other boys to express thanks and explained the first three of the sacred rituals. The boys always met together without any prearranged plans, and when this occurred one day again, The Fatherless One said, "Boys, I will now leave." The boys wished to clasp his hands, but he refused, because he said that it wouldn't be right since he was already dead. "I was killed where I was. No one believed me of what I spoke. There is one thing I've left out to teach you. You can now go to this Bowl Game." He then taught the boys the Bowl Game, and as the children were progressing with the game, the spirit departed. He had risen toward Heaven. He was the boy with no father. There was no name for that child. This is the same spirit which they call Christ—going toward sunrise to preach to other people. The entire episode was "the first dispensation." This first dispensation lasted for some time. But people forgot the legend until Deganawi'da? revived the Great Spirit among the Iroquois. So it carried on until the people from overseas brought many evil things, and in imitating these here, the people did not realize they were committing sins against the Great Spirit. Then Handsome Lake received the message that the people should repent

made by hammering a knife blade into a piece of wood and using the whole as a scraper is very popular for preparing this particular dish.) Sometimes the scraping is done at home and only the kernels brought to the Longhouse, while at other times the deaconesses scrape in the cookhouse the morning of the ceremony. The kernels are then dropped in lukewarm water and boiled until mushy. Salt, butter, and fresh red beans are added, as well as some corn flour if the corn has not been shredded finely enough to thicken the soup sufficiently. A few years ago the dish was embellished with squirrel meat, which today may be replaced by chicken and chicken broth if the deaconesses feel so inclined. This dish is considered a delicacy, and people look forward to it a great deal.

of the four cardinal sins which the palefaces had brought, firewater, witchcraft, contraception, and the dance.[15]

Those ceremonies which appropriately accompany the four sacred rituals—such as naming, giving up the dead, and making deacons—are also performed. The people themselves remind each other that they, too, must continue to fulfill their obligations and duties, and ethical lecturing is in order at the Green Corn Ceremony.

The first day of the Green Corn Ceremony at Sour Springs opens with the Thanksgiving Address, followed by a tobacco burning in the cookhouse, which is witnessed by the chiefs, speakers, and deacons, but not by the ordinary people, who remain behind in the Longhouse. (Some informants say that the tobacco burning takes place on the second day of the ceremony, and there may be local variation.) The participants and onlookers ought to be in costume, since Green Corn is an important ceremony and one of the three requiring "dressing." (In general, observances dedicated to the Great Creator, particularly the four sacred ceremonies, should be conducted in "Indian clothes." This indicates respect for the Great Creator.) At the tobacco burning the speaker offers thanks for the food which was given and which is ready to be harvested; he further gives thanks that the assemblage meets once again; and he instructs them to put away all everyday work for the length of the ceremony. When the officials return to the Longhouse, a Feather Dance set of the earthly type is danced. Then a traditional speech to the deacons admonishes them to work together and to remember their duties. A second set of the Feather Dance, selected from the songs concerning the Upper Pantheon, is offered to the

[15] The identification of The Fatherless One with Christ is made because Christ, too, had no father; Christ, too, was dead when he reappeared to the disciples; Christ, also, had disciples with whom he consorted and to whom he taught esoterica; and Christ, also, gave "dispensations." Not only the content but the very choice of vocabulary indicates a high degree of acculturation. Since Mr. General is the principal educator at Sour Springs and disseminates his beliefs, one must not underestimate the importance of his version. Speck (1949: 127-9) attributes belief in an almost identical etiology to the Cayuga, although Mr. General was most probably his informant too. However, even among the Sour Springs Cayuga, The Fatherless One is not always equated with Christ but may also be Deganawi'da?. A legend about the Big Dipper, for example, relates that there was a boy, Deganawi'da?, who had no father. He wanted the seven boys he played with to bring a kettle, a ladle, corn, beans, and some soup. The parents of the boys, however, would not allow them to have these items, and Deganawi'da? declared that he had foreknowledge that matters would turn out this way. Nevertheless, he wished them to sing and dance. The parents heard them, and one of the mothers thought she heard them "way up." She looked, and they were going up, so remorse overcame her and she rushed out with the kettle, which the boys grabbed and took up with them. Deganawi'da? told the boys not to look back. The mothers cried, and one boy did look back and fell, and where he fell a tree grew at the Bay of Quinte. (If one cut into this tree it would sometimes bleed, and if one killed it another would grow in its stead. This was the "Life Tree." If a hunter remained out too long one could cut this tree; if it bled, the hunter had died, and if not, he still survived. Today, however, the tree is not bleeding, but the bark is red.) The other six boys and Deganawi'da? continued to heaven and became the Big Dipper. Speck (1949: 50) recorded an almost identical tale, but does not identify The Fatherless One, and the story concerns the Pleiades rather than the Big Dipper.

Great Creator. The Feather Dance is the first of the four sacred rituals, and everyone ought to participate, preferably in costume, in order to amuse our Creator. Women should have anointed their heads with sunflower oil, but, in fact, this is not done any more. The Thanksgiving Address finishes the day's ceremony. The meat which the men have "hunted" has been in preparation by male cooks most of the previous night and morning and is passed in small chunks to the congregation. The women have roasted the husked large white corn on top of a stove or in a fire and then have shelled the kernels and cooked them in the beef stock with salt and fresh, ripe red beans (osahe?da?õ'we, "real beans," or more accurately, "native beans"). This soup is poured into the pails which members have brought and in plates for anyone who wishes some immediately or who neglected to bring his pail. Feast cookies of all kinds and corn bread are also distributed. Thimbleberry juice (na'ēnõ) is the appropriate drink when it can be obtained. The ceremony should be concluded before noon, but in practice the "doings" get under way somewhat after 11:00 A.M. and last till mid-afternoon.

The second day of the ceremony opens with the Thanksgiving Address, followed by an explanation of the second of the four sacred rituals, the Adõ'wa, which is the personal chant of the men. At one time the Adõ'wa was most probably a narration of personal exploits, but today it is considered a deeply moving religious dedication, and the men are extremely serious throughout, even if the words of the song appear somewhat inconsequential. Each male member should, if he is able to sing, acquire his own song. If a man likes a particular Adõ'wa song, he may adopt it as his own, whether the original singer is living or dead. Thus, several people may simultaneously own the same song. However, once one adopts one song (or several), one uses it repeatedly, so that even children can identify songs and owners. Some of the songs consist of burden syllables, while others express sentiments such as "now I am walking, I am giving thanks to his appointees" or "I am now singing my song." Before each repetition of the song the singer addresses a prayer to the Great Creator, thanking him for the ability to perform, for his creations, his goodness, etc. At Green Corn the first Adõ'wa song is that of the Great Creator, which is of the Stirring Ashes genre. A man (preferably in Indian costume) impersonates the Great Creator and sings "his" (the Creator's) song. The impersonator rises at his seat and explains that "Our Maker wants it to be this way; people on earth should do as in heaven" (i.e., sing Adõ'wa). The impersonator than moves to the center of the house, stands and sings a few measures, and then continues singing while pacing deliberately counterclockwise between the two stoves. At irregular intervals the singer pauses to thank the chiefs and officers for their good work and to encourage them to continue. He then declares that now the same ritual is "open" to all the people, and that each should, if at all able, perform his own Adõ'wa song. Any man can thereupon rise, state how thankful he is to have been spared to witness this ceremony again and be permitted to offer his song, and declare how grateful he is for the "help" everyone is giving; and then repeat the singing of the song, pausing at irregular intervals to offer up prayers thanking the Great Creator,

Handsome Lake, and as many of the Pantheon (in descending order) as he wishes. Should anyone feel unable either to speak or to sing, he may take a ritual friend "around with him," and the friend fills in those parts which the person feels incapable of performing. Such an act is considered "very nice" of the friend and the proper behavior toward one's ritual brother. It is also considered polite if the spectators of either moiety "help" a person sing his Adŏ'wa, by starting with the singer, keeping time by clapping in a two-two rhythm and chanting "haek, haek," and at the conclusion of the song giving a whoop (a fragment of the war whoop which probably once followed the Adŏ'wa).

The program then turns to the needs of the congregation, for should any child or adult need an Indian name, the deaconess of the moiety desiring a naming informs the speaker, who now bestows the name with a speech. (At Sour Springs naming a person is the duty of his own moiety; at Onondaga and Seneca the opposite moiety performs the rite.) If a male is being named, an Adŏ'wa will be sung for the child (or man) (see p. 213 *infra* for a description of the naming ceremony). The impersonator of the Great Creator then repeats the Stirring-Ashes-type Adŏ'wa of the Creator, once again thanks the Creator that he was able to "pass" the rite for him, and announces this part of the ceremony "closed now."

The third sacred rite is then announced, namely the Skin Dance. Costumes should be worn for this dance, and the men leave to change in the cookhouse. They reappear with a "holler" and begin the dance from the doorway. These circle dances are interspersed with prayers of thanksgiving, recited in the center of the house at the performers' bench by a speaker from each moiety. The prayers concern themselves with thanksgiving to each of the spirit forces mentioned in the Thanksgiving Address, the only difference being that the recitation begins with the Lower Pantheon and proceeds to the Upper Pantheon, and then a speaker from the opposite moiety continues with the earthly spirits, beginning with the lowest and proceeding to the highest of them (for a full description of the Skin Dance at Sour Springs, see Speck, 1949: 138–41). This dance was also at one time a boasting song of military exploits (antiphonal "hollering" reminiscent of a "whoop" yet remains), but today it, also, is consideredvery sacred and solemn.

Next, a sermon on the proper behavior of each to each is customary, with admonitions to be good and kind, to help the sick, and to help one another. Then the program returns to the concerns of the congregation, and bereaved spouses and ritual friends relinquish, in a formal ceremony, their dead relatives (see p. 250 *infra* for a description of the release of the dead). A grieving widow or widower ought not attend the Longhouse until this public release has been effected, by means of a speech by the speaker and the handing over of the suitable cloth to the nearest surviving matrilineal relative of the deceased.

Next, deacons are invested and charged with their duties (see pp. 83 *supra* for a description of the installation of deacons). The speaker then orders the distribution of the food, which is the same as on the previous day. Final announcements concerning the congregation, as well as the announcement of the two deacons for each moiety who are to collect the stakes for the following morning's Bowl Game, end the activities. The Thanksgiving Address is repeated briefly as the house empties for the day.

The third day of the Green Corn Ceremony is a "clan" day, which means that men and women enter through the door which is associated with their clan rather than with their sex, and also that they seat themselves on the Wolf or the Turtle side according to their moiety affiliation. For the calendar year starting with the Bush Dance, this is the first ceremonial day on which moiety seating is adopted. Ideally, the speaker should have instructed the congregation of the proper seating the previous day, enumerating the clans in each moiety, but this is often neglected today. However, no "dangerous" consequences beset the individual if he enters the wrong door or sits with the opposite moiety.

The principal event of the third day is the fourth sacred ritual, the Bowl Game, and since it is one of the major "amusements" of the Great Creator, the participants should be costumed. The preceding afternoon, or even early that very morning, two deacons on each side made the rounds of the households of their moieties and collected from each a "stake." At the Longhouse, the deacons pair stakes of equal value, one from each moiety, tying the two items into one bundle and placing the set of bundles in baskets under the south window. Should there be unequal numbers of items, so that pairing is impossible, the final unmatched items are returned to the owners. The stakes for the Bowl Game for the Great Creator should be in the following order of preference: wampum, Indian costume, lacrosse sticks, turtle rattles, clothing, Indian beads, other items. Money is not in good taste but is sometimes used. Also, one person on each side bets a small string of two to four beads of wampum of any color for the entire side, which is hung on a nail high above the players. This stake is contributed in addition to the personal stake for the game and is a sign of the special reverence of the bettor, for the more valuable and treasured the article, the more spiritual credit accrues to the bettor. All items should be offered in a spirit of sacrifice rather than of competition, and it is spiritually more beneficial to lose than to win (although, empirically, winners always looked very happy about their acquisitions). A loser is compensated for the earthly loss of his item, because the essence of the article immediately ascends to heaven, where it waits for the arrival of the bettors after death. One always says, "You'll see it back—it will come back to you." The two moieties compete against each other, and when a moiety wins the Bowl Game, each member of the winning side walks over to the baskets of paired stakes and chooses his own by sight, retaining his stake as well as winning the item tied to it. The individual (male or female) on the winning side who bet the wampum for his side may keep both strings, and they become his personal property.

Once the stakes have been "put together" (athadiya'drē?), the ceremony proper starts with the Thanksgiving Address and then proceeds to the game itself. The bowl (which is kept by Ida General), the six black and white peach stones, the 101 white beans, the flat cushion which supports the bowl in play, and the flour bags to kneel on while playing are all placed halfway between the Wolf and Turtle sides under the south window, and the two head deaconesses and their male seconds (who watch for accuracy of play) sit facing the game with their backs to the north wall. Two chiefs are asked by their respective head deaconesses to initiate the game, and, with three whoops before the first throw, the Bowl Game gets under way. Also, if the game lasts more than one day, at the beginning of each day, everyone gives three whoops reminiscent of war whoops. Similarly, when the game is over the whoops are again emitted. Throughout the game, the players should be encouraged and spurred by enthusiastic yells of "yehhe," and when a player is replaced the opposite moiety yells "hu, hu." The moiety of a player, while he is shaking, calls for scoring throws of either all white, all black, or "a kill." The animated expressions of enthusiasm leave almost all the congregation hoarse and with sore throats at the end of a prolonged game. However, their interest brings merit and is pleasing to the Creator. The rules of the game stipulate that the first person to bounce the bowl containing the six peach pits should be the chief who gave the last losing shake at the previous Bowl Game. Thereafter anyone, male or female, may shake, but in practice the deacons and deaconesses are called up first. The scorekeeping positions should be rotated among all the deaconesses, but one deaconess holds the beans of her moiety for the duration of the entire game, and should the game last more than a day she takes them home with her at night. Beans are kept in a white handkerchief and ought to be counted and observed only to the extent that one calls for a chief to "be up" for the losing moiety at the last throw.

The scoring rules are as follows: When all six peach pits turn up one color after being jounced in the bowl, five points are scored; and when five pits turn up one color and a single bean is of the opposite color, then one point is scored. With the scoring of each point, a bean is transferred to the player who won the point, and the object of the game is that one moiety should accumulate all 101 beans. At the beginning each player is allotted six beans, the other 89 beans being placed in a pool. When a player wins six beans from his opponent, the captured beans are placed in the pile held by the deaconess of the moiety. The loser is "retired" and is replaced by another player from his moiety, who receives six new beans from the pool of 89. This procedure continues until the pool is exhausted, and thereafter the winner of a point receives a bean from the pile of the opposite moiety until one side captures all the beans. A successful throw by an individual allows him to make a second throw before relinquishing the bowl to his opponent.

The Sour Springs bowl is about 4 inches high and slightly over a foot in diameter. It has a natural light-wood finish and faint red-paint markings on the inside sectioning the bowl into quarters. These markings, however, are said to have no significance. The Bowl Game which is played at Midwinter has identical rules, and the seed-betting Bowl Games have the same rules except that the number of beans to be won is smaller. The game may also be played for sport, with "knocks" on the forehead as stakes, but then it is purely secular, though the scoring and rules are similar to the ritual game.

The game is believed to progress under the direct supervision of the Great Creator, who controls its vagaries and continues it as long as the fluctuations please and amuse him. He ends it immediately when he wishes, and "the beans all of a sudden all go one way, and it is over." (The "expected" [or mean] duration of the game can be approximately calculated by a standard method of solving the so-called gambler's-ruin problem; see Feller, 1950: 279, 289. About 3,400 tosses of the bowl is the expected duration, which is about five and a half hours if one allows around ten tosses per minute. It is, of course, possible for the game to last a longer or a shorter time, and one can calculate the probabilities of various deviations from the expected duration.) People should play the game cheerfully and patiently, with no show of annoyance if it lasts for an unusually long time, since the game is regulated by the Great Creator, and it is pursued for his amusement only. Furthermore, it is a "sacred affair," and people should show no malice or anger and should have no evil thoughts. The outcome of the game is ritually immaterial, but there are, it is said, medicines and charms which influence the peach stones and cause the side of the manipulator to win or prolong the game extraordinarily. Such magical medicines are extremely sinful, indeed; and recipes, if known, are not divulged. That there is emotional involvement in the outcome of the game is evidenced by the occasional unauthorized fights which occur over some throws, by the fact that a chief must end the game for the losing side (for a chief is ex officio peaceful), and by the amount of careful watching and debate over the game. Despite the belief that the Creator regulates the game, and only he knows when it will terminate, men carefully watch the oscillations of the counters with semiscientific interest, and claim to have insight into the behavior of the beans. In 1955, for example, when at the end of the second day of play the Wolves were left with 83 beans and the Turtles with 18, opinion on the Turtle side proclaimed definitively that since the Wolves were unable to capture all the beans after two days of playing, "their luck and beans will go straight out that front [Wolf] door." (Some believed that the Turtles would win because more children from the Turtle moiety had been given names the previous day than from the Wolf moiety.) Actually, the counting of beans at the end of each day is prohibited, but this restriction is widely ignored.

As soon as the game ends, a Feather Dance is performed, to give thanks for the completion of the game. Seating switches over again to the sexual division; and speakers release the congregation from the ceremonial obligations, "give back" work things and playthings, and return the "doings" to the women. The Thanksgiving Address is repeated, and food is distributed. Roasted-white-corn mush with lard and sugar is the correct ceremonial food, in addition to any of the meat and soup remaining from previous days. Feast foods and breads are also distributed. If the Bowl Game ended unusually quickly after an hour's play, the Dyŏnhe'hgŏ (Our Life Supporters) Ceremony will be performed immediately; otherwise, women will schedule it for a week later.

OUR LIFE SUPPORTERS CEREMONY

This food-spirit ceremony (dyŏnhe'hgŏ, sometimes translated "Our Sustenance") is scheduled by women after the Green Corn Ceremony, just as the Bush Dance is scheduled after Midwinter. The purpose is once more to entertain the food spirits and to thank them. The program is the same as in the other food-spirit ceremonies— Feather Dance, Women's Dance, Standing Quiver Dance, Corn, Bean, and Squash Dances. The food served is sweetened cracked-flint-corn soup.

HARVEST CEREMONY

The Harvest Ceremony is scheduled by the women for late October or early November and indicates that the agricultural season has come to a close. The designation for the ceremony means "we put our sustenance away" (ẽsaagwathõwi's?a õnthẽndi's?ẽnhõ), that is, the harvesting is finished; and once more the food spirits are entertained and thanked, with special attention to "our winter food."

The program begins with the Thanksgiving Address and a Feather Dance set dedicated to the earthly spirits, especially the food spirits. The women's songs are performed next, just as at Seed Planting, differing only in that the short prayer preceding the individual song gives thanks for the completed harvest rather than asks for a successful growing season. As at Seed Planting, men may substitute their Adõ'wa songs for the planting songs. The standard set of food-spirit dances follows, and finally there is a speech by the speaker on the good luck of the preceding agricultural year. The ceremonial calendar is once again handed back to the men, "to hunt for meat," because the next event, the Midwinter Ceremony, is scheduled and conducted by men. From the Harvest Ceremony on, all attention is focused on the preparation of the main ceremonial event of the year, which should be scheduled roughly four new moons later (but often occurs sooner than this). Tea meetings and meetings to raise money for the meat, to supplement the "hunting" proceeds, are now planned, and responsibilities are delegated to the members. The Thanksgiving Address and the passing of sweetened corn soup made from cracked, colored flint corn end the ceremony. (At Onondaga, however, a False Face Ceremony may be scheduled after this event and before the Midwinter Ceremony.)

MIDWINTER CEREMONY

The Midwinter, or New Year's, Ceremony is the climax of the calendric rituals and the most important Longhouse event of the year. At Six Nations it is called Ganaha'owi (Stirring Ashes) in reference to the Stirring Ashes ritual which occurs during the first two days of the proceedings. Midwinter is the ceremony which has been related to the Huron dream-guessing and curing festivals, which the authors of the *Jesuit Relations* termed the Feast of the Fools or Carnival of the Wicked Christians. At that time the ritual centered around dream guessing and dream fulfillment, curing, and shamanistic displays accompanied by some forms of possession (Thwaites, 1899, 42: 155–69, and Fenton, 1936: 4–5); but today the dream-guessing feature has atrophied to a minor item in the program, which may or may not be observed. However, some of the beliefs concerning the imperativeness of guessing the dream, when the rite does occur, are indeed reminiscent of the beliefs ascribed to the Hurons in the seventeenth century. Death is said to follow failure to guess the dream or to perform what was demanded in the dream, just as the Hurons used to believe. Shamanistic displays per se are also omitted today, though one might legitimately classify some of the medicine-society rites as derivative from the shamanistic complex.

Midwinter, today, is notable for its inclusive ceremonial observations. Almost every aspect of Longhouse activity is represented, including preaching from Handsome Lake. The ceremony falls into two distinct parts, the first of which is concerned with curing and personal well-being, and is most probably the descendant of the old dream festival; while the second is concerned with the four sacred rituals and the food-spirit observances and is the result of the fusion of the teachings of Handsome Lake with the agricultural calendric observances. Primary emphasis throughout both sections, however, is upon the well-being of the individual himself. In the first section the individual looks to the health of his person, spiritual and physical, in the second to the harmony of the universe, so that all may "work together" for man's welfare. To this end, not only the Great Creator but all the spirit forces require the attention of man, for only then will they reciprocate throughout the coming year. Furthermore, during the previous year the spirit forces did fulfill their duty to the assembled members, and they must be thanked with appropriate observances. The old idea that the people are distraught in mind, due to an accumulation of ceremonial obligations and directives revealed in dreams (see Fenton, 1942: 15), has been replaced by a more generalized idea of merely fulfilling one's ceremonial duty "at this time of the year," so that man may stay well and the universe may remain contented and in an orderly condition.

The dating for this ceremony should be entrusted to the two head deacons, who theoretically observe the movement of the Pleiades (ohgḗ'nya?) after the celebration of the Thanksgiving Festival in the fall. In reality, the course of the Pleiades should have been watched throughout the year, since they roughly delimit the agricultural seasons. The setting of the constellation in April (in the northern sky) indicates the appearance of warmer weather and the planting season, and some of the women at Six Nations still do, in fact, watch for the setting of the Pleiades when planting their gardens. The reappearance of the constellation in August heralds fall and harvesting. However, this constellation may best be seen during the actual winter months, and it is not surprising that the middle of the year is counted from the time that it reaches the zenith. Actually, it is not a bad approximation to the winter solstice. When the Pleiades are observed directly overhead at sunset, the middle of the winter has been reached; and the fifth day after the first new moon thereafter (the five days being added to allow women to complete the menstrual period, which is believed to coincide with each new moon) should begin the Midwinter Ceremony. However, Handsome Lake is said to have observed that the Midwinter Ceremony should begin five days after the first new moon following the white man's New Year, and since this date is easily determinable from any white man's calendar or almanac, this method of determination has been exclusively adopted. In fact, the date is determined and announced at the Thanksgiving Ceremony. The Cayuga Longhouses and usually also Seneca Longhouse still adhere to this dating, but at Onondaga the ceremony has recently been advanced a month in order to allow those members who might otherwise have to report for work off the Reserve to be present for the observance. Many people were dissatisfied with this liberty in the scheduling of the event, but it indicates the power of individual personalities and the resulting variation.

Often a Longhouse will sponsor a chiefs' convention before the Midwinter Ceremony, so that the members may have an opportunity to confess before beginning the ceremonial activity, since speakers at the opening day advocate that all "be clear of sin when the Longhouse 'doings' are on." However, if one has not gone to a confession at a convention, one may go to a deserted place in the country, usually identified as a swamp or crossroad, and confess privately there, especially if the transgression has been a serious one. If neither of these courses was taken, the individual is told to confess and repent in his mind, and not to feel that people talk about him or don't like him. The admonition against paranoia is an interesting admission of one of the commonest traits at Six Nations, and one from which much "sin" arises. Individuals constantly imagine that "someone" doesn't like them, and they practice or contemplate practicing a liberal amount of counter-witchcraft. The most common proof of having an enemy is that one becomes ill, and revenge is not always withheld. Naturally, Handsome Lake is on record as opposed to such practices, and, therefore, one should lay them aside before entering into the Midwinter ceremonials.

Until a few years ago the opening of the Midwinter ceremonial season was proclaimed in each household by the arrival of "Our Uncles" (ethino'?sẽ), two messengers (who need be neither chiefs nor deacons) dressed in "Indian costume," who stirred the ashes in the stoves of the visited member, sang the Stirring Ashes song, and announced in a formal patterned speech the arrival of the ceremony. One of the Uncles sang, the other instructed. (At Six Nations the Uncles are not termed "Bigheads" and are not conceived of as being distraught in mind, nor are they robed with buffalo skins or cornhusk chains as at some of the New York State Seneca settlements; see Fenton, 1936: 4; 1942: 15.) The content of the message was that the Stirring Ashes and Midwinter Ceremonies have arrived; that all should be thankful to have been spared to attend once more; all should work together to help each other at this time; all should pass their dances; and all should "lay up" their toys and work things, for only Longhouse matters should enter the mind until the work things and playthings are restored. Today, however, the event is heralded by the ordinary messengers who visit each house and simply announce the forthcoming event. At the three Longhouses down below, Our Uncles still "go around," but the appropriate costume both on the rounds of the homes and in the Longhouse consists of "dead clothes" (see p. 235 *infra* for a description of "dead clothes") with some extra ribbons and decorations rather than "Indian clothes." It is the only occasion, aside from actual burial, at which the "dead clothes" are worn.

Approximately 50 years ago, the Stirring Ashes Ceremony at Six Nations took place at night, accompanied by musket shots outside, but now (due to the troublesome intrusion of alcohol) the Midwinter Ceremony begins around 11:00 A.M. at Sour Springs and in the afternoon in the Longhouses down below (where one must allow enough time for the Uncles to make their rounds in the morning). No costume is worn, with the exception of the "dead clothes" of the Uncles "down below." Entrance and seating are according to clans, so that the two moieties sit at opposite ends of the house as at the Bowl Game. The program of the first day is dedicated to stirring the ashes in the lighted stoves in the Longhouse, which symbolizes stirring up the congregation and also is the "pass dance" of the Great Creator.

The program opens with the Thanksgiving Address by a speaker from one moiety. It is followed by an explanation of the events to come by a speaker of the opposite moiety, who thanks the Great Creator on behalf of all assembled that they were spared to be present and hopes that they will all be present a year hence. He explains that the Great Creator has given the Stirring Ashes rite to the Indians, and that now Our Uncles are "coming through," visible to all in the Longhouse. Since the Stirring Ashes ritual is really a "pass dance" belonging to the Great Creator, the congregation sees itself performing on his behalf. Consequently, the speaker admonishes, "Everybody must stir, just as if Our Maker were here stirring the ashes." The speaker also reminds the congregation to take off their hats and kerchiefs, because the ashes will then be on one's head to make one well. This is an interpretation borrowed from the False Face Medicine Society, the curative aspect of whose "pass dance" lies, in part, in rubbing ashes over one's head. In the Stirring Ashes ritual no ashes are placed on the head of any individual, but the ceremony has nevertheless come to be interpreted more as a curing rite than as a "stirring up of the people." The Indian names of Our Uncles are then announced, as well as the names of the deacons who should pass the paddles with which the congregation stirs. These paddles are long-handled, crudely carved wooden blades with various clan and moiety symbols painted or burned on the blades. Ideally, they should be burned in the fire after each stirring, and new paddles should be constructed for the following year; but today they are stored in the attic of the Longhouse, and few people bother to make new paddles, even though making new paddles brings personal merit to the carver, especially if he has embellished the paddle in color. An individual should be handed a paddle whose decorations correspond to the clan to which he belongs; but this also is ignored today, and, in fact, even the moiety designation is ignored. One man, a Turtle, upon being handed a Wolf paddle seemed disturbed at this negligence and declared, "I could have thrown it away"; nevertheless, he used the paddle to stir the ashes.

At Sour Springs Our Uncles rise from their seats, are handed paddles, and proceed to a lighted stove (beginning at the Wolf and Turtle stoves in alternate years). There the Uncle assigned to speak delivers the patterned message: toys are to be taken away from children, sewing from women, and work from men; all should give their whole strength and mind to the Longhouse events; all should participate, and should any be unable to bear the icy weather outside that day, they should never-theless participate in the ritual by "going around" inside; the Great Creator gave this ritual, it is his "pass dance," and all must help. Then the speaker asks to be excused should he err in his duty, and the second Uncle takes over to sing the Stirring Ashes song. There are today approximately 30 Stirring Ashes songs. (Bill Buck and Roy Buck, both among the most erudite performers at Six Nations, agree that the number of songs known was 30. They were not able to sing the entire set, however.) Singers are at liberty to choose any one they like, though individual songs are said to have been at one time the property of different clans. As the singer chants the song (unaccompanied by any instrument), the two Uncles stir the ashes which have been raked to the front of the opened stove, letting them run over the blades. Still singing, they walk to the opposite stove, where the ashes are similarly stirred. This procedure of chanting and stirring is repeated once more at each stove, and then Our Uncles give up the paddles to the deacons and are seated. The actual number of stirrings is arbitrary. Variations from three to six stirrings are common, depending on the desire of the chanter. At the Longhouses down below, the costumed Uncles arrive from outside the Longhouse, as if they had just come to notify the congregation of the Midwinter Ceremony (even though they have previously stirred ashes in the homes), but otherwise the ceremony is the same as at Sour Springs.

Paddles are then handed to small groups of members, alternately to a group from each moiety, each of which exits, following a speaker and a singer, through its own moiety door, goes about the house counterclockwise, and enters at the door of the opposite moiety. The members of the group proceed to the stove on the side on which they entered, form a semicircle about it, and listen to the words of the speaker who gives thanks for being allowed to stir this year and hopes to repeat the stirring next season. The singer then sings the Stirring Ashes song, and all stir the ashes and then slowly move to the opposite stove where the ashes are also stirred. Again, the number of times that the ashes are stirred is arbitrary, but the groups usually visit each stove at least twice. The deacons in charge of distributing the paddles use their discretion as to the composition of each group, the average number being about six for a small attendance, more for a larger crowd. After everyone has been given a chance to stir the ashes, the Thanksgiving Address is repeated, and the next day's events are announced. People are instructed to bring their lunches the next day, because after half the day, the meeting will be open for "pass dances" for the people. If a chiefs' convention has been held at one of the other Longhouses on the Reserve, the Sour Springs representative to that convention now reports on the success of the preaching and the number of confessions, and he hands back to the wampum-keeper the wampum of the Longhouse which was used in the confession rite. No food is served at the Stirring Ashes ritual. The entire ceremony ought to be completed at noon, but it usually lasts until 1:30 or 2:00 P.M.

The second day of the Midwinter Ceremony proceeds just as the first, except that Our Uncles do not open the Stirring Ashes ritual, since they "came through" the day before. However, each of the small groups stirs as on the first day. When all have had a turn, Our Uncles return to give thanks for the performance once more, to stir the ashes, and to sing their song a final time. These should be the same Uncles who opened the meeting the day before. Then a speaker announces that "we will turn the paddles over" or "lift the paddles," (i.e., conclude the ritual). All the deacons in the house are asked to stand around the Turtle (east) stove, while the speaker (usually one of the Uncles, if the Uncle was in this case a deacon) impersonates the Great Creator and thanks the people for having helped to "pass" his dance. The singer also impersonates the Great Creator and sings the Stirring Ashes song which belongs to the Creator alone. The deacons stir twice at each of the stoves, give up their paddles, and the part of the day dedicated to the Great Creator is over. It is interesting to note that when the Great Creator is impersonated and when his song is sung, deacons rather than ordinary people must stir the ashes. It is one more example of the exalted position of the deacon in the Longhouse.

The remainder of the day, as well as the following day, is now "open for the people," which means that the "pass dances" of the members themselves may be performed, since everyone helped perform the dance of the Great Creator. While the people eat their lunches (which they have brought), the speakers encourage all to "pass" their dances, promising equal efficacy whether the dances be "with food" or "dry pole" (see p. 179 *infra*). "Our Creator has made it so that we should help one another," the speaker continues, and he explains the procedure involved in the public observance of the personal ritual obligations. "And," continues the speaker, "no one must leave just because his dance has been passed, but you must all remain and help each other." The remainder of the day, often until 6:30 P.M., and the entire third ceremonial day are devoted to the execution of the various individual and family obligations. At Lower Cayuga, where the attendance is somewhat larger than at Sour Springs, one more day is often needed to satisfy all the demands for rites. No two "pass-dance" days are identical, since the program depends on the particular needs of the individuals present, and the scheduling of the events is flexible. However, the types of observances and the procedure are standard and patterned.

Members today conceive of three types of public "pass dances" as appropriate to the occasion. First, there are the periodic observances which derive from obligations incurred by joining, for *legitimate* and *natural* reasons, one of the formalized medicine societies. (For a description of the recurrent obligations of medicine rites, see pp. 274–5 *infra*.) This means that the individual must have joined the medicine society because he was ill, or dreamed he should join, or made use of the society in forming a ritual friendship (see pp. 218–24 *infra* for a description of a ritual friendship), or was asked to join for miscellaneous reasons such as expert knowledge of the ritual or songs. If, however, membership in the society was sought for reasons even remotely associated with witchcraft or hunting-charm medicines (for example, if the individual joined because he had in some way acquired or inherited the charms, and not because another party had caused him sickness through witching and charms, for in the latter case membership in the society is legitimately sought on account of illness), then any observance of the obligations to the society should not be displayed at the Midwinter Ceremony. Actually, discrimination between natural and suspect causes for joining a society is often a difficult matter. At Midwinter, however, each individual decides for himself, for he initiates and asks only for those "pass dances" which he feels would not incriminate him. People are extremely shy about explaining the origin of many of their associations, and there is suspicion of almost all society membership, especially of membership in those societies which are known to be "strong" (have powerful and "particular" medicine) and in those which are commonly associated with hunting charms. In fact, suspicion about the motivation for joining one of the more powerful societies, such as the Hĕna'i?dos (Shake Pumpkin Society or Medicine Man's Society), even when it was actually done for perfectly legitimate and natural reasons, can prevent a public "pass dance," although the obligations derivative from membership in this society are periodically fulfilled at home. If, however, an individual joined the Hĕna'i?dos Society for reasons of illness, and then joined the False Face Society because it is intimately connected with the Hĕna'?idos Society, there is no prohibition against a public performance of the False Face "pass dance." The second type of appropriate observance is that which calls for a social or ceremonial dance, or for one of the four sacred rites, or for a ceremonial game, because at one time one of these had been performed for or by the individual, due to an illness, a dream, formation of a ritual friendship, or other legitimate reasons. Again, none of the suspect, "witching"-type games (such as the Bowl Game with wood counters or the football game using a flaming football) will be performed publicly, despite their "natural" acquisition. Performances of these first two types may, at Midwinter, be the actual cure or initial execution rather than the renewal of the rite. In such cases food should be provided, unless an emergency prevents the proper preparations. ("Passing" a dance "dry pole" is condoned only in the Longhouse; for if a "pass dance" is performed "dry pole" at home, there is a good chance that the spirit associated with the society would be hurt, and harm would occur to the individual who had so slighted "his medicine.") The third type of observance is one in which a person asks to have any ritual, song, dance, or game performed, not because he wishes to "pass" his dance and fulfill an obligation, but merely because he desires to offer it as a particular devotional act. This last type is most often exemplified by the performance of an Adõ'wa song or by a dance for the entire family. Although no specific results are expected from the execution of such a ritual, nevertheless, the individual tacitly hopes for some unspecified "merit."

Basically, all three types of "pass dances" are believed to be medicinal in nature, and consequently, the individual who "has the dance up" always assumes a role which indicates that he is being "cured." The patient removes his kerchief so that the medicine may be on his head, particularly in False Face curings where ashes are rubbed upon the head (he does not remove the ashes for three days); the patient throws the first snow snake; he throws up the ball in the football and lacrosse games; he shakes first in the Bowl Game; he ducks under the tug-of-war stick in the tug-of-war game; he dances immediately behind the leader of the opposite moiety in all dances; and he makes known his Indian name. All these actions are part of the medicine itself and essential for its efficacy. The moiety opposite to his always assumes the role of primary administrator of the medicine and acts as the one "who takes care of things." (For a description of the content of the "pass dances," see Speck, 1949: 64–126, and "Medicine and Witchcraft" *infra*.)

The procedure for arranging for a "pass dance" is best explained by an example. If a Turtle woman wishes one or more rites performed for her, she first informs the head deaconess of her own moiety that she wishes this rite performed and that she will have it either "with food" (in which case she will have brought all the appropriate food) or "dry pole." Also, if any esoteric ceremonial item is necessary, such as a stick for the tug-of-war game or a football for a football game, the person usually provides this item, too. (The same procedure is followed by a Wolf member in his moiety. Members usually inform deacons of their own sex, but this is not essential. A man may, if he wishes, communicate his desire to a deaconess on his own side.) The head deaconess then crosses over to the opposite moiety and informs the Wolf head deaconess that one of her members, whose Indian name she mentions, wishes a certain rite. Should this rite call for female performers the deaconess then arranges for principals (for example, for a leader of the Women's Dance). Otherwise, she will ask the Wolf head deacon to arrange for performers for the rite, to see to the spacing of the benches for the singers and actors, and to assemble the necessary accoutrements. (The head deacons and deaconesses may engage helpers [other deacons] to facilitate the procedure, since often the job of arrangement is too much for them.) The Wolf head deacon is also told the Indian name of the patient, since this must be announced to the congregation. The speaker for the day is then informed of the arrangements, and he announces to the whole "crowd" the particular rite to be given next and the Indian names of the patient, the singers, and the leading performers. The Turtle patient then moves over to the Wolf side of the house where the rite will be performed for her, or if it is a dance, the Turtle patient will follow immediately behind a Wolf leader. Although the lines of communication are clear, there is nevertheless an air of informality about the arrangements for each rite. No particular order is prescribed. Three Turtle patients may precede a Wolf patient, or there may be an alternation of moieties, or two events may occur simultaneously, one outside and one inside the Longhouse (for example, a football game may be going on outside while a Women's Dance is danced inside), or one in each moiety area. Events are scheduled on the spot, according to convenience; and the arrangements often require much whispering, consulting, searching for qualified performers, changing of costume, borrowing of performers from the opposite moiety, and borrowing equipment. Although the more esoteric items are usually supplied by the patient, the congregation is expected to arrive at the Longhouse bringing along masks and burlap sacks for disguises, lacrosse sticks, snow snakes, and musical instruments, in case they may be "called for." All such services are involved in "being helpful," for one should help others "pass" their dances successfully, even if one is not personally planning to have a rite. However, this rather haphazard arrangement is bound to result in shortages of necessary items of equipment.

When dances are required which need no particular performers—such as social dances (here they are of course in a medicinal context and not considered social), or the Feather Dance, or Skin Dance—everyone who is able, from both moieties, is expected to participate, though a member of the moiety opposite to that of the patient leads the dance. The greater the number of people who dance, the more pleasing is the dance to the patient and to the spirit forces involved. When the rite demands specialists, such as does the Eagle Dance, the head deacons designate the participants and personally ask each one to perform. It is considered incumbent on everyone to respond gladly to such a request. The head deaconess (or head deacon) indicates who is to receive the portions when food is distributed at the end of a rite and who is to participate in those society rites for which there are more potential actors than the sponsor can feed. The Otter Society rite, for example, presents such a problem, since the only activities are sprinkling the patient with water with a cornhusk bundle and eating fish, and there are many more eligible members of the society than the patient provides for. Since every participant must share in the food, and since not to reward a participant, if food is distributed at all, would be both bad taste and "dangerous," a choice of actors has to be made. However, when a society has a rite in the Longhouse, such as a Bear Dance, only the leaders, the performers, and those who spew the patient with berry juice must be rewarded. Anyone may enter the dance line itself when the "dancers go around," and these people, with the exception of the leaders, can safely be left unrewarded. In general, the days devoted to the "pass dances" are among the busiest and most trying for the deacons.

All the arrangements for "pass dances" must be made with care, since they deal with medicinal spirits, which are always potentially dangerous. Even though the Longhouse is the proper locale of the "pass dances," and dangerous medicines and witchcraft are outlawed in the Longhouse, there yet remains a feeling of uneasiness that some harm might be committed whenever a "pass dance" is performed. The casual observer might describe the "pass-dance" days as among the favorite and most light-hearted observances at the Longhouse, and indeed the attendance is excellent on those days, and the congregation actively takes part in many of the rites with apparent gusto; yet there is a definite undercurrent of extreme anxiety about performing the dances with a minimum of deviation and satisfying the spirit forces. A member thinks about and plans the "passing" of his dance in advance and is nervous when the dance actually comes up in the Longhouse. He wishes to see it "done right" and will discuss the "pass dance" after it has occurred in all its details and ramifications. "Pass dances" touch upon the most "particular" and emotionally worrisome aspect of a person's life, and therefore they must be treated most carefully and with seriousness and respect. A small offense may cause great harm, both to one's physical health and to one's luck. Incidentally, attendance at Sour Springs increases markedly from the first Stirring Ashes Day to Pass Dance Day. The first day usually draws 20 to 50 people. On the second Stirring Ashes Day, half of which is devoted to "pass dances," at least 50 people come; whereas the third day of the Midwinter Festival, dedicated to "pass dances" only, usually draws 150 people.

It is at this time also that a dream may be "hunted" (shagodiihwĕnhagos), which means that a dream which occurred in the five days between the last new moon and the opening of the Midwinter Festival is eligible to be guessed. (Dreams which occur during the rest of the year, if recurrent, should be taken to a fortune-teller for diagnosis and prescription.) The dreamer (male or female) tells his dream to a deacon or deaconess on his side, who then decides whether the dream is worth guessing. On the whole only a particular type of culturally patterned dream is deemed appropriate, namely, a dream in which the person finds himself in a dangerous predicament and is helped by the aid of another person who hands him a saving object. Many such dreams involve drowning, swamps, or encirclement by natural obstacles. Those dreams which concern dead people—and these are very common—are cured by dead feasts and are not believed to be helped by guessing, so that deacons usually disallow them. However, once a dream is judged eligible, the dreamer is taken "across the fire" (to the opposite moiety), where the chiefs and male deacons attempt to guess the dream. In difficult cases the guessers are given hints by the deacon who has brought over the dreamer. (Speck, 1949: 122, claims no hints are given; however, the contrary seems to be true today.) When the dream specifically identifies an individual, this person, if present in the Long-house—whether male of female, on the same side as the dreamer or on the opposite side—is asked to guess first; only if he should fail is the dream taken across to the chiefs and deacons. It is believed that all dreams which are considered must be guessed, else the dream will come true, and if one dreamed of a disaster, one is subject to that disaster. For example, Esther Jamieson recounts a tale told to her by her grandmother, in which a dreamer dreamed that he fell into a swamp and was helped by the swamp weed (ha'ŏhgwa). However, no one guessed, and he finally revealed the dream himself. The following spring, this same person was discovered drowned, with his head resting on the very swamp weed he had foretold. The empirical evidence for such beliefs is naturally difficult to determine, but this does not diminish adherence to the beliefs. Interestingly enough, the *Jesuit Relations* disclose similar beliefs among the Huron. A dream had to be guessed, and the content given to the dreamer, else he would destroy by fire any article within reach, including houses. Often, not only had the content of the dream to be guessed, but the individual insisted on a re-enactment of the dream. Failure to guess the content of a dream was considered extremely ominous (Thwaites, 42: 157, 165).

The guessers, with their heads lowered, take turns in trying to determine the content of the dream. As soon as the correct solution is proposed, the deacon who brought over the dreamer gives a whoop, and the dreamer goes back to his seat.

The guesser is then obliged to fashion or procure for the dreamer a miniature imitation of the object which he guessed and which figured in the dream. If no particular object appeared in the dream, the dreamer is at liberty to choose an object he would like to have carved. Most frequently it will be a miniature False Face mask, which is also the appropriate item in cases where the dream was merely "frightening." (A miniature mask may or may not have the mouth and eyes cut through, but this stylistic variation seems to be merely a matter of preference of the carver. Contrary to Speck's, 1949: 84, report, this does not differentiate a witching from a dream mask.) Other common objects are Husk Faces, snow snakes, corn pounders, lacrosse sticks, ears of corn, sticks like those for the tug-of-war game, canoes, paddles, knives, and ladders. These objects then act as protective charms throughout the lifetime of the individual ("they watch one," saya?darō). They must be "taken care of," however, or else their feelings might be hurt, and they might cause the owner illness. "Taking care of" simply involves an attitude of respect and the preservation of the item in a small silk (or silklike) wrapping in a safe place. If such a charm should "act up" and cause the owner any trouble, some tobacco must be burned for it, and sometimes the miniature masks are adorned with small bags of tobacco as are the real False Face masks. Potentially, these charms are also dangerous in that they may be used as agents in witchcraft: should one burn tobacco and ask the charm (particularly a miniature False Face or Husk Face mask) to perform an evil deed, for example, to cause illness to an enemy, it will carry out the orders. This characteristic gives the miniature masks a semisecret and fearsome aspect. All objects which are procured as a result of dreams ought to be buried with the dreamer at his death and should be inconspicuously placed in the coffin. However, this rule is often ignored, because relatives like the small sculptures and wish to keep them, despite the knowledge that it is a dangerous practice and that it is often diagnosed as the cause of illness (see p. 242 *infra*).

In the early evening the speaker announces the events of the coming day, which signals to the members that the "pass dances" must soon terminate, in case all of the members' requests have not already been fulfilled. Perhaps one or two more dances are passed; and then the Thanksgiving Address and miscellaneous announcements (e.g., reminding the Cayuga members to collect their Cayuga interest money) close the ceremonies for the day. No food is served the congregation beyond the special foods distributed during the day to participants in the various rites.

On the fourth day of the Midwinter Ceremony a white dog used to be burned (see pp. 185–7 *infra*). Lately, however, this has not occurred, and consequently there is no ceremonial activity on this day, and the deacons go to the Longhouse only to "scrub" it. (At Lower Cayuga Longhouse the fourth day is usually necessary for further "pass dances." Scrub Day there is the afternoon of Feather Dance Day.) The floors and benches are washed with lye, the stoves are cleaned, the cookhouse is set in order, wood for the fires is prepared, water is drawn for the meat to be boiled that night, etc. These tasks are rather unpleasant and strenuous; for instance, water often has to be scooped through a hole hacked in the ice and then carried a quarter of a mile to the cookhouse. It is considered meritorious to assist the deacons in these tasks, but they are a test of the ability of the deacons to work together and show devotion to the Longhouse. Lately, at Sour Springs, male deacons have been rather negligent, leaving the women to carry the water, make the fires, and scrub down the Longhouse.

At night the male deacons assemble in order to cook the meat for the following day. At present a side of beef is delivered in the afternoon, which the men chop into pieces on the large tree-trunk block in the cookhouse. The pieces are then dropped into water and cooked till edible. The remaining soup is saved until the next day, when the women use it as a base for the corn soup. The male cooks should stay at the Longhouse and cookhouse all night, dancing the Feather Dance "in order to wake themselves up and warm themselves." Today, however, if more than one cook remains, they are apt to sleep on the benches, after some singing of "Indian" songs for the sake of companionship. However, even after sleeping, one should as a minimum token of respect dance the Feather Dance as soon as the sun rises.

About 65 years ago, it is said that names were given on the fourth day at Sour Springs. Furthermore, the Life Supporters dances were performed at this time. The program was dedicated to life-sustaining things (food and medicines) and consisted of the same observances as those of the Dyŏnhe'hgŏ programs which survive today (see *supra*, pp. 156–7). At Lower Cayuga, a set of Life Supporters dances (Women's Dance, Standing Quiver Dance, Corn and Pumpkin Dances) are inserted even today between the two Feather Dances during the fifth day of the ceremony. In 1955, the Wolf moiety at Sour Springs thought that it would be "nice" to schedule a set of the Life Supporters dances at the same time, but the Turtle deaconesses were strenuously opposed. They claimed that Sour Springs ought not follow "down-below" practices (and the leading Wolf deaconesses come from "below"), and if the dances were to be resurrected at all, they should be performed on the fourth day, Scrub Day, as was once done. Bitterness ensued over this procedural point, with an immediate and predictable formation of factions. No agreement could be reached; and finally, in characteristic fashion in case of disagreement, the dances were omitted altogether. Even though this seems a minor point of protocol, it illustrates the emotional attachment to procedure and to local variation. Furthermore, it throws light on the problems of the deacons. They are supposed to "work together"; but after this incident the relations between the two deaconesses involved were severed for a while. Everyone deplored the shocking discord, yet all took sides.

The fourth day, and certainly the fifth, marks a shift in the emphasis of the Midwinter Ceremony. The informants say: "Now the second part of the doings are on." From a concern with curing and personal well-being, attention now turns toward the agricultural hierarchy and toward thanking and supplicating the Great Creator, although matters of concern to the individual are not suppressed. It is felt that the first three days are "for the people" (despite the fact that the Stirring

Ashes ritual is the Great Creator's "pass dance") and the following days are primarily for the sake of the Great Creator; though if one considers motivation, all the observances are ultimately for the good of the people.

The last burning of a dog took place at Seneca Longhouse in the late thirties, though some informants thought it was 1941. Nevertheless, Longhouse members insist that the ceremony has not been definitely abrogated but rather is being held in abeyance pending the reappearance of a dog of prescribed breed. The requisite dog is described as "pure white with a short pointed face and long fur, and it is neither a collie nor a terrier." No one gives an exact description (Fenton, 1942: 17, thought the breed in recent years "sometimes had spotted ears"), but everyone is unanimous in the opinion that the "right" dog hasn't been seen around and perhaps has by now died out. Indeed, there are those who claim that Handsome Lake had already pointed to the extinction of the breed and declared that therefore no further dogs ought to be burned. These same informants, however, admit that Handsome Lake also saw the burned dog in heaven, where he was following the "man with wounds on his feet and hands" (i.e., Christ), and that Handsome Lake thought the ceremony was a good practice. The various interpretations concerning Handsome Lake and the white dog arise from the apocryphal and diverse versions of the Code. The Parker version (1913: 75) describes Handsome Lake's reunion with his dog during his journey to heaven, "and it appeared just as it had when he had decorated it for the sacrifice in the . . . [New Year's Ceremony]. Then said the four [Angels], 'This thing attests to the value of our thank offering to the Creator.' " This version is also repeated at Six Nations, concurrent with the version that Handsome Lake outlawed further burnings. There is also a highly rationalized version, showing Christian influence, which the famous Longhouse speaker, John Isaac, taught, namely: "White people burned sheep as a sacrifice, and the Indian wanted to sacrifice, too, so he used a dog." However, the dog is not considered a sacrifice, but more of a messenger and a present to the Creator. The Canadian government, through the local Indian Office, has let it be known that it considers this ceremony to be a "cruel pagan ritual," and has exerted considerable pressure on the Longhouse to outlaw the burnings. This, too, may help explain the sudden extinction of the requisite breed, although even before the cessation of the ritual, dogs were scarce and performances irregular.

If the Creator had sent a dog, then chiefs, warriors, and deacons met the night before the scheduled ceremony in order to apportion the requisite tasks among themselves. Men were designated to kill the dog, dress him, carry him into the Longhouse, and carry him out to the fire; and the speakers and singers were also appointed. Each detail was anticipated, so that the ritual would function smoothly. Decorations for the dog, such as wampum and feathers for his head and ribbons for his legs, were also collected from the congregation the day before.

At four o'clock in the morning the appointed ones met again, a speaker recited the Thanksgiving Address, and the preparations began. The dog had to be strangled so that no blood appeared, since he was supposed to look as alive as possible.

Then he was decorated in the cookhouse with wampum, ribbons, feathers, and a daub of Indian rouge on each cheek, which represented three Angels. The interpretation of these spots as representing three of the four Angels comes from a version of the Code preached at Six Nations. Fenton (1942: 17) mentions that the dog had three stripes of red paint on each cheek and a half circle toward the ears. Perhaps the fact that there were three stripes (at Onondaga Longhouse) led to the interpretation that the daubs represented three Angels. None of the ribbons may be red in color, since bright red is considered inappropriate on a dead person, and the dog was treated just as if he were a dead person. He was carried into the Longhouse through the men's door—"as if he were walking"—and laid on the singers' bench at the center of the house with his head to the west. Both of these traits occur in the burial of people.

The congregation arrived just before sunrise, around seven o'clock, and the ceremony began at the first break of day. A messenger, dressed in Indian costume, arrived from a near-by house, uttering three hoots, "hui, hui, hui," which indicated that the Great Creator was on his way to the Longhouse. The impersonator of the Creator then appeared at the Longhouse, circled once outside the house in a counterclockwise direction, and entered the house. During this peregrination he sang his "dream song," which is similar to a Stirring Ashes tune. Inside the house the "Creator," still singing, four times circled the bench on which the dog was lying; then an appointed speaker stopped him and said that a gift had been made to the Creator by the people, and that this gift was a hammer (gadji'hwa?). "No," said the "Creator," "anyone wishing to say a few words must do it in the right way." This indicated that a hammer was not the appropriate gift nor the answer to the dream song. Stopping the impersonator of the Creator and suggesting items to him were a simulation of dream guessing, and the correct answers indicated the items which should be given to the Creator, just as the item of a dream should be given to the dreamer.

After this exchange of guessing and answering, the "Creator" resumed singing his dream song as he circled about the bench four more times. A second time he was stopped, and the speaker said, "The people on earth have made a gift—Indian tobacco." This was a correct response, and the appointed "hollerer" (the same who announced the arrival of the Creator) then emitted a hoot like the one which announced the arrival of the Creator, except that this time the hoot indicated that the correct item had been guessed. The "Creator" also replied, "I will thank the people on earth with an Adõ'wa that they have given tobacco." Thereupon, the "Creator" sang his Adõ'wa song, and once again circled the bench four times, singing his dream song. A third time he was stopped and told, "The people on earth have made a gift to the Creator—a white dog." This, too, was a correct response; the hollerer hooted again, and the "Creator" confirmed it again. "I thank the people with an Adõ'wa that the gift has come to me," he said, and he immediately sang his Adõ'wa. For the last time he circled around the dog four times, and still singing his dream song, he left the Longhouse through the door which belonged to the moiety having the "lead" for that year. The appointed pallbearers for the dog followed, carrying the dog, and then the congregation filed out, too. All followed the "Creator" once around the Longhouse and to the fire. There a speaker repeated the tobacco invocation while he offered the promised tobacco to the "Creator," the speech being almost identical with the one offered at present on Skin Dance Day. (During those years when the white dog was burned, the tobacco invocation was omitted at Skin Dance Day, since it had already been offered at the pyre of the dog.) Then the dog was placed on the fire and sent to the Creator. When all was finished, four men sang their Adŏ'wa songs in order to give thanks for the fulfillment of their obligation. Then, before the sun had fully risen (around eight o'clock), everyone went home.

Both the tobacco and the dog were offered to the Creator as "gifts" and as tokens of thanks and respect from the people, but with both offerings there once more was the implied supplication that in return the Creator should continue to bestow life-giving things on man. Also noteworthy is the reciprocal politeness shown between Man and the Creator, for each thanks each for his offerings. The white dog is believed to be "a messenger to the Creator of what the people want," as well as a gift from the people. It should be conceived of as fulfilling functions almost identical with those of the Indian tobacco and as endowed with similar efficacy.

The fifth day is widely designated as Ohstowa Day, because the Feather Dance (ohstowa?go'wa) is the outstanding event. The Feather Dance, as one of the four sacred ceremonies, is here performed specifically to please the Great Creator and to thank him for his benevolence throughout the past year. The mood of the congregation is attuned in reverent thankfulness to the sacred Upper Pantheon. Gone is the anxiety of the "pass-dance" days, and gone is the need for extreme "carefulness." Dancing the Feather Dance is eminently pleasurable, and with the addition of meat for the first time at Midwinter the attendance reaches its peak. Three hundred and fifty is the average attendance on this day, which is consistently the highest of any ceremony whatever.

Seating once again follows sex lines, with entrance through men's and women's doors and not Turtle and Wolf doors. Attenders ought to be costumed in "Indian" dress, since it is respectful to "dress" for the sacred rites of the Great Creator. Indian dress should be worn for the remainder of the Midwinter Ceremony, because both the next day, Skin Dance Day, and the following day (or days) of betting are also dedicated to the Great Creator. (Actually, preachers at Six Nations declare that "Indian" dress should be worn at all Longhouse festivals, but the essential times are Strawberry, Green Corn, and Midwinter, when one or more of the sacred rites are performed for the Creator. Conventions should also be attended in costume. Many people, however, do not own any "Indian" dress, and the majority come in street clothes. No penalty accompanies noncompliance with proper dress, but if one does dress as prescribed, one is considered "more respectful.")

The Thanksgiving Address opens the ceremonies, usually around 11:30 A.M., though again the ceremony should be terminated at noon. A Feather Dance set of the Upper Pantheon follows, which the performers try to make lengthy and inclusive of most of the songs in the series. The best performers in the house are chosen for this set, and participation at this time is considered an honor. At Sour Springs, in 1954, the set of Upper Pantheon dances lasted half an hour, and often a set will last even longer. At Lower Cayuga Longhouse young boys and girls lead the first Feather Dance, but at Sour Springs a costumed man leads. Deacons customarily dance at the front of the lines, although this is not obligatory.

After the first set it is customary to deliver a sermon to the congregation along the lines of a Handsome Lake exhortation. Members are urged to lead good lives, to refrain from gossip and slander, etc. At Sour Springs such a pronouncement is delivered in Cayuga and then translated into Mohawk for the benefit of those members who are not able to understand Cayuga. Since such a procedure is not often followed, one may note the relative importance attached to this sermon. Speakers become emotional, often allowing themselves to include factionalistic, chauvinistic, and messianic statements. Grievances are repeated, positions stated, and the congregation is also stirred to emotional expression. A preacher at this time may be as florid as he desires, for it is one of the occasions on which "good, kind talk" is prized. Naturally, the customary thankfulness to the spirit hierarchy is also expressed.

A second, earthly Feather Dance set follows, also lengthy. If the same performers again provide the music, they are apt to change places—that is, the leader of the last set now takes the secondary role, following the songs initiated by his partner. Everyone is expected to join in both Feather Dance sets, since they represent an offering to the Creator.

The Thanksgiving Address is repeated again, and the ceremonial foods are distributed. The corn soup of cracked flint corn boiled in beef stock with salt and beans is distributed around the women's stove, and the deacons hand each member his pail filled with the hot soup. (Ceremonial foods are salted at Six Nations now. Speck, 1949: 41, evidently was told the contrary.) The meat is passed in chunks from trays and baskets along with the feast foods which the women have baked and donated. Since Midwinter is the most important ceremony, and this is the first day for food distribution, the choice and variety are usually excellent. People would be ashamed to attend the Longhouse without bringing a substantial contribution, and consequently there is much baking the day before. Women place much emphasis on their "baskets," which are mostly made of decorated black-ash splints. They fill them with cookies, and deaconesses reward "people with baskets" by placing a variety of baked goods in each basket before allocating the food for distribution to everyone. Ceremonial foods should never be touched or distributed before the proper time in the regular course of events, and even the tasting of a cookie is improper. The moment of distribution is therefore eagerly awaited and causes a noticeable thrill among even the adults.

The following (sixth) day is known as Skin Dance Day, since the Skin Dance is the outstanding event. Again the day is mainly dedicated to performances of sacred rituals which belong to the Great Creator and are designated to entertain and please him. Seating is according to sex division, and people come dressed in costume. Men should once more have stayed at the cookhouse all night cooking meat, though in fact the meat from the day before is simply served again, so that there is no need to cook a second time. Consequently, only some deacons will have arrived at the Longhouse early in order to light the stoves and the fire in the cookhouse. (However, at Onondaga Longhouse meat may be cooked as often as on three separate nights.)

The program opens with the Thanksgiving Address, followed by an explanation of the ceremony at hand and a lengthy tobacco invocation. Two speakers, one from each moiety, are appointed to offer the prayer, and they step to the Turtle stove, surrounded by deacons. Speck (1949: 131) mentions three deacons from each side. However, in 1954 12 deacons flanked the speakers. Probably all deacons are eligible to accompany the speaker to the stove. Once again a special prerogative of the deacons is displayed. First the Wolf moiety speaker usually expresses thanks and attention to the Lower and Upper Pantheons, and then the Turtle moiety speaker continues by noting all the earthly spirits. The content of the prayers once more follows the itemization of the Thanksgiving Address. Each spirit force is individually recognized and thanked for its services and then asked to continue them another year. Also, all ask to be spared to see another successful spring and to meet again the following year. As each verse is finished a pinch of Indian tobacco is thrown into the fire, for it is the tobacco, together with a whoop, which attracts the spirit forces and the Creator and conveys to them the words of supplication and thanksgiving. At Onondaga and Seneca the tobacco invocation is performed outside the Longhouse over a small fire, or, if it is too stormy, in the cookhouse. No whoops accompany the burning at either of these Longhouses. At Sour Springs the ceremony is usually conducted around the Turtle stove, though Speck (1949: 131) mentions that in 1933 it was also performed outside. (He mentions "near Turtle moiety door and cookhouse. . . ." However, that must have been the Wolf door. In 1954 and 1955 the invocation occurred indoors.)

After the tobacco burning the second sacred ritual, the Adõ'wa, is performed. As at Green Corn the first song is that of the Great Creator, sung by an impersonator, who circles twice round, sings the song eight times, and gives eight speeches of thanks. Then the Adõ'wa rite is open to the people. Even though the number of songs and recitations is optional, no person matches the length of the Adõ'wa of the Great Creator. Again, as at Green Corn, friends may traverse the Longhouse, side by side, as they sing their Adõ'wa. Since names for boys are bestowed with the singing of an Adõ'wa, the naming ceremony occurs at this point. Both girls and boys are named, though in the case of a woman a chanted speech alone bestows a name. (For a fuller description of naming, see p. 210 *infra*. At Lower Cayuga Longhouse names are not given on Skin Dance Day but on a special day set aside for this purpose before the Stirring Ashes ritual. This is also done at Coldspring, according to Fenton, 1936: 22.) At the end of the personal Adŏ'wa and naming rites, the impersonator again sings the Great Creator's song, thanks the people for their attention, and closes the second sacred rite of the day.

The third sacred rite, the Skin Dance, is then announced. A water drum and a horn rattle are used in the Skin Dance, and its name is said to derive from the drum covering. The Skin Dance is another one of the rites which is believed to have been a war dance and boasting song at one time (Speck, 1949: 138). Since this ceremony, like the Adŏ'wa, War Dance, and Eagle Dance, involves stopping the singing, delivering a speech, whooping, and striking for silence, it is reasonable to classify it as an erstwhile boasting song. Neither boasting nor war are condoned by the Handsome Lake tradition, and it was an interesting metamorphosis to transform the boastful texts to paeans of thanksgiving. After the announcement the players are selected, both of them from the same moiety, unlike in the majority of the dances, in which there is one performer from each moiety. (At Onondaga Longhouse the moiety affiliation of the players is not important, but the men must be costumed.) War whoops are heard outside the women's door, and the costumed male dancers enter the Longhouse. (At Onondaga one song is sung before entrance into the Longhouse.) Each song is initiated by a short whoop by the leading dancer and an echo by the men behind him. At the end of the song, all members dance in a circle counterclockwise until the next song begins, with men dancing first and women joining the line at the end. An introductory set of Skin Dance songs is completed, and, then, after one dance of the second Skin Dance set, the Wolf speaker steps to the performers' bench, signals for the cessation of the song, and chants the first verse of the thanksgiving invocation to the Lower Pantheon. After this verse the dance continues, then stops again to permit the speaker to move up in the pantheon and offer his respects to the Sun and Moon, and so on through both the Lower and Upper Pantheons. The speaker from the opposite moiety then repeats the procedure, beginning with the lowest of the earthly spirits and moving up in the hierarchy till he has completed the customary listing. The content of these chants is almost identical with that of the tobacco invocation at the beginning of the day. The entire series lasts 40 to 60 minutes. (See Speck, 1949: 138–41, for a further description of the Skin Dance.) Performers, speakers, and dancers may help themselves to berry juice or water placed at the performers' bench throughout the dance.

At the end of the dance, announcements are in order, as well as the personal observance of "giving up the dead" by widows or widowers. (See p. 250 *infra* for a description of "giving up the dead.") The speaker then announces who will collect the bets for the Bowl Game the following day, and he also reminds the congregation that the seating and entrance will once more be by "clans." It is at this point that a conscientious speaker should enumerate the clans and the side to which each clan belongs. The Thanksgiving Address is then repeated, and the same ceremonial foods as on the previous day are passed to the congregation. In the afternoon and the next morning the bets for the Bowl Game are collected.

The final (seventh) ceremonial day, Betting Day, is primarily devoted to the last sacred rite, the Bowl Game. The stakes are paired off in the Longhouse, and the wampum staked by each moiety is hung on a nail over the south window. After the opening Thanksgiving Address and the explanation of the ceremony for the day, four whoops are given, and the Bowl Game begins as at Green Corn time (see pp. 170–2 *supra*). The same rules apply now as then, and the game lasts until all beans are won by one moiety. The winning moiety then again gives the whoops, and a Feather Dance set is danced to celebrate the ending of the game and to thank the Creator for having ended it, for the day was dedicated to pleasing the Creator by playing "his game." The stakes are passed to the bettors of the winning moiety, and a speaker announces a change (a "cross over") to seating according to sex.

A speaker will then "free" the people from their ceremonial obligations and return to them their work and pleasures, and to the children their toys. Also, they may now go out again, for during the ceremonial period, no member should visit outside his home and his Longhouse. (Morgan, 1901, 1: 206–7, mentions entertainments with dancing at private homes and snow-snake games during the Midwinter Ceremony. Both are forbidden at Six Nations today.) Children are kept out of school, and going to a dance would be a major sin; though when the Bowl Game lasts too many days, the congregation becomes impatient, and it is then said that the prohibition on going out applies only to the "most important days," Feather Dance Day and Skin Dance Day.

Once more a sermon is preached giving thanks for having been spared and supplicating for the means of life for another year. Also, once more, the congregation is exhorted to work together, to follow Gaiwi'yo, to be united in mind, and, in general, to "travel the right road." The Midwinter Ceremony ends with the Thanksgiving Address in brief form and the distribution of food—sweetened cracked-flint-corn soup and feast cookies. If any meat still remains, it is passed once more.

The over-all spirit of the Midwinter Festival may accurately be summed up by the statement of Sam Jamieson, Chief Deyothowe'hgō:

> At Midwinter we ask the Great Creator to continue giving life-giving things to sustain men, and ask him for our sustenance; one works into the other. At Green Corn and Thanksgiving we thank him for what he gave. It is good. Our religion is good. And so it goes each year. When people come and see the forms only, it is silly to them, but it is not silly when you understand it; it is good. It is this way with the Indians all over the country.

THE GOOD MESSAGE IN THE LONGHOUSE

INTRODUCTION

As I have pointed out above (pp. 133 ff.), the term "Longhouse religion" applies not only to the calendric agricultural observances but also to an ethical and moral system and a cosmology introduced by the Seneca prophet, Handsome Lake (1735–1815). It is this ethical and moral system and this cosmology which properly constitute the subject matter of the "Gaihwi'yo," the Good Message. However, when Handsome Lake awoke from a trance in 1799 to utter the first of his prophetic revelations—now incorporated into the body of dicta, anecdotes, and laws which comprise the Good Message—he did not introduce a radically new ethic. Rather, he propounded a doctrine taken largely from the existing body of Iroquois religion, which he had reinterpreted and syncretized with the Christian, and particularly Quaker, teachings familiar to his community. (For a most interesting and well-documented account of the origin and viability of the Good Message, see Deardorff, 1951: 79–107. Deardorff believes the Message to have been born "of a miscegenation of Quaker with old Seneca stock," which hybrid was acceptable to the local audience.) Fortuitous historical and cultural circumstances, as well as the familiarity of its content, undoubtedly aided the viability of the Good Message, until today Gaihwi'yo has been so assimilated into the generalized Iroquoian religion that the entire religious complex is designated as "Gaihwi'yo." However, there are two observances which deal specifically with the words and deeds of Handsome Lake and which cannot be classified as belonging to the agricultural complex described in the preceding section, yet they form an important part of an individual's religious life.

These observances are the Six Nations convention and the chiefs' convention. Both are primarily meetings for the purpose of reciting the Good Message of Handsome Lake, which today involves the revelation as described by the Prophet himself and memorized and transmitted through several lines of preachers,[16] an explanation of the necessity of the revelation, and certain biographical details about the life of the Prophet and the circumstances of the revelation to him. Associated with the recitation of the Code are personal confessions and moral exhortations to lead a "good" life. It is at these meetings that the specifically ethical, moral, and cosmological considerations are emphasized for the practitioners of the Longhouse religion.

A Six Nations convention is one of the meetings of the biennial circuit which begins every fall at Tonawanda and which is observed in turn at each of the other nine participating Longhouse communities, plus the Sour Springs community in those years in which it elects to join the circuit (see p. 36 *supra*). The Longhouse communities participating in the circuit today are Tonawanda, Allegany, Catta-

---

[16] Parker suggests that the succession of recitations was the following: Handsome Lake taught Owen Blacksnake and James Johnson; Blacksnake then taught Henry Stevens, who in turn instructed Edward Cornplanter, who wrote the "Code" as recorded by Parker (1913: 19). Deardorff (1951: 99) traces the history of the Coldspring recitation today backward from DeForest Abrams, to Oscar Crow, to Jackson Titus, who might have heard it from Handsome Lake. At Six Nations it is said that David Thomas learned from Dave Sky, who learned from John Gibson, who learned from his grandfather, who heard Handsome Lake. At Six Nations it is also claimed that there was no gap in the preaching between Handsome Lake's death and the next recitation in Canada, as there supposedly was in the United States. However, Deardorff has shown (*ibid.*) that the latter supposition is incorrect, and that James Johnson, the grandson of Handsome Lake, was not the reviver of the Code in 1840, but that the Code was being preached as early as 1818 at Tonawanda.

raugus, Onondaga Castle, St. Regis, Caughnawaga, Muncy, and the four Long-houses of Six Nations. The name "Six Nations convention" does not refer to the Six Nations Reserve, but to the ensemble of all the Iroquois tribes. A chiefs' convention is a recitation of the Code which is sponsored by a particular Longhouse community for local edification, though at Six Nations it is customary to inform all the Longhouses on the Reserve that a convention will be held. However, the message is delivered orally and informally by a messenger who is "sent around," and wampum tallies are not used. At Sour Springs, where a preacher from Muncy has recently been much in demand for the local conventions, the Muncy community is tacitly invited whenever Hilton Nicholaus is engaged, though none of the Muncy members has lately come with him. When a local convention of this type is held, the attenders are not considered "guests,"[17] nor must any particular hospitality, such as housing, be provided. There are, however, some chiefs' conventions which, while not really Six Nations conventions, are not confined to the local Longhouse nor to the Longhouses on the Reserve. Such a convention is sponsored by a single Longhouse, but all the other Longhouses usually considered in the circuit are invited, and wampum tallies are sent out to legitimate the invitation. The sponsoring Longhouse undertakes complete responsibility for the visitors, housing and nourishing them for the duration of the recitation. Onondaga Longhouse, for example, sponsored such an event just before Strawberry time in 1953, and declared the convention "a great success." Not only does a congregation gain spiritually from such a convention, but it is also calculated to impress socially. In general the same procedure is followed at all the conventions, except that a preacher at the Six Nations convention must have official validation as a Gaihwi'yo preacher from the "Sanhedrin" at Tonawanda, whereas the preacher at a local convention may be locally chosen and need satisfy the sponsoring congregation only. Deardorff (1951: 99) used the apt term "Sanhedrin" for the committee of chiefs and preachers at Tonawanda which passes upon the qualifications of a preacher of Gaihwi'yo and which decides whether his version is orthodox. Candi-

---

[17] The concept of "guest," particularly one who is a stranger, is important in Iroquois culture. An elaborate set of mores concerns the proper treatment of a guest, e.g., clan identification, introduction with handshaking, hospitality patterns (which include sharing all of the host's food and belongings in order to escape a suspicion of witchcraft), joking about permitting a guest to sleep with the appropriate spouse, and, on the part of the guest, elaborate thanking for the hospitality shown. Guests should be announced and treated as important personages; and on such occasions as when the opposite moiety comes "on the road" to a Condolence or when any delegation arrives, the rules concerning guests are also applicable. Supernaturals are treated similarly. For example, the Creator was announced and treated as an honored stranger at the White Dog Festival, the False Faces are preceded and announced by the Husk Faces, the dead who attend any dead feast are treated as honored guests, etc. In part this pattern may be traced to the time of the village settlements, when delegations walked many days to deliver messages or condolences to their brethren. At that time hospitality not only sustained but also assured safe conduct. The concept of a peaceful guest, who may come and go unmolested, was also stressed by Handsome Lake. Before that, people say, "we liked to fight," and treachery was not unusual.

dates must preach a complete Gaihwi'yo, usually lasting four days, and are often very hesitant about "taking the test," though great prestige accrues to any man who can pass. Usually a novice preaches first at his own Longhouse and then is "invited" to preach at Tonawanda. This means that the "Sanhedrin" has heard of him and wishes to validate another preacher. It would be considered very forward to appear at Tonawanda and "ask" for validation.

CHIEFS' CONVENTIONS

The local chiefs' conventions are held more frequently than the others, and they may be scheduled to satisfy a variety of needs. The chiefs, deacons, or speakers of a Longhouse may at any time decide that the congregation needs a spiritual stimulus—that people "are slipping," or absent from the Longhouse too much, or sinful, or demoralized—and therefore they schedule a recitation of the Code "to bring them back to the Longhouse way." A particular omen may demand that a recitation be held. For example, in 1955 at Tonawanda the convention wampum, signifying all the nations, broke in two while the preacher held it during the recitation. Handsome Lake supposedly said (according to the speaker at Tonawanda, in whose hands the wampum broke) that a sign would be given if the Longhouse were in danger of breaking up, and the breaking of the wampum was interpreted as this sign. Consequently, a special convention was sponsored by Tonawanda Longhouse, with invitations to all the chiefs, and there were most earnest exhortations to "attend to the affairs of the Longhouse." Representatives from the various Longhouses were particularly asked to report to their home Longhouses and to warn the population. Nevertheless, there were those who insisted that the wampum had broken due to natural causes, such as the age of the strings supporting the beads, rather than due to the imminent decay of the Longhouse.

Most commonly the chiefs' conventions are called to provide an opportunity for spiritual purging before participating in the major Longhouse ceremonials. At Six Nations it is believed most important to attend a convention before the Strawberry Ceremony in spring, because the spiritual purge complements the physical purge so desirable before the oncoming new season and before partaking of the "first fruits." Listening to the Code and confessing afterward "cleans one out," which means that the individual is sanctified and made worthy of participation in the calendric rituals and worthy of contact with the spirit forces. The Strawberry Festival also coincides with the first message of the Prophet (see *supra*, p. 36), and therefore it is particularly appropriate to commemorate his gospel at that time by listening to a recitation. Midwinter is almost as important a time for a convention, since a person "should give up his sins" before entering into the sacred rituals of the Midwinter Ceremony. Also, a convention before a major ceremonial cycle inspires the population to give more attention to their Longhouse, as the commands of the preachers are still fresh in their memory.

Finally, it is the duty of a Longhouse to sponsor a Good Message recitation occasionally, because it shows respect to Handsome Lake and the Creator and also because it allows the people a chance to hear the sacred words. The congregation appreciates being given an opportunity to hear Gaihwi'yo much as a Catholic appreciates being allowed to partake of a sacrament; it is a privilege, and therefore gratitude is felt toward the Longhouse which sponsors the meeting. Personal thankfulness to Handsome Lake and to his expositor can be indicated immediately after each day's preaching at confession time. The act of confession, aside from offering the sinner absolution, is considered the most affirmative declaration of allegiance to the religion of the Prophet and a concrete indication of the effectiveness of the preaching. A preacher is judged by the number of people he is able to move, to cause to confess their sins, or perhaps to convert to the Longhouse. The more confessions, the more renowned is the speaker; and each confession is counted and reported to the Longhouses which sent representatives. Particularly at present, when the Longhouses are under much pressure to acculturate, the congregations like to point to the large number of confessions and affirmations of faith which occur at local conventions. (In 1955 at Lower Cayuga Longhouse 80 people confessed at the convention just before Midwinter. At the Strawberry convention at Sour Springs in 1956, 46 people confessed.)

Seating at a chiefs' convention is according to sex, with no particular necessity to divide according to moieties within the sexual division. Conventions are stratified according to age and status rather than moiety; the invitations and salutations refer specifically to chiefs, officers (deacons of the Longhouse), those "other than officers" (the congregation in general), children, those that are creeping, and those on the cradleboards (infants). The separation of chiefs and officers is reflected in the seating; for either they sit on the front benches, as in the usual ceremonial events, or they sit apart opposite the preacher in the center of the house. In all cases, officers, even more than the general audience, should wear Indian dress (not "dead clothes") to a convention, and officers and chiefs should listen to the dictates of their religion more assiduously than the ordinary person. The special seating is a device for elevating the official personnel of the Longhouse and for maintaining the prestige of the chiefs, despite the derogatory comments about chiefs attributed to Handsome Lake by some of the preachers. (For example, Hilton Nicholaus maintains in his version of the recitation, that "one of the chiefs with Handsome Lake converted to Christianity, and therefore the chiefs are of two minds and have a difficult time going to heaven." Joe Isaac and George [?] Gibson are said to have mentioned this, too. This supposed conversion is considered detrimental to the chiefs, who should, according to the Longhouse view, have their wampum and antlers removed if they join the church [see p. 92 *supra*].)

The meeting opens with a Thanksgiving Address and an explanation of the nature of the convention. The speaker is handed all the wampums to be displayed and used during the convention, which always includes the Longhouse wampum of the sponsoring community, as well as any brought by representatives of other Longhouses. At Six Nations, whenever the Onondaga Longhouse sponsors a convention, Seneca Longhouse also contributes its wampum, and conversely; and when Lower Cayuga sponsors a convention, Sour Springs usually contributes its wampum, and vice versa. Thereafter, the preacher is led from his seat to the special central position from which he is to preach. At Six Nations all the Longhouses prefer that the preacher face east, "because the sun rises in the east"; but facing south is also permissible, since "the path from heaven to the Longhouse comes from the south." Facing west or north is not considered appropriate, and Hilton Nicholaus was corrected when he began speaking, facing north. A preacher is always attended by a "guardian" (who ought to belong to the moiety opposite to that of the preacher) who leads him, introduces him, sits next to him throughout the recitation, hands him the wampum and the strawberry juice (in case the speaker wishes to refresh himself during the preaching), indicates when noon has come so that the recitation may end, and attends to any needs that the preacher may have. A preacher should continue without interruption through a recitation until it is time to stop. The text of the recitation mentions that it begins at "breaking-daylight time," but eight o'clock is considered the ideal time to start. In practice, however, meetings begin about 10:00 A.M., which in part accounts for the number of days necessary to complete a recitation of the Message. Preachers must stop promptly at noon (1:00 P.M. Daylight Saving Time), and if they have a late start, the recitation may last five days. Three to five days is the common duration, and at Six Nations recitations have lately run four days at all the Longhouses.

The content of the recitation may, in its general form, be found in Parker's *Code of Handsome Lake* (1913) which is a translation of the version written by Edward Cornplanter in 1903. There is at present, however, no standard version of the Message which is preached by all preachers, or indeed by more than one. Each preacher has his own version, learned from various predecessors who also had their own versions, and embellished and interpreted as the preacher repeats the Message year after year. Furthermore, the emphasis of a recitation may vary according to the purpose for which the chiefs' convention is called. The specific needs of each congregation are assessed, and the appropriate sections of the Code are emphasized. Thus, the section on marriage and fidelity might be stressed to one congregation, while the section on the evils of liquor might be stressed to another; or, if the chiefs' convention was called to impress the congregation with its duty to the Longhouse and to prevent defection to the churches on the Reserve, the preacher might be told to stress the sections in the Code referring to the ultimate salvation of Longhouse members as opposed to the eternal doom of Christians. Much of each version is apocryphal and exegetical and circumscribed only by the capabilities of expression of the preacher. The manner of delivery is declamatory, and a preacher may interject as much zeal as he feels appropriate. However, even a minor deviation of dogma might make a considerable difference in the culture of a locality, for the words of the preacher are among the most definitive determinants of the ideal culture. Since preachers presume to report the exact dictates of Handsome Lake and to interpret these dictates even as the Prophet would have them interpreted, it follows that people must pattern their actions and beliefs on the preaching if they wish to follow Handsome Lake. And, indeed, one of the commonest answers to a question of "Why . . .?" is "Because it says in the preaching. . . ." Nevertheless, informants do realize that various preachers use their own versions. Some Longhouse members, for example, will not go to a Good Message recitation by one of the Six Nations principal preachers, even though they attend when he speaks at other times. It is claimed: "He preaches funny. He puts in things he shouldn't and leaves out others, and though he passed in the States in his first tryout, he was never asked back to preach in the States." Also, informants recognize when various speakers "preach alike." Thus, George Gibson, John Isaac, and Hilton Nicholaus are said to have preached in a similar way, though they spoke Seneca, Cayuga, and Oneida, respectively. Dave Thomas, incidentally, speaks in Onondaga; and Ezekiel Hill, a Seneca preacher who lived at Six Nations until his recent death and was often called upon to preach, used Seneca, Onondaga, Cayuga, and Mohawk at will.[18]

At the end of a morning's preaching, the Thanksgiving Address is again delivered, and then the congregation dances a set of Feather Dances in order to indicate its gratitude to the Creator and to the preacher. Again, the leading dancer should, for the sake of respect, be clothed in Indian dress. Then the sponsoring Longhouse treats the members attending to lunch, although it is often considered appropriate that the attenders "help out" by bringing food to contribute to the communal meal. At Onondaga, in 1956, the food was typically American—canned goods, bread, and Freshie (a commercial powdered soft-drink preparation popular in southern Ontario, like Kool-Aid in the United States)—but the prestige of a Longhouse increases if it is able to present real "Indian" corn soup to the conventioneers.

After lunch the attenders are recalled to the Longhouse for confession and supplementary explication of the morning's text. Again, the Thanksgiving Address begins the meeting. Then the speaker explains the confession to the assemblage, the two benches which hold the confessors are centered in the house, and the two confidants (those who take confession from the people) are handed the wampums of the Longhouses to be used during the confession. These two men need not be from opposite moieties, and their only qualification is that they are able to speak the requisite words. The confidants rise first and confess their sins in public, which usually takes the form of a simple declaration of being sorry for having done wrong. Absolutely essential for confession, however, is the holding of the wampum, for it is the wampum which impresses on the individual the sanctity of the occasion and which helps to convey his contrition to Handsome Lake and the Creator. It is often recounted that the individual will shake involuntarily during confession so that the wampum rattles, bead against bead. Such confessions are adjudged to

[18] Preachers active at Six Nations today are Dave Thomas, H. "Chief" Cusick, Huron Miller, and Hilton Nicholaus, who is from Muncy, an Oneida reserve. Notable Six Nations preachers now dead were George and John Gibson, John Isaac, Dave Sky, Tom Aaron, Joseph Jacobs, and Ezekiel Hill.

be most sincere. That there is often much emotion in confession is beyond doubt. Men and women weep, offer lengthy explanations of the cause of sin, and resolve, with feeling, to "go a straight road." Usually, one of the confidants delivers a sermon to the congregation, urging them to keep their promises of repentance and, especially, not to drink. Those who wish to confess then take their places without prior arrangement, women sitting on the bench nearest the women's side, men on that nearest the men's. Both men and women sit facing inward, that is, facing each other. One confidant steps to the right end of the women's bench, the other to the right end of the men's bench, and each moves down the line from his right to his left, "taking confession" as he goes. Each confessor rises in turn, holds the wampum extended to him, and, either softly or audibly, mentions his confession to the confidant. Many of the confessors seem to take a marked interest in the wampum which they hold, fondling it, inspecting it, and in general giving indications of curiosity and awe at so long a string. The wampum is then handed back to the confidant, who briefly absolves the sinner. After all the occupants of the two benches have confessed, they return to their seats, and a new set of people take their places, until all who so desire have been afforded the opportunity to "cleanse themselves." In all probability confession was an old trait reinterpreted by Handsome Lake to fit into his New Religion (see Speck, 1949: 52, for a discussion of confession in North America; also Spier, 1935, and LaBarre, 1947), and even today the public confessions at the conventions do not wear a particularly Christian aspect in that sins need not be enumerated and penances are not imposed. After all have confessed, a speaker once more enjoins them to adhere to Gaihwi'yo and to "keep their promises." The Thanksgiving Address in brief form is recited, and the remainder of the food is then redistributed to be taken home. Social dancing in Indian style may be scheduled at night, particularly on the last day of the convention, but at the Onondaga convention in 1956 this was not done.

On the following day the procedure is repeated, the preacher continuing his recitation from the exact place he ended the day before. The number of days necessary is determined by the amount of time the preacher needs to finish his version of the Code. A single individual does not usually confess twice, and it is hoped that there will be different personnel confessing on the successive days.

At the conclusion of the convention, greetings are again sent to the congregations of other Longhouses whose members attended the meeting. At the chiefs' conventions the greetings are usually addressed by the chiefs to the chiefs. The following is the version used by Alexander General, who, one must remember, is an ardent advocate of the chiefs' jurisdiction in all Longhouse matters.

> We are the chiefs here and wish to send greetings to the chiefs from where you came from, and we hope all is well with the chiefs when they hear our greetings. And the same we wish to the hodri'hõnt and the godri'hõnt, and people other than officers. And we send greetings to the children, to those that are creeping and to those on the boards. We send greetings to those that remain at home in their beds, those that are unable to come.

Notable again is the stratification of society. When delegates return to their home Longhouse, especially to a Longhouse which contributed the use of its wampum to the convention, they report those statistics which are deemed important: how many people confessed, which wampums were present, and how far the speaker progressed in his recitation each day. Any untoward event, such as the breaking of the wampum, and any special incidents of the representatives' trip should also be mentioned. In this way interest in the community of all the Longhouses is maintained at the individual fires, and the number of confessions is taken as evidence of the vitality of the Longhouse religion. A report of a successful convention at one Longhouse inspires the desire to hold a similar convention at the home Longhouse.

SIX NATIONS CONVENTIONS

The motivation and procedure at the Six Nations conventions are the same as at the chiefs' conventions, except that the invitations and the programs are more organized and formal. In preparation for the Six Nations conventions, Tonawanda Longhouse "sends word" (either through a personal messenger or by mail) to Onondaga Longhouse each year, to inform the Reserve of the date of the initial Tonawanda meeting, which usually occurs in late September. Onondaga Longhouse sends messengers to the remaining Longhouses on the Reserve, each of which makes an effort to send a representative to the meeting. The invitations are symbolized by the distribution of small notched tally sticks with about eight white wampum beads attached. (The exact number of beads is immaterial, but depends on the available supply at the host Longhouse when it fashions the sticks; see Beauchamp, 1907: Fig. 2). One tally is given to a major officer of the Longhouse, such as the wampum-keeper or the leading chief associated with the Longhouse, and one is given to the preacher who has been invited to speak at the "Central Fire." The number of days until the scheduled meeting is represented by the peaks left once the notches have been cut. Ideally, a peak should be cut with a knife by the representative each day until all have been leveled or cut off, and that is the day he arrives at Tonawanda. A calendar, however, is more convenient, and even if a notched tally is delivered today, the representative is apt to appear with the stick at Tonawanda (often with the date written on the stick) and in one swoop cut off all the notches.

Each Longhouse which plans to send a representative to Tonawanda schedules a meeting, the name of which means "push the boat on the journey" (or "the people left behind shove the boat"). This meeting is primarily attended by deacons, but the ordinary people really ought to participate. Here a delegate is chosen and formally authorized to represent the Longhouse community throughout the preaching circuit. He is told to "be seen at the gatherings" and to act as he personally deems proper should any question come up for decision. He is explicitly instructed to attend all the meetings, and he must report back faithfully. Official delegates often feel their responsibility deeply. However, the ideal of attendance at all the loci of the year's circuit is seldom fulfilled. Most listeners from a visiting Longhouse will follow to one other Longhouse, or at most two, and even the preacher may preach to only part of the circuit, being replaced by another after two or three recitations. Nevertheless, the repeated hearing tends to inculcate the delegates with the preaching, and Longhouses often send a member whom they believe to be desirous of learning the recitation.

The Six Nations convention usually starts on a Sunday in the Tonawanda Longhouse, with the entire Tonawanda community acting as the fire-keepers. They sit on the south side, the visitors on the north. When all the representatives have assembled, a Tonawanda speaker asks how many invitation wampums have been returned; whereupon each delegate rises, declares whom he represents, and tells how many people "the wampum has brought" (how many members of his Longhouse have accompanied him to Tonawanda). He returns the wampum cut from the tally stick, offers his monetary contribution to the convention, and "brings the message before the fire-keepers" stating whether his Longhouse will also sponsor a recitation that year. The dating and co-ordination of the various recitations is mentioned, though final settlement is often in doubt until the last day of the convention. The speaker then announces the number of people who came, thanks them for coming, and says he expects the missing invitees to arrive momentarily. This is followed by the Thanksgiving Address. Thereupon the attenders rise while the fire-keepers circle the house counterclockwise, shaking hands with each of the guests to greet them. Finally, the fire-keepers announce that they are moved to say something more. A patterned address now follows, which is usually delivered by Corbett Sundown.

The substance of this address is as follows (though the text was not obtained from Corbett Sundown): It begins with a narration of Handsome Lake's birth at Cornplanter Reservation, of his four years of preaching at Allegany, and of his sojourn at Tonawanda where, according to this version, he preached two years. He decided to return to Tonawanda when he felt that he did not have many more years to live, because he wished to be buried next to his mother. However, he finally died at Syracuse. For eight years the preaching lapsed. (See Deardorff, 1951: 97, for a historical analysis of the facts, including a refutation of the interim loss of the Code.) Then the gona'thriŏnt of Tonawanda looked at the people and saw that they were beginning to go back to the days before Handsome Lake (i.e., fall into sinful ways). So they went to the man who had sat next to Handsome Lake as he preached (the traditional caretaker of the functionary) and asked whether he would not preach in the steps of Handsome Lake. At first he answered no word. They waited a time and then had another meeting, and asked the caretaker again. This time he answered, "I will try what I remember, and what comes into my mind." The women then went to the council and reported the news that the fire was started again. And so the man started preaching. (Morgan, 1901, 1: 220–1, identifies the preacher as Jimmy Johnson, grandson of Handsome Lake; Parker, 1913: 19, identifies him as Owen Blacksnake; and Deardorff, 1951: 97, again gives historical data.) And while he was preaching, two men arrived, the yadatha'wak ("father and son," identified in this context as symbolizing the Mohawk and the Oneida). After dinner at the council, it was decided to hear the two men's voices. They said that when they were on their way they had come to a spring and found wampum lying on the banks of a spring stream. They did not touch it, as they thought it must belong to someone. But then they had had a dream, and they were told that those wampum beads were for his great fire and must be taken to the place at which a fire was then going. Thus, they returned to the stream and brought the wampum, and that is what we have today (a reference to the strings of wampum kept at Tonawanda and displayed biennially at the convention). "This is the first fire since the death of Handsome Lake," said the yadatha'wak, "and this is where we are leaving the great fire of the Creator." A chief's council was then held, at which the message had to be approved, the decision being left to the chiefs of that reservation (Tonawanda). "Since that time, when the fire started to burn, it always had coals, the fire was never covered, and the smoke always reached the heavens, bringing the teachings of Handsome Lake." The convention was left in the care of the people and chiefs of Tonawanda, who looked around to the south, north, east, and west, and thought that Tonawanda was halfway to "all around." The great fire was always burning. Every year, when ready, one pokes and renews it, and every year the teachings of Handsome Lake are preached. All the Longhouses around must come and renew what they know about Handsome Lake's teaching. This way Handsome Lake's teachings will never go down as long as people still believe in his teachings.

The speaker representing the fire-keepers then continues, saying that the people of Tonawanda are still carrying on their duties. They have stirred the fire and renewed it, and the great white smoke has reached heaven. They have appointed their runner to deliver the message to all the Longhouses of the Five Nations. And today all are together in one house. The Seneca people have done their duty, and return to the people of the Five Nations the duty to see that it is put through. (Despite the fact that the convention is called "Six Nations convention," most speakers still think and talk in terms of the "Five Nations.")

A procedural session follows immediately. The preacher is decided upon (actually a foregone conclusion), his caretaker is appointed, the speaker for the meeting is selected, the number of days of the convention is fixed, and then the Thanksgiving Address finishes the program. From now until the final day of the convention the initiation of events is the duty of the Five Nations (the visitors). Only three "words" (duties) are left with the fire-keepers: to take care of any death either at the convention or in the community, to announce the arrival of a messenger from another reservation, and to start the Feather Dance at noon. Of course, the fire-keepers also house and feed the visitors as a matter of hospitality, but this is not considered part of the ritual of the occasion.

The next three days and often Thursday morning are taken up with the preaching of the Good Message. At lunch some confessions are made, in the afternoon business meetings are held, and social dancing occurs at night. On Thursday afternoon, the Five Nations again "return the meeting" to the fire-keepers. The delegate for the visitors essentially repeats the speech given by the Tonawanda speaker on Sunday and also thanks the fire-keepers for fulfilling the duty which was first put upon them when they met together. Then a résumé of the activities at the various Longhouses is called for. The fire-keepers state the number attending at Tonawanda at Midwinter and Green Corn and tell whether a local preaching had occurred during the preceding year. All the other delegates then report the same concerning their Longhouses. Finally, the fire-keeper states that all have now heard how each Longhouse upholds the religion and still thinks of the Great Creator. The Thanksgiving Address ends the convention.

It had been customary to bring forth the wampum biennially on the Wednesday of the convention (Deardorff, 1951: 100, says Thursday), if that was a clear day, and to display it to the congregation. However, in 1959 the convention members decided that thenceforth the wampum might be displayed on a Monday, Tuesday, or Wednesday, depending on the decision of the chief delegates from each Longhouse. The day on which the wampum will be shown should be selected randomly and "by a whisper," so that the congregation as a whole will not be able to anticipate the appearance of the wampum. The purpose of the innovation was to stimulate attendance at all the days of the convention, for it was felt that the people would come primarily to see the wampum. Also, the stipulation that the day be clear seems to be interpreted less stringently now, for if there are merely streaks of clouds but the sun is not completely hidden, the wampum may be shown. Of course, if it is an overcast or drizzly day, the wampum remains in hiding. When the wampum fails to be shown during the regularly scheduled biennial year, an attempt is made "to bring it out" the following year. If the weather is then clear during the third year as well, it is possible, at least in principle, that the wampum is seen two years in succession. The wampum strings and belts are mnemonics concerning the religious teaching of Handsome Lake; the hierarchy of chiefs, deacons, and people; the events after Handsome Lake, and the proper behavior of people. They also contain predictions as to the future, particularly if the Good Message is to lapse; thus, if one does not wish to "bring on the end [of the world] fast," one must uphold the religion and "attend to" the Longhouse. The wampum is said not to be "read right out" today; it is claimed that too many feelings would be hurt, because the prescription of the belts concerning how peace chiefs should and should not behave is "quite sharp."

The week after the convention ends at Tonawanda, the circuit of recitations continues at other Longhouses. One year the circuit includes Tonawanda, Caughnawaga, St. Regis, Onondaga Castle, Allegany, Onondaga at Six Nations, and also Sour Springs, if it felt it could afford to join (see *infra*, pp. 35–7). The following year the circuit will encompass Tonawanda, Cattaraugas, Oneidatown (sometimes called Muncy), Seneca Longhouse at Six Nations, and Lower Cayuga. Again Sour Springs may or may not have elected to join that year. Currently, there is some agitation to change the pattern of participation. It is felt that too many recitations fall in the first mentioned group, making attendance at all of them costly. Furthermore, there is some feeling at Tonawanda that Sour Springs, and also Seneca and

Lower Cayuga, should be more firmly tied into the biennial cycle. At Six Nations, however, there is a definite rejection of this view. In particular, the Seneca and Lower Cayuga Longhouses would like to curtail their participation. Each of these Longhouses wishes to participate in the Six Nations conventions only once in four years. Over a four-year period the schedule would then be Onondaga, Seneca, Onondaga, Lower Cayuga. This would leave Onondaga's role in the biennial cycle undisturbed but would lessen the burden of the expense accompanying a convention for both Seneca and Lower Cayuga. Sour Springs wishes to retain its complete freedom of action, without any promise of systematized participation. When the time arrives for a Longhouse in the circuit to sponsor a convention, it should send wampum tallies indicating the date of the meeting, just as Tonawanda Longhouse did for the initial meeting. Each Longhouse should have a representative present at every other convention of the circuit, and it is his duty to contribute the use of the wampum of his home Longhouse to the convention. Again a community of Gaihwi'yo followers is emphasized.

THE CONSERVATIVE INFLUENCE OF GAIHWI'YO

The effect of the conventions is definitely conservative and cohesive. At the conventions, more than on any other occasion, the participants are imbued with ideas of special salvation as long as they adhere to Gaihwi'yo and the "Longhouse way," and of damnation as soon as they deviate from the rules of conduct prescribed by Handsome Lake and endorsed by the Great Creator. The Message has all the symptoms of a messianic creed, and, historically, Handsome Lake was indeed one of the prophets so prevalent at the beginning of the nineteenth century in New York State. He shares traits not only with the prophets of other nativist and anti-acculturative Indian movements, but also with the intellectual climate of northeastern America of his day. His creed promises eternal happiness to his followers and punishment for all others. "The road of the church people ends at church, that of the Indian in heaven," says the preacher. Furthermore, the prophet and his following are declared intrinsically superior to the white man and the white man's prophet: Gaihwi'yo preachers aver that God sent his son to earth to see what people are like and to distribute good Christian news. However, the people tortured and killed him. So he went back to his father and told him about the torture he had undergone, and his father said it was up to him whether he would let white people into heaven. So his son said: "No, they will never go to heaven, but they can have heaven on earth." It is explained that by saying white men "can have heaven on earth," the preacher indicates that white men can travel and have pleasure in the world more than the Indian, but for the Indian pleasure comes after death. This is a typical expression of the nativistic message of a minority group, which sees salvation for the impotent group after death at the expense of the oppressive and overbearing successful group. The Prophet himself is extolled beyond the Christian prophet, in that the Code now relates that when Christ met Handsome Lake in heaven, Christ inquired how many people believed in

Handsome Lake. To this the Iroquoian prophet answered one half. Christ thereupon admitted that Handsome Lake was much more successful than he himself had been. "When *I* preached they only killed me." At this point, also, Christ retells how his father knew what had happened and left it up to him to determine whether his tormentors ought to be admitted to heaven. "My decision," Christ tells Handsome Lake, "was that they should never enter this heaven. When the time comes they will see me above the clouds, and I shall show the marks they made on me. My marks on my body, hands, feet, and breast shall be as fresh as when new." (See Beauchamp, 1907: 414–5, for a similar version.) Handsome Lake, however, implies that all those who conscientiously follow *his* teachings will be allowed into heaven, and those are, of course, all Indians. The Prophet also provided an eschatology for his disciples, by which they would know when the world would end. Belonging to Handsome Lake's cult and practicing it brings privilege, preserves the world, and also delays the disastrous end of mankind.

Longhouse adherents revere the Code, not only because of these messianic and nativistic traits, but for the collection of rules of conduct which the Great Creator wanted the Indians to observe. It is the "Indian religion" brought back according to the explicit wishes of the Great Creator to the once wayward and sinful Indian. A much greater percentage of Longhouse activity is attributed to the influence of Handsome Lake by the Longhouse adherents than can fairly be ascertained by the historian who analyzes the Longhouse complex today with a view to separating out various strains. In fact, Longhouse adherents claim that were it not for the Message of Handsome Lake, which instructed them concerning their duty to the Creator, they would have nothing Indian left; they would be corrupted by the sins which the white men brought and which unwittingly they adopted. These beliefs are inherently conservative as to what they believe to be their old Indian heritage, including all that occurs in the Longhouse. That a belief in the Good Message also aids in the retention of much that is not in the actual text of the preaching of the Message is a corollary of the general fusion of Gaihwi'yo and the Longhouse rituals.

One area of the older Iroquois culture, however, has been radically changed rather than preserved by the teaching of Handsome Lake—namely, the cosmology. The old cosmological tales as recorded by Hewitt (1926), such as the stories of Flint and Sapling, are almost never recounted at Six Nations today, either as serious accounts of the origins of things or as "stories," and it is hard to find an informant who even remembers many of them. In one way, the lapse of the cosmological tales is surprising, since they have a strong affinity to the culture as it survives today, and the conservative Iroquois is still familiar with the incidents and psychological quirks which enter into the tales. However, a partial explanation for the loss of the old cosmology may be found in the fact that the cosmological tales had little ethical content and little direct relationship to the values of the culture. The cosmology and eschatology of Handsome Lake, however—which are largely Christianized and replete with the flower-bestrewn path to heaven, the wide and narrow roads, a punisher with a tail and cloven feet and horns on his forehead, and with boiling oil and molten metal in hell—are directly related to the ethical prescriptions of the Code. Thus, if a man beats his wife, he shall be ever-lastingly tormented in hell; if a man plays a violin on earth, he shall imitate this action with a hot bar of iron upon his arm in hell; etc. The cosmology in this way has a definite function of making the demands of the Great Creator more vivid, and in fact it is incorporated into the sanctions of the culture. As Mrs. George Green says: "It [the Code] has lots of legs, that is why preaching is so long. It tells how we should carry ourselves, and explains how the sin part and good part goes." The religion of Handsome Lake is more "advanced" than the older Iroquois re-ligion, at least according to those classifications of religions which consider a syn-thesis of cosmological and ethical elements to be more highly evolved than a religion in which these are separate. In any case, the "hell-fire" character of Handsome Lake's cosmology and eschatology has provided an extra sanction for the Long-house religion, which helps account for its momentum.

Finally, the social structure of Six Nations Reserve itself heightens the dichotomy between Gaihwi'yo followers and the rest of the Reserve. Members classify each other as Christian or as Longhouse; and if one is Longhouse, in order to escape from the stigma of being a "pagan," one simply calls oneself a Gaihwi'yo follower. Hence, the comparison between Handsome Lake and Christ, which is so widespread at Six Nations, is a perfectly natural one. To the Longhouse members the wishes of God were transmitted through Handsome Lake, to the Christians through Christ. Because the Message is so definite a codification of the ethics and cosmology of the Longhouse member, it is easy for a member to identify himself with it and to point to it as his religion. "Gaihwi'yo is my Bible" is a perfectly understandable concept to both Christians and Longhouse members at Six Nations. Under pressure a succinct doctrine, recited *in toto* at specified times and claimed to be the revealed religion, is a convenient vehicle of explanation to the dominant culture.

THE ORTHODOX LIFE CYCLE

INTRODUCTION

THE previous chapter described the religious institutions associated with the calendric observances in the Longhouse, and also the moral and ethical system which has become integrated with these institutions. In order to complete this study of Iroquois conservatism, it is necessary to examine those institutionalized ways of behavior characteristic of the personal actions of the individual as he proceeds through life. It is this personal, but not idiosyncratic, behavior of the Longhouse member which is discussed in the remaining chapters. The present chapter considers most of the prescribed behavior and institutions of the life cycle. However, because the institutionalized actions concerning the health and "luck" (which is closely related to health) of the individual are so important and provide so many of the sanctions of the entire culture, they will be described separately in the following chapter.

The institutionalized personal behavior of the conservative Iroquois is connected in a number of ways with his Longhouse participation. In the first place, as indicated before (p. 133), certain activities concerning the health and well-being of the individual are an integral part of the Longhouse complex. Furthermore, going to the Longhouse and professing to be a Gaihwi'yo follower (and there seem to be no cases in which an individual professes to be a Longhouse member but denies a belief in Handsome Lake) implies an "Indian" way of life, and this has a definite meaning to each individual. When a preacher at the Longhouse exhorts that one should adhere to "Indian ways," the member of the congregation knows, or has some understanding of, what is meant. Of course, the exact way in which a person interprets such a command and actually does act in a conservative manner is a private matter. In each case it is dependent on the belief of the individual, his knowledge of older traits and institutions, his education, his exposure to the old culture and the acculturated community, etc. "Acting as a good Indian should" never means exactly the same thing to any two persons; but because there is social interaction, and because the same tradition belongs to most of the residents of the Longhouse community, there is a general area of agreement as to how one should act "in the Longhouse way." Even when specific actions are not mentioned in the Longhouse exhortations, there are "old" ways of behaving which are proper and which please the Creator and Handsome Lake and the spirit forces. And, in pleasing the forces that be, the individual is guarded against evil consequences which would befall him if the prudent Indian action were omitted. In this way, the sanctions invoked in the Longhouse reinforce and perpetuate traditional ways of behavior outside the Longhouse; and, conversely, if one has been brought up in a traditional way of behavior, there are sanctions which will enforce attendance at the Longhouse and respect for the doctrine of Handsome Lake.

Finally, some of the personal actions important in the life of the Longhouse member are performed in the Longhouse itself as part of the public ceremonies—such as naming, forming ritual friendships, and giving up the dead—and in this way they are shared and preserved. If a personal action is not only considered important for the individual himself, but is a part of the program of the entire community, it is much more likely to be observed, since a slurring of the act would cause instant public suspicion. This is particularly so among the Iroquois, where mutual action, cooperation, "togetherness," and reciprocity are highly valued. Social pressure for, and social sharing of, personal observances are conducive to the retention of these observances, and the Longhouse leadership is aware of this fact, much as any minister of a church is cognizant of it; they use their knowledge in order to stimulate those activities which they deem necessary for the maintenance of the institutions they cherish. Thus, figuratively speaking, the Longhouse "takes an interest" in the personal actions of its members, so that the daily actions of Longhouse members are definitely related to the system of beliefs and actions conserved in the Longhouse religious community.

BIRTH AND EARLY CHILDHOOD

BIRTH AND PREGNANCY

The birth of a child is not an event calling for much in the way of special observances, and there seems to be little evidence that this was at any time the occasion for an important *rite de passage* among the Iroquois. Murdock (1934: 311) implies the same. He finds that "Iroquois women have little difficulty in childbirth and usually work up to the last. A few experienced women render the necessary assistance." The traditional position of delivery, still found occasionally today, is in kneeling position. Since the Canadian government has provided a free hospital on the Reserve, and since many Indians have medical insurance, almost all current births occur in the Reserve hospital or in near-by towns, according to standard hospital procedure. Only the most conservative Longhouse followers refuse hospital treatment, and in such cases a midwife is called in to help in the delivery of the child. As far as could be determined, there are no taboos or cautions concerning the afterbirth, manner of delivery, or manifestations at birth, with the exception of a caul. When a child is born with a caul, it is believed to be endowed with extraordinary power, usually of a clairvoyant or magical (in the sense of witching) nature. Such a child, "if properly taken care of," will be much respected and somewhat feared if indeed it grows up to practice either witchcraft or fortunetelling. "Properly taken care of" means that the child should be secluded from sight and "hidden" most of its childhood, or at least very carefully protected,[1] which to my

---

[1] Hewitt (1903: 142, 255) related birth with a caul to the concept of "down-fended," which meant that cattail down was strewn about the area of seclusion, and no one could enter the sanctuary without disturbing the down. The motif of achieving special power if hidden from sight is a common one, occurring in the cosmological tales (for example, in the story that Deganawi′da's mother was born with a caul and was "down-fended" and hidden until maiden-

knowledge is never done today at Six Nations. However, the very knowledge that a person was born with a caul creates a tendency to treat the person somewhat more carefully and deferentially than most. At Six Nations it does not seem necessary to save the caul, as Fenton (1953: 70) implies is the case at Tonawanda.

Conception and pregnancy are also not particularly stressed. The most important belief concerning conception, that it occurs only at new moon, has been mentioned previously (p. 137). A pregnant woman is subject in general to many of the taboos imposed on a menstruating woman; but in neither case do they apply to the husband or the immediate family except in extreme ritual matters, and hence there is no great hardship involved. Pregnant women should not use the common drinking cups at the Longhouse, nor should they hold babies, for both actions would cause others harm (see pp. 159, 161 *supra*). Nor should a pregnant woman associate with hunters or with medicine men or watch the making of medicine, since the animals would be scared by the contaminated hunter and the medicine would be spoiled. "Particular" medicines are especially sensitive to contamination by a pregnant woman.

Geophagy is quite common among pregnant women, although some geophagy is practiced by the population in general, mainly by women. Pregnant women may participate in most functions, except that skinning mink is forbidden, for the smell of the mink supposedly causes abortions. Furthermore, there are some folk beliefs concerning the behavior of the mother. She should not sit in a doorway nor turn her back in a doorway, for this is said to indicate a bridge or difficult birth. Nor should she sit on her foot, as this might cause the child to be clubfooted; and if she sits with her leg bent up the child might be crippled. These beliefs are clearly based on analogical reasoning.

BIRTH CONTROL

Abortion is strictly forbidden by Handsome Lake and must be confessed, if only on one's dying day. Nevertheless, the practice of abortion is known, and abortive medicines are frequently made at Six Nations but kept fairly secret. One such common preparation is made of boiled sassafras shoots, accompanied by a tobacco burning to give the shoots power to abort. Young girls seem to believe that five-grain quinine pills will induce abortion, and these may be secured in the drugstore. Also, it has been said, girls sometimes attempt to lift very heavy objects in order to induce abortion.

Contraception is also strictly forbidden by Handsome Lake, but the rhythm method of contraception is practiced correctly by many Longhouse members, even by those who associate conception with the new moon. Commercial contraceptives

---

hood) and occurring today in such societies as the Little Water Medicine Society. In general, any strong power or medicine should be hidden (see Fenton, 1953: 70, 113–4, and Fenton's remarks in Hewitt, 1944: 80). Professor Floyd Lounsbury observed that the Oneida at Green Bay, Wisconsin, used the word for "down-fended" (deyeno'da'dõʔ) to refer to a sheltered child.

are also used by many of the Longhouse population today, particularly by men, if they are able to afford the expense. Once an initial child has been born, however, the most common method of contraception is to prolong the breast feeding of the child. It is, incidentally, demand rather than schedule feeding. Informants are aware of the fact that often menstruation does not occur during nursing, and they explicitly mention nursing as a method of spacing children. Studies of the effectiveness of nursing as a contraceptive method are extremely hard to control, though some demographers have estimated 60 to 70 per cent effectiveness. Even if this is an overestimation, continued nursing does reduce the birth rate somewhat. Spacing of approximately three years is considered desirable, and the average duration of breast feeding is two years for girls, one year to one year and nine months for boys. However, there are cases in which children have been breast fed for as long as five years. Once a child is weaned, the parents should wait two to three months before attempting another pregnancy, "to get strength back." Lately, however, many mothers either bottle feed from birth or after a short period of breast feeding, and the earlier emphasis on the spacing of children has faded. The birth rate seems to be rising at Six Nations as elsewhere in the world.

Early Training

Early child care is rather uniform at Six Nations, there being no particular distinction in this respect between the Longhouse population and the remainder of the Reserve. Children today are not put on cradleboards, although cradleboards may still be found at Six Nations—mainly as mementos of the past. Toilet training is easy, and no attempt at discipline is made until after the child is able to speak, certainly not till after the eighteenth month and more frequently not till after two years or two and one-half years. Weaning among the Longhouse population is accomplished by placing a chicken feather on the breast or blackening the nipple in order to frighten the child; or by causing an unpleasant taste by using onions, salt, pepper, or nontoxic liniment; or simply by stopping breast feeding one day. A current belief at Six Nations is that it is good to end weaning during the "fish days" (horoscopically designated), "for then one is not sick." This, of course, is a borrowed trait.

Children are liked and desired (even when illegitimate), and parents are generally lenient to them. Protective attention toward them is rare, and display of affection is restrained. Children are allowed a good deal of independence as they grow up, their supervision often being in the hands of older siblings. The Code of Handsome Lake (Parker, 1913: 33–34) is very specific concerning the sinfulness of punishing children excessively, and the suggested method of chastisement, the use of cold water, is even today the culturally accepted method. When a child misbehaves, he is sprinkled with cold water; when he fails to improve, he is doused with cold water; and when he is still obstinate, he should be taken to a running stream and threatened with immersion or actually dipped. Temper tantrums are also treated by sprinkling water. In each case the water is considered a "medicine." If, however, the water methods do not bring the desired results, the child should be hit three, four, or five times with a red-willow whip, for red willow is again considered the appropriate "medicine." Any other method of punishment, such as slapping a child, is incorrect, because "it fixes the child's mind to fight back," whereas using water or a red-willow whip makes use of the "power of the medicine to correct disobedience." Severe punishment of children is also said to bring disease to the punisher, particularly vomiting of worms and hysteria ("hollering").

Procuring a willow switch is handled in the same manner in which any medicinal herbal agent is obtained. Indian tobacco is "given" to the first plant of the species, and an explanation of the intended use (always including the Indian name of the patient) is offered; and then any exemplar of the species is picked as the medicine. Thus, it is the "medicine" in the red willow rather than the "spanking" which corrects the ways of the child. Ideally, the mother should always be the punisher.

That some chastisement is considered essential for the training of the child is shown in the following two stories current at Six Nations (as told by Alexander General):

A set of parents had only one offspring, a boy. They loved their child, and as he grew he could ask for anything he desired, and the parents would do as asked. Whenever the child acted as he pleased, the parents would not say anything. They just looked on because they loved him, and they would not abuse him. When the boy grew up he was involved in all mischief, but he was never punished. The child then became sick, and one day (by now he was a young man) he said to his parents, "Take me out to the woods, I'm passing on." The father carried him out, and when they came to some bushes the boy said, "Would you straighten the crooked young bushes." The father did so and managed to get them fairly straight. The boy then said, "It's fairly good, now you straighten out this other tree." The father said that it was too big now to do so. Then the boy said, "You see now what you have done to me. You have let me have my way all along, and you never told me and punished me. You should have tried to straighten me out. You should have straightened the crooked whip. Even as the tree, I am now perishing, and it is all your fault." So this boy died, because of the parents who did not tell the children.

Furthermore, children are said not to go to heaven if they are not punished with the red-willow whip. The etiology for this belief is contained in the following tale:

Once there lived a woman who had only one girl, and she was very "stingy of her" (treated her very carefully). The girl was only five years old when she got sick and died. The woman then dreamed that the little girl came back. "Ma, I want you to whip me, so I can go home. I can't go there if you don't lick me. You take three little switches and go to the grave and lick me." They coaxed the woman to go to the grave and whip the child over her grave. But when the woman went there, the little hands were sticking out of the grave, and that is where she whipped her, and she was told that her little girl had a good home. That is the reason you have to lick children to make them mind. Maybe it's true.

NAMING

Any child born at Six Nations today is given a common name and a surname, under which it is registered on the official tribal rolls. However, the child of a Longhouse family should also be awarded an "Indian" name at the first opportunity, namely at the first Green Corn Ceremony or Midwinter Ceremony at which the child can be presented in the Longhouse. Naming a child in the "Indian" way is a double initiation. Privately, it certifies the new individual as a functioning member of his mother's family, for the name is supposed to be a lineage or clan name from the maternal family, and publicly it certifies the individual as a member of the Longhouse community. Naming in general symbolizes the adoption of an individual into the society, and when an outsider is adopted, the principal indication that the individual has been accepted by a family and by the community is that he is accorded a family name by his immediate sponsor. In particular, naming a child publicly shows that the mother identifies herself with the Longhouse "Indian" community and wishes to provide her child with the means for entrance and participation in this group.

Informants often compare naming to baptism, and, in fact, like baptism it has a ritual as well as an essentially initiatory purpose. A name is considered an indispensable part of one's ritual personality, since all references to an individual in the Longhouse should be by his Indian name (in keeping with the use of Iroquoian languages in the Longhouse), and all invocations to any spirit force on behalf of an individual must likewise use the Indian name. Medicinal cures, whether they be herbal or societal, necessitate mentioning the patient's Indian name to the curing agent, and most of the informants agree that a cure is seriously endangered if there is no Indian name. Often, if a cure is performed for a non-Longhouse member or an unnamed individual, he is first given a name, and then cured. It is permissible to omit the Indian name only in the most extreme cases, when there is no time to bestow a name before embarking on the cure. In those cases, it is contended, the cure will be effective if the individual believes in its effectiveness sincerely; and it is assumed that he will acquire a name at some later date, particularly if the cure is successful and the individual shows enough gratitude to the Indian ways to become a member of the Longhouse. However, possession of an Indian name is considered so vital to a cure that many non-Longhouse Indians retain an Indian name just for those occasions on which they might become ill enough to require "Indian" medicine.

Use of the Indian name is considered appropriate at almost all activities which are believed to be in the old tradition, and Goldenweiser's (1914: 469) contention that a person is not addressed by his Indian name is definitely untrue today. The only name taboo which is known to some informants today is that the name of a dead individual should not be used until after the funeral; but even this taboo is not universally observed, despite the fact that matters of death are very "particular." On the contrary, it is considered respectful to use the Indian name of a person, both for reference and in address. In many instances, members of two or three generations ago are known today only by their Indian names, and this is considered both proper and "real Indian." The Indian name of a person almost represents his orthodox personality. (This is a trait with world-wide distribution [see Frazer, 1943: 244], which previously had not been particularly attributed to the Iroquois.) When, for example, a diagnosis from a fortuneteller is needed, and the patient is not able to go himself, his name may be "taken" together with some Indian tobacco, and the fortune may safely be told *in absentia*; or if a cure is performed for an individual who cannot attend, perhaps because he is in the hospital, the use of his Indian name during the ceremony will adequately substitute for and represent the absent person. Furthermore, at a curing ceremony at home or in the Longhouse, not only the patient, but the performers and assistants should be indicated during the invocation and during the announcement by their Indian names. One of the commonest Longhouse incidents is that the speaker is hurriedly informed of the names of the performers or patients by the deaconesses. The whispering which seems perpetually to surround the speakers is often merely a communication of these names. Throughout the life of an individual his name is an important adjunct to his actions: should a ritual friendship be made, the name must be used; should a mask be commissioned, the "face" ought to be told the name of its owner; should goods be distributed at a tenth-day feast, the recipient should be called up by his name; should aid be needed, it can best be obtained by appealing to the donor by his name; and so forth.

Names are usually chosen by the mother of the child from among those which she can *remember* as having belonged to a deceased member of her matrilineal family of the same sex as the child, for intrinsically it is impossible to identify the sex and clan association of many of the names. Ideally, a name should not belong to more than one person at a time, but often today several people either from different or identical clans (though different families) bear identical names. (However, no disagreements, like those reported by Goldenweiser, 1914a: 366, seem to arise from such a situation today.) New names are not composed today, and sometimes parents have difficulty in remembering appropriate old ones. In such a case the mother may ask the family matron (if there is a matron who holds a chief's wampum in her family or clan), or she may ask the head deaconess of her moiety for a name in her clan. Often the mother consults with the eldest woman in her immediate matrilineal family (her mother, grandmother, or aunt), since it is a sign of respect toward the elder to seek her advice and approval with reference to a name. It also seems to be a recognition of the fact that the name belongs to the whole family rather than to the individual who is choosing. If a name is still not forthcoming, any knowledgeable person (usually known as a "keeper of names") may be asked to contribute a name, even if this person is a male, though at one time it is said to have been exclusively a woman's task to assign names. However, it is frequently at such "borrowings" of names that the clan associations are confused. The "keeper of names" simply remembers names as such, rather than the names belonging to each clan. Thus, today it is often difficult to determine which clan "owns" a certain name, and the Indian name is not so much the symbol of membership in a particular clan as an affirmation that the bearer is Indian and wishes to be identified as such. (This is one further example of the declining importance of the clan and the corresponding increase of "Indian" loyalty or loyalty to the Longhouse community; see pp. 33-4 *supra*.)

The Indian names vary widely in meaning, from those susceptible to such modern interpretations as "a lot of old tin cans lying around" and "picking up rails," to those with meanings such as "she spoils everything" and "beautiful hanging flower." The last is a favorite woman's name, while men like those with such meanings as "level skies" and "twenty medicines." In general, people express preferences for complimentary or idyllic names, but actually the meaning of the name has no importance whatever. Being called "Spoiler" is not a matter of opprobrium, and at most the recipient is a little sorry not to have a "pretty name."

At one time many of the names indicated status, for example the chiefs' names or the hereditary deaconship names or the Ohgi'we matron names, but today this aspect of naming is becoming more and more obsolete. Almost none of the "baby names" (which are the ordinary names assigned to the population) carry a connotation of an occupation, a status, or a privileged position; and most of the names which at one time indicated an office have been lost, or, if the name remains, the associated office is not known. Very few of the matrons, deacons, medicine-keepers, society officers, or warriors today have a name which indicates their position or was accorded to them because of the position. (See *supra*, pp. 76–71, for a discussion of names associated with hereditary deaconships. Also see pp. 79–80 for a case in which it is not clear whether a certain name is a "baby name" or a name indicating the office of a chief's matron.) However, it is worth mentioning that the names associated with the chiefs are carefully preserved.

Usually a person now keeps his "baby name" throughout life, though occasionally the "baby name" may be discarded ("put in a box"), and a second name assumed. This may occur when a person is fifteen or sixteen, though today it is not linked to puberty, as seems to have been the case at one time. Also, one may discard a name at any point during one's life, though the practice is not favored. The discarded name is considered "free" and may be bestowed on any clan member during the lifetime of the initial recipient, for he is considered to have relinquished all claim to the name. "Giving up" one's name and assuming a new one is a formal occasion: the announcement must be officially made in the Longhouse by the speaker during the regular naming days, and the individual involved must be "stood up." This is so that the community will know the new name of the individual in case his services are needed, since an appeal for aid should use the Indian name of the person petitioned. This is in fact given as one reason why a name should not be changed, for the petitioners, not knowing the new name, might not be able to ask for help convincingly.

Naming occurs in the Longhouse on the Adŏ'wa Days of the Green Corn and Midwinter Ceremonies, the second and sixth days of the ceremonies respectively. However, lately at Lower Cayuga a special day for the naming of children has been set aside before the first Stirring Ashes ritual (see *supra*, p. 189). When a name is to be given to a baby in the Longhouse, the mother should inform the head deaconess of her own moiety of the name and of her desire to have it formally presented. The deaconess should be informed both for the sake of courtesy and so that she may make the necessary arrangements for the child. At the Cayuga Longhouses the deaconess arranges with the speaker of her own moiety to chant the naming speech, while either she or the mother stands in front of the speaker with the child in her arms. At Onondaga and Seneca Longhouses, the deaconess arranges with the head deaconess of the opposite moiety to take the child and have that speaker chant the naming address. The important trait again is to "stand up" the individual being named, so that all may see and take note, and it is this act which validates the ceremony. The content of the naming speech emphasizes both the personal and the community functions of the named individual, and it is approximately as follows:

Our Maker has said that we should now do it this way at this place, that names should be given to all who come to travel the road on earth. The . . . [mention the name of the clan, e.g., Bear] family is fortunate that this offspring [reveal sex of child through the form of the word] has come to them. Now you warriors will hear the name . . . [insert name]. Now you [addressed to the child] may have the fortune to travel about later in time and to be able to perform tasks which our Creator has established. If you are called by name [to help], you will do so. That is how it shall be.

If the child is a boy, he will furthermore be handed to an Adō'wa singer, any man who can sing being acceptable, of the same moiety as the speaker. The singer then holds the child while he paces the house, singing his own Adō'wa and speaking the ritual lines between songs. This song then may become the Adō'wa Song of the baby, but it is not compulsory for the child to adopt that song. No such ceremony is performed for a girl.

If the child has been adopted, the speaker will take cognizance of this fact by mentioning that "the name is hung around the neck." Ideally, in such instances, the name is not passed on to a member of the child's family of procreation, for it is only bestowed upon the child for the duration of its life, and at death ought to be returned to the clan which contributed the name.

It often happens that a name is bestowed when the individual is older or even adult. In such instances the speaker recites rather than chants the naming speech, and he frequently adds some words of admonishment and some rules of behavior toward the Longhouse community. A grown boy is led by the Adō'wa singer rather than carried.

At the end of the ceremony, the person simply returns to his seat. Although the ceremony does not appear momentous, and no presents are distributed to the speaker or Adō'wa singer, the occasion is judged to be extremely serious, and it is said that "children enjoy getting their names." Thereafter, the Indian name just bestowed will be exclusively used for all reference to that individual in the Longhouse or at any other ritual event. Even the announcements concerning social dances will refer to the individual (if he leads a dance, for example, or plays an instrument) by his Indian name.

LATER CHILDHOOD

As children grow up, they either play among themselves or idle about the house. There are few toys and little supervision. Some cornhusk dolls are made for children,[2] but the hoop-and-javelin games and the snow boat (see Morgan, 1901,

---

[2] Possessing a cornhusk doll in the house has a further purpose, for it is believed to insure the house against theft. (Nevertheless, most houses are locked during the absence of the owner. Sometimes a broom is still placed against the door on the outside, to indicate that the owner is away from home.)

1: 287–90, 293–4) have been practically obsolete at Six Nations for 15 years. Boys usually acquire snow snakes, bows and arrows, and lacrosse rackets, and both boys and girls engage in much softball. Boys do some hunting and muskrat trapping, but the methods are modern Canadian. Trapping may be quite profitable for the boys, as muskrat is eaten and the fur is used or sold in the general stores on the Reserve. (The retail price of a skin ranges from $.95 to $1.50, depending on the quality.)

Children help with chores at an early age. Girls cook and keep house, and often an eight-year-old girl will be "hired" by an invalid or an elderly person to run the entire household. Boys chop wood, fetch water, and care for livestock. Elder children also care for younger ones. The children tend to be rather self-sufficient and to keep to themselves. Seldom does one see temper tantrums.

School is now mandatory for all children, so that on the whole there is little difference between the formal education of the Longhouse child and the Christian Indian child. However, all teachers agree that the Longhouse children are more disciplined in behavior and that they attend docilely, even though they are frequently uninterested in the curriculum, and despite the prejudice among their orthodox parents against learning to read and write (see *supra*, p. 40). There is not much fighting or competition between children. During vacations older children try to get work in the neighborhood, usually tobacco or fruit picking or light factory work. All the children on the Reserve seem to be much addicted to comic books, which usually constitute the only reading matter in the home for the child.

Longhouse children follow one distinctive custom, and that is a form of trick-or-treat at New Year. Although the trait of a New Year's exchange of presents was probably introduced in colonial times by the French, the kin groups involved are typically Iroquoian. The treat, in the form of fried doughnut cake men, should be collected from a relative whom one calls "agadõ'nih" and baked for a relative whom one calls "kheya'ʔdaweh." However, the practice is not extended to all the eligible relatives in these categories. The most common arrangement is that children will call on their paternal aunt (father's sister) and their paternal cross-cousins (father's sister's children) in order to obtain the doughnuts, while adult women will bake for their own brother's children or maternal cross-cousins (mother's brother's children). One usually bakes for one's own or descending generations and collects from one's own or ascending generations. Although the doughnuts are primarily baked for children, there are some families in which the practice is continued throughout life. Exactly why the agadõ'nih and kheya'ʔdaweh are involved in this exchange is not known today, nor is any particular significance attached to the practice. If informants are pressed for an explanation, they interpret it as a children's delight.

PUBERTY AND MENSTRUATION

One may infer from the folklore that men at one time endured tests or demonstrated their skills at puberty. Waugh (see Randle, 1953: 632) recorded a story, "Thunder Man as Puberty Spirit," in which power was sought by boys at puberty: "In olden times they used to take a boy who had arrived at puberty away out into the woods, so far he could not go back home. They would leave him there alone for ten days with a single cob of corn. At the end of that time they would return. . . . The boy would also make a friend of one of the larger animals and receive good luck from it." In this particular story the Thunder Man confers powers on the boy. (See also Fenton, 1953: 93, who quotes Curtin and Hewitt, 1918: 139–42, on an eagle-shooting ordeal at puberty.) When girls reached puberty, it is said that they once were isolated in a hut for a year and forced to sit facing the walls. Food was taken there by a guardian woman, but otherwise no human contact was allowed during that interval.

The general menstrual taboos arise out of the belief that women during the first three days of menstruation are "poisonous" and "dangerous" in contact with men, hunters, babies, pregnant women, medicines, and ritual items. Whereas they need not be secluded, menstruating women ought to keep to themselves and not come into intimate contact with a person or an item which might be harmed, nor should they plant corn. In particular, a menstruating woman should not prepare, touch, or look at medicine, for not only will the "power" of the medicine be spoiled or "killed" instantaneously, but harm might come to the patient who takes the medicine and to the woman herself. "Strong" medicines, such as Little Water, are said to act on women who are not very "strong" (physically) and induce menstruation a week early. Therefore, a woman who yet has a week before menstruation is expected but who is considered "sickly" ought not "be around" when the medicine is being used. In fact, those who administer Little Water usually say that preferably all women of menstrual age should leave before the medicine is used. When a woman is admitted (and there are accounts according to which it is women who are the custodians), it is claimed that she is "strong" enough to withstand the danger or has passed the menopause. A menstruating woman should not be present at a society meeting which purports to cure, for though there may not be an herbal or other tangible medicine present, the entire procedure "is medicine," and her presence would "spoil" the "power" inherent in the performance. For example, False Face performers are supposed to burn their hands on the hot coals if a catamenial woman is present. Contamination by a menstruating woman has a vitiating effect on any ceremony, whether in the home or in the Longhouse, and "the poison in the woman spoils the power" of ritual items and ritual foods. The Midwinter Ceremony is scheduled five days past the new moon in order to allow women to complete menstruation and participate in the Longhouse cures.

A menstruating woman should not drink from the same glass or bite on the same bread as a man, nor should she kiss, sleep with, breathe upon, touch, or cook for one. At one time a five-day period of isolation was prescribed, but this has now been shortened to three days, and in actuality few women obey even this curtailed prohibition. There is some inconsistency between the Cayuga belief that women are taboo while menstruating and the belief that conception occurs at menstruation, both taking place at the new moon.

As is to be expected, the ultimate sanctions which enforce the menstrual taboos are in the sphere of health. It is believed that if a child is kissed by a menstruating (or pregnant) woman or drinks from the same cup, it will "get cross and cry." Men and babies, male children in particular, who drink from the same cup as a menstruating woman are in danger of developing bloody diarrhea and bleeding piles, a belief based on an obvious analogy. (The type of piles induced through contact with a catamenial woman is called thōwakwaa, and it is distinguished from hohe'tsintgēs, which is the naturally caused disease.) These symptoms may occur years after the transgression has been committed, and regardless of whether the contact was accidental or intentional. Also food prepared by a catamenial woman is supposed to produce cramps in the more sensitive men. Contact of a catamenial woman with a pregnant one is supposed to induce menstruation in the expectant mother and thereby to cause abortion. It is for these reasons that menstruating women are admonished to provide their own drinking vessels when they do attend the Longhouse. Actually, women seldom bring their own cups unless visibly pregnant, probably being shy about admitting that they are menstruating or pregnant and that they are attending the Longhouse in these conditions. Men never bring their own cups, except that at one Strawberry Festival, a visiting male anthropologist, who seemed squeamish about the sanitary factors involved in drinking from the communal dipper, produced his own cup immediately after the speaker had warned of the menstrual taboo. Naturally, the congregation dissolved in merriment. Incidentally, the expression used to mention the menstrual taboo in the Longhouse is the same as that for catamenially induced piles, thōwakwaa ("it—sickness—is catching"), while in ordinary address to indicate menstruation one says, "djisanō-hwa'kdēnih swēhni?da'tshō? ('you are sick again with the monthly recurrence')."

A further reason for fearing menstruation is that the main ingredient of "love medicines," which will cause either insanity or bad luck, is menstrual blood. Consequently, one should not indiscriminately take a drink from a stranger. There are also certain special dangers to the menstruating woman herself. For instance, she should not walk in the woods, for snakes would follow her, and she should not comb her hair, for it would fall out.

Not all the taboos mentioned above are observed by all the Longhouse community, and, indeed, many function in the ideal rather than the real culture. Women frequently ignore the restrictions, if only out of embarrassment of admitting that they are menstruating.

There are two general countermeasures against the effects of menstruation. The first is the application of the ubiquitous neutralizer, skwa'ēda (a tea made of coltsfoot, *Tussilago farfara*), with which the person or object is washed; and the second is that the woman should wash her hands in ash water before attempting any cooking or before touching any important object. In both cases the neutralizers act as counter-medicine to the "poison" of menstruation and render the endangered objects or persons safe. There is a special counter-medicine which cures the catamenially induced piles, namely a tea made of the whole plant of gana?wē'tha? (hepatica, *Hepatica triloba*). To test whether a woman is menstruating at any particular time, a small piece of ironwood may be placed in bed with her, and if she is indeed affected, the ironwood will bleed by morning, and the pithy heart of the wood will be black and dead. Men frequently admonish girls to be sure to report their condition accurately, for their reports can always be tested by this means. To relieve menstrual cramps herbalists usually prescribe tea made from the whole plant of smartwood (*Polygonum hydropiper*) and a tea made from a whole fern (?) plant (including roots) called gahnēdade'?dah. The latter is a blood builder, an anti-anemic agent, and a purifier, and is useful because "women must have lots of blood because they menstruate." Tea of mayweed, or camomile (*Anthemis cotula*), and tea made from mayflower (*Epigoea repens* [?]) are also administered to ease cramps. The latter is also believed efficacious for preventing excessive bleeding at menopause.

Menopause is not marked by a *rite de passage*; women who have passed the menopause are allowed to handle medicines more freely and to attend the rites of the more "particular" societies, such as the Hĕna'?idos and Little Water Societies.

RITUAL FRIENDSHIP

One of the most important institutionalized events in the life of a majority of the orthodox individuals is the acquisition of a "friend" (ado'?thra?). This common institution involves the establishment of a formal, life-long relationship between two people with culturally defined rights, obligations, and statuses. A person may acquire any number of such friends.

There are three main occasions which call for the formation of a ritual friendship— sickness, a dream, and an extreme nonsexual affection for another person. Forming a "friendship" through "sickness" is perhaps the most common occurrence. In this case, a sick person consults a fortuneteller, and he is told that the cause of his disease is the lack of a friend (often expressed as "you're lonely for a friend") and that the acquisition of a friend is sure to cure him. The fortuneteller usually hints in generic terms at the individual who should be asked to form the friendship, but in such a way that the patient has very little difficulty in identifying a particular person satisfying the description. Some examples, all from actual case histories, are as follows: "There should be a young girl, about her [the patient's] age, who lives close by"; "there was an old man who did not like the child [the patient] so much and of whom the child was scared"; "he [the patient] needs a friend who is a tall, big, fair, young boy"; "there is a dead child, and she [the patient] should make friends with the child's mother's sister"; "she [the patient] should make friends with a good woman"; "she [the patient] should make friends with a woman who had stayed overnight at her house with a child." The fortuneteller also prescribes a ceremony or rite which should accompany the occasion and implies that only the formation of a friendship by a particular rite and with the person indicated will effect the desired cure or result. Therefore, the dictates of the clairvoyant are always meticulously followed. No significance is attached to the specific observance which accompanies the formation of a friendship. It is simply assumed that that is "what the patient needed." The most common observances which accompany the formation of a ritual friendship are the Women's Dance, social dances, the Bowl Game in shortened form, the War Dance, and Adõ'wa. If the person is more seriously ill, a society dance is often recommended along with formation of the friendship.

When a friendship results from a dream, the dream usually indicates both the friend and the ceremonies which should accompany the formation of the friendship. If a dream is at all specific, the patient will aim to duplicate its content as much as possible.

A typical example of a dream which leads to a friendship, and which was reproduced as accurately as possible at the time of making friends, is the following: The informant, in 1951 or 1952 around Strawberry time, dreamed that he was walking alone in a deserted place, when suddenly crushing cliffs surrounded him on all sides and began approaching him. The faster he ran, the faster the mountains in front closed in upon him, and the mountains in the rear rushed up from behind. All of a sudden he saw a certain man, dressed in Indian costume, coming toward him and telling him to take his hand and follow him, to jump when he jumped, to run when he ran. He followed the advice, jumped, and strangely rose above the clashing rocks, where he saw verdant fields; and on a ridge sat another acquaintance, also dressed in Indian costume, singing four Feather Dance songs and eating corn soup. Four costumed men (all recognized) from Six Nations were dancing to the music, and as the dreamer and his escort reached the plateau, they too joined in the dancing and were saved. (Four is the most common Iroquoian pattern number.) The informant then asked a noted ritualist to interpret the dream. The interpreter thought the dream could be held over until Midwinter time, and one could see what to do then, but shortly afterward he died. In the following summer the informant dreamed the identical dream. He now became worried and consulted another ritualist, who informed him that the dream no doubt portended disaster (death or bad luck) and that he should immediately make friends with the indicated person, as it was the last opportunity for help. This person concurred in this diagnosis. Consequently, the very next day, all the participants were invited to the informant's house, and the dream was duplicated as much as possible. The two men became "friends," and yard goods were exchanged. The singer seen in the dream played the rattles; while the four dancers of the dream, together with the dreamer and his guide (now his "friend") danced the Feather Dance. All were asked to wear Indian costume, and the same songs were performed as in the dream. Corn soup was served just as in the dream. The only addition to the events of the dream was that the interpreter was asked to burn some tobacco and to explain the proceedings to the assemblage. The informant claimed he had "good luck" thereafter.

If the dream is indistinct or merely "bothersome," the patient will seek the aid of a fortuneteller to elucidate the specific stipulations.

Friendship due to affection may be concluded at any time through the wishes of either party involved, and is merely a way of formalizing a close relationship between two persons. Code preachers, it is said, used to mention that it is sinful to contract formal friendships for opportunistic reasons, such as the wealth or potential usefulness of the "friend." Friendships for the sake of social climbing or exclusiveness are considered equally sinful. Voluntary friendships should be concluded for the sake of true affection only, and even then the friendships which are incurred to cure a disease are considered the "best" ones. These general notions are still a part of the ideal culture at Six Nations today. When friendship is formed on account of affection, no ritual need be performed, but sometimes the parties decide to have a social dance or perhaps to sing an Adō'wa song, dance the Feather Dance, or eat corn soup together to celebrate the occasion. The first two relationships—friendship through sickness or dreams—may be formed regardless of the sex of the individuals involved, but friendship for the sake of affection is most common between members of the same sex. Whereas it is not forbidden to form a cross-sexual friendship, it is not considered exactly proper, particularly if the parties are of equal ages. Ritualized friendships are considered to be consanguineal relationships, and this is probably the reason why friendships which might be construed as involving sexual attraction are questionable. Clan considerations are immaterial, since a friendship may be formed either with a member of another clan, a member of one's own clan but in another family, or even with a member of one's own family, for example, with one's own grandfather. The latter case, however, is usually one which has been prescribed, "due to sickness," by a fortuneteller.

Ritual friendship is said to come from the mutual associations of warriors in a war party. However, Handsome Lake is said to have condemned friendships formed for the purpose of fighting and to have substituted associations for mutual aid, particularly in case of the illness of one of the partners. (Parker's version of the Code has no mention of this, and therefore it may be apocryphal.) Whether a friendship association actually did exist among warriors is now hard to determine, but it is interesting to note that the informants themselves conceive of a specific shift of function from war to curing. Alexander General describes the change in the following story:

At the time when the Confederation was established and the laws between the Confederate nations had already been made, the warriors were dissatisfied because they had no part in the Confederacy. Consequently, they went on war parties to various settlements, scalped there, and finally returned. The chief then asked them why they had done this, since the Good Tidings of Peace had already been established. They said that they had no part in them. Various people then started guessing what it was that the warriors wanted, and some guessed correctly that the answer to their wishes was that they wished friendships for the purpose of going to war, because warriors were of the war party. The Code of Handsome Lake, however, condemned friendships for war purposes or making friends in order to subdue another people. Friendships should be for the sole purpose of loving one another and doing good for people, and helping when one is sick. Ever since that time friendships have become more contagious.

The same general ideas are usually "preached" to the friends at the time that their friendship is formalized, either at home or in the Longhouse. A speaker stands up, and both friends stand while the standard instructions to them are recited. Alexander General's version (as translated by him) is as follows:

Relatives now present, it has been conferred upon me to address a few remarks through these persons that have now become friends. I would now draw your attention to those who desired to make friends. I would draw your attention in connection with the Message of the Great Spirit. We have heard how they used to make friends in former days. We have been asked to change our attitude toward our own people. Friendship is for the sole purpose of having love and respect for other people. You are forbidden to carry on the way they used to carry on in former days. As they used to do whenever friends were traveling or were gathered in a group, they used to boast themselves of the physical strength that they had, which made the people fear. I forbid you to do as they did before. You are now to do only the wishes of the Great Creator. You are to have love and respect for other people, and also when you call on your friend's relatives, you are to treat them as your own relatives, and I decide that the friends are to do likewise. And should, at any time, a friend become ill, the other is to go and help him with whatever he requires of help. That is the duty of friends as long as they are to survive on earth.

If the friendship is formed because of a disease or a dream, this fact is mentioned in the speech. The particular text given here is used when the motivation of the friendship is affection. Each friend will have given the speaker a length of cloth (shirt material for a man, printed cotton for a dress for a woman), which is now exchanged between the parties. This present represents "a word," meaning "a word of honor" or "a contract" to keep the friendship, and it is an integral part of the ceremony. However, there are occasions, such as when a friendship must be concluded "in a hurry" due to the urgency of the sickness, when one or perhaps both friends lack the present. In such cases "it is promised," which means that the parties formally obligate themselves to procure the material as soon as possible. In fact, however, this promise is sometimes not fulfilled, particularly not by the party who was asked to make friends, since he feels that he is already doing the supplicant a favor. Very likely, though, after a few years, or at the next sickness, this neglect begins to "bother" the negligent party, and a fortuneteller often "sees" that an obligation has not been fulfilled. The material is then hurriedly procured and presented. Once a friend has received the material, he may dispose of it in any manner he desires and need not keep it as a charm or token of the friendship. The present itself is unimportant; only the fact that it is given is of importance. Sometimes the speaker also burns some Indian tobacco.

If any ceremony or rite is to accompany the friendship it is also performed at this time, and it is this rite which should be periodically repeated by the friends throughout their lives. These may be performed at home at any time or in the Longhouse at the Midwinter Festival (see *supra*, pp. 178–9). Thus, if the War Dance accompanied the formation of the friendship, either or both of the friends should call for the War Dance at the Midwinter Festival, and they should sit side by side throughout the performance, though the ceremony ought to be repeated despite the absence of one of the friends. Even after the death of a friend and after he has been "given up" (see p. 250 *infra*), it is still respectful to call for the ceremony which accompanied the formalization of the relationship. In part, the repetition of the rite reminds the parties of their obligations and expresses their mutual respect, but an equally important purpose of the periodic reiteration of the rite is to show respect for the relationship of friendship as a "medicine" (in contrast to showing respect to the human beings involved). This is particularly so in the case of those friendships which were contracted for therapeutic reasons, for then the relationship is conceived explicitly as being "medicine." If this "medicine" were ignored, it would very likely cause a recurrence of the initial disease, or perhaps a new disease which would have to be diagnosed. Fortunetellers often claim just such an etiology for a sickness, and the neglected friendship rite is then immediately performed. Forming a friendship is thus a serious matter, which should be treated respectfully, since the obligations are immediately tied to the ultimate sanctions of disease and bad luck. People should, therefore, not enter into a friendship frivolously or too precipitously, although instances in which a friendship is refused to a supplicant do not seem to occur.

Ritual friendships may be formed at any age, from babyhood till death, but in all cases the mutual obligations and rights are the same, even as they are identical regardless of the cause of the friendship. The primary characteristic of a "friendship" is that the parties involved are considered to be related to each other as if they were siblings, and all the social relations which ideally accompany the sibling relationship should be followed between the friends. They should address each other by sibling terminology, and each must address the family of his friend as if it were his own consanguineal family. Children in particular often mention that they have two or three mothers or fathers. They mean that they have consanguineal parents and also the parents of their friends, to whom they actually refer as "mother" and "father." Some fortunetellers even prescribe friendships not so much for the sake of acquiring a "friend," as for a supposed need of the child for another parent. A further extension of the kinship terminology is the use of "aunt" and "uncle" by a child in referring to a ritual friend of one of his parents. Friends must also observe between themselves and their respective families the incest taboos which apply to siblings. A typical example is that of a girl who as a baby had formed a ritual friendship with an ailing child. Approximately 15 years later, this girl wished to marry the brother of her friend. However, this was definitely disallowed by her mother, who said it was exactly as if she were marrying her own brother, and, consequently, the romance was broken up. Interestingly, the same uncertainty which characterizes the incest taboos and marriage regulations in the normal course of social relations also persists in the determination of eligible marriage partners in families which are related through friendships. Thus, some informants hold that it is forbidden to marry into the matrilineage of a friend; whereas others maintain that all those relatives of the friend to whom "close" kinship terms are applied, including anyone classified as agadō'nih or kheya'ʔdawēh by him, are ineligible as marriage partners, regardless of whether they belong to the friend's mother's or father's matrilineage (see pp. 31–2 *supra*). Similarly, it is uncertain how far a friendship relation between two people extends to the families of the parties. Is the entire family of orientation obligated, or is the father exempt? Some people maintain that only the matrilineages of the friends are involved, while others hold that all relatives to whom "close" kinship terminology applies are obligated. Finally, there are various interpretations regarding the extension of the relationship to the families of procreation of the friends. Spouses usually show a marked degree of respect toward the friends of their own marriage partners, but on the whole affinals are not considered to be bound by friendship relations. The ideal culture stipulates that if a female "friend" of the wife visits the home of the couple, the friend ought to be allowed to sleep with the husband. However, all informants agree that they would not, in fact, condone the practice. The topic, incidentally, always occasions much laughter.

Even as brothers and sisters should at all times help each other, so should the friends and the immediate families of the friends. Once more there arises the question of who is to be included in the designation "the families of the friends," and once more two answers are given. Some informants confine the mutual obligations to the matrilineal relatives, while others extend the obligations to the groups whom they designate agadō'nih and kheya'?dawĕh (and, of course, any closer relatives, such as parents, siblings, etc.). Nor is there a strict correspondence between the extension of the incest taboos between the families of friends and the extension of the obligations of the families of the friends. An informant may say that the incest taboos apply only to the matrilineal relatives, yet he may extend the obligations of mutual aid to the kindred of the friends, or vice versa. As is natural, however, the friendship and obligations are observed much more rigorously by the two principals (the friends) and by their close matrilineal kin than by the more remote relatives to whom duties and rights are extended.

Whereas in the real culture there is a great deal of understandable variation from the ideal of sibling solidarity, friends, on the whole, do attempt to be loyal to each other. In fact, the closest and must trustworthy relationship between any two human beings should be, and often is, that of ritual friendship. Friends confide in each other more than do siblings, and to break the trust of a friend is considered the most serious of transgressions. No matter what the circumstances, it is the friend who ought to share in sorrow and aid in distress. This applies not only to social and economic affairs, but pre-eminently to medicinal and supernatural ones. If a person is ill, the friend should see to it that the appropriate feast is held. If the person is in a white hospital, the friend should have his fortune told *in absentia* and should perform the necessary "Indian" ritual. If food, cloth, or other ritual materials are needed for a feast or a society rite, the friend should help provide them. If a hunting charm (see p. 285 *infra*) is present in the family, it is the friend in whom one confides and asks for help. At Six Nations, where curative and supernatural events play so important a role in the life of the orthodox individual, a ritual friend is therefore both a spiritual and economic asset.[3]

A friendship once formed is indissoluble until the death of one of the friends, and even then, according to a current legend, the friends are loath to part. The story relates that in olden times a person died, and his friend had himself put into the casket and went with him. When he got to heaven, he was told, "You are not ready yet— when you are, you'll meet your friend. Go back." So he went back, and people heard

---

[3] Friendships between two humans with supernatural endowment and between a human and an animal are common in the folk tales of the Iroquois. The friends usually help one another in critical situations, such as overcoming a wizard or witch, concluding a contest successfully against overwhelming odds, or maintaining life in a difficult situation. Here, too, the friendships are formal associations rather than mere cases of affection between the two partners (see Randle, 1953: 616).

him "holler" in the grave and let him out. He told his story, and the moral is: "Don't be too sad if your friend dies; you will meet him again." Until the tenth-day feast (see p. 245 *infra*) strict mourning should be observed, which includes abstinence from any meeting, including curing rites and Longhouse ceremonies, maintenance of reserved and sober conduct, and nonparticipation in the cooking, grave digging, etc., for the dead (just as the matrilineal family and moiety of the deceased are prohibited from helping). The surviving friend is subject to the latter prohibition even if he belongs to the moiety which makes the preparations for the dead, namely, the moiety opposite to that of the dead person. However, excessive grief is not condoned in Iroquois culture (see p. 245 *infra*) and the institution of friendship shares with the marital relationship the trait of "giving up the dead" (see p. 250 *infra*). This means that the relatives of the deceased, in their own name and in the name of their dead kinsman, and the surviving friend formally terminate the friendship and sever any obligations which the relationship might have imposed upon them. The living partner is "released" by the matrilineal family of the dead at the tenth-day feast, and as a token of the release is given a length of material (enough for a shirt for a man, enough print cloth for a dress for a woman). Though the living friend is released, he still continues a modified mourning until the one-year feast, even as should the matrilineal family, and he should conduct himself soberly and not participate in riotous occupations. In some instances the living friend is released at the one-year feast rather than at the tenth-day feast, either because the friends were so attached to each other that the survivor prefers to be bound to his friend for a full year and to observe strict mourning for the friend for the longer interval, or because the family of the deceased does not wish to give the survivor his freedom for a whole year. The former motive is censured because excessive grief is shown, and it is not considered appropriate "to hold on to the dead person" too long; and the latter motive is criticized as "looking bad," as if the surviving relatives were possessive. The living friend usually releases the dead and his family at the first appropriate Longhouse event after the tenth-day feast, which means either at Strawberry time, Green Corn, or Midwinter; until this event the surviving friend ought not attend the Longhouse at all, but thereafter he may again participate in all rituals. A length of cloth again symbolizes the release of obligations, this time passing from the surviving friend to the closest matrilineal relative of the deceased (see p. 251 *infra*). After this public abrogation of the friendship, all ties of consanguinity are broken, and the survivor and his family are allowed to marry into the dead friend's family. The obligations to assist are also repealed, although it is considered polite to show respect and continued consideration toward the family of an ex-friend. In fact, a polite form of kinship terminology is often retained in that the elder members of the family of the friend are still addressed as "grandfather" or "uncle" or "aunt." However, this is a purely gratuitous act, indicative of good breeding rather than obligation. Should one of the parties neglect to effect the release, it is believed that sickness or bad luck will befall a member previously involved in the relationship, nor will this member necessarily be the surviving friend.

MARRIAGE

Although there is great emphasis upon marriage among the acculturated group at Six Nations, marriage to the orthodox Longhouse follower is today, as it has been traditionally, a relatively minor *rite de passage*. However, whereas at one time the mothers of the marriage partners arranged the marriage and formalized the contract by an exchange of food (Morgan, 1901, 1: 311–13), the choice today is definitely that of the partners involved. There is, of course, a natural amount of parental supervision and anxiety concerning the marriage of a child, but in most cases it is a negligible factor. Handsome Lake is said to have decreed that parents should guide the marriage of their children, and the more orthodox informants believe this sincerely, but when an actual situation confronts them they are loath to take active measures against any particular choice of their children, even though they may disapprove. Children are early told of the particular marriage taboos which their parents believe in, and the advice may or may not be followed, depending on many factors. (For a discussion of such taboos at Six Nations today see pp. 30–2 *supra*.) The choice of marriage partners is an area of life in which the real and ideal culture diverge widely, so much so that some marriages have taken place between children of two sisters. One man, for example, was married to his own matrilineal cousin, which was considered "bad," and any misfortune which occurred in his family was attributed to this marriage. However, he was in no way ostracized and later even occupied ritual positions allowed only to particularly "good" men. Courtship today is a casual and haphazard process in which the partners have almost unlimited freedom of choice. The only consistent pressures upon the younger members of the Longhouse are to obey the strongest incest taboos, namely to avoid marriage with any relative classified as agadō'nih (father's kinsman) or kheya'ʔdawĕh (fraternal offspring, reciprocal of agadō'nih), and to choose mates who also belong to the Longhouse. The latter is important, since the greatest loss of Longhouse membership results from inter-faith marriage.

An inter-faith marriage between a Longhouse girl and a Christian man almost invariably alienates the girl from the Longhouse during the lifetime of her husband. If she outlives him, she may, however, return to the Longhouse. Even Longhouse men tend to drift toward the church if they marry into a "church family." Since it is generally recognized on the Reserve that the social prestige of the church is higher than that of the Longhouse, it is difficult for all but the most convinced of Longhouse followers to maintain their Longhouse affiliation in a church environment. Conversion of a Christian partner to the Longhouse occurs only in those cases in which the spouse has an important position in the Longhouse, or in which the Christian partner becomes convinced through the stronger personality of his spouse or through some curing rite that the Longhouse way is the more desirable. The Canadian idea of choosing a marriage partner for the sake of "love," regardless of religious affiliation or of consanguineal or ritual relationships (e.g., a "friendship"), has very much invaded the thinking of the younger generation. Also, the particular dating habits current even among the Longhouse population, which consist of car rides, movie dates, skating or sports dates, parties, and clandestine drinking dates, are not conducive to parentally supervised marriages. "Going quailing" (looking for a dating partner) is an absorbing pastime for most adolescents, and marriage usually results from such dating.

Once a choice has been made, the partners very often merely "get together," and forthwith consider themselves married. This was definitely the pattern among the older generation living today, and they furthermore maintained that according to the Code, "God (Shõngwaya?di'hs?õh) marries one when a child is born." Such common-law marriages are frequent and are considered absolutely valid by the community, even though no public pronouncement or ceremony commemorates the occasion. Today, when the importance of registering on tribal rolls and also the customs of the acculturated group are influential factors, Longhouse couples may request a formal Longhouse marriage, which, while it is not considered a common-law marriage, yet avoids the services of a minister or a Canadian justice of the peace. For a brief period, 1954–57, the local Indian Office required that a legal marriage be performed by a Canadian justice of the peace. Reserve members led a vigorous fight for the abolition of this ruling and were successful (see pp. 95–6 *supra*). Longhouse marriages may be accomplished in either of two ways. The couple may simply ask a "speaker" from the Longhouse, who is tacitly understood to be a chief, to "speak" to them; or the couple may utilize the services of Patrick Longboat, a Longhouse speaker (but not a chief) from Lower Cayuga Longhouse, who was designated by the elected council to perform legal marriages "according to Longhouse custom." (Jesse Jamieson had been similarly designated by the elected council to perform Longhouse marriages for members of Sour Springs, but at his death he was not replaced by another Sour Springs official. Sour Springs, which is currently very much under the influence of protagonists of the hereditary chiefs, is opposed, in general, to an official validated by the elected council.) Although both methods constitute legal marriage in the eyes of the government, the administrators in the Indian Office show a definite preference for marriages performed and recorded by Mr. Longboat rather than by a hereditary chief. Consequently, there is a tacit distinction between first- and second-class Longhouse marriages, with those performed by Mr. Longboat being considered more "proper," legitimate, and binding. To dissolve a marriage formed with the aid of Mr. Longboat necessitates legal proceedings and a judicial divorce, whereas those marriages performed by a Longhouse chief can merely "break up." Consequently, at the Indian Office and among the more acculturated members of the Reserve, and even among some of the Longhouse members, there has arisen the conception that a marriage by Mr. Longboat is not a common-law one, whereas one performed by a chief is; and, as a result, some couples both utilize a chief and also pay Mr. Longboat for a marriage validation. Naturally, this causes dissension, and the chiefs and more orthodox members are incensed. For a while, the hereditary council also designated members who were empowered to conduct valid and binding marriages. (Jacob General and George Davey, now both deceased, and Joe Logan were among those appointed.) This was at first more or less a concession to Indian Department pressure for registration with the Indian Office, but later, after the elected council was established, it became an expression of protest by the displaced hereditary council. Added to the struggle for recognition of the Longhouse as a responsible way of life is the struggle over the powers of the chiefs, and the particular case of Mr. Longboat has caused further factionalism between the liberal and the orthodox Longhouse members. He is considered by some to be unfaithful, since at one time he served in the elected council, and also because he allows his services to be endorsed by the elected council. All in all, the particular marriage arrangement chosen by a couple identifies them with a particular faction in the Longhouse and influences their later relations in the community. Naturally, the type of marriage preferred by the majority of the orthodox Longhouse community is that in which a chief or "speaker" is called upon to talk to the couple, whereupon the two consider themselves married. Today there is, of course, an official registration of the marriage with the Indian Department, and most of the Longhouse members are resigned to this "invasion of Longhouse rights."

The essentials of an average Longhouse marriage are simple. The wife's family usually cooks a Canadian meal and invites some of the family and friends; little ritual food is required, in itself indicative of a lack of tradition for this occasion, although corn soup and corn bread are always appreciated as "treats." A few families also remember the traditional corn-wrapped wedding bread and may serve it to the visitors as "wedding cake" (see Waugh, 1916: 223). The extent of the invitations is a personal matter, but, unless the family is attempting to rise socially, not many people are invited. After all have assembled, the Thanksgiving Address is recited. Thereupon various members may speak to the couple (who are seated and dressed either in plain or Indian clothes), admonishing them to fulfill their promise of faithfulness, to love their family, and not to discriminate against the parents of either partner. The principal speaker, the one assigned to validate the marriage contract, then rises and "stands up" the pair, as is the custom in the Longhouse in any formal validation. The pair clasp hands, and the speaker admonishes them to follow the advice of the previous well-wishers and to abide by his words. The man and then the woman answer that they will obey the dictates of the speaker. Thereupon the visitors and attendants shake hands with the pair and personally wish them well. Dinner is then served at the table. No moiety or lineage duties are observed.

Lately, however, in emulation of the elaborate wedding ceremonies, dances, and receptions of the Christian elements, some Longhouse families have increased the social aspects of a marriage ceremony. Thus, in 1956, the wedding of Lorna Jamieson (the daughter of the head deaconess of the Turtle moiety of Sour Springs Longhouse, who incidentally is ultraorthodox) was announced by printed invitation: "Mrs. Esther Jamieson requests the honour of your presence ... at three-thirty o'clock, Sour Springs Longhouse near Ohsweken. Reception six o'clock, Sour Springs Longhouse. R.S.V.P." It was claimed to be the first wedding and reception at a Longhouse and was proclaimed a great success. It will be interesting to see how many follow suit.

Separation and divorce are easy as far as the Longhouse population is concerned, in spite of condemnation by Handsome Lake and the preachers. It is mainly the Indian Office which refuses to recognize mutual separation and consequent common-law remarriage. Having been married previously is otherwise no handicap to a further marriage, whether the person has children or not. Even illegitimate children are no barrier to marriage or remarriage. They are accepted and not discriminated against, except in those families which attempt to emulate the Christian acculturated elements (but even among these families the incidence of illegitimacy is high). Small children usually stay with the mother; older children are sometimes given a choice, but otherwise they accompany the parent most able to provide for them. Often, particularly in large families, the children are divided, some remaining with the mother, others with the father. Here, therefore, is an area in which the ideal culture, as represented in the Code or by Longhouse preachers, is commonly and institutionally flouted even by the most devout of Longhouse followers. This, too, may indicate only peripheral interest in the marriage *rite de passage*, as well as a lack of historical tradition. What is felt to be important is only that a couple live together for a length of time and "raise a family," regardless of the paternity of the children or the legal validity of the union.

DEATH

CONCEPTIONS OF DEATH

Death, both as a concept and as an actuality, is today of paramount importance and interest to the Iroquois, and in fact it can fairly be said to be one of their overwhelming preoccupations. Not only are all of the practices associated with death labeled "particular" by the Iroquois, but death represents consciously and unconsciously the ultimate sanction for much of the culture. Thus, if one is not respectful to "old" ideas and customs concerning the spirit forces, one will become ill and die; if one does not give proper respect to medicine, animals, and plants, one will become ill and die; and if one does not hold feasts as directed, one will most certainly die. But above all, fear of death is the sanction which enforces the observances owed to the dead themselves. Since the dead have power, nothing could be more dangerous to the living than to neglect them, for their natural method of punishment is to cause disease and death.

Although thoughts, dreams, and prophecies are filled with omens and matters of death, there is no well-formulated ontology of death, and no one representation or philosophy of death is maintained to the exclusion of others. Death is many things to many people, and the relationships between the various ideas are indeterminate. In part this may be explained by the incorporation, but inadequate integration, of ideas concerning death from various historical periods and various sources; for superimposed on an early concept of death as related to coldness are ideas derived from the Jesuits, the eschatologies of several Christian sects, and from Handsome Lake. However, the multifarious conceptions of death also result in part from the wide extension of death as an ultimate sanction. Since the mechanisms of political, economic, social, and military control have become weakened as means of enforcing adherence to customs and beliefs, those of disease and death—which are ever present, despite the inroads of a dominant culture—have gained in importance. Conceptions of death consequently have been perpetuated and elaborated without regard for mutual consistency.

One of the commonest characterizations of the dead is that they are "souls." However, there is no uniform concept of a soul. One informant holds that it is the heart and that this is what leaves through the opening in the coffin, and she translates the word "sadō'nhethra?" (which ordinarily means "your heart") as "your soul." Another uses the word "thwa'isra?" and translates it as "immortal soul" or "spirit." Parker (1913: 61) gives a resumé of ideas of the soul. Among those which he mentions and which still persist today are:

"Every soul has a path to its destiny after death.

Every soul retains its personal identity whatever form it may inhabit.

Soul differs from life.

When life leaves the body the soul generally does, though not always immediately but may linger for ten days.

The soul may pass from a living body and enter any object or go to any place to acquire wisdom and returning reveal it to the person in dreams or visions."

The soul may take the form of a light, a will-o'-the-wisp, or a vapor, or it may imitate the shape of a body even though it has no substance. When it intends to do evil, a soul may assume the shape of any animal or even of a thing, such as a whirlwind. Faithful followers of Gaihwi'yo believe that the souls of the dead either go to the pleasant eternal abode or are damned to tasks symbolic of their misdeeds in the domain of the "Punisher." The former group follow the heavenly path (along the Milky Way), on which there are beautiful flowers, bright lights, fragrant odors, and a refreshing spring, and they approach a house through which they enter forever to the beyond. Here, it is intimated, matters are much as on earth, except that everything is pleasant and magnificent. However, while they believe that the souls "have gone beyond," they still speak of the souls as being "around" at times. Fenton and Kurath (1951: 144–5) say that "the Iroquois who follow the Longhouse way believe that although the main soul goes the long trail to the land of the dead beyond the setting sun, the ghost spirit hangs around the reserves." However, I have found no evidence for a belief in two distinct entities—the main soul and the ghost spirit—which have different destinations.

Some informants conceive of the dead as people who are similar to the living but invisible to them. When they say "the dead are around" at a feast or a dance, they mean literally that. The dead hover above or dance amid the living, and they participate in reaching for the ribbons at an Ohgi'we just as they might have done while alive, except that under ordinary circumstances they are invisible to the living performers. Occasionally, however, the dead may be seen at the Longhouse, and it is just such a vision which is said to have converted the Longhouses down below to passing food clockwise rather than counterclockwise. Fifty years ago, it is said, a man who was in the habit of attending many of the Ohgi'we noticed that as the women were circling counterclockwise, the dead were dancing between them clockwise. Since that time food has been passed toward the left, or clockwise, at dead feasts, rather than counterclockwise as at regular feasts. In fact, there are many associations of the left side with the dead.

Still others believe that the dead are skeletons, caskets, ghosts, or vampires, for these are the shapes which commonly appear to the living in their dreams when they are being warned or given messages by the dead. Any or all of these characterizations of the dead may influence the actions which are performed when a person dies, and the elaboration of burial and mourning rituals is due in part to the superimposition of various conceptions of death.

Hewitt and Fenton (1945: 303), in their descriptions of the Condolence Council, and Parker (1913: 105–6), in the Legend about the coming of Death, characterize Death (as distinct from the dead) as "that demonic Being that is faceless, Death—the Great Destroyer" (see also Hewitt, 1944: 65–85). One of the ideas current among the Iroquois is that of predestined death, and it is probably this "demonic Being" (acting somehow in conjunction with the Great Creator) who is responsible for predestination.[4] The personification of death is also common in myths and in some of the folklore, and it may even be this agent which inflicts the "14 hurts or wounds" on mortals at the death of a chief and which must be exorcised by means of the Requickening Address (see Hewitt and Fenton, 1945: 303).

However, it is not this personification of death which is considered most dangerous and "particular" by the Iroquois, but rather the dead themselves. The Iroquois' fear of the dead is neither a fear of death in the abstract nor a nameless fear of something unknown, but is a specific fear of the "power" of the dead. The dead can affect the living, though there are different conceptions of their means of so doing. Sometimes it is simply said that "the dead touch you," and it is this which does harm. Some informants hold that not even touching is necessary; the dead may simply wish an individual to be ill and die, and, unless countermeasures are immediately applied, the person is indeed in grave danger. There is particular danger from the dead when someone has just died. This need not mean that the recently deceased person wishes his mourners any harm. The reason is rather that when a dead body is present, others of the dead then tend to be "around," and it is easy for the mourners to provoke them unintentionally unless precautions are taken.

The elaborate and varied conceptions of death are important and fearsome to those who have them, and these conceptions are injected into the burial and mourning observances. A wake, a burial, a tenth-day feast, and a one-year feast are not merely ceremonies designed to console the mourners and dispose of the dead, but

---

[4] Fenton (1941b: 89–90) discusses the role of the concept of an allotted life span, but he attributes the determination of the length of time to the Great Creator. It is considered sinful, particularly according to the Code, to shorten this allotted life by suicide, and the punishment is the condemnation of the spirit of the dead person to travel on earth only.

they are also occasions at which the community takes cognizance of, and acts upon, those ideas of death which function as sanctions for the culture in general. The community does not fear that the body might be inadequately treated or the mourners left distraught, but rather that the power of the dead will take vengeance for the neglect of a culturally prescribed detail. Consequently, the details of a burial must be executed with respect and precision. Any participation in the process exposes the participant to risks and dangers. If he is lucky he will not be harmed, but he is gambling with his luck while he has contact with the dead. Even if there is no immediate manifestation of harm, an individual may show the effects of a transgression concerning the dead years after the event.

THE COMMUNITY DEAD FEAST

Even when the souls of the dead have gone beyond and are not apt to be provoked, a certain amount of respect must periodically be accorded to them and to the bones they left behind. No matter how well satisfied the dead may be, they must be remembered and given food or presents. This applies to the dead of the entire community as well as to those of a family. If such observances are neglected, illness and death will strike the transgressors. Furthermore, if a community moves, or if the bones of the dead are moved, the dead must be informed. The institutionalized fulfillment of these duties occurs in the periodic Dead Feast, or Ohgi'we Ceremony (often called the "Feast of the Dead" or "Carry-out-the-Kettle"), held by the entire Longhouse community. Fenton and Kurath (1951: 143–65) have given a detailed account of this ceremony at Six Nations (Onondaga and Sour Springs Longhouses), and consequently it will be discussed only briefly here.

Each Longhouse has attached to it a society which is composed primarily of women, ideally with equal representation from the two moieties, who are called "Ohgi'we women," and who have as their duty the scheduling and execution of the semiannual Ohgi'we Ceremonies. The society is led by one "head lady" from each moiety, who should receive her position hereditarily (in the maternal family). She should also be awarded a name characteristic of the position, which at the death of the incumbent is passed on to her successor. Today, however, most of these names have been forgotten, although not so generally as those which accompany other positions in the society. The names associated with the head positions of the Sour Springs Ohgi'we Society are still remembered. The name which accompanies the Wolf position, now held by Susan Johnson, is Gayẽʔgwa'adji (Black Smoke), and the name which accompanies the Turtle position, held by Sarah Isaac Clause, is Kᵃhya'dõs (Writing). Assisting each head lady, and also serving the society as a whole, is a man chosen from each of the moieties by the Ohgi'we members of that moiety. These men are called hane'hwaʔ ("he-skin"), and they hold the office, which is not hereditary, for life. Other members of the society belong because they believe the positions are inherited in their families, because they dreamed that they should join, or because they were commanded to join by a fortuneteller. Membership for the latter two reasons should not be passed on to other members of the maternal family of the incumbent, but at times this is ignored, and just as there is a multiplication of hereditary deacons, so there is of Ohgi'we members who claim membership hereditarily. Induction occurs at the Ohgi'we Ceremonies, where the new members are announced and "stood up" by the speaker.

In spring and in fall, when no crops are in the fields (for an Ohgi'we is believed to bring frost, due to the presence of the dead), the head ladies meet to plan an Ohgi'we Ceremony. Sometimes a Longhouse feels that it cannot afford to sponsor two Dead Feasts in one year, and in that case one may be omitted. Once a decision has been made to hold an Ohgi'we, the head ladies call a meeting of the rest of the society at which two women are chosen to collect food and ritual paraphernalia (especially cloth or money to buy cloth) from the community. After a while a second meeting is called, and if enough material has been collected, a date is decided upon, and the hane'hwa? inform the community of the date of the Ohgi'we; otherwise, there are further collections and meetings before a date is set.

On the day of the Ohgi'we the members of the Ohgi'we Society, together with other conscientious members of the community, clean up the graveyard of the Longhouse, burning the brush, tidying the markers, and planting new plants; and then they eat a communal lunch at the Longhouse and dance a few social dances. This indicates respect and attention to the dead and also indicates a sense of responsibility toward the community. The hane'hwa? and head ladies then make ready the Longhouse, cook for the midnight and morning meals, divide the materials which are to be distributed, see that the large Ohgi'we drum and tobacco are kept with the ritual paraphernalia, and in general prepare for the ceremony.

All the community Ohgi'we should be held at night, not in the afternoon as is now the custom for many of the personal Ohgi'we ceremonies. Even the latter, in principle, ought to take place at night,[5] but since this is inconvenient, most sponsors of personal Ohgi'we abbreviate the ceremony and have it in the afternoon, unless the disease is particularly serious. At times even an entire Longhouse may schedule an Ohgi'we in the afternoon (often due to the fear of excessive night drinking on the part of irresponsible persons congregating outside), but orthodox members frown on this practice. It is said that the afternoon Ohgi'we started because at a

[5] At one time ceremonies were performed at night, but Handsome Lake outlawed this procedure to avoid intoxication at the ceremonies. He divided the day into periods watched by various agents. It is believed that the Great Creator looks upon the earth from sunrise until noon. At noon he turns around, and the Angels take over the watch of the earth until the middle of the afternoon. Thereafter the "dead" (i.e., their souls) travel about the earth until midnight, whereupon the Evil Spirit roams the earth. However, for the sake of all-night Dead Feasts the dead are around till the first rays of sunrise, and, indeed, it is thought that "dead people may be around all the time, but we can't see them because they are behind leaves." (Speck, 1949: 17, has a slightly different interpretation of the "spiritual modes": sunrise till noon is allotted to the living; noon till sunset to the dead; sunset to midnight to good spirits; and after midnight to the evil spirits.) Longhouse ceremonies ought to be completed before noon, while the Great Creator is still looking, though they invariably continue into the afternoon these days, since the congregation is "slow in getting started."

reservation in the United States the Christians overturned the food and stole the materials of the Longhouse people. When the superintendent was asked for help, he promised police aid only during the daytime, and consequently the time of the ceremony was changed. Soon thereafter "it even appeared in the preaching that the Ohgi'we could be in the daytime." The lower end of the Reserve then started daytime performances, and the custom spread to the upper end. The story is probably apocryphal, but interesting in that the informants themselves recognize nonsupernatural historical changes. Nevertheless, Mrs. George Green adequately expresses the opinion of the majority of the conservative members when she says:

Since the dead come out to be amongst the living toward morning, they should be given a chance to mingle with the givers of the feast. The main purpose is to satisfy the dead and give them a chance to grab for the ribbons in the morning. If this is not done the whole is no good. Having an Ohgi'we in the afternoon looks as if the people come only to get the food and cloth rather than to please the dead.

The ceremony itself ought to be a truly communal undertaking. All the participants should actively "unite their minds" and sing and help and dance together for it is the unanimous effort of the entire community which is pleasing to the dead and benefits the whole nation. Actually, the ceremony is only for the benefit of the Longhouse community and any visitors. However, the informants always refer to the communal Ohgi'we as the "Ohgi'we for the nation," to distinguish it from family or personal Ohgi'we ceremonies, to some of which the entire Longhouse community is invited. Again, one notices the common motif of "togetherness" and participation. The Ohgi'we is supposed to have the effect of making every member of the community "sleep well and feel well."

The program is as follows: the Thanksgiving Address, an explanation of the "doings," a tobacco invocation at the women's stove, a performance of the cycle of Ohgi'we songs and dances, the "Carry-out-the-Kettle," the "midnight" lunch, social dances, distribution of lengths of cloth and handkerchiefs, social dances once again if time permits before daybreak, "Halfway of the songs," the ribbon and candy distribution as members file counterclockwise around the Longhouse outside, and the final food distribution. The order of the events and the length of any of them may vary, but this is the general pattern. Again, for a detailed description of the program, the principals involved, and the distribution of goods see Fenton and Kurath (1951).

Death of a Common Member

Introduction. The Ohgi'we is the only ceremony dedicated to all the dead of the nation collectively, and the rest of the observances discussed here concern either an individual dead person or, at most, a designated group of dead. But whether attention is focused on the collective or the individual dead, the attitude of the Longhouse members remains consistently respectful and careful. A single dead person must be treated just as "particularly" as the host of ancestors who intermingle with the performers at a community Ohgi′we. Consequently, funeral customs are of major importance to the Longhouse members.

Any occurrence of death must be recognized ceremonially, but that of a chief or of a close uterine relative of a chief involves a more complicated condolence ceremony than that of an ordinary person. Therefore, the death of a common member of the Longhouse will be treated first, and then the additional rites for a chief will be briefly discussed.

Preparation for death. Although death may strike a person unexpectedly at any time, particularly since it is widely thought to be predestined, relatives and friends are often given indications of an approaching death. Such a sign, which is, however, not a causative factor in the death, may come either in a dream or through a culturally recognized omen. The most common of the omens is a bird, which travels swiftly to foretell disaster, though often a bird simply brings a message, and one cannot tell whether it is good or bad until the presaged event occurs. An owl seen or heard, a whippoorwill near one's house, a wild pigeon flying into the house, a woodpecker pecking at the house, a bird flying into a window pane, or a hen crowing like a rooster—all may presage death.

Mrs. George Green was warned twice by wild pigeons that someone would die. One day while she was sitting at the table eating, a dove flew into the dining room under Mrs. Green's chair and then flopped under the chair of her mother as if dead. When they got up to catch the bird, it flew out the door. One week later Mrs. Green's mother was dead, though she had been very well. (She was, however, quite old at the time.) On another occasion a dove flew into the tree in front of her house, and she had her husband chase it. Less than an hour later a man bore the news that the shopkeeper at Johnson's store had died. "The bird had come straight, first to give the message."

Owls in particular are so feared that it is best not even to mention them in an ordinary conversation; talking freely of them would be foolhardy and would tempt fate. The appearance of ghosts, lights, skeletons, or snakes on the path, as well as numerous other folkloristic symbols, also may mean the imminence of a death.

One informant saw a light on the ceiling and a skeleton at the foot of her bed one night, but for fear that the ghost might hear her speaking she did not awaken her husband to tell him. Suddenly, three days later, her mother's father who was more than eighty years old, died of heart trouble. She thought that the ghost had been an omen. Another informant heard the stairs creaking one night, and the next morning she learned that a relative who had lived with her as a child had been killed at a stone quarry. She took the creaking as having been a sign of the approaching death, for "the relative came to her once more."

Since the omen gives no indication of who the doomed person may be, nothing can be done but feel fear.

It is always to be hoped that one will be so fortunate as to die in one's own home, and death in a foreign land is considered punishment for past sins or an evil life. Debates often arise in the council about whether the band should pay for the transportation of the corpse to the Reserve for burial, for there is a strong feeling, shared even by Christians, that "the body should be brought home." To ameliorate the misfortune of death away from home, Indian tobacco is sometimes sprinkled on the spot where a person died by accident. Versions of the Code mention that the faithful shall die in their sleep, and the fact that Handsome Lake did not do so is at times adduced to show that he was an impostor (see Parker, 1913: 59, for a similar statement).

If a person is at home and death is imminent, he should confess his sins, particularly any associated with witchcraft or the use of "medicines" for illicit purposes (such as a lacrosse or snow-snake game), for should the person hide these, he would die a "hard" death.

After confession, the "dead clothes," which everyone ought to have ready at all times, should be hung in sight of the ailing person above the bed. If he has been unable to prepare his own dead clothes, help in preparing them should be sought from a member of the opposite moiety. The dead clothes of a woman consist of a white cotton undershirt, a cotton half slip with a drawstring, black or navy wool broadcloth leggings, a skirt of the same material, two printed colonial-style cotton dresses (so that the dead may have a change of clothing, though the dresses are worn one on top of the other), a neckerchief, a ribbon belt, a ribbon to tie the hair (or to be placed in the coffin in case the person's hair is too short to be tied), and a pair of "dead moccasins."

A dead moccasin is cut with a seam up the center front rather than with a tongue inset over the top of the foot as in the common moccasin worn during one's lifetime. Also, the shiny side of the deerskin is turned outward in the dead moccasin and inward in the ordinary moccasin. At one time the men's and women's designs differed, but today, when only a few people remember how to make a moccasin, the same pattern is used for both sexes. Mrs. George Green, who makes dead moccasins, will do so without charge if the deerskin is provided; otherwise she will charge $2.00, as compared to a charge of $5.00 for making an ordinary pair. The moccasins have no decoration and are tied.

All the cloth must be sewn, and no buttons or pins are to be used at all. Not only are the latter considered to be white man's goods, but a pin, being made of metal, is said to weigh down the soul so that it would be earth bound and unable to ascend to heaven. Nor must any of the clothing be decorated with beads, for they also are "too heavy" and would confine the soul to the earth. Decorations of ribbons (which are essential items in any "Indian" wardrobe and are deemed to be the truly Indian decoration) and embroidery are permissible, but neither the material nor the decoration should be brightly colored. In particular, nothing of a red color should ever be put on a dead person, although pinks are perfectly acceptable.

The funeral wardrobe of a man consists of an undershirt; a breechcloth; leggings, slit on the outside, trimmed with ribbons, and sometimes tied to a belt at the waist; an overshirt of patterned print cotton reaching to just above the knees; arm-band ribbons which are tied above the elbow; leg-band ribbons tied below the knee (though in the "down-below" communities the leg bands are sometimes omitted); a long ribbon which is draped over the left shoulder, brought down and crossed over the right hip, and tied in a bow at the left hip, so that the ends hang down from the waist; a silk neckerchief folded into a triangle and knotted in front; a scarf bound about the head and also tied at the left side, with the ends hanging down; and moccasins. The same strictures concerning color and decoration apply to men as to women. The reason why all items are tied at the left is that "when one gets to heaven the dancing is always clockwise, or toward the left, and the sash knot and ends should always hang on the outside of the dance circle." Here is another instance of the "dead going around to the left"; and the Skin Dance and Feather Dance in particular are danced clockwise in heaven. Also interesting is the conception that in heaven the soul has the same form as the fully dressed body.

A generation ago the failing person would be dressed just before he died, but now he need only be able to look at his prepared clothes as he dies. Seeing them hanging neatly above one's head is supposed to give a feeling of security and reassurance that one is "ready to go." The fact that most people are not so prepared causes Mrs. George Green to comment: "We different now, just like a cat would die now."

The wake. Once dead, the body should not be left alone in the house for even a minute. A messenger should be engaged, from the moiety opposite to that of the deceased, who should fetch helpers to bathe and dress the corpse. Sometimes the mourners themselves perform these tasks, but strictly no members of the family of the deceased should perform these duties, and members of the moiety opposite to that of the deceased should be called in for this purpose. When the dressing is completed, three "hollers" should be given, and the corpse should be placed so that his head lies to the west. Canadian law now requires that the corpse be embalmed, and therefore an undertaker is called to take the body and to return it in time for the wake. Sometimes all the preparations of the dead, including dressing in Indian clothes, are performed by the undertaker. Traditionally, a plain pine box was ordered from the casket maker on the Reserve, but today the undertaker sometimes supplies a modern coffin. A v-slit is made at the head of the pine box in order to allow the soul to escape. When a metal casket is used, a symbolic knife scratch suffices.

Jake Henry, Howard Johnson, and Bob Martin were notable casket makers, and even today a few families order a box from Jake Henry to be delivered to Mr. Styres, the Six Nations undertaker. These home-made caskets had no nails or other metal parts and were mainly undecorated. The coffin maker, too, should ideally belong to the moiety opposite to that of the deceased. However, the tendency today is to sell "fancy" coffins to all the Reserve, including the Longhouse members, despite the fact that they are not considered proper. Social prestige has become an important factor in matters of burial, and often a burial will cost several hundred dollars. The benevolent societies (see p. 39 *supra*) will pay $100 of the cost, while the rest is borne by the family and often is owed to the funeral director for years. Not long ago all funeral expenses were paid in yards of material (three to five yards to each person who rendered services), but modern economic conditions have practically eliminated this.

The soul usually does not leave this earth, and perhaps not even the body, until after the tenth-day feast, and consequently the dead should not be left alone, particularly not until the funeral day. The family stays at home during the day, and friends and relatives are invited to the wake for the night. Wakes are held the first or second night after death, and in order to indicate particular love and respect for the dead they may be held both nights. The messenger who "tells around" of the death also invites members to the wake, saying, "You are requested to come to keep the light lit." He also procures the equipment (kept by a designated member of each Longhouse) and the caretaker, or helper (hadyenawa'se), to run the wake, if he does not act as the caretaker himself. Also, in preparation for a wake, the family should hire two cooks of the moiety opposite to that of the deceased to prepare the "midnight lunch," which is served both to the mourners at the wake and to the deceased. Since the soul of the dead is on earth for at least ten days, the dead person must be treated as if he were still alive. Food must be served him; a place for him must be set at the table; and all the speeches must be phrased as if the person were still among the assembled ones. Should the deceased be carried in or out of the room or the Longhouse, it should always be done feet first, "as if he were walking in."

Although a wake ought to be held for any person who dies, including a baby "who has uttered one cry" (i.e., was not stillborn), it is not one of the indispensable observances. Since the particular game now played at a wake was borrowed from the Delaware, the omission of a wake is usually rationalized by saying, "Well, it's Delaware, it is not Iroquois." Wakes are not held on reservations in the United States, and, consequently, when a member from a United States reservation dies in Canada, he may be buried without a wake.

When the mourners arrive for the wake, around 10:00 P.M., they hand the food which they are contributing to the caretaker and then either seat themselves in a circle around the room, or, if they expect to participate in the wake game, in two rows of chairs arranged facing each other. At one time the two moieties played against each other, but today moiety seating is not observed in the game. The immediate family is always absent from the wake until the final song in the morning. Close relatives are defined as "those in the same house." This means the relatives in the same matrilineal family as the deceased, and also those who physically live in the house with the deceased, such as a spouse (although the attendance of a spouse is optional). The close relatives should not take part in the wake, because they should be "in darkness and grieving," and "it would look funny to see people enjoy themselves" (i.e., at the wake games). The close relatives of the deceased should keep silent as much as possible.

The body is kept in the room, head to the west, in the open coffin, and the mourners may get up to pay their respects and have a final look. Lately, however, some wakes are held at home, while the body remains at the funeral parlor, and this is not believed to affect the efficacy of the wake, nor is the procedure changed.

After most of the mourners have assembled, a shortened version of the Thanksgiving Address, directed mainly toward the Great Creator, opens the observances. It is followed by a condolence speech to the mourners, delivered by any competent speaker. Wake speeches are not highly patterned and standardized, and consequently various speakers are noted for their individualistic style of address. Dave Thomas is said to give emotional speeches designed to make the mourners cry; Bill Thomas, Pat Longboat, and Alexander General give much more conventional, constrained speeches in the manner of the Longhouse orations. Alexander General's version is as follows:

It is our duty to come and help the mourners, the people that have sustained the loss of their beloved one. We would ask the mourners not to grieve and not to feel too severe for the loss we have sustained. For we know that the Great Spirit, our Creator, has not given us perpetual life. We all have suffered more or less the same of our beloved ones, and therefore we should sympathize with the people that have suffered this loss of their beloved one, so that they will not grieve too seriously. And they have asked us to come to keep a wake until day breaks. We therefore ask you, who are now assembled, that you will carry on this wake in a respectful manner, within the house and around the outside.[6] Then we now begin the rite to keep ourselves awake.

After the speech the wake game is played. At one time this was the Bowl Game played with deer buttons and later with peach pits, but today a Delaware gambling game is substituted. Informants on the Reserve still remember when the Iroquoian Bowl Game was played, so that the Delaware "mitt-and-stick" gambling game is a rather recent innovation. John Beaver, the uncle of Joseph Isaac (who himself died in 1920), died in Delaware territory on the Reserve probably around the turn of the century, and his body was kept by the Delaware, who played the "mitt game" during the wake. It was after his death that the "mitt gambling game" is said to have spread to all the wake observances on the Reserve. The songs which accompany the game are also borrowed from the Delaware, and Iroquoian performers are not able to understand the meanings of the songs, though they do not consist of burden syllables only.

Each wake is "run" (supervised) by an appointed helper, who is in charge of the progress of the game. The rules vary from occasion to occasion, depending upon who "runs" the wake and how the scorekeepers have been taught to keep score. Neither the exact rules nor even the outcome of the game is essential to the proceedings, since the purpose of the game is simply to assist in staying awake all night. However, the general pattern is unmistakable, and the songs are easily recognized. The wake game is played between two teams, which consist of an arbitrary number of people of either sex. At one time the teams reflected the moiety organization, but lately this has been neglected. The game is a kind of hide-and-seek, a version of the common moccasin game of North America. One side hides a small object in one of four moccasins (or socks, mittens, gloves, or a combination of these articles) placed on the floor between the two rows of players. Members of

[6] The reference to "outside" is aimed at adolescents congregating and drinking in cars outside at the scene of the wake.

the opposite side try to guess the location of the hidden object, each in turn pointing with a pointer stick to the moccasin which he believes contains the hidden object. When the object is found, the side of the successful searcher becomes the hider, and the side which previously hid the object becomes the searching side.

At Sour Springs the permanent wake paraphernalia consist of six small ball bearings used as counters and one larger ball bearing which is the object hidden in the gloves and moccasins. Edric General keeps these for the community, and he lends them to any family which needs them. The 3-inch wooden counters, 50 for the death of a child, 100 for the death of an adult, are fashioned just before each wake by the wake official, as are the large pointer stick and the drumstick used in the drum accompaniment of the wake songs. These items must be fashioned anew for each occurrence because they must be burned in the morning in the final stages of the game. The family sponsoring the wake provides the moccasins and the mats (or blankets) under which the counter sticks are placed when won by a side. The drum may be borrowed from anyone, whether a relative or not. Incidentally, Fenton (1950: 35–6) mentions a "cane with a crook for use in the Moccasin game at a chief's wake," collected by Hewitt in 1916, but at Six Nations there was no evidence of a mnemonic cane. The only cane was the rude pointer stick, fashioned from any ordinary branch and burned at the end of the ceremony. It is said that at one time the instruments used to accompany the wake songs were a notched and an unnotched stick (rasping sticks), but today the Delaware and the Iroquoian singers at Six Nations all use the drum (see Conklin and Sturtevant, 1953: 286).

The details of the game are as follows: Two persons, one from each team, "choose up" by placing hand over hand on the pointer stick, and the side whose representative comes out "hand on top" is the first side to seek. Four songs initiate the game. A member of the losing team then hides a ball bearing under or in one of the moccasins and chooses a wake song. He may sing any one of 30 songs now remembered, and as soon as the song is recognized, the entire hiding side helps to sing, while a drummer on the hiding side accompanies the song. There is no order of choice, and often the same song is repeated time after time, especially when the participants are not versed in many of the songs. Approximately two dozen different wake songs are remembered by one of the singers. This is probably as large a set as any one person knows today; most performers know only two or three. The song continues over and over until the seeking side has successfully located the hidden object, at which point the song is broken off abruptly. The members of the seeking side take turns at guessing, but the ball bearing is hid anew by the same hider after each guess. When a person guesses incorrectly, he passes the pointer stick to his neighbor. When there is a correct guess, the hider indicates the success by hitting the moccasin on the floor, so that the object makes a loud sound. At this point the teams switch roles: the drum and ball bearing are handed to the new hiding side, the pointer stick is given to the new seeking side, and the whole procedure of hide-and-seek is repeated. The new hider is the neighbor to the right of the last person to hide on his team, and the new seeker is the neighbor to the left of the last person to guess on his team. The drum is passed to the neighbor on the left if he can play it, otherwise it tends to be held by the head of the side. There are two scorekeepers, one for each side, who sit at the head of the two rows of players and move the counters according to the guesses of the seekers. At the beginning of the game, all the counters are in a pool. As the game progresses, according to Alexander General's set of rules, a ball bearing is laid aside each time a seeker misses, and when six of these have been moved to one side, representing six consecutive misses, a counter is awarded to the hiding side from the pool. After the pool is exhausted, counter sticks are transferred from one side to the other; in this respect, the rules of the wake game resemble those of the bowl game (see p. 171 *supra*). Because winning is unimportant, there is considerable individual variation in the details of scoring, depending upon the individual scorekeepers, and at times the scorekeeper may even get tired of "moving the sticks," and scoring is ignored. Even though the game is strictly intended only to pass time and to keep the mourners awake, there is often some cheating. Hiders keep the marble in their hands or up their sleeves, and scorekeepers attempt to favor their own side. At a wake sponsored by a family belonging to Lower Cayuga Longhouse, the scorekeeper apparently awarded the hiding side a wooden counter each time the seeking side missed, and awarded the seeking side a counter when the hidden object was located. There were no auxiliary counters, such as the ball bearings, in evidence. In all the communities the purpose of the game is merely to help to stay awake, so that when all the counters are won by one team, they are simply placed in the pool again, and the game is resumed. Often, however, a whole night passes without a side ever amassing all the counters. The game continues uninterruptedly until midnight, at which time the speaker announces that there will be a small rest. "Lunch" is served, including a plate for the deceased. The food consists of ordinary home-made feast fare for which no special preparation is prescribed. After the "lunch," the speaker announces that "we will now proceed where we left off, we will carry on till day breaks." All the counters are again placed in a common pool, and the game continues as before, although with only three moccasins.

Toward morning, just as dawn appears, all inhabitants of the house must be awakened, and both sides sing the "cry (or crier) song" (dewashēthwa'ʔtha?). During this song only two people play the game, using only two moccasins, and each time a person misses, a wooden counter stick is burned in the stove by the wake official. However, because it is believed that a death will occur within the family in that very year if the "cry song" lasts a long time, the official will burn several sticks at a time to shorten the game. (Down below, if the deceased is a woman, two women play; and if a man, two men play during this last song, alternately hiding and searching.) Both squat on the floor over the moccasins, and since the game is fast and intimate, no pointer stick is used. When all the counter sticks have been burned, the pointer stick is broken in two and also burned, and then the drumstick. At one time a gun was shot off in the morning, but this has now been discontinued. The "skin" head is then taken off the drum, and is "put up" (stored in the house in a safe place) until the tenth-day feast, whereupon it is returned to the owner and may be used again. Of course, if the wake is repeated the second night, the skin is replaced and the drum "tuned up" for the second wake, but thereafter it is kept until "freed" at the tenth-day feast.

All the inhabitants of the house must be aroused for the "cry song," and all the participants must be awake, for the deceased is close by and is dangerous to anyone sleeping. During this song all participants, and particularly the mourners, weep bitterly, for it marks the departure of the deceased. The speaker once more gives the Thanksgiving Address in brief form. Again only the sections which are dedicated to the Great Creator and which give thanks for the privilege of the assembly and health of the participants are used. If the funeral time has been set, the date is mentioned, and the participants are asked to communicate the information to whoever may ask. Once more there is stress on wide community participation. Should food remain from the lunch, it is either passed to the participants or served to them "on the table," or both (see p. 247 *infra*).

The guests leave, and the family takes over the deathwatch. The food which was served to the dead, and from which the dead is believed to have extracted the essence, is given to the first visitor who arrives in the morning or to a strager or to a "poor" person, or it is simply discarded (given to a dog, buried, or thrown into a swamp). A dead person should participate in all meals served in the house from death until the tenth-day feast. No other person may occupy the accustomed place at the table of the deceased in the interval. However, food need be placed on the plate only as long as the corpse is in the house and at the tenth-day feast.

Burial. At one time Iroquois burial was a scaffold, or tree, burial, or simply an abandonment of the corpse in a shack, and numerous folk tales still discuss this type of disposal. For example, see Randle (1953: 632), who also notes that Waugh included five versions of "The Vampire Corpse" in his Six Nations collection. Today, however, the only method of disposing of corpses is grave burial, and the popular story, "The Vampire Corpse," is related at Six Nations to indicate that this is the only proper type of burial.

Mrs. George Green and others related the story much as it was told to Waugh in 1915 (*ibid.*: 632): A family had lived in a lodge, and when a death occurred, the dead person was left while the remaining members stole away silently, abandoning the entire hut. Later these members or others in the community were led back to the lodge where either they were attacked by a vampire, or the old corpse was found "eaten out in the stomach" or "with blood on the face." The explanation is that this was the work of the dead who were not buried, or that wolves had reached the dead because they were not buried. In either case a discussion of burial method follows, with the conclusion that henceforth the dead should be interred rather than left in an abandoned house or given a scaffold burial.

The grave should be dug by a fellow member of the deceased's Longhouse, but one who is preferably of the opposite moiety. The grave must not be dug earlier than the morning of the interment, for an open grave is disrespectful to the dead, in that it might imply that the mourners are eager to be rid of the corpse. According to the "Indian way," says Mrs. Green, one is supposed to "hold on to the dead and keep them with us as long as possible." Consequently, the very last thing to do is to dig the grave. Furthermore, a grave left open overnight is believed to cause another death in the family. For example, a few years ago a woman was buried at St. Johns with Christian rites, and the grave was prepared the day before burial. One week after her death two of her grandchildren became extremely ill (in a coma), which her husband attributed to the opened grave. "They did wrong by the old Indian belief," he said, although he is a very acculturated Christian Indian and a high-steel construction worker in the United States most of the time.

On the morning of the funeral the corpse is provided with a "lunch" consisting of corn bread 2 inches in diameter, which has been baked in ashes ("the dead people's way") rather than cooked in water. (This type of corn bread may also be eaten as a delicacy; see Parker, 1910: 68.) No beans or salt are ever added. This corn bread is wrapped in a handkerchief and placed in the hand or elbow joint of the deceased to be eaten on his journey. (Church people sometimes place oranges in the coffin of the deceased as the "lunch." Although this is not considered proper by the Longhouse population, it is an understandable substitution, since oranges are expensive and highly valued at Six Nations.) Furthermore, many of the smaller personal, ceremonial, or medicinal artifacts which were made specifically for the welfare of the individual, or which passed to the individual in connection with a supernatural decree or through the instructions of a fortuneteller, should preferably be buried with the individual, and should be placed in the coffin as inconspicuously as possible (under the body, for example). Thus, the stick used in the medicinal tug-of-war game, the football used in the football game, the eagle wand, the snow snake from a medicinal snow-snake game, and the miniature False Face masks from dream guessing are typical objects which should accompany the deceased in death just as they did during his life.

Speck (1949: 123) mentions that in one case the miniature mask was buried with the dreamer. This ought to be done in all cases. Thus, a curing rite was required for a granddaughter (SoDa), because a miniature mask had not been buried with her grandmother. The circumstances were as follows: The grandmother and her sister had identical dreams that there was a deep gully, and there was water in this gully. It was a windy day, and a False Face and a Husk Face helped both to avoid falling into the gully. This dream was "looked into" at Midwinter and duly guessed, whereupon two miniature masks were made. The grandmother kept both of them in a little sack, but when the grandmother died, her little mask was not "taken along." This, a fortuneteller diagnosed, caused the misfortune and made the granddaughter have fainting spells. (Note that the illness affected a son's child, who is not in the matrilineal line of descent. It is characteristic of medicine or charms that they work on both sides of the family.) A long and elaborate feast was held for both small masks, in which the entire history of the case was recited, the masks were asked for forgiveness, tobacco was burned, tobacco was tied to both masks, and False Face and Husk Face songs were performed by masked performers. The food served was False Face mush, roasted for a black miniature mask; and also "dead" corn bread, because a Husk Face likes corn bread and because the owner of the Husk Face was dead, and with a dead person one buries corn bread baked in ashes. It was further promised that one miniature mask would be buried with the grandaunt, and one with the sick girl. However, the grandaunt once again took both masks home with her. The procedure and program of the entire ceremony had been carefully delineated by the fortuneteller.

False Faces and Husk Faces, as well as the musical instruments of the curing societies, are not deemed proper objects to accompany the dead, even though the person may have acquired these in the same manner as an eagle wand. These objects must be disposed of at the tenth-day feast, where they should be given to a suitable heir who can use them "properly." Simply "keeping" them will bring disease and bad luck to the hoarder, even if he is a legitimate heir, such as a child of a deceased woman. Hunting charms should also be buried with the dead who once owned them, and, indeed, burial with the owner is one of the "safest" methods of disposing of charms and medicinal objects. If such burial should fail to take place—and despite the potential dangers, relatives often refuse to give up the objects, because "they are stingy of them"—the family can reasonably expect some illness and poor luck from the presence and improper care of these objects. Similarly, if the deceased had been an herbal curer, all his or her "medicines" should be buried separately in the earth. They may be dug up again after the ten-day mourning period and used by another specialist, if he is sure of the proper usage. However, by far the safest course is to bury the medicine and leave it buried, because "it might be dangerous" after the rightful owner has died. Medicines are individualistic and dangerous, and might work only for the "doctor" who originally owned them and knew how to use them. But in this case, too, relatives are loath to discard a useful material, and some keep the medicines and merely purify them by smoking them with pine branches and the burnt root of skwa'ĕda (coltsfoot), after the tenth-day feast. Occasionally, an individual will express a wish to "take along" his favorite snow snake or walking stick, and such desires are granted. However, no informant at Six Nations could remember seeing any wampum in a coffin, as has been reported in the literature and is found in archeological excavations.

A meal is usually served at noon to the gravediggers and mourners. Then, before setting out for the final Longhouse rites a speaker, belonging preferably to the home Longhouse of the deceased but to the opposite moiety, usually comes to the house of the deceased and once more consoles the family and mourners in a formal address. If a competent speaker of the opposite moiety is not available, a speaker must be borrowed from the moiety of the deceased. Such a speaker acts as a "two-faced," and he is returned to his own moiety with thanks (see p. 48 *supra*). The spouse, children, ritual friends, kheya'ʔdawhĕh, agadŏ'nih, and other mourners are condoled in that order in much the same words as at the wake. Then the procession to the Longhouse begins.

At Sour Springs the body is carried in and out through the women's door, while at Lower Cayuga and Seneca the east door is used for the entrance and the west for the exit. In all cases the foot end of the coffin is carried in first to simulate "walking" into the Longhouse, as if the person were "still with us." The coffin is opened and placed in the center of the house on the singers' benches, the head westward and the feet eastward. At one time there was such emphasis on verisimilitude and "being with us still" that the undertaker was compelled to unscrew the entire lid of the coffin at the wake and at the Longhouse, so that it looked as if the person were reclining on a couch. Lately, however, the undertaker has been relieved of this chore at most of the funerals.

Seating for a funeral is according to sex. A second condolence address is given by the speaker who had consoled the bereaved at home earlier. He says that perhaps some relatives had not heard the words expressed at the house, and therefore he condoles them again. Furthermore, he condoles the entire moiety of the bereaved, specifying as usual each of the ranks in the hierarchy: the deacons, the people, the children, and those on cradleboards. If the deceased belonged to a title-owning family, the chief of that family is particularly condoled. Then, the moiety of the deceased replies briefly in kind, avowing that the loss undoubtedly affected not them alone but also the condoling side. The speaker then announces that the people may now have a last look at the departed relative. All the speeches are phrased in such a way as to indicate that the deceased is still among the people, passing through the Longhouse a final time on his way to heaven. Going up to the coffin for a last look is considered extremely important, and orthodox members insist that the body must be brought into the Longhouse and must be visible. (This causes friction at times, such as when the undertaker refused to bring a corpse which had been submerged for several months in the Grand River into a Longhouse. The "head push" of the Longhouse protested violently and feared that the soul might therefore be unable to enter heaven.) At Sour Springs the women ("because they are the mothers") circle the coffin counterclockwise first, followed by the men, and then followed by the family of the deceased, which is not separated by sex. Down below, women circle first if a woman died, men if a man died. After all have circled, the speaker announces that the coffin will be closed and the remains laid to rest. The coffin is carried out feet first, again as if the deceased were walking. Mourners then follow the coffin to the burial ground of the Longhouse, where the speaker delivers the last address. He indicates that now the departed has arrived at the final resting place and henceforth will be entrusted to the Creator. The mourners have done their duty as decreed by the Creator, and they should now release their hands from the dead. Alexander General adds: "We have now returned the remains to earth, which the Creator made to create man by earth. So the remains shall return back to earth." Mourners are instructed to return to the house of the deceased on the tenth day after death for the tenth-day feast. The coffin is lowered, again with the head to the west, and two shovels of earth are symbolically placed on the lowered coffin by a member of the moiety opposite to that of the deceased. Sometimes a single wreath from the family is added, and the mourners depart. Gravediggers complete the interment. It is generally believed that it will rain if an "old person" dies, "because those left behind are not so sad, as the dead cover up their tracks." Therefore, if a death occurs, rain is usually forecast for the funeral day.

Until the tenth-day feast there should be a general period of mourning for the entire community of the home Longhouse of the deceased, and no games should be held at that Longhouse.

The tenth-day feast and the one-year feast. Wherever the Iroquois culture is verbalized—for example, in the folklore and legends—the expression and repression of excessive grief are familiar motifs. Prolonged displays of despair are depicted as the natural, untutored reaction, which, however, according to the teaching of the culture hero or the new prophet, ought to be tempered and limited to a shortened period. In the legend of the founding of the League, for example, Deganawi'da? persuaded Hayō'hwatha? to moderate his grief by means of wampum strings and the sympathetic recitation of a condoling address (Parker, 1916: 24). Today the Requickening Address restores the bereaved kindred to a normal state and admonishes them to observe a more balanced expression of suffering than the erstwhile tearing of vestments and mutilation of the body. The funeral, tenth-day, one-year, and "giving up" speeches all enjoin the mourner not to dwell on his loss beyond a reasonable measure. Functionally, excessive mourning would interfere with the operation of the culture, and the injunctions to be moderate are sensible, particularly in view of so many tales of grief-induced debility and of the great emphasis on death. The institution of the tenth-day feast is described as an innovation promulgated by Handsome Lake in order to limit the dejection of the mourners. According to Mr. General:

> Before Handsome Lake the people mourned continuously and no more forgot the first loss before there would be another death, and the mourning would continue. It caused a troubled mind or suicide. Handsome Lake had a vision that the people should discontinue the mourning after ten days, and if they exceed that time they commit a sin, because it causes them to impair their health. Now the mourners do follow up the advice.

Parker (1913: 56–7, 108–9) also finds these sentiments in sections of the Code.

The tenth-day feast, therefore, formalizes the conclusion of the period of deep mourning though certain obligations of mourning still remain for the spouse and ritual friends, who abstain from complete social reintegration until they have "given up the dead" at the next appropriate Longhouse ceremony (p. 250 *infra*). The obligation of the one-year feast also remains (p. 251 *infra*). The tenth-day feast marks the final departure of the dead from the earth, for many believe that the dead person hovers about the vicinity in "ghost" form for ten days after death. "Ghost" form specifically means that the dead, when visible, assume a bodily aspect precisely like that of the living. Many individuals claim that they have at times seen dead persons and that they looked just as they did during their lifetime. The belief in the presence of the dead is so strong that special provisions are made to protect the weaker members of the assemblage. Children in particular are described as "not strong enough" to withstand so much contact with the dead, and consequently precautions must be taken to safeguard them. It is safest to tie a half-inch band of deerskin around the left wrist of a child (often for children up to fifteen years of age, though it is mandatory only for children under four), which the child wears throughout the period of contact with the dead (i.e., at all dead feasts and from death until the tenth-day feast). Once the dead have left, the band, which prevented them from approaching the child, is simply discarded.

Should there be no deerskin bands at hand, snipping a small amount of hair from the top or front of the child's head and burning it fulfills the same purpose, because the dead do not like the smell, and sometimes both methods are used simultaneously. Yet another method of safeguarding, particularly for children at the death of their mother, is to sew a snippet of hair of the deceased into a small cloth bag, and to pin this to the clothes of the child during the ten-day mourning period. Not only does this provide the necessary protection, but it is also meant to keep the child from becoming too sad. Another category of people who are represented as "not strong enough" in respect to withstanding the ill effects of the dead are menstruating women, but here the remedy is simply to keep them away from possible contact. Only after the proper "feast" on the tenth day is the dead person able to leave in peace. For this reason the event is considered vital, and the neglect of a tenth-day feast is a dangerous gamble, seldom dared by a Longhouse family. Without the feast the dead would most probably "be bothered" and would be forced "to be around," which is extremely dangerous to the living, for the chance of contact with the dead is naturally much greater if they are "around" and displeased on account of disrespectful treatment than if they have left for the final journey. Furthermore, the dead are very "particular" about the tenth-day feast, with the result that any neglect of the prescribed event could cause illness and bad luck for generations among the kindred of the dead. Indeed, many of the diseases of Christian families are diagnosed by the Longhouse fortunetellers as stemming directly from the neglect of a tenth-day feast of some relative. Alexander General even goes so far as to state that in his opinion more Christian than Longhouse families are forced to pass small dead feasts, which is the common remedy for a neglected tenth-day feast, because the Christians are so unmindful of their obligations to the dead. Mr. General's statement expresses the common attitude rather well:

> Neglect of feeding the dead by feasts causes sickness. One must at all times treat the dead with proper respect, so that they do not harm the living. "Indians" put the dead to rest after ten days or a year, with material. The dead are treated as if they were here for ten days and then released, and they are not so vindictive then and do not hurt or afflict the living much. Nor do they come back to make the Indian sick. But Christians don't do this, and therefore they are more bothered and must give more feasts. More Christians give feasts than Longhouse people.

This is an indication of the importance attached to the tenth-day feast, for it is usually a Longhouse fortuneteller who diagnoses the cause of the Christian's illness, and the omission of the tenth-day feast is so obvious a transgression that it is often designated as the cause of an ailment which might easily be ascribed to quite a different cause were a Longhouse patient involved. Of course, if a Longhouse family did neglect a tenth-day feast, there is no doubt that any disease and bad luck in that family would immediately be traced to this indiscretion.

In practice the execution of the tenth-day feast is comparatively simple, with very little need for paraphernalia or specialists. The importance of the event is definitely philosophical and emotional, and the participants emphasize *that* the event must be observed rather than how elaborately it is to be performed.

A tenth-day feast ought to be arranged by the matrilineal relatives of the deceased, one of whom supervises the feast and is referred to as the "matron." (This does not mean that she is the custodian of a chief's title.) Usually, she is the sister, mother, mother's sister, or mother's sister's daughter of the deceased. However, if there does happen to be a chief's title in the matrilineal family, then the matron of the chief is often asked to perform the duty, since she is looked upon as the ritually most important member of the family. The matrilineal relatives "hire" the messenger and the cooks and engage the speaker, usually the same people who helped at the wake. The matrilineal relatives should also decide upon the distribution of the estate of the deceased, for a husband or wife is, theoretically, ineligible to participate in the division of either the personal articles or the lands of the dead. In practice, however, only the personal articles of the dead are distributed today by the family at the tenth-day feast, particularly since all land transfers must be approved by the elected council and the Indian Department at Brantford. However, at the more orthodox ceremonies the speaker may mention to whom the lands will eventually be deeded. In preparation for the tenth-day feast, the personal effects are bundled and tied by the matrilineal relatives into separate packages, ready to be bestowed upon the helpers, "hired" personnel, friends, and heirs, and these packages are readily visible to the visitors.

Theoretically, all the members of the Longhouse community are invited, as are all the relatives of the deceased, but in fact only those people who knew the deceased and the family well or who aided in the funeral proceedings attend. In general, those who go to the funeral also go to the tenth-day feast, particularly since an invitation to the tenth-day feast is automatically extended at the grave to all funeral participants by the speaker. Those who attend usually contribute to the "feast" for the dead by bringing baskets of edibles, but contributions are not mandatory. The two cooks hired by the matrilineal relatives of the deceased help them prepare the doughnuts, scones, pies, cookies, corn soup, and other feast foods. In the Sour Springs community the visitors are first given a meal "on the table," which means that each person sits at the table for a complete meal of corn soup and any other foods the family may be able to afford. As soon as a person has finished eating, he rises and takes his seat somewhere else in the room, and his place is filled, at the instruction of one of the cooks, by another visitor. There is very little, if any, conversation during the feasting, and all participants are reverent and solemn. Throughout the meal a place has also been set for the deceased and provided with a normal portion of food, which is kept until the next morning, when it is either given away or disposed of. The extra place setting for the deceased constitutes "feeding the dead," and it is the crucial trait of the "feasting-the-dead" pattern. The dead are always described as "being hungry," and keeping the food overnight gives them a good chance to absorb the essence of the nourishments. In the communities down below the "feasting" at the tenth-day feast is confined to the passing of food at the end of the distributory ceremonies of the occasion, but here, too, the deceased accumulates his share of the food, which is also kept until morning.

A definite distinction is always drawn between eating "on the table" and merely "passing food," even though the actual food may be identical. The two traits are conceptually very different to the participants, and eating "on the table" is considered a more formal and solemn observance. Since the average family can accommodate at most eight or ten people at one time at their table, the procedure often takes several hours. A notable trait of the entire "feasting-the-dead" pattern is that, at all times, the living must also be given the appropriate food for the particular dead feast. The mere offering of food to the ghosts of the deceased does not constitute "feeding the dead."

The matron who runs the tenth-day feast indicates to the speaker that he should begin the formalities of the occasion. A speaker should never, out of respect to the family, be a member of the family, and preferably he should belong to the moiety opposite to that of the deceased. If the deceased was married, the speaker will explain that the first attention must be toward the distraught and "untidy" spouse, who until this moment has been in deep mourning and ought to have been in a corner of the house not noticing any of the guests or talking to any person. (Although the mourning spouse formally observes avoidance patterns at the tenth-day feast, he should have been accompanied by a matrilineal relative of the deceased until the funeral is concluded.) The grief of the spouse must be assuaged by the closest matrilineal relative of the dead, who must also release the spouse from mourning obligations toward the deceased and the kindred of the dead. To symbolize the reintegration of the mourner into society, this matrilineal relative "cleans up" the spouse by combing his hair with a new comb and by presenting him with the means to reappear among humans. Since he has symbolically been said to have rent his clothing, he is given material for a garment (enough cotton print for a dress for a woman and white shirting for a shirt for a man), a silk scarf, a handkerchief, and the comb with which he was combed. Even though the spouse need not thereafter avoid the company of humans, he must yet observe a modified type of mourning until he, in turn, has released the dead and the matrilineal family of the dead from their obligations, and until he has publicly declared that he shall "give up" the spouse (see p. 251 *infra*). Occasionally, it happens that the spouse is not released at the tenth-day feast, and a variety of standard reasons may be adduced. The most common ones are that the family of the deceased cannot afford the material at that time and therefore waits until the one-year feast; that the survivor does not wish to be released from his spouse so soon, for his love and grief are too intense as yet; and that the family of the deceased harbors ill feeling and purposely neglects to release the spouse for motives of revenge, since the unreleased partner is then unable to move about freely but must continue in mourning. However, all of these situations are considered in poor taste.

The distribution of the personal effects of the deceased now follows. The speaker kneels near the pile of articles, and he begins to recapitulate chronologically the last days and death of the deceased. First he mentions each visitor who came to see the departed during the last illness and says that for this kindness the family would like him to have a final keepsake. At each of these patterned speeches the matron hands the preassigned item to the speaker, who holds it in his hand during the announcement and then returns it to the matron, who hands it to the recipient. The matron then whispers the name and deed of the next beneficiary, and the speaker may say, for example:

> This evening is the tenth day. We now think the people outside should hear our voice. We are going to talk to the person . . . [Indian name of the individual] that gave us help when this first happened in our house. When death happens in the house, our minds are blackened. We can't think clearly. We have to look outside to the person who has a mind which is clear to help us. That is what happens when death comes. We stood outside, and our minds rested on a woman who we thought was willing to help us. So this evening we are thinking she'll hear our voice. First we plead and ask her to stop thinking of what has happened to us, and change her thoughts. We are asking her to start thinking about what our Creator has made a ruling to do. We know she is one of the people that is upholding our religion, and now she'll start carrying on and upholding our religion. And there are a lot of gatherings going on among our neighbors. Now there is nothing between us, but she may carry on her duty to help her neighbors. Now what little thing she [the deceased] had, she'll [the helper] keep to remind her, and this is our voice. It is going toward this woman that sewed clothes for the dead. So now she can take her reward.
>
> (This is the speaker's own translation.)

Each of the helpers during all the funeral, wake, and tenth-day feast preparations is thus rewarded. For some there is a standard "fee," such as three yards of material for the messenger, the cooks, the man who "ran" the wake, the speaker at the wake, the speaker at the funeral, and the speaker at the tenth-day feast. The gravediggers were formerly paid in material, but today they usually demand cash ($15.00). In such cases the payment is not made at the tenth-day feast, for only traditional payments of material, handkerchiefs, or scarves are ceremoniously made. Nor is the money of the deceased distributed at the feast, although the speaker may mention the principal beneficiaries. Finally, the remaining belongings are distributed to the ritual friends, friends, and relatives of the dead, in particular to the kheya'ʔdawēh and the agadõʼni. All earthly things should be thus disposed of, for if an item is left undistributed, and perhaps coveted by an unauthorized heir, it may easily be the source of much later harm, particularly if it happened to be a ritual artifact.[7]

[7] Such artifacts may cause disease and bad luck in the family of the person who has kept them. In particular, if a deceased owned any ritual artifact which he himself had procured by illegitimate means, or if he owned a hunting charm, his nearest of kin will be reluctant to dispose of it at a public ceremony. Such items are particularly "dangerous" to later generations, and many of the diagnoses of the fortunetellers point to such items as the source of later difficulties. It is interesting to note that the illegitimate retention of nonritual artifacts seldom is offered as the cause of trouble. There is a definite feeling that a ritual artifact should be inherited by a person who is able to make intelligent use of it, and that harmful (witching) artifacts should be disposed of at death. Death is an excellent time to discard hunting charms, since they will not "turn" on anyone then, but once they are possessed by a new owner they again have a legitimate field of operation, namely the family (and by this is meant any person on either the maternal or paternal side who is designated by kinship terms) of the new owner.

When the goods of the deceased have been distributed, the family "feasts" the dead again, and the cooks and helpers pass feast foods to all the guests. In the communities down below, if a visitor has contributed a basket of food for the tenth-day feast, the cooks usually fill the basket separately with a selection from the donations of food prior to the general distribution. The distribution of food at Sour Springs is to the right, but in the communities down below the food is passed to the left, "because it is a dead feast." The distribution follows roughly the same pattern as at the festivals in the Longhouse. The cook or helper moves about the room, either handing each person in turn his share or letting him take one of the items from a basket, so that everyone is given an equal share. Each time a basket is passed around, one of the items is set aside and accumulated on behalf of the deceased, whose share is then kept overnight and disposed of in the morning. Aside from the usual feast foods (cookies, scones, corn bread, cake), the offerings may also contain oranges, chewing tobacco (which is distributed equally to all, regardless of whether one chews or not), and candies. Even though the guests take home most of the food which is passed them, they should nevertheless take at least a token bite, so that "the dead can eat off it, too." If there are any dirty dishes, such as piepans, they should be left unremoved and unwashed until the following morning, "so that the dead may eat off them."

The speaker ends the feast by recapitulating the purpose of the event to the dead, stating that he hopes the dead will be satisfied. The guests go home, and mourning is officially ended. The drum which was used at the wake is also "sent home" now.

The spouse and the ritual friends of the dead, however, observe a modified mourning until "giving up the dead" (or more strictly, "giving back the dead to the relatives"). During this period the mourner may go out and may associate with members of the community, but should avoid participation at the Longhouse and at pleasurable social events. A restrained, modified, semi-mournful attitude is demanded until the release at the Longhouse. "Giving up the dead" always coincides with Adõ'wa Day, which at Sour Springs is the second day of Green Corn and the sixth day of Midwinter. At Lower Cayuga, where an extra day of "pass dances" has been inserted, the Midwinter Adõ'wa Day is the seventh day of the festival (see pp.169, 189 *supra*). Sometimes, if a death has occurred shortly after Midwinter, the survivor may not wish to wait until Green Corn and may give up the dead at Strawberry time instead. In one instance a woman even gave up her husband at the tenth-day feast instead of waiting for the Longhouse event. She claimed that being a head deaconess, she was needed at the Longhouse and therefore could not afford to be absent until Midwinter time. However, she was criticized by the community, which felt that she merely used an excuse to avoid observing the partial mourning and staying at home. On the other hand, another head deaconess did abstain from attendance at the Longhouse until she had released her husband at Midwinter time. There are also cases where the survivor "holds on" to the deceased for two or more years, due to a reluctance to become "unmarried." One such widow was criticized for her untoward mourning and "stinginess of her husband."

On the occasion of "giving up the dead," the survivor brings three yards of cloth (wrapped in paper) to the Longhouse and hands it to the proper Longhouse official (a deacon or deaconess), who in turn hands it to the speaker of the moiety of the survivor. The speaker, while holding the present, rises and pronounces the formal speech of release, at which time the survivor also rises in the Longhouse, so that all may observe and take note of the present. The speaker addresses the matrilineage of the deceased, and he explains that now the survivor "has put nice varnished boards over the grave" and that this completes his duties toward the deceased and the family of the deceased. The speaker then "sets the living out on the road" and releases all his ties to "the public." In other words, the widow or widower is now free to remarry, and the ritual friend may marry into the family of the deceased. The length of material is then handed to the official again, who conveys it through the appropriate person to the nearest available matrilineal relative of the deceased— e.g., a brother, sister, or mother's sister.

Even though mourning has been renounced twice, the spouse, ritual friends, and immediate family still tend to curtail their activities until the one-year feast for the dead. This feast, at which the dead is "fed" one more time, occurs on the first anniversary of the death, for it is thought that the soul of the dead, perhaps in ghost form, returns to earth again on this day. Consequently, the matrilineal family of the deceased prepares to "feed the dead" and invites the immediate family, the spouse, the family of the spouse, and friends and neighbors to share in the feast. It is again interesting to note that unless the feast is shared, it is not considered valid. Feast foods are cooked in preparation for the event, although the visitors also contribute to the feast by bringing food. The one-year feast is less formal than the tenth-day feast. Seating and moiety rules are not carefully observed, and the speaking, cooking, and passing of food may be performed by any available persons. A speaker is invited, who opens the ceremony by burning Indian tobacco in the stove in order to call the attention of the dead to the feast. The dead, who is addressed by his Indian name, is informed that he has not been forgotten, that he is being "fed," and that it is hoped he is content. He is begged not to harm any of the mourners, since all the rituals have been carried out to the best of their ability. Then the food is distributed as is customary at death feasts, to the left at the "down-below" communities, to the right "up above." Again an equal share is retained for the dead, which is discarded on the following morning. The dishes again are left unwashed until the morning after the feast.

If, however, at the anniversary of the death, the family feels economically unable to perform a one-year feast, the ceremony may be "promised" by burning tobacco and stating this fact. In such cases the feast may be held as soon as the family can afford it. Some families let the event slide, hoping they can avoid the feast, but it is safe to assume that before long someone will become ill, and a fortuneteller will diagnose the cause as the neglected one-year feast. It is immediately held after such a diagnosis, since worse is feared if the deceased is not propitiated. Thus, even though this feast is a very simple rite, it is backed by the strongest sanction of the culture, namely, sickness that neglect of the event may cause.

Tutelo Ceremonies

If the deceased at Six Nations was of Tutelo descent or had been adopted by a Tutelo in a formal spirit-adoption ceremony, then the mourning customs must reflect Tutelo as well as Iroquoian institutions. The Tutelo nation was adopted by the League, and specifically by the Cayuga, in 1753, and there are today at Six Nations, according to Speck (1942: 3), approximately 50 to 60 persons (seven family groups) who recognize that part of their ancestry is from this Siouan tribe. Whereas in general this group has been integrated into the culture of the Iroquois, there nevertheless remains the distinct belief, both among these Tutelo and among all the Longhouse groups on the Reserve, that the Tutelo nation must not be allowed to die out, and that at the death of any Longhouse adherent among the Tutelo there must be substituted another individual who will perpetuate on earth that aspect of the personality of the deceased which identified him as being "Tutelo." The spirit-adoption ceremony, which should be observed either on the ninth night after death or within the year after death, accomplishes this aim, for it transfers the Tutelo nationality from the deceased to the person adopted in the ritual. This individual is thereafter bound to observe all those cultural traditions which are believed to be peculiarly Tutelo, and upon his own death his "Tutelo nationality" must be transferred to yet another person. Many of the adoptees are Iroquois, so that the cultural designation "Tutelo" today does not necessarily imply Tutelo ancestry; but as far as those who follow this practice are concerned, Tutelo adoption bestows genuine Tutelo nationality, regardless of birth, and thus the Tutelo are sustained among the population.

If the death occurs in summer, a spirit-adoption ceremony cannot be performed at once, because the dead would cause frost to ruin the crops. The family therefore holds a fourth-night feast on the fourth night after death and also a regular tenth-day feast on the tenth day, and promises the dead that the spirit-adoption ceremony will be held as soon as possible. If the death occurs in winter, however, the fourth-night feast is omitted, and the adoption ceremony takes place on the evening of the ninth night after death, with the distribution of the inheritance immediately preceding it. The tenth-day feast is then omitted, since the adoption ceremony lasts from the ninth night into the morning of the tenth day, and since there is ample feasting of the dead. Because the adoption ceremony is a very expensive ritual, the family of the deceased may not be able to sponsor the event on the ninth night after death and instead may simply "promise" (by burning tobacco and stating the promise) that the ceremony will be performed as soon as feasible. In that case, the fourth-night feast and the tenth-day feast are held just as if the death had occurred in summer. People often attempt to postpone the scheduling of the spirit-adoption ceremony, but at the onset of illness they become "frightened" and begin planning the event. Thus, the Tutelo rites are retained through the same powerful sanction of disease as the Iroquoian rites for the dead.

Since the Tutelo rituals, and in particular the spirit-adoption ceremony, are economically taxing, many of the Iroquois would like to dispense with their execution. However, the Tutelo are now depicted as having been a supernaturally powerful nation, capable of considerable witchcraft, and since this power has been perpetuated in the Tutelo dead as well as in those Iroquois who are adopted as Tutelo, people fear that the discontinuance of the rituals pleasing to the dead would cause harm. Stories exist about both the fourth-night feast and the spirit-adoption ceremony, which concern specifically the lapsing of these ceremonies and the supernatural command for their reinstatement.

The fourth-night-feast songs, it is related, had been discontinued by the Tutelo long ago. One day the wife of a man died, and he went out into the woods. There the spirit of the dead wife met him and instructed him to sing the fourth-night songs. The man said that he had not sung the songs in so long that he could only remember part of one song and none of the rest, and no one else knew any. The spirit of the dead said not to worry, since she would help. Thereupon the man went back to the village, told his story, and gathered the people around to sing. They burned tobacco, as instructed, to help them sing and began. Miraculously, they remembered all the songs. Ever since then tobacco is burned to ask for help from the dead, though "lots of us know the songs now." Incidentally, the magical assistance by the dead or by a supernatural in the reconstruction of a presumably forgotten ritual is a very common motif in the Iroquoian folklore.

The story of the spirit-adoption ceremony, as told at Six Nations today, recounts that one day the Tutelo Indians had a meeting to decide how they might stop the "dressing-up" (spirit-adoption) ceremony, since it cost so much and was so much trouble. It was then decided that the best way was to get a good runner to run far out and hide the "stuff" (ceremonial paraphernalia associated with the spirit-adoption ceremony). So, a man was hired who ran fast, and he took the stuff straight to the sunrise and kept running until noon. There he came to a large pine tree with two large roots stuck out facing the sunrise. The man made a hole 4 feet deep and buried the objects so that no one would find them. He then came back. "Now it is hidden, now we can quit," he said. And so they quit for years and years. One day, however, a man was out hunting, and he went so far that he had to stay overnight. He made a little fire and thought he'd stay. He was sitting quietly, when he heard an owl way far away, and in another direction another owl. Then he heard them coming closer, and when they were near him they began to fight. Both fell within the light from his fire, and he could see them rolling around. After fighting, the owls went their separate ways. He wondered what had happened at home; perhaps there was sickness. [Owls are a notorious sign of death and disease.] Then a woman spoke behind him and said: "Don't turn around; it wouldn't do to see me. I am a Tutelo Indian, and I have been dead for years and years, and they never 'dressed' me into another, and so I have turned into an owl. That is what happened. I am married to a real owl, but he abuses me. You saw how he licked me, my husband. I can still get away if I am really 'dressed up.' I can become a person again, though not come to life." The man said that it would be hard, since no one can sing now. She said that one old man could still sing one song. "When you sit down, one man will sing and will burn tobacco and ask us dead to help him remember the song. We'll do it. Another thing is that it [the ritual "stuff"] is hidden, but it can be found. Hire a young man who is a good runner to start running in the morning, facing the sunrise, and keep running until he reaches a clearing at noon and sees a stump with two big roots sticking out toward the sunrise. Dig there; it must be 4 feet, and it will be there." The man agreed to try. He returned to his village, gathered all about him, and told his story. [Here the informant repeated the entire story.] Consequently, it was decided to hire a runner, and if, indeed, he found the "stuff," it would be true. The runner did find the things, gathered them, and returned, and so they said it must be true. Another proof was that an old man (ninety years old) said he could still remember one song. He therefore was asked to play the drum, and another man burned tobacco and asked the dead to please help to sing. "If it works," they said, "it must be true." They gathered, cooked, sat down to sing, and sang all night. Therefore, it must be true, "and we keep on and go ahead."

Both tales were told by Jake Henry, who thought he had heard them from his father, William Henry, who had been dead 47 years and died at a reputed one hundred four years of age. Jake Henry has himself been "dressed" as a Tutelo many times and is able to sing all the song cycles.

The fourth-night feast is not to be confused with the Four Nights Ceremony (ge'i niwahsōnda'ge) of the Tutelo, which is a harvest ceremony at one time repeated at four private Tutelo homes on four successive nights in October (Speck, 1942: 118–9) and still performed in part at the Longhouses down below during the Corn Testing Festival (see pp. 156–7 *supra*). The fourth-night feast combines the traits of an Iroquoian dead feast with some allegedly Tutelo procedures, including a series of songs, and is envisioned by those who hold it as "the Tutelo ceremony for the dead." The method of invitation, the cooking, and the feasting of the dead are in the familiar Iroquoian pattern, but no moiety considerations are involved. Anyone may cook or sing, and no distinction of seating separates the clans. Usually, the messenger and cook who help the family at the wake and tenth-day feast also help at the fourth-night feast. Relatives, friends, and neighbors are invited, and they are expected to donate food for the ceremony. The head singer, usually the drum player, is responsible for assembling "the gang" of singers, the number of whom preferably should not be less than eight and should be divisible by four, since four is the pattern number of the Tutelos. (There are at least a dozen well-known singers of Tutelo songs at Six Nations today.) A speaker who burns the tobacco and a tobacco custodian are also appointed. When all have assembled, two opposing benches are arranged in such a manner that one of the benches occupies the same place as had the coffin, and this bench holds the food. The relatives and singers sit on the opposite bench, and without plates and utensils ("this is Tutelo," say the informants) they eat the feast foods. In particular, a knife taboo must be strictly observed, as the dead are believed to cut themselves as they hover about tasting the food and touching all the objects. No knife should be left lying near the food, and if an item must be cut, the knife should be removed immediately after use. The appropriate foods are meat boiled until it breaks to pieces (also described as "Tutelo"), potatoes, corn bread, rice, doughnuts, cookies, pies, cakes, and berry juice, but not soup. After the singers and the members of the family have eaten at the benches (other guests not being fed at this time), tobacco is burned in the stove, and the dead are implored to lend their aid to the singing and to be satisfied with the "doings." The singers then take their seats on the two benches and, accompanied by a water drum and a cow-horn rattle, sing without interruption the 80 songs in the cycle, the meanings of which are now unknown. It is dangerous to fall asleep during the performance, because one is weak and easily harmed by the touch of the dead while sleeping; and it is also dangerous to leave the room, because of the large number of the dead clustering outside. Since the Tutelo are depicted as a supernaturally powerful people, a considerable amount of fear accompanies the execution of any Tutelo ceremony, particularly the dead feasts. Furthermore, the performers claim that Tutelo feasts are dangerous because the Iroquois really do not know how to perform them properly nor do they know what it all means, and, consequently, they must be particularly careful not to antagonize the dead unnecessarily. The tobacco custodian, who holds a small bag of Indian tobacco, should drop four pinches of tobacco on the floor "for the dead" at each mishap, be it a mistake in singing, the late arrival of a member, or the inadvertent dozing of a guest. Death might otherwise overtake the transgressor. During the last song all the remaining feast foods are passed clockwise (because it is a dead feast) to all the guests, and the singers are each given a basket of food as "payment." (The "eat-all" trait is also common to many Iroquois feasts.) The speaker then thanks those assembled for their participation, and all go home. Dishes are left till the next morning as in all the dead feasts.

The Tutelo spirit-adoption ceremony is the most complex ceremony at Six Nations today, with the exception of the Chief's Condolence. The essential point of the ceremony is that the soul of the deceased is recalled to earth for the duration of the night and is informed that it will be represented on earth by an adoptee who is given the name of the deceased. It is the last time that the soul of the deceased consorts with the living, and at the first break of day the relatives wish it a tearful good-by. (If the spirit-adoption ceremony is held before the one-year feast, the dead does reappear yet another time; otherwise this is, indeed, the last time one can be certain of the presence of the spirit.) Also present during the night are any other deceased Tutelo who may have wished to attend the ceremony, but these too vanish at the first rays of the sun. Naturally, so many returned dead make the ceremony extremely "particular," and it is therefore executed with great precision. Speck (1942) has given a detailed description of a spirit-adoption ceremony, which agreed well with my observations on the two occasions on which I witnessed the ceremony.

The obligation to perpetuate the existence of the Tutelo by means of the adoption ceremony is felt acutely, and an omission of the rite would be considered an enormous miscarriage of trust. The sanctions are the more stringent because the transfer of nationality is so closely concerned with the wishes of the dead, and violating this injunction would be dangerous, indeed. Furthermore, there is the supernatural sanction related in the origin story (see pp. 252–3 *supra*), which intimates that any deceased Tutelo who is not "reclothed" in the adoption ceremony will be turned into an owl; and it is widely believed that such obviously discontented souls harm the living by causing bad luck, disease, and death for generations to come. Therefore, even though the ceremony necessitates a large expenditure, many performers, and prolonged planning, the survivors of a deceased Tutelo and particularly of an adoptee, usually hold the spirit-adoption ceremony. Any willing individual may be "clothed" and adopted as the earthly representative of the deceased Tutelo. However, no one enjoys assuming the risks inherent in the ceremony, which is attended by hosts of dead Tutelo, each one of whom might take offense at a mistake or an omission, and no family voluntarily assumes the obligation of perpetuating the spirit-adoption ceremony. Hence, the sponsoring family often searches for someone who has been previously adopted, and it is not unusual to find individuals who have been adopted four or five times. Such individuals know how to conduct themselves during the ceremony and in addition assume no new duties by being adopted once more. Also, when such an individual dies, only one new person need be "clothed" on his behalf, and thus the total expense to the community is diminished, while the obligations toward the particular dead who might cause harm are fulfilled. This skewing of the supposed original "Tutelo" purpose in favor of fulfilling the Iroquoian death prescriptions indicates that the Tutelo spirit-adoption ceremony and the fourth-night feast have become parts of the death pattern of the Iroquois rather than remaining isolated Tutelo institutions. Or, alternatively, one may speculate that the reason these ceremonies are still retained is that they are related to that part of the culture of the Iroquois which is upheld by the strongest sanctions, namely "careful" treatment of any ritual which concerns the dead.

THE DEATH OF A CHIEF

When a death is that of a chief, or even of an individual whose matrilineage claims a chief's title, the loss is recorded in a ritually more elaborate manner.

First, should a chief be on his deathbed, not only his "dead clothes" but his "antlers" (the string of white wampum which legitimates his title) must be hung over his bed.

Parker (1916: 108) relates that "while yet the dying lord is suffering in the agonies of death, his brother lords will come and remove his deer's horns from his head and place them beside the wall. . . . While the lord is ill we will place a string of black wampum at the head of his bed. . . ." Today at Six Nations there is some confusion among the matrons as to which wampum string should be hung above the bed during the illness. In practice, various matrons follow their own ideas; some hang up the white, some the purple, but none both. Although it seems, from Parker's account, that the purple is meant to be displayed over the bed of the deceased, the more prevalent opinion at Six Nations is that it is the white string which should be hung up.

Because the title of a chief ideally should pass from the living to the living, a chief who is not expected to survive his illness should be formally relieved of his duties during his last days. A speaker from the opposite moiety is summoned to explain to the dying chief that he will honorably lay aside his antlers, but should he recover he will once again possess them.

Three characteristic mourning cries are pronounced at the death of a chief, and since his passing is of concern to the entire League, his deputy must be sent at once to announce the grievous news to the opposite moiety of nations, since it is they who officiate at the mourning ceremonies. Consequently, the deputy takes from his matron the purple string of the chief's wampum, and, carrying the string, he "runs" to the fire-keeper of the opposite moiety of nations, proclaiming the mourning shouts every few hundred yards, particularly at the gates of the houses of Longhouse members on the way. (Today the deputy usually drives to the home of the fire-keeper, but even so the death shout is emitted from the car window at the homes of Longhouse followers. The death cry must never be uttered in vain, as it would cause the death of a chief.) Gadji?nŏnda'whyŏ is the fire-keeper for the Four Brothers, Honŏwiye'hdŏ for the Three Brothers, but should the appropriate one of these chiefs not be accessible, the wampum may also be delivered to Haga?a'ēyŏnk for the Four Brothers, since he shares the position of fire-keeper with Gadji?nŏnda'whyŏ, and to Thadoda'ho? for the Three Brothers, since at Six Nations he is the most prominent chief. The fire-keeper (or his substitute) keeps the purple wampum string until the Installation Ceremony, after which it is returned to the matron. Meanwhile it is his responsibility to prepare for the condolence of the bereaved moiety. The fire-keeper should say that he will "come on the trail of his grandfathers" in three days time to console the bereaved brothers, whereupon the deputy should answer that he would prefer if the "clear-minded" moiety (i.e., the moiety which did not suffer the loss) would arrive in ten days for the consolation. (This is supposedly a reference to the change of custom effected by Handsome Lake, for if the Condolence were to take place after only three days, the mourners would be unable to contain their grief thereafter.) At the funeral of a chief the speaker must be furnished by the "clear-minded" moiety of nations, rather than by the opposite moiety of clans within the deceased's Longhouse as with an ordinary citizen. In other words, the death obligations for chiefs are between the Three Brothers and Four Brothers and hence are internation obligations.

On the tenth day after the death of a chief, the chiefs and speakers of both nation moieties assemble at the home of the deceased in order to condole the mourners. This ceremony, which is a tenth-day Condolence, is to be distinguished from a Chief's Installation, which is referred to in the literature as a "Condolence Council" (Morgan, 1901, 1: 109). It seems reasonable from the descriptions in the literature (Morgan, *ibid.*, and Beauchamp, 1907) that traditionally there was only a single ceremony, at which the deceased chief was mourned and the new chief installed; but now, because of delays in installing a new chief, there are two distinct ceremonies. The Three Brothers and the Four Brothers are seated in two opposite rows, with no particular ordering within the moiety seating (probably because so few chiefs actually come and because often the chiefs are unable to recite the 14 verses of condolence and hence must be joined by speakers). Between the rows is suspended a stick containing the 14 strands of Condolence wampum belonging to the "clear-minded" moiety. Any stick is suitable. At the Condolence which I attended Joe Logan offered his walking stick for the purpose. Theoretically, each moiety should own a set of Condolence wampums. However, the Four Brothers today must borrow a set from Alexander General, which he maintains belongs to the Cayuga nation, and even more specifically to Sour Springs Longhouse. He claims to have completed the set himself, since it was incomplete when Jacob Isaac handed it to him (see p. 87 *supra*). The current set in use among the Four Brothers at Six Nations is constituted as follows:

(White beads are marked w; purple or dark beads, sometimes brownish, are marked P.)
1. Eyes (or Tears)—30 beads: alternating two w one P ten times.
2. Ears—34 beads: alternating one w one P 17 times.

3. Throat—36 beads: five sets of two P one W, one W, four P, two W, two P, three sets of one W two P, one W, one P, one white striated.

4. Intestines—36 beads: three sets of three P and three W, three sets of three W and three P.

5. Resting Place—36 beads: two P, seven W, two P, four W, eight P, nine W, four P.

6. Darkness—26 beads: 13 P, 13 W.

7. Loss of Sky—35 beads: eleven W, 15 P, nine W.

8. Loss of Sun—25 beads: three P, 19 W, three P.

9. Grave Cover—60 beads: two strings of beads, one having 29 P and the other 31 P.

10. The tenth string is the one called Twenty Matters, which is said to have been the fine for homicide (see Fenton, 1946: 120). This string is used only at the time of a Chief's Installation and never at a tenth-day Condolence. There is some doubt about the number of these strings at Six Nations and their use. The rules governing this string are ideally as follows: At the Installation the "clear-minded" moiety sends its set of Condolence wampum and the Twenty Matters to the mourners, who then immediately send back (with the proper message) to the "clear-minded" all the wampum strings except the Twenty Matters. If the next Chief's Installation happens to be that of a chief from among the previous "clear-minded" (who now are the mourners), then the condoling moiety returns the Twenty Matters to the current mourners, who keep the set until the next installation. Thus the set alternates between the two moieties. However, if it happens that the second death occurs in the moiety which mourned the time before, then they secretly return the wampum set "by a whisper" to the "clear-minded," so that it can be handed to the mourners in the Longhouse installation, after which time they (the mourners) again keep the string.

When the writer inspected the set of wampum used by the Four Brothers (i.e., the set which Alexander General says really belongs to the Cayuga nation at Sour Springs Longhouse), there was no wampum string to represent the Twenty Matters. Mr. General claimed that it was currently held by the Three Brothers, since the last chief to have been installed was a chief from that moiety. These rules would work well if there is only one Twenty Matters string at Six Nations, and Mr. General's explanation for the absence of the string would also be reasonable. However, Fenton (*ibid.*: 122) and some of the informants thought that each moiety has a string to represent the Twenty Matters; Mr. General said that it was his string which was being held by the Three Brothers, and Mrs. Buck, when she described the Three Brothers set of wampums, also described a Twenty Matters string for the Three Brothers. She described it as consisting of two white, three purple, one white, five purple, three white, nine purple, two white, five purple, two white, and four purple beads. Mr. General said his string was "mixed purple and white," but since it was not at hand he could not describe the bead sequence. If there are two strings, and if the above rules are followed, it is hard to explain why Mr. General had neither of them. Furthermore, Roy Buck, who is a Condolence preacher, claimed that there should be only one Twenty Matters. Consequently, it seems unlikely that there are two in use.

11. Chief's Fireplace—31 beads: all are W.

12. Deaconess—33 beads: eight P, 16 W, nine P.

13. Two Nephews—22 beads: eight P, one W, one P, two W, one P, two W, one P, six W.

14. Troubled Mind—24 beads: ten P, 14 W.

15. Candlelight—27 beads: four sets of four W and one P, one W, one P, four W, one P.

Mr. General provided the titles for the individual strings. Hewitt and Fenton (1944: 65–85) list similar designations and also give extended versions of the sentiments accompanying each string. However, if the strings were at one time meant as mnemonics, they do not serve this purpose at present. In fact, not only must the speaker learn the verses of "requickening," but he must also memorize the order of the strings, since the sequence of beads in each string means nothing to him. To help the speakers order the strings in the "proper" manner, the Four Brothers set has attached to each string at each end a "foot" (a small leather tab) which is fringed with the appropriate fringes to indicate its place in the sequence of strings. Furthermore, a number has been written on the leather to clarify its position.

The writer did not see the Three Brothers Condolence wampum, but obtained information from Mrs. Helen Buck, who borrowed it in order to copy the number of beads. The titles are her interpretation and illustrate the local diversity, as do the differences in the composition of the Three Brothers set and the Four Brothers set. Her description of the Three Brothers Condolence wampum is as follows:

1. Tears—19 beads: three sets of one P one w, one w, six sets of one P one w.
2. Hearing—18 beads: alternating one P one w nine times.
3. Throat—31 beads: alternating one w one P 15 times, one P.
4. Yellow Spots—46 beads: four sets of one P one w, 19 sets of one w one P.
5. The Chair, or Seat—no data.
6. Darkness—43 beads: two sets of one P one w, six P, five sets of one P one w, eleven sets of one w one P, one P.
7. Loss of Skies—51 beads: 25 sets of one P one w, one P.
8. Loss of Sun—39 beads: 19 sets of one P one w, one P.
9. Grave—39 beads: all P.
10. Twenty Words of Comfort (Helen Buck says that this is used only in the appointment of a new chief and at no other time. See the discussion above of the Twenty Matters string in the Four Brothers set.)—36 beads: two w, three P, one w, five P, three w, nine P, two w, five P, two w, four P.
11. Logs from the Fire (Confederacy)—100 beads: two strands, each of 50 w.
12. Deacons—112 beads: two strands, each with 45 w and eleven P.
13. Two Close Associates (Nephew and Niece)—48 beads: two P, two sets of two w three P, one w, four P, two sets of two w six P, two w, four P, two w, six P, one w.
14. Great Threat (Poison)—35 beads: three w, 16 sets of P and w.
15. Light (Torch)—15 beads: one P, one w, one P, three w, three sets of one P two w.

The speaker for the "clear-minded" moiety recites the 14 verses of the Requickening Address, sending the appropriate strand "across" to the mourners with each verse. (For the text of these verses see Hewitt and Fenton, 1944: 70–8.) These words enable the mourners to clear their bodies and minds from the great loss which they have suffered and to restore them again to the ranks of the sane. When all verses have been concluded, the mourners return the same sentiments and the strands to the "clear-minded," for though the latter were not directly involved in the loss, they too have suffered, and are considered to be "a minor mourner." The form used for the Condolence and Requickening at the tenth-day feast is the same as that used for the Condolence at a Chief's Installation, except that the strand called Twenty Matters and the associated sentiments are omitted. (For an extended description of a Chief's Installation see Fenton, 1946: 110–27.)

At the conclusion of the Condolence, the family of the deceased feeds, "on the table," the chiefs, speakers, and members of the family, serving first the "clear-minded" guests and then the others. The meal should be an ample one, including corn soup, meat, and "feast" desserts, such as pies and doughnuts. The pattern of eating in shifts, with very little conversation, which is followed at the tenth-day feast in the Sour Springs community (see p. 247 *supra*), is followed at all the communities in this instance.

After the meal, a speaker from among the "clear-minded" moiety of nations distributes the belongings of the deceased. The procedure is the same as that of an ordinary tenth-day feast, except that the moiety division is one of nations rather than of clans.

If the chief had been adopted as a Tutelo, the Condolence may take place on the ninth day, followed by the distribution of goods and the spirit-adoption ceremony, as in the case of an ordinary citizen.

At Six Nations this procedure of condoling and "requickening" on the tenth day after death (or the ninth for a Tutelo) is practiced not only for the death of a chief but also for the death of members of the matrilineage of a chief. In such an instance, the chief's mind is pictured as being so darkened that only the formal expression of condolence with wampum can relieve him sufficiently for the further execution of his duties. Consequently, the death is of concern to all the nations, and the ceremony is performed. In the communities down below the death of any member of the matrilineage of the chief necessitates a Condolence, but at Sour Springs all but the most orthodox families limit the Condolence Ceremony to the death of one of a chief's "covering" (his matron, deacon, deaconess, or deputy). The mourning cry is not emitted in these instances, and the opposite moiety of nations may be informed by any messenger rather than by the chief's deputy.

MEDICINE AND WITCHCRAFT

INTRODUCTION

WHEREAS the calendric observances of the Longhouse, the moral and ethical precepts of the Handsome Lake religion, and the surviving social and political institutions are important to the orthodox individual, there is no aspect of culture which so dominates his thought and actions as does the concern for his personal health. "Health," as it is currently conceived at Six Nations, includes not only physical well-being, but also the maintenance of life, mental ease, and good luck. And, while each individual believes that he is entitled to these endowments, he also believes that they are constantly threatened and that he must therefore determine the nature of the threat, engage in various precautions, and take counter-measures throughout his lifetime in order to maintain them. Indeed, the belief that his health is constantly endangered is so universal and obsessive a tenet of the modern Longhouse member's life view, that overtly and covertly it motivates much of his behavior and provides many of the values and goals which give meaning to his daily round of activities.

One can even go further and say that matters of health are the focus of the con-servative culture at Six Nations. No other concept is more crucial in the ideology of the Longhouse member, more comprehensive in its ramifications, or more com-plex in its expression. Almost all the basic prescriptions trace back to some principle that "if x is not done, there will be damage to health." This is clear, for example, in the motivations for helping one another perform the routines of the society, such as aiding the Longhouse organization, going to bees, attending the animal-society meetings, and bringing donations to feasts. Individuals often go to "doings" not only to help their neighbors, as is stipulated in the ideal culture, but also because they fear the consequences, in the form of disease and ill fortune, of failure to fulfill their obligations. The basic fear of damage to one's health also motivates the Longhouse members to perpetuate the animal societies and the various ritual feasts, because the tutelaries and the ritual objects involved are believed to take revenge upon the nonattentive member. The same is true for any of the death ceremonies (see pp. 228–61 *passim*). The people themselves realize that the fear of disease is part of the motivation for their actions, for they often commented, "If it weren't for sickness, no Indian would have feasts or dances." That every person, every animal-society tutelary, and every soul of the dead is sensitive about any slight is never doubted; and that such a slight can precipitate an assault upon the health of the transgressor or his relatives is also never doubted. Indeed, such feelings on the part of the offended are considered perfectly natural. That the dead and the spirit forces, which are animistic and animatistic agents, should react in this typi-cally human manner seems not only consistent but self-evident. There thus exists an almost paranoid undercurrent of suspicion, in which each person sees his health and good fortune and even his life threatened by someone or something, and it is this anxiety which motivates much of the behavior of the individual. Adopting the terminology of Kluckhohn (1941: 124–8), one could accurately say that the "basic configuration" of the modern Iroquois culture at Six Nations is concern with health. (To the extent that the sanctions are realized by the practitioners, Kluckhohn would call them "patterns." The concern with health provides both the "whyness" and the "whatness," both the inner coherence of the patterned actions and the rationalization of the actions.) Furthermore, as the individual and the culture are increasingly threatened by outside forces (poverty, tuberculosis, white pressure, discrimination, prohibition of old culture patterns, etc.), the individual finds corroboration for his fears, and they become correspondingly reinforced.

Leighton and Leighton (1942) made quantitative observations on a similar process among the Navaho. There, too, as living conditions became more difficult, the population felt itself threatened and manifested its anxiety in a nonrational and unrealistic uneasiness concerning health and body. Although no quantitative study was made at Six Nations, no single protracted conversation is remembered in which the topic of anxiety over health did not arise unsolicitedly.

That such a system of fears is conducive to conservatism, even under changing conditions, has been pointed out before and will be explored further.

The current theory of health and disease is a widely ramified one, reflecting various complexes incorporated at different times and from different cultures and not particularly well integrated. However, there is exhibited in the current "pathology" a rough hierarchy of diseases, progressing from natural physiological diseases to those caused by the dead, the tutelaries of the medicine societies, or the supernaturals, because of some injury to them, to those which are caused by hunting charms and by witching. There are also various conceptions of therapy, so that a diseased individual may try several cures either seriatim or simultaneously. One type of therapy is to discover—via a dream or a fortuneteller—what the causal agent of the disease is, and then to apply the correct countermeasure. Another type of therapy is to try one or more of the various standard specifics for the symptoms, without first seeking out the cause. The commonest pattern is that the patient, unless he has prior reason to suspect a specific powerful cause, first attempts a cure appropriate to the lowest causative agent, and only if that fails does he postulate more and more powerful agents and apply more and more dangerous cures. Since many of the ailments are either psychosomatic or organic but not responsive to the traditional herbal cures current at Six Nations, the anxious and ailing individual sees himself perfectly justified in suspecting a more obscure and more potent force working for his destruction.

Finally, it should be pointed out that the line between medicine and witchcraft is blurred and tenuous. In part, this is because the apparatus and techniques used in the two areas are roughly the same, and a legitimate medicine becomes witchcraft by means of a small distortion. In part, also, the overlap of medicine and witchcraft is due to the fact that almost all witching—whether in self-defense or in revenge—is concerned with life, health, and fortune, which are "medical" matters.

INDIAN MEDICINE

To the modern Longhouse member at Six Nations the world is panmedicinal, and his practical pharmacopoeia is limited only by his knowledge. Individuals frequently express the wish to extend their knowledge of the pharmacopoeia, and they are eager for innovations. However, they rarely experiment with new items but would rather wait for instructions through dreams, for then they feel assured that the spirit force of the item or some supernatural imparted the knowledge. Such revelations are consistent with many of the origin tales for the medicine societies and for medicinal procedures, in which the animals or the supernaturals involved tell humans what procedures will elicit their aid. In their own words, "everything is medicine for us on earth, for us people, if we know how to use it." The conception implicit in this world view (which is also manifest in the Thanksgiving Address, see *supra*, pp. 133–40) is an animistic and animatistic one, for it is the spirit force of each item, each plant, or each supernatural which is the active medical component. As Marett and Lowie have pointed out, animism and animatism are not necessarily religious, "and they become religious only in so far as the emotional attitude characteristic of religion clusters about their objects" (Lowie, 1948: 134). This observation is to the point here, for though the concept of the spirit force is the same in this context as in the Thanksgiving Address, the spirit force is neither supplicated in a religious manner nor does it respond as a religious agent. By using the proper technique—usually the donation of Indian tobacco and an invocation—one can summon a spirit force, which responds to the request for aid by allowing its medicinal power to cure the supplicant. Thus, if one takes an herbal medicine, for example, sweet flag (*Acorus calamus*), to relieve a sore throat, it is not only the herb itself which relieves the soreness, but also the spirit force of all sweet flags. Usually, the spirit forces are understood to be amenable to all such requests, provided that the petitioner reciprocates the favor by a suitable acknowledgment, which might range from mere gratitude to elaborate recurrent ceremonies.

In general, all the herbal medicines which cure by virtue of the *legitimate* power of the spirit forces of the ingredients are called onõh'gwʔathra, and a dispenser of this type of medicine is termed shade'djẽʔt or hanõhgwʔathrõ'nih. This terminology for "medicine" and "doctor" always implies that there is involved no element of sorcery, no item from a medicine bundle, and no hunting charms. In contrast to onõh'gwʔathra is that medicine which depends on magical or illegitimate agents or which is applied in those medicine societies derivative (according to the informants themselves) from older shamanistic or hunting societies. All medicine, no matter how common, is considered to possess "power" (power to cure and to withhold a cure), and therefore it should be treated with a measure of respect. However, onõh'gwʔathra is classified as the least powerful, least "dangerous," and least "particular" of the types of medicines. "Dangerous" and "particular" both refer to the probability of offending the spirit force in such a manner as to precipitate disease, bad luck, or death through even a slight breach of technique. The statement that onōh′gwʔathra is not "particular" does not, however, imply that its application is an unimportant procedure, for obviously the substitution of an incorrect plant may well lead to poisoning. Consequently, onōh′gwʔathra may be handled without disastrous consequences by any ordinary person who believes himself adept at "doctoring" (though even a person who practices therapy on this level is often suspected of witchcraft). There are, therefore, at Six Nations today a large number of people who have knowledge of at least some of the common herbal cures. Colds, fevers, gastrointestinal disorders, poisonous bites, rashes, burns, and poisonings are generally treated by the average householder with a standard herbal specific. (See Fenton, 1941a, for identification and description of most of the common herbal remedies.) When a somewhat more complicated disease develops, one has recourse to the known herbal specialists. These specialists—the stereotype depicts an "old woman," although they may be of either sex—have become known for their general skill or perhaps for success in treating special diseases. One was known to be a specialist for bladder obstruction; another for piles and skin diseases; still others for tuberculosis and appendicitis. In each case the doctor had been known to produce successful cures.

Whether the medicine is collected by an amateur or by a specialist, the techniques are identical. Spring and fall are the preferred seasons for the collection of plants; however, any time of the year is acceptable except "when the lightening bugs are out" (June and July), for it is thought that in midsummer the roots are hollow, thus reducing the strength of the preparations. Nevertheless, if a plant is needed during midsummer, it is procured and used, although an extra dosage is added in an attempt to achieve the usual strength. The collector should go out early in the day, and, to the first exemplar encountered of each desired species, he should give some Indian tobacco and respectfully inform it that a specimen is desired as a medicine for disease x for person y. The tobacco which is offered to the plant is the most important tool of the herbalist, for it is the tobacco which transmits the message to the spirit force of the plant, thus permitting the individual specimens to be effective. The tobacco is also a reciprocal gift to the spirit force. In an emergency, herbalists use medicine collected without tobacco, but it is considered to be very weak indeed. The Indian name of the designee should be mentioned, but if the medicine is not intended for any particular person, the plant should be informed that the medicine is being collected for future use for "anyone at all." Thereafter, any other specimens may be procured. However, should any untoward signs appear immediately before or during the collection of the plants—such as a snake crossing his path or the appearance of a hearse, an inebriated person, or a menstruating woman—the collector should either turn the other way or preferably refrain from collecting that day, since the medicine picked after such an incident is at best not of full strength and possibly even dangerous. Of course, a woman must never collect medicine during her menstrual period, for medicine is particularly prone to spoilage by any contact with a catamenial woman (see pp. 216–7 *supra*). Due to the danger of damaging the medicine by an ominous encounter and also in part due to fear of being suspected of witchcraft, collectors usually pursue their tasks in secret. Once home they are quite willing to admit having collected plants in the morning, though there exists, particularly among the specialists, a certain reluctance to divulge the location of the plants and the ingredients of the medicines.

After the plants are brought home, they may be used immediately or dried and stored. Ideally, medicine should be prepared fresh each day, but since the majority of the oral herbal medicines are made into teas, participants find it bothersome to prepare daily portions and often prepare larger quantities to be used over a period of several days. The wastage of the plants should be burned or buried, for if it is seen lying about the house of the herbalist, people are believed to say, "That woman has been making witch medicine again."

Medicine should be dispensed without charge to all those who have need of it and who ask for it. Obviously, this is not a satisfactory arrangement for the herbal specialists, and payment is now expected either in money or goods or by an exchange of herbs, although most of them affect a show of reluctance when payment is offered. When a medicine is given to a patient, the herbalist always includes instructions concerning its use, and in case of severe illness he may even supervise the treatment.

One of the most common institutionalized uses of herbal medicines is the annual spring purges of the Longhouse males. (See Parker, 1913: 77, for a description of similar spring purges and sweat baths.) It is believed that even as nature begins anew in spring, so should the human being, and he should purify himself so that the new year may be started with renewed vigor and cleanliness. The purification involves "cleaning out the blood and the bowels," and the treatments usually include tonics of a cathartic nature as well as emetics. The older the boy, the more rigorous is the treatment, but after a man has reached middle age, he may relax its strenuousness. Men who engage in much ceremonial and ritual activity particularly should undergo purging. The more strenuous cleansings last three days, during which time the person attempts to vomit frequently and also to sweat. Sweat baths and lodges are remembered by the Iroquois, and even though today no lodges are built, men do try to induce sweating along with the purges. The medicines used are mainly herbal preparations, sometimes prepared by specialists and sometimes simply prepared privately. The commonest emetics now used seem to be teas made of bloodroot (gane'hgwas, *Sanguinaria canadensis*), wild iris roots (*Iris versicolor* or *Iris prismatica*), roots of jack-in-the-pulpit (gahõ'hsra?, *Arisaema triphyllum*), and red whip (red-willow bark). The jack-in-the-pulpit tea is made from dried roots which have been powdered, and it is this powder which is dissolved in boiling water and given as the "tonic"; it is known that the roots in themselves are poisonous. In addition to these emetics, the patient also imbibes a laxative, such as prince's pine, or pipsissewa (*Chimaphila umbellata*) tea, May-apple tea (*Podophyllum peltatum*), or pine-bough tea. All herbs should have been picked in the standard medicinal fashion, with tobacco offered to the first of the species. The prepared tonics made by the herbalists usually combine several of these herbs, so that the patient will have a maximum flushing of the system. Ideally, one should not mix the Indian medicines for purging with any "white" medicine (although some of the tonics which the herbalists prepare have ingredients which were bought in a drugstore). Usually the dosages are followed by taking water. Food should be shunned during the "spring-cleaning days," and the patient should conduct himself "carefully." He should not come in contact with a contaminating agent (such as a menstruating woman, a spirit of the dead, or a hearse), and he should be somewhat hidden, at least to the extent of staying at home. After the patient is thoroughly emptied and weak, he takes body-building tonics, which are believed to be either blood building or nonspecifically therapeutic ("to make a man feel good"). Sassafras is the common "blood medicine," but a tea made of buckthorn bark, black dogwood, berry alder, and alder thornbush is also popular, for it is said to have the property of stimulating the appetite. The institution of purging in the spring is a private matter, and each person sets the limits of his purge, although there is definitely a feeling that a strong and protracted purge is good and more beneficial than a mild one. At the time of execution, the treatment is usually kept a secret, but informants are quite willing to relate afterward that they took the spring purge that year. The same kind of purging occurs before important lacrosse games and foot races. At one time, in fact, such treatments were almost standard before games. No prayers, songs, or meetings are associated with purging medicines, and no tobacco is burned when the medicines are used.

The boundary between the natural herbal preparations and the more magical ones is often indistinct. The more sophisticated herbal specialists say that their medicines contain ingredients which have great power and which can be procured only under special circumstances. An example is the remedy for "summer complaint" (intestinal flu) called onrahsʔago'wa ("large rooster comb"), which is a pine-tree fungus. This medicine "calls one with a clucking noise high from a pine tree," and in order to be an effective agent it must be shot. Furthermore, it must be shot immediately, else it will "run and hide," and, therefore, it is very scarce. After being shot, it is detached from the tree, dried, and given as a powder in a cup of water. This medicine seems to "holler" after having been administered, just as when it was found, for when the writer took a dose, all three people who knew about it independently heard it "holler" at night in the tree outside their house, although the tree was not a pine but a maple. Also, it is said to presage a death in the family by "hollering" in its storage container. Knowledge and use of this type of medicinal agent—seminaturalistic, semimagical—usually qualifies its dispenser to be called "a real doctor," with the implication that the preparations are slightly tinged with the magical, but not as seriously as witch medicines or hunting-charm medicines. Since such medicines are dispensed rather secretly, and since a certain amount of esoteric knowledge is involved in their preparation, it is not difficult to see how suspicion of witchcraft might be attached to the herbalist. It is also not inconceivable that these herbalists do at times allow themselves to become implicated, perhaps unwittingly, in the preparation of witchcraft or counter-witchcraft. A basic maxim for the Iroquois might be: "whoever is close to Indian medicine is close to witchcraft."

WHITE MAN'S MEDICINE

Since the Reserve is not isolated and most of the Longhouse population has contact with the neighboring townspeople, and since Canadian doctors and a free hospital have been operative at Six Nations for a long time, the population is fully cognizant of the pharmacopoeia and medical practices of "the white man." Consequently, along with Indian remedies there is a special category of medicine termed "white man's medicine." This includes patent medicines, standard pharmaceuticals (such as aspirins and vitamins), and prescription medicines, as well as the services of the chiropractor, the general practitioner, the surgeon at the Toronto hospital, etc. Which of these drugs and services are used and how carefully a person distinguishes among them are, of course, private matters, depending on the beliefs, knowledge, and experience of the individual.

Since the educational level of the Longhouse member is not high, and since any close association which a member may have with the surrounding white population is apt to be with individuals who are equally unsophisticated scientifically, it is not surprising to find a wide use of patent and drugstore preparations. These are widely advertised (and almost every Reserve family is exposed to radio, television, placard, or newspaper advertising) and can be procured without the inconvenience and embarrassment of consulting a white doctor. Some of the most common preparations currently popular are Dr. Thomas' Electric Oil, $.49, for sore throats, cold sores, and loss of voice (and recommended also for cattle, horses, and poultry); Dr. Chase's Nerve Food, $.77, for "poor nerves" (and containing, according to the label, $\frac{1}{120}$ gr. of strychnine, $\frac{1}{32}$ gr. arsenic, and $\frac{3}{40}$ milligram of vitamin B_1); and Geritol, $3.29, for giving energy, building strength, and renewing the blood of elderly people (and characterized as a "vitamin and iron preparation"). Furthermore, one or more of such standard remedies as aspirin, vitamin preparations, laxatives, antiseptics, ointments (Vick's products being particularly popular), and throat lozenges may be found in most orthodox homes, often placed immediately next to an "Indian" herb tea. The precise extent to which any individual uses such products is again a private matter, depending on his income, knowledge, and tastes. It is not, however, an index of his orthodoxy and devotion to the Longhouse, since some of the most dedicated members, who also participate actively in the medicine societies, indulge in the greatest number of drug products. Rather, the use of such medicines is related to the degree of hypochondria of the individual. For example, at the sickbed of a deaconess who is undoubtedly one of the "strongest" Longhouse advocates, there were counted at one time 14 drugstore products ranged beside four "Indian" preparations; furthermore, on that very day she sponsored a medicine-society rite and also had her ailments diagnosed by a fortuneteller, who suggested that witchcraft was involved and prescribed magical countermeasures. She merely complained of "feeling bad," but it was later decided by the hospital that she suffered from diabetes and tuberculosis. Incidentally, the Indian preparations she used at the time were black snakeroot (*Cimicifuga racemosa*), prince's pine (*Chimaphila umbellata*), sweet flag (*Acorus calamus*), and egger root (?) called niya'skae in Cayuga. Another striking example of the adoption of "white man's medicine" is that the singers of a medicine society, even of so "particular" a society as Hĕna'ʔidos, relieve their throats during and after the rite not with the well-known accessible "Indian" remedy of sweet flag, but with Smith Bros. cough drops. Yet another example is that of one of the most erudite of the practicing herbal specialists, who is always intensely interested in the descriptions and uses of "white medicine," and in addition to buying and prescribing them outright, has used many of them as ingredients in her "traditional" mixtures. Another herbalist, who at the age of ninety was still the "spring tonic" specialist of the Reserve, was said to include "store" items in her preparation, whose composition she learned from "the old people." Thus there is evidence that the incorporation of medicines and herbs procured in the neighboring pharmacies has a long history at Six Nations.

In the ideal culture, the orthodox Longhouse creed prescribes abstinence from any of white man's inventions, and furthermore there exist such maxims as "white man's medicine and Indian medicine don't mix," "white man's medicine is for the white man, but Indian medicine is for the Indian," and "you can't cure Indian diseases with white man's medicine"; but in the real culture there is widespread use of white medicine and much interest in it. Perhaps an explanation for the ready acceptance of white medicine is that it is so far removed in context from anything which the Iroquois consider "particular," "dangerous," or magical that they are able to consider it quite pragmatically. Although the Canadian doctors are termed "honatjina'hgasõʔ" (medicine men), there are in this context no overtones of witching or magical practices, and the medicines which they dispense are considered to be closer to Indian herbal medicine than to anything "particular" and "dangerous." When white man's medicine is used there is no attention to the spirit force of the medicine—for it has none—no tobacco is given or burned, and no taboos need be observed. White man's medicine is procured for cash, doctors are paid money (if not by the patient, then by the Canadian government), and no other reciprocity or expression of gratitude is required. If a person dies at the hospital, the accusation is always that the doctors are incompetent, but never that they are malevolent. If a medicine fails to take effect, then it is because it was erroneously prescribed, because it was administered too late, or because "white man's medicine does not work on Indian diseases."

The classification of diseases as "Indian" or "white" is quite loose, and there are diverse ideas on when to apply Indian or white medication, indicative of the varying degrees of acculturation among the population. In the real culture there are only a few special instances (for example, when the Little Water Medicine is being applied) in which there are binding restrictions against the use of both Indian and white methods, and thus an individual need not decide in every case how the disease should be classified. He therefore may prefer to postpone a decision and try to gain the benefit of both medicines. If both are used the credit for a cure is likely to go to the Indian medicine, and the discredit, in the event of failure, to the white medicine or to the mixing of the two. However, most Longhouse members are now willing to concede that there are some diseases, not typically Indian, which are better treated in the hospital, and the increasing attendance at the Ohsweken or surrounding hospitals is testimony to this concession.

The medical staff of the Ohsweken hospital has multiplied about sixfold in the last ten years, and despite the claim that old Dr. Davis did the work of five of the current physicians, the Reserve as a whole is undoubtedly getting more medical attention. A public health nurse and a social worker also check on the population and especially the school children. There has lately been an effort, for example, to test each resident for tubercular infections, which had been endemic on the Reserve. However, as is to be expected of all institutions on the Reserve, there are active factions who are violently for or violently against the hospital and its staff and method of treatment. The Longhouse population, on the whole, is one of the factions opposed to the hospital administration. Many claim to be discriminated against because they are "Longhouse," and they say that they cannot understand the "foreign" doctors, nor can the doctors understand them. (In Canada, immigrant physicians must serve one year of internship in a government post before they may be licensed, and there have been doctors of many countries at the hospital. The Indian population refers to the hospital as "the United Nations" and is very prejudiced against the non-Canadians.) Nevertheless, almost every resident of the Reserve has had some contact with the hospital, if only with the out-patient clinic.

Ultimately, the choice between "white" and "Indian" treatment remains a personal and private matter, to the extent that parents often refuse to take the responsibility for the treatment of their children. For example, one mother asked her nine-year-old daughter whether she would like a heart operation, which the Ohsweken hospital considered essential. The child thought not, and the operation was postponed until the child changed her mind. Fenton (1941b: 101) reported a similar attitude among the Seneca of the United States.

The fact that a person allows himself to be treated at the hospital does not indicate that he abandons a search for the cause of his disease, for the purely physiological explanations of the Ohsweken physician are not always persuasive. Longhouse members do talk in terms of "germs" and "high blood pressure," and on that level they understand natural cause-and-effect relationships. However, they continue suspiciously to wonder why they, as particular individuals, are subjected to the disease. This is especially true if the disease is lingering and hard to cure, or if the hospital is unable to diagnose why the patient "feels bad." Surely, there must then be something causing the disease which white man's medicine cannot understand and does not have the historical perspective to appreciate, and it is therefore necessary to find the true etiology of the disease (a typically "Indian" cause) and apply an "Indian" treatment. To determine the true etiology one has recourse to an Indian specialist, namely, the fortuneteller.

FORTUNETELLERS

Fortunetellers—aksa'ktõ or gyõngyõhwẽdja'nya?, "they looking after our land (i.e., affairs)"—are individuals whose primary function is to determine the causes of diseases, but who have a secondary, though important, function of prescribing cures. There are also some fortunetellers who specialize in locating stolen or lost objects, such as clothing, cattle, horses, and spouses, but these will not be discussed because they are not primarily concerned with health.

The only prerequisite for either a man or a woman to practice fortunetelling is the elusive one of being properly endowed by the Great Creator. A strong indication of this endowment, though by no means a necessary one, is to be born with a caul. Ideally, there are some disqualifications. Chiefs, preachers, and Longhouse speakers ought not engage in fortunetelling, but in the real culture this is ignored. It is not at all clear how the practicing fortunetellers become aware of their own powers, but it is unlikely that a normal member of the conservative community would practice without conviction, for there are strong warnings against such presumption. A reflection of these warnings is found in the Code (Parker, 1913: 49–50), which relates that when Handsome Lake was asked to divine on behalf of his half-niece, he protested that he had not yet been so empowered by the messengers. He was, however, persuaded to tell fortunes against his will and against the will of the Angels. At Six Nations it is said that "the people bossed him into fortunetelling, else they could not have feasts." The warnings against unauthorized fortunetelling are reinforced by a general fear of improper contact with medicines and supernatural agencies, which are characterized as being "too dangerous to fool around with." Although the ability to tell fortunes is considered to be a gift of the Creator, the details of the art are often supposed to be learned from older practitioners, and skill can be increased by "practicing" (in analogy to ritual speaking or singing).

The fortunetellers vary in reputation. Not only do patients claim to distinguish "real fortunetellers from fakes," but they attribute particular abilities to individual fortunetellers, for instance, skill in detecting witches or in discovering "unsatisfied" rituals or "unfed" masks. To a large extent, the reputation of the fortuneteller is derived from the plausibility of his diagnoses and prescriptions, which always contain elements familiar to the patients. There is probably also a certain amount of empirical foundation to the reputation of a fortuneteller. A convincing fortuneteller may be very effective in helping to cure an ailment which is psychogenic, and a record of past successes will enhance his reputation, thereby increasing his effectiveness in dealing with a new psychosomatic case. (The high incidence of psychogenic illness was apparently recognized by Dr. Davis, who was for many years in charge of the Canadian government hospital at Ohsweken, and who sometimes told patients that they did not need any white man's medicine, but should have a feast.)

In order to have his illness diagnosed, the patient goes to the house of the fortuneteller, or if he is unable to go in person he sends a representative, usually a relative or ritual friend. The visit is unannounced and may occur at any time of the day, and it is usually made in secret. The fortuneteller is told the patient's Indian name and is offered Indian tobacco; and when the patient has sent a representative, the fortuneteller is usually handed an article of clothing belonging to the patient, which serves as a surrogate for him. The trouble is described, together with relevant descriptions of circumstances and previous attempts at curing. Thereupon, the fortuneteller will make a diagnosis by any method he thinks appropriate, the most common techniques being the use of tea, card reading, dream interpretation, and scrying. Among the fortunetellers practicing at Six Nations in recent years, several (both Longhouse and Christian) use tea; some use tea and cards; and others make use of dreams. Since scrying is usually concerned with witchcraft it is not advertised as the fortuneteller's medium. (See Fenton, 1953: 57, for an account of similar practices at Tonawand Reservation.) There are also many ritualists who are willing to give advice and interpret omens, but these do not claim to be "real fortunetellers."

Perhaps the commonest method today is the use of tea. In general, as soon as the client enters, the fortuneteller boils water on the stove, and in the ordinary tea equipment of the family brews a tea (either green or black). The tea is poured into a cup, the cup is emptied, and the remaining leaves are examined. The precise details of procedure by which the cup is emptied vary from individual to individual. One practitioner had the patient invert the cup onto the saucer, and then he poured the tea back into the pot, repeating the procedure several times until he received a "good picture." Others allow the patient to drink the tea and then invert the cup onto the saucer. Still others ask their patients to drink the tea from the saucer. One, in a rather unorthodox manner, looked at the steaming tea in the saucer and ignored the leaves completely. Despite her Christian convictions and unconventional procedure, she was highly regarded as a fortuneteller throughout the Reserve. Incidentally, she was perhaps the only fortuneteller who would occasionally recommend a visit to the Ohsweken hospital instead of an Indian remedy.

The writer was never present at a card seance and consequently does not know what precise methods are used. People report simply, "She looked at cards," and they are not particularly curious about the mechanics of the operation.

When dreaming is the means of diagnosis, the patient tells his complaint one day and reappears the next morning to hear the fortuneteller's findings. One who used this method required that a piece of the patient's clothing be left overnight, and he said that he places this under his pillow while dreaming. Another who also uses the dream method says that he wraps the "Indian" tobacco which the patient brings around "the medicine," which he has in reserve and may prescribe, and places these under his pillow at night.

In scrying, which is usually reserved for more serious investigations involving suspicion of witchcraft, a root, "small like a fingernail," of a plant reputedly having dark-grey flowers and growing near a creek or river is used. The plant is called dyōhwĕdjawa'ʔgo ("base of the earth"). Its identity is not known, nor was the plant ever pointed out to the writer. The root is rubbed into a saucer of water and observed. If it floats and turns counterclockwise it is a good omen, but if it sinks or turns clockwise (the direction followed in dances of the dead) it is a bad sign. Fortunetellers also "see people and medicine" in the water and give prescriptions accordingly.

The fees, aside from the Indian tobacco, are usually 25 to 50 cents. However, fortunetellers often prescribe their own medicines, especially when the diagnosis revealed witchcraft, and these may be expensive. Thus, one had medicine ranging from $15.00 to $60.00, while another, who is the most successful fortuneteller in the vicinity of Six Nations Reserve, charges up to $50.00 for medicine. (Her medium of investigation is cards, and her reputation must be remarkable, for although she is Christian, Reserve residents travel a distance of 60 miles to consult her.) Still another, when he prescribes expensive medicine, is willing to accept payment on the installment plan.

The fortunetellers tend to prescribe standard cures for a few characteristic symptoms. Among these are False Face Dances for facial paralysis, Red False Face rites for nose bleeding, Otter rites for sore, red eyes, Bear Dance for hysterical spitting or clambering along the wall, formation of a ritual friendship for "lonely" children, snow-snake or ball games for sore legs, and Little Water Medicine for internal injuries and broken bones. However, the body of specific Indian cures for specific ailments is quite limited today, contrary to some of the reports in the literature (e.g., Speck, 1949: 59), and there is considerable latitude even within the standardized part of medical lore. Each consultation with a fortuneteller is a unique case, for not only is the method of diagnosis at the discretion of the fortuneteller, but he is free to vary the standard prescription because of the particular circumstances of the patient and his complaint. Thus fortunetelling is an individualistic activity which may be properly characterized as an art, and each practitioner has his own style.

It is essential to the success of a fortuneteller that his diagnoses and prescriptions appear plausible to his patients. This is accomplished primarily by formulating the diagnoses in terms of concepts which are familiar in the traditional Iroquoian culture, and prescribing Iroquoian herbal remedies and rituals as cures. Thus, in the art of fortunetelling there is freedom in selecting and combining elements of medical lore, but those elements are almost always drawn from a circumscribed domain of concepts and practices. The fortuneteller also achieves plausibility by adjusting his recommendations to the seriousness of the patient's trouble. A simple and inexpensive remedy is usually prescribed for a minor ailment, but if the sickness is lingering or if the patient is obviously very concerned, the fortuneteller is likely to "see" a powerful and perhaps supernatural causative agent. In such serious cases he may indicate that a medicine-society feast has been neglected, or that a mask has not been given tobacco, or that a menstrual taboo has been broken, or that a member of the family who died long ago is "hungry" because of improper treatment at the tenth-day feast, or even that some one is practicing witchcraft against the patient. The fortunetellers have wide knowledge of personal affairs on the Reserve and often have very good memories, and therefore they may be aware of specific ritual negligence on the part of the patient; a direct or indirect reference to this omission may awaken the patient's conscience and suggest the remedy. Even when a member of the Reserve attempts to be his own diagnostician, he may guess that the cause of his disease is supernatural. Thus, one woman dreamed about her dead husband while suffering from a leg and neck ailment. Since she was a Christian and had given her husband a Christian burial, it seemed quite clear to her that the reason she was "being bothered" was that she had failed to release her husband in the customary manner of the Longhouse. Consequently, she decided to hold a dead feast and release her husband, and the morning after this was done she felt quite relieved. A final reason for the plausibility of the fortuneteller's recommendations may be found in their reliance upon the principles of analogy, re-enactment, and association. The fortunetellers certainly have no explicit formulation of such principles, but they are inherent in the normal *modus operandi* of fortunetelling in a way which appears natural to the practitioner and to the patients. For example, one patient "wriggled like a fish with pain" when he had sciatica, and the fortuneteller prescribed an Otter feast, which seemed reasonable because one eats fish at this feast and also because the otter is in constant motion. An example of re-enactment is the prescription of a dead feast for another patient after he dreamed of lines of caskets and skeletons which claimed to be hungry. Another instance of the principle of re-enactment occurred when a young girl (who was undoubtedly hungry) dreamed of a white chicken, and the fortuneteller prescribed an Eagle Dance on the grounds that a white chicken is eaten at this ritual. (See also pp. 218–9 *supra* for a further example.)

The cure prescribed by the fortuneteller may be herbal medicine, magical medicine, or even "white man's medicine"; and it may be friendship formation or any one of the standard songs, feasts, dances, games, medicine-society rites, and ceremonies (such as the Tutelo adoption ceremony or one of the four sacred rites). Sometimes more than one of these is prescribed. Usually the fortuneteller avoids prescriptions which would impose an extreme financial burden on the patient and his family, except under extreme conditions such as repeated witchcraft. Prescriptions which are more expensive than the circumstances seem to require can discredit a fortuneteller, and even subject him to the suspicion of having ulterior motivation. In one case a fortuneteller's business has fallen off sharply because of this. When the cure prescribed is of a ritual nature, the patient is obligated to repeat the rite during the remainder of his life at intervals of one to three years. This is particularly essential if the patient was initiated into a medicine society, for after being cured he must reciprocate to the tutelary, or spirit force, of the society in order to avoid "hurting its feelings." Neglecting the periodic repetition of the ritual may result in a recurrence of the original disease or in a new disease. In this way one ritual obligation can lead to another, and an individual may acquire a large number of them. Since such ritual obligations are an economic burden and are also a latent threat to health, on account of the possibility of lapses in carrying them out, there is considerable fear of a fortuneteller who is too efficient at "digging up the past" (i.e., finding neglected rituals in the family of the patient).

Fortunetellers occupy a position of particular authority in the Longhouse community today. They are respected for their supernatural endowment and their knowledge, and they are feared because of their intimate association with "dangerous" forces. To a population which tends to be hypochondriac their services are considered indispensable, and it would be rash to ignore their prescriptions. It is likely that some fortunetellers abuse their authority and are a disruptive influence, especially when the diagnosis is witchcraft. On the whole, however, the fortunetellers have an over-all cohesive influence. Their prescriptions nearly always involve elements from the "Indian" culture, and these prescriptions are given force by the intense concern with health which characterizes the Longhouse Indians. It is possible, therefore, that the fortunetellers do more than any other single group to maintain the conservative culture on the Reserve.

DOINGS

The General Pattern

One of the commonest types of medical activity on the Reserve is what the population calls "to have something up" or "to have a doings." (These terms are also used generically to refer to ritual activity of any sort, whether sponsored by an individual or by the whole Longhouse community.) "Having something up" includes any of the observances of ritual activity designed to further the health and welfare of the individual sponsoring the event, whether it was prescribed by a fortuneteller, was self-imposed, or represents the execution of an inherited or recurrent obligation. Also, whether the "doings" which the person "has up" is merely a single set of songs, one Bowl Game, or something as elaborate as a Tutelo adoption ceremony, the general pattern of execution and the conception are the same.

The general pattern of these medical observances is as follows: The patient and his family, in most cases his matrilineage, are the sponsors of the event. The patient invites, often by sending a messenger, a group of Longhouse members—friends, relatives, neighbors, or people known to "pass" the same observance—to participate in *his* ceremony, and includes among the invited a number of specialists versed in the execution of the intended ritual. A speaker formally opens the ceremony with the Thanksgiving Address, stressing the section known as "forewords" (see p. 134 *supra*), which reminds the assembled of the value of "togetherness" and mutual participation, and adding any or all of the remaining sections of the Address he believes appropriate. Then the speaker explains why people are assembled, mentions the Indian name of the patient, and gives a sketch of the circumstances leading to the current occasion. This résumé may be in considerable detail, recounting the first anxiety about the illness, the previous attempts at curing, the types of medicine applied, and any doings which preceded this one. If the event at hand is part of a recurrent obligation, the speaker will mention this, giving descriptions of the previous observations of the ceremony. The speaker then mentions, by their Indian names, the participants in the ritual: the one who acted as messenger, those who will burn tobacco, sing, dance, and cook, and he who is speaking. He will also explain the procedure of the ritual briefly. All are thanked for their attendance and asked once more to unite in helping the patient. Next, the patient must provide some Indian tobacco, which is burned in the stove by the speaker or by a special tobacco burner. When the ceremony involves the use of rattles, masks, or other ritual paraphernalia, they are initially placed with the tobacco around the stove and ring the stove while the tobacco is burned and the invocation recited. The main ritual follows, and the patient is prominently involved according to the conventions of the particular ceremony. In dances he customarily is the second in line, immediately following a person of the opposite moiety. In games, he usually makes the first move and thereafter merely watches. However, in cases of emergency (if the patient is at the Ohsweken hospital, for example), the ceremony may be performed *in absentia*, provided that this contingency is "explained" during the tobacco burning. At the conclusion of the main ritual the speaker once more thanks the participants, recapitulates the event, and repeats the Thanksgiving Address in a brief form. Food is then passed out to the performers and the onlookers, and if the ceremony is an observance involving the dead, a plate is set aside for the deceased.

The ideas concerning the obligations of the doings are also rather uniform. Once an individual has decided to "put up a doings," he should attempt to collect the requisite paraphernalia as soon as possible, for an undue delay would cause a deterioration of his condition. But if, economically or circumstantially, this is not feasible, the patient may give a "hurry-up" ceremony, which is a curtailed version of the prescribed event. Such a hurry-up ceremony may also be performed in critical cases, when the patient is judged to be in danger of death if the ceremony is not performed immediately. The appropriate presents, feast foods, or specialists may all be dispensed with or replaced by the best available substitutes. In such instances, the patient should register his intention to perform the unabridged ritual as soon as possible. In actuality, however, this promise is often disregarded until the patient's conscience becomes "bothered," and he has a relapse of the initial illness, or until he succumbs to a new disease and attributes this to the initial neglect. A responsible person will not neglect to fulfill this obligation at some time, for such neglect is of potential danger not only to himself but to any member of his immediate family (both matrilineal and patrilineal) for generations to come. In fact, one of the most frequent diagnoses made by the fortunetellers is that the ailment stems from just such a neglected obligation in the family of the patient. Particularly if a medicine society, a dead person, or a ritual object was involved in the original obligation is there danger that the tutelary, soul, or item will "turn on," "bother," or "eat" another member of the family. The possibility of hereditary punishment for the transgressions of one's ancestors is an important concept in all the medicine rites, and the danger increases as the rituals are judged to be more "particular."

Yet another concept germane to all the doings is that there should be maximum involvement by the attending members, with all actively participating in body and mind. In addition to contributing one's skill (singing songs, burning the tobacco, and making speeches), one must "keep in mind" throughout the performance the hope that the medicine will help the patient to recover. Only through the "united minds" and the united good will of the attenders can the "medicine" attain maximum effectiveness. This conception is closely related to the idea that everything about the ceremony, each part and the whole, "is medicine," and that if one part is not functioning, the medicine is weakened to that degree. When everyone participates properly, the ritual has a general beneficent effect. While it is true that the ceremony is specifically for one patient, all the participants and guests gain some benefits by their attendance. In part this is because a doings is something peculiarly "Indian" and therefore in itself good. In part also, particularly in medicine-society rituals, it is because the tutelaries are always depicted as craving attention. Consequently, they are pleased when their songs and dances are observed, and they manifest their pleasure by not causing the participants any "bother." It is therefore considered polite, when passing a doings, to invite those people who must pass the same doings for their own benefit, for in sharing the patient's ceremony they too gain protection.

According to the participants, the single most important trait of the medicinal complex is the use of "Indian tobacco." "It is the head of everything," "it is our plead," they say, indicating that tobacco is the validating agent of a doings. Or, as one expressed herself: "If only one thing can be had for a dance or a feast, you'd get good results if you just burn the Indian tobacco. It is the good, strong tobacco. It has strong power. If you don't have Indian tobacco you can try the ordinary kind, but I ain't saying it's right." Only if Indian tobacco is burned or given will the spirit forces and the tutelaries be able to hear the plea of the patient, and only if they lend their aid will the performance be "real medicine." This is the reason why the speaker repeats the entire history and purpose of the ceremony during the tobacco burning, explaining to the spirit force what he has just explained to the populace. Furthermore, since all beings are believed to crave tobacco, the tobacco is given as a reward to the agent for the services desired from it. Finally, the tobacco is proffered to the spirit force in return for forgiveness of any mistakes in the ritual which might displease it.

Another very important trait in the medicinal complex is that of feasting. Associated with every doings is the concept that both the agent implored and the members attending must be "fed." In fact, it is precisely the hunger for food and tobacco on the part of many of the animistic and animatistic agents which necessitates the doings in the first place and obligates the patient to repeat the ritual, ideally at yearly intervals. This is especially true for the following agents: the animal tutelaries, which are said to "get hungry" for the particular foods associated with their societies (berry juice in the case of the Bear Society, fish in the case of the Otter Society, etc.); the dead, who crave feast foods; and the hunting charms, which need meat if they are not to "eat" the suffering patient. Furthermore, the food constitutes the reciprocal payment to the supernaturals, to the performers, and to the other people who attend, for their respective parts in the ceremony. Incidentally, the first and most costly distribution is usually made to the performers, and it is they who receive the pig's head whenever one is used.

In both of the two common ways of determining the appropriate type of doings—through the instructions of a fortuneteller and by the dreams of the patient—any combination of tasks could in principle be prescribed, since the theory of the cure is "to each according to his needs." In fact, however, the fortunetellers and the dreaming patients draw from a definite set of conventional observances, which are prescribed with only minor individual variations and which can be executed by the available trained personnel. The most important types of medicinal observances, roughly in order of increasing power, are modified Longhouse events, ritual games, dead feasts, medicine-society rituals, and the Little Water Medicine. All of these are to some extent derived from other areas of the culture, though in this context all are definitely "medicine." It is especially to be stressed that none of these are religious in character, contrary to the reports of some of the older literature (Morgan, 1877: 97, and Parker, 1913: 113 ff.). Although the procedure and the conception of all these types of doings are generally the same, as has been described above, each of them will now be described briefly in order to indicate its individual characteristics.

ADAPTATIONS OF LONGHOUSE EVENTS

Among the commonest prescriptions are those drawn from the Longhouse ceremonies and events. In such a case the fortuneteller or the dream specifies that the patient needs one or more of the familiar Longhouse rituals, and also specifies what food is to be served the participants in the doings. None of these rituals is the function of a special society, but each one belongs to the common experience of the Longhouse community, and any person who is able to duplicate the performance as seen in the Longhouse may be called upon to "help."

Each of the four sacred rituals—the Feather Dance, Adóʹwa, the Skin Dance, and the Bowl Game (pp. 166–72 *supra*) is often prescribed. When this happens the patient may wait until Midwinter and pass his ceremony in the Longhouse on Pass Dance Day, providing feast foods, if it is the first time he "passes" the ritual. Usually, however, he invites to his home at night the personnel capable of performing the ceremony, preferably though not necessarily including members of the opposite moiety. Indian costume, which is appropriate in the Longhouse for these ceremonies, is not necessary for the medicinal performance at home, unless specifically demanded by the fortuneteller. In the case of the Skin Dance and the Feather Dance, it is ordinarily not necessary to perform the complete set for the sake of the patient, and if the Bowl Game is played, only 20 to 30 beans are used. In the case of the Bowl Game the patient ought to have made for him a bowl, peach-pit dice, and counters (and sometimes even a special pillow for bouncing the bowl) to be used at all subsequent observances (see p. 180 *supra*). Usually, the same foods are served as those associated with the ritual at the Longhouse.

Further borrowings from the Longhouse program which are believed to be appropriate in the medicinal complex are the Stirring Ashes song, the tobacco-burning invocation, the War Dance (taken from the Thunder ritual), and the women's planting songs and dances. The planting songs are often used along with some other ritual, instead of being the entire cure. Of these songs the Women's Dance and the Standing Quiver Dance from the Life Supporter's cycle (see p. 156 *supra*) are pre-scribed most frequently, particularly for women. When a planting song is used for a doings, a small rattle should be obtained as a charm.

Parker (1913: 126) mentions a Thõwi'sas Society, with which the planting songs were asso-ciated, in his list of medicine societies. There is no such society at Six Nations today, although designated women keep a Thõwi'sas rattle and some claim a hereditary right to its custodian-ship. There is no injunction against using these "pass dances" for men, and at the Longhouse a Women's Dance is sometimes announced for the benefit of a whole family. However, it is usually a woman who "calls for" the dance as a personal rite.

Also considered appropriate are the more traditional of the social dances, though these are mostly prescribed as adjuncts to some other obligation, such as forming a ritual friendship. Newly introduced dances, "show" dances, and the "naked dance" (Speck: 1949: 151) are not thought to be appropriate for a curing ritual. Of all the social dances the older Fish Dance (gayo'wa) seems to be the most popular current prescription at Six Nations. The Delaware Skin-beating songs and dance (ganehwa'e) in which a leather or rubber strip and two paddles are used, have also become incorporated as a curing ritual. (See Speck, 1949: 147–58, and Kurath, 1951, for the details of these songs and dances.)

Finally, judging from the number of individuals who have at one time "made friends" in order to help an ailing member of the community, one concludes that this is a very common prescription (see pp. 218–22 *supra*). Strictly speaking, ritual friendship is not borrowed from the Longhouse program; but the relation is almost invariably within the Longhouse community, and it is often formalized in the Longhouse.

GAMES

Ceremonial games constitute a second category of currently employed curing rituals, although some of them are related to the Longhouse rituals. The Bowl Game, derivative from the fourth sacred ceremony, has been discussed above. Field lacrosse, associated with the Thunder Ceremony, is frequently prescribed in con-junction with the War Dance. The teams are divided according to moieties, and the patient must duck under the crossed lacrosse sticks enclosing the ball before the beginning of the game. This act is considered the essence of the "medicine," al-though the game must then be played until one side has three or sometimes seven goals (or in other versions, until a total of three, five, or seven goals have been scored by both sides). As in the Thunder Ceremony in the Longhouse, it is immate-rial which side wins. The ball, which is made of rags, is then presented to the patient by the person in charge of the performance, and it should be kept throughout the lifetime of the patient and used in all further games on his behalf. The players are feasted by placing their food, False Face mush and cookies, on the spot at which they finished playing.

The football rite is almost identical, with the patient throwing out the ball to begin the game and also keeping the rag ball as a charm. The game may be played either by young men against old or by opposing moieties. Again the outcome is immaterial to the curing, the most important act being the initial throw by the patient. Cookies and False Face mush also accompany this game.

The tug-of-war game, with both sexes participating, is played by opposing moieties holding onto a small wooden stick, about 1.0 to 1.5 inches in diameter and 12 to 20 inches long, which again should be owned by the patient. He should pass under the stick at the beginning of the game, for this act represents the main part of the "medicine." Cookies are passed to the participants.

The snow-snake rite consists of allowing the patient to throw the first snake and then having other participants attempt to "beat" (outdistance) his throw, usually with two snakes each. No medical importance is attributed to the farthest throw in the game. If the patient is a man, he should own the snow snake, but if a woman, she should procure a small replica as a charm. Cookies reward the players in this game, too.

Speck (1949: 116) mentions a game involving a chipmunk rite, and informants do remember the name; but it seems to be obsolete at Six Nations at present, and I was not able to verify the details which Speck described. He, too, notes that "the rite is now rarely called for and performed."

INDIVIDUAL DEAD FEASTS

The dead are powerful, and human relations with them are "particular." Consequently, transgressions of mortuary obligations pry upon the consciences of negligent persons and apparently even cause psychosomatic ailments, which are characteristically described as "just not feeling well." Culturally patterned recurrent dreams (e.g., skeletons, caskets in a line, and familiar deceased persons calling for food) occur with remarkable frequency, and the dreamers concede that they are "bothered by the dead." In these cases, as well as in the case of any disease which occurs after a known omission of a death ceremony, a fortuneteller or the patient himself will prescribe a "dead feast," in order to "feed" the eternally hungry dead.

The most common of the dead feasts, and, indeed, the commonest of all the personal observances at Six Nations today is the small dead feast (niwa′a tihakō′-srah). This feast, like all dead feasts, is performed only when no crops stand in the fields, for a summoning of the dead, which is one of the characteristics of these feasts, is supposed to bring a killing frost. However, during the winter months there is no observance so popular and so frequent at Six Nations as the small dead feast. During the week of February 2, 1954, for example, a leading ritualist performed three dead feasts for members of the upper Reserve. A rather facetious statement constantly quoted by Longhouse members is: "We're so poor in winter because we have all those little feasts." Its popularity is due in part to the fact that the feast is a countermeasure for so many possible transgressions, in part to the conception of the dead as excessively desirous of attention, and in part to the simplicity of the ceremony, which requires no specialists except a speaker, who also burns the tobacco, and a woman who can cook the feast foods.

One characteristic of a dead feast for a relative is that the sponsor should make a particular effort to invite members of his matrilineage, because all may then share in feasting an ancestor; the dead are also said "to bother on both sides of the family," and patrilateral relatives should therefore attend if they are able. The program of a small dead feast opens with the customary introductory remarks and explanations to the participants. It is followed by a tobacco burning, at which the speaker explains the situation to the deceased, bids him accept the apologies of the patient for his transgression or his neglect in feeding, and offers as proof of contrition and attention a share in the food which has been prepared. In return it is hoped that the deceased will be satisfied and will refrain henceforth from bothering the patient. If a release of the dead or an exchange of ritual objects has been planned, this is effected after the tobacco invocation. (Interestingly, at almost all the small dead feasts which the writer attended, the participants did not take much notice of the tobacco burner and his mission. They were usually busy arranging the food, or they smoked cigarettes while listening, or they simply waited out the invocation in apparent apathy.) The speaker then ends the meeting with the customary words; and the food is passed to the dead, for whom a plate is reserved and set aside until the next morning, to the speaker, to the patient, and to the guests. The distribution is usually in a clockwise direction, to indicate that a dead feast is being performed. (Some people at Sour Springs claim that it may also go counterclockwise, but on the occasions on which this feast was observed in the Sour Springs community the passage of food was clockwise.) The dishes must be left until the next morning, as is common to all mortuary observances. A mild knife taboo prevails at the small dead feast, since the dead might be cut as they hover about tasting the food. The foods served are corn soup, corn bread, doughnuts, cookies, and general "feast" foods. Oranges, apples, and chewing tobacco are included in the distribution. Attenders take home with them in pails and bags any of the food they were unable to eat at the home of the patient, for nothing should be left over.

There are at Six Nations two other dead feasts, slightly more elaborate than the ordinary small dead feast and dedicated respectively to a "bearded white man" and to dead children. The first of these is called thodi?gostohõ and seems to have a local origin myth. As told by one narrator (whose mother occasionally "passed" this feast), the story is that the men of the community saw a man who was hungry and had a long beard come to the people. They said he was a white man and had lived near the graveyard. The people gave him food. Then, many years after his death, he was seen again, and the people fed him again. He had a long beard, and therefore the feast is called "long-beard white man feast." The narrator said that she did not know whether this actually happened or whether it had been revealed in a dream. Fortunetellers now prescribe the feast mainly for elderly people, and they in turn should invite other elderly people to participate. The feast follows the same pattern as the small dead feast, except that the food is served "on the table."

A spoon, but neither a knife nor a fork, may be used. The lights should be dimmed slightly, but when the writer attended the feast, this rule was neglected. The food on that occasion consisted of corn bread, cold pork slices, potatoes, gravy, biscuits and butter, tea, cooked rice with raisins, and apple pie. Corn soup was omitted, but since the patient was impoverished, the feast represented a considerable sacrifice. (The ailment being treated was only a cold, but one which had lasted three weeks.) The feast for dead children is almost identical with the small dead feast, except that it is described as more "particular"; no cutlery at all should be in evidence, and both corn bread and corn soup are mandatory.

Three other major mortuary ceremonies are prescribed for patients at Six Nations: the Tutelo fourth-night ceremony (see pp. 252–5 *supra*), the Tutelo spirit-adoption ceremony (see pp. 252–6), and the personal Ohgi'we (see pp. 232–3). The first two of these are always performed in their entirety when used as medicinal rites, but the personal Ohgi'we may be considerably shortened from the version used for communal benefit in the Longhouse. Also personal Ohgi'we are often performed in the afternoon rather than at night. An Ohgi'we can be prescribed for diseases suspected to be caused by a specific dead person, by one's ancestors, or by the dead collectively. Since even an abridged Ohgi'we entails a considerable expenditure, it frequently happens that an entire matrilineal family will sponsor one, and all will share the benefits therefrom. The Ohgi'we differs from the other dead feasts in that it is ideally the prerogative of a special society (see p. 231 *supra*), although nonmembers may participate. In fact, many of the performers themselves are not members of the Ohgi'we Society and have never had to pass the feast themselves. A detailed description of a typical Six Nations Ohgi'we is given by Kurath (Fenton and Kurath, 1951).

MEDICINE SOCIETIES

The medicine societies of the Iroquois are among the most fully described of their institutions (e.g., Fenton, 1940a and 1953), and consequently it will suffice here to sketch only their main characteristics and functions. At Six Nations there are currently extant eight societies which are conceived strictly as medicine societies: Bear, Otter, Eagle, Buffalo, Husk Face, False Face, Pygmy, and Shake Pumpkin (Medicine Men's or Hēna'ʔidos). Each has its distinctive tutelaries, origin myth, paraphernalia, ritual procedure, membership, and methods of effecting individual cures, and all but the Otter Society have music associated with their rites.

There are also three other societies often listed as medicine societies but which, for various reasons, are not grouped with the eight above by the Longhouse members. First there is the intrusive United States society, Gaihōnda'dŏ (Word Shaking), which has songs similar to the set sung by the Pygmy Society, but which observes a different ritual. The most noted performer of the Gaihōnda'dŏ songs at Six Nations learned them from a resident of the Tonawanda Reservation in New York State. Because the ritual is rarely performed and is dependent upon a singer who is able to lead the set, and because many of the upper community think the ritual is primarily a tjinhgẽ'da (hunting charm) dance, it has never attained the standing of an organized society at Six Nations, despite the fact that several women are able to "absorb" the songs competently. In the United States there is a cycle of songs performed immediately after the conclusion of the Gaihõnda'dõ and called Deswahde'hõ, which Parker (1913: 126) lists as belonging to a women's medicine society (though the performers were all men) called "Deswadenyatiõndottu." This cycle is never performed at Six Nations, and the society does not exist there. Secondly, there is the Ohgi'we Society, which is a society satisfying most of the criteria outlined above. However, because it concerns itself so much with the semiannual feasts for the whole Longhouse community, it is not thought of exclusively as a medicine society, despite the fact that much of its activity does involve curing individuals. Finally, there is the society which sings for the sake of renewing the strength of the Little Water Medicine. Whereas it is true that all members who partake of the Little Water Medicine are subsequently members of the Hẽna'?idos Society, the reverse is not the case, and to group the two societies as if they were the same (Speck 1949: 100) is not correct. The singers for the Little Water Medicine do not at any time perform their songs for an individual person, but rather repeat them, at most only three times a year, for the medicine alone.

Although the medicine societies have, in most of the literature, been designated as "secret" societies (and often they are given an incorrect religious interpretation as well), this is not strictly true, or at least not in the case of the societies at Six Nations. It is true that their doings are not widely advertised, particularly not to the outsider, but this is not so much that the society is "secret" as that the "power" of the tutelaries and of the doings as a whole is considered to be so great that a person who is not a member might be harmed mentally or physically. That this is not an idle fear is proved by the numerous instances in which uninitiated individuals have actually become hysterical in the presence of the societies and their tutelaries. For example, this has happened to a number of people in the presence of False Face and Husk Face masks, not only while attending a private curing ritual, but also when watching them perform publicly in the Longhouse. These hysterical possessions are always cured by initiating the individuals into the society. The instances in which the hysterical persons calmed down as soon as ashes were placed on their heads are too numerous to disregard, and obviously one is dealing with a culturally patterned phenomenon. The exclusion of outsiders from the societies is thus not for the sake of cliquishness but for their protection. Furthermore, the exclusion is not strict and usually applies only in those societies which are considered to be "particular," namely, the Hẽna'?idos and Little Water Medicine Societies, and only to those people who are considered "weak" (i.e., unable to confront the power of the curing rite without becoming possessed or otherwise harmed). Characteristically, children and menstruating women, as well as high-strung women who have not reached the menopause, are considered too weak to attend the medicine-society meetings. Menstruating women are excluded also because of the danger of spoiling the medicine. In general, however, the restrictions are so relaxed that almost anybody can observe and hear a curing rite of a medicine society from an adjoining room. In any case, none of the medicine societies is secret in the sense that it ever rejects an individual. Anyone who has "need" of the society—which merely means a prescription from a fortuneteller, or a dream which indicates that one should join, or a symptom such as possession in the presence of the society performance—may join. And "joining" simply means having the society perform its ritual in one's behalf and assuming the recurrent obligation of "passing" the society's dance at home or in the Longhouse.

In general, then, the function of the medicine societies in the medicinal complex is to be the trustees of certain rituals for the benefit of the whole community. By perpetuating these rituals they can act as intermediaries between the tutelaries and any individual who needs the aid of the tutelaries. A society's performance as a whole is the medicine, and it is more powerful and "particular" than any of the other doings so far discussed. The songs of the more powerful societies should not be sung "in vain." "It is too particular to fool with," is a common statement. Both because of the power of their medicine and because of their permanence and institutional status, the medicine societies are popular and prominent on the Reserve. However, it should be pointed out again that both in conception and procedures, the performances of the medicine societies are very similar to the other doings.

It is interesting that performers of the ceremonies of most of the societies need not themselves be members. The exception is Hēna'ʔidos, but even it allows nonmembers to participate in case of emergencies or if suitable rationalizations can be found.

For example, if one is a member of the False Face Society, one may attend the Hēna'ʔidos also, because "the False Faces come in at the end of Hēna'ʔidos and are related. They are the next in power" (i.e., the latter part of the Hēna'ʔidos ritual incorporates an appearance of the False Faces). And if one merely belongs to the Husk Faces, it is rationalized that one may attend, because Husk Faces are related to False Faces, who in turn are related to Hēna'ʔidos.

Boys may "pick up" the songs while they are young and help sing for years before having to join the society for one reason or another. Since active ritualists sing in many societies, the obligations which would be incumbent on them were they formally to "join" each one would be rather strenuous. Sometimes, however, an illness of a performer is attributed to his not being a member or not being "strong enough" to have contact with such powerful medicine. When this diagnosis is made, the performer usually joins the society in which he has been singing, and some singers do finally join a formidable number of societies. Perhaps the leniency with which the Six Nations medicine societies accept the participation of nonmembers is simply an indication of the scarcity of trained specialists (for fewer and fewer of the boys "pick up" the song cycles) and an instance of flexibility under difficult circumstances. Whatever the reason, the fact does show that the societies are not exclusive or "secret."

Although the ideal culture is very specific about enjoining the medicine societies "to help at all times, without cost and with alacrity," the matter is not so simple in the real culture, where a patient has to deal with individual representatives of the medicine society rather than with the society in the abstract. The community of an individual is primarily the community of his home Longhouse. An individual who needs the services of a medicine society therefore turns naturally to the "gang" at his Longhouse, which knows the required song cycles.[1] If he is not in good standing with this group, he may have to look to another Longhouse for aid or perhaps will have to pay for the required services (see p. 45 *supra*).

Of all the societies the Little Water Medicine Society deserves special note, because of the unique conceptions concerning the medicine of which it is the guardian. The Little Water Medicine, or gano'da, occupies a special place in the pharmacopoeia of the Iroquois, for of all the beneficial medicines it is depicted as the strongest and at the same time as the most dangerous. Etiologically, it derives from a common motif: the presentation to the good wounded hunter of a medicine which will restore him to health, together with a set of songs and a procedure for its administration. In the etiology of Little Water Medicine, each animal tore from its own body a living part, and today the preparation of this medicine is said to require a living part of an animal. An allied medicine is now reported at Six Nations, called Dekhni'hwadō'nthra ("the second place"), in which only ingredients taken from birds are essential; it is kept as a supplementary medicine with the Little Water Medicine bundle. The actual formulae of the Little Water Medicine vary with different informants, but a typical one includes the live flesh of an animal taken near the heart, the heart of a loon, the heart of a bird, and mixed herbs. Only an infinitesimal amount is needed for each cure, and when it is administered it is dropped into water which the custodian dips from a running stream in the direction of the water flow. The method of preparation of the medicine is not known at Six Nations, and the two Longhouses which keep the preparation on hand have lately gotten their supply from Cattaraugus for $25.00 to $35.00.

Since the ingredients of the Little Water Medicine are "so strong," there are a large number of strict injunctions concerning its custodian, the patient, and the medicine itself. The custodian should be an absolutely good man: he should never kill anything, not even an animal, he should never drink, he must be at the service of his community at all times, and above all he must never have had anything to do with any hunting charms. When the patient receives the medicine, he must take extreme care to be hidden for four days, to smell no smoke, not even Indian tobacco smoke, to drink only basswood tea, to eat only unleavened flour and water mush, and to remain in a darkened room; and he must upon recovery "pass" a Hĕna'?idos feast to release the medicine and indicate his gratefulness. Finally, the medicine

---

[1] As is natural in any society, certain associations have formed between members who habitually sing together, practice together, have cooperative work relationships, etc. These soon become known as "so and so's gang." The unofficial leader of this miniature informal singing society will often contract for the services of his entire group, and it is convenient for patients to arrange their doings through him. Each Longhouse has associated with it one or more such "gangs" for most of the societies. Sour Springs, however, is currently "poor" and must often rely upon members of the communities down below.

itself must be kept wrapped in a bundle with the 4 yards of material given to the custodian by the last patient and with the flute used during the rite which renews the strength of the medicine. Should any person die after having taken some of the portion of medicine kept by the custodian, the entire batch is spoiled. However, the power is restored to the spoiled medicine at the meetings of the Little Water Medicine Society (held semiannually at Lower Cayuga and three times a year at Onondaga). It is this medicine society which is devoted to "keeping" and "taking care of" and "singing for" our "great Grandmother, Gano'da."

These characteristics, especially if compared to the etiology and treatment of hunting charms, described below, suggest that the Little Water Medicine is, in fact, a hunting charm, carefully groomed to "work for the people." When, however, such a suggestion is made to any knowledgeable person, the answer is that "it is entirely different, it is a medicine and not a charm, and it works only for the good."

HUNTING CHARMS AND WITCHCRAFT

More powerful than all the curing rites except Little Water, and more dangerous than Little Water because they are prominently associated with evil, are those observances involving tjinhgē'da. Tjinhgē'da derives from hunting charms and medicine bundles, and today at Six Nations, where knowledge of both of these complexes is vague and confused, the characteristics of tjinhgē'da are likewise confused. Basically, a tjinhgē'da is a bone said to be taken from an animal while the creature was yet alive and fashioned into a charm to aid in hunting. This was accomplished by burning tobacco, asking the object for "power," and feasting it in return. Thereafter, throughout the life of the hunter the charm had to be "taken care of" and fed regularly, preferably with some portion of each kill. While the ancestors of the modern Iroquois still hunted, all was well, for the charms were used to good purpose, and hunters knew how to "take care of them," and both the charm and the hunter were "well satisfied." However, when the white man arrived and destroyed the game, so that hunting was no longer practiced, the charms could not fulfill their original purpose, and the hunters forgot to take care of them and to feed them. Consequently, these charms, which are handed down in the (matrilineal) family, become hungry, "turn on" the hunter and his family, and begin to "eat" them. Being "eaten" always involves falling ill, succumbing to bad luck (especially to accidents which maim), and eventually dying. It is said that such a hunting charm will "eat" through a whole family, beginning with the matrilineage, shifting after their extinction to the father's lineage, and finally eating the owner of the charm. The fact that some families experience several deaths in a short time is given as evidence of this process of depredation. Furthermore, when people had hunting charms but no legitimate purpose for which they might be used, they burned tobacco and implored the charms to help them gain illegitimate ends, such as achieving wealth, harming an enemy, or unfairly winning a lacrosse game. As a result it is now said that all the hunting charms are "spoiled" and have become evil and a means of witchcraft. Any family which is known to have inherited such a charm, or even to have once possessed one, is therefore under the suspicion of witchcraft. Tjinhgē'da is thus sometimes thought to be a menace to its possessor and sometimes a source of illegitimate power, and these two conceptions are often intermingled and confused.

There are today several families at Six Nations which openly admit that they did at one time own such charms (usually a fortuneteller has told them so), and in order to protect themselves they now give periodic feasts. Should they neglect to do so, the charms would indeed turn on them and eat them. Also, once a charm of this nature is known to be in the family, the ailments of its members are frequently traced to it, and it becomes necessary to "pass" the dance which will satisfy the charm. The appropriate "pass dance" for such ailments is a rite called gana?djae?-go'wa which has a ritual pattern very much like that of the Hēna'?idos Society, though there are differences in the two sets of songs. Only a few ritualists know the variant sets of songs. It is interesting to note that those who do know the songs are reluctant to attend and sing a gana?djae?go'wa, even though the sponsor protests that the entire proceeding is purely medicinal and prophylactic, divorced from all intention of witching; such protestations, in fact, prove nothing, since no one would ever admit that he intended to practice witchcraft. The ceremony is rarely performed, and most of the families who legitimately sponsor an initial gana?djae?go'wa for a hunting charm prefer thereafter to continue the periodic feeding of the charm by "passing" the ordinary Hēna'?idos Society feast or the "hurry-up" feast called ksa?ō (see p. 287 *infra*). The Hēna'?idos Society feast is considered an essential adjunct to the gana?djae?go'wa (just as it is for the Little Water Medicine rite) and is required in order to "release" the initial medicine.

To invite the singers and attendants for a gana?djae?go'wa, the sponsor should clearly explain his purpose and give a week's notice, "so that one may think it over." With each invitation a pinch of tobacco must be sent, which the invited returns and burns in the stove when he comes to the meeting. It is considered both polite and safe to invite only those people who "pass" a similar feast (for these are supposed to be more able than others to withstand the power of the hunting charm), but in fact others are also asked. Although most such feasts certainly have a legitimate medicinal purpose, the Longhouse population is extremely anxious about attending, and many of the invited refuse to attend. "That's dangerous, them kind, you can't play with that, no joking here, no sir" (all one exclamation); "I call it witchcraft in English"; you can't talk foolish about it, it really will stay in my brain so long as I live"—these are three typical reactions which were received in the discussion of such a tjinhgē'da ceremony. The anxiety is not necessarily that the sponsor of the feast will use the illegitimate power of the charm to harm the people whom he has invited, but that they may be unwitting accomplices in witching someone else, which would expose them to counter-witchcraft. Finally, there is a general fear that any contact with tjinhgē'da, or even the presence of a "bundle" (which is the hunting charm wrapped in material or in a bag, in the manner of the old medicine bundles), will contaminate the innocent. If one does attend such a ceremony, one must be extremely careful, since of all medicines the hunting charms are the most "particular." Mistakes in the ritual must immediately be rectified with tobacco, and even then the ritualists remain anxious.

The program of the ceremony follows that of the Hĕna'ʔidos Society, with men playing "shake-pumpkin" rattles and a single water drum. Sweet, small white beans are the characteristic food of all tjinhgē'da feasts; they are served in the break periods between songs and at the end of the ceremony, and are supplemented by a pig's head, corn soup, Hĕna'ʔidos mush with large white beans, and strawberry juice. In all other respects—opening statement, tobacco burning with invocation, and ending statement—the ceremony is like any curing rite.

Closely allied to the ganaʔdjaeʔgo'wa ceremony is the "hurry-up," or substitute, ceremony, called ksaʔõ, which may be "passed" when a person feels he cannot afford the more elaborate ritual, or needs a feast in an emergency, or simply has it prescribed to him. This feast is designed expressly to "feed" the charm, and it is an "eat-all feast," performed in the dark and with no utensil whatever being used (and no table, so that the participants eat on the floor). Invitations are extended with tobacco, even as for the ganaʔdjaeʔgo'wa. Sweet white beans and meat are the main foods, and that which cannot be eaten is thrown into the stove. Participants do not take home a pail as at all the other Iroquoian feasts.

Currently, there are numerous variations on the theme of tjinhgē'da, each one described as a "bundle" or a "charm," and each one suspected of being an instrument of witchcraft. Thus one hears them described, though usually not by members of the families in which they reside, as the heart of a giant lizard, gainawe'hdi (probably derivative from the Hĕna'ʔidos songs); or as small deer skeletons; or "live meat" called gʔawa'hõnheʔ (often depicted as a live heart, capable of fusing again after being cut); or as a snake section; or even as a root, stone, or seed. There is also a minor hunting charm, second in power, made of the heart, liver, or wing of a bird rather than of an animal. It is said that a snow-snake rite may be substituted for the minor tjinhgē'da obligations.

Two further objects are consistently identified as erstwhile hunting charms now used exclusively in witchcraft, both of which are still fed to prevent their turning upon and eating their owners. One is called oʔnē'yõnt (or oʔnē'yĕt) and is a small stone, alternatively described as a small piece of dried meat, kept wrapped in silken rags. When placed in a saucer of water, this stone is said to give power to the water to work evil on anything it contacts. The method of use described is to dip a handkerchief into the tainted water and sprinkle it in a room while pretending to fan oneself; the drops then affect anyone in the room. The other object is a beetle, or "fatal insect," called ganõhõ'thwaht, which affects a person who steps on it by "eating his face" or settling in his neck and spine. A set of songs called ganogē'hyõn (?), interpreted as "devil dance" (?), is the countermeasure against the beetle. It requires a drum and a horn rattle and was supposedly taught to a few Six Nations practitioners by Chauncey Johnny John of Allegany. The food appropriate for this ritual is flint-corn soup with meat.

As noted above there is widespread suspicion that any person who openly passes a tjinhgē'da feast for his own protection is in fact actively engaged in witchcraft. A further anxiety, shared by most of the Longhouse population, is that any medicinal feast may be a tjinhgē'da feast. Certain types of substitution in the ritual—using whiskey, serving sweet white beans as a feast food, or less obviously, mentioning the intent of using the ritual for tjinhgē'da while burning tobacco—or even burning some supplementary tobacco at another place at an earlier time to apply to a forthcoming doings, are believed to change a legitimate event into an instrument of witchcraft. Some instances of variation in ritual which are highly feared as witchcraft are the Bowl Game with a variant set of counters and rules of scoring, and the football game reputedly played with a flaming ball, which is kicked only and not tossed up by the patient at the start of the game. However, the sponsors of such games characterize them as purely and legitimately medicinal. For example, one of the deaconesses, who periodically "passes" the variant Bowl Game, says that it was prescribed to her by a fortuneteller as an adjunct to making friends.

The bowl and dice and method of play, as well as the moiety division and pairing of bets, are as in the standard game, but scoring is managed by a male scorekeeper, who sticks the carved wooden pegs into two pots of soil. (Down below there is a version with one pot.) The counters consist of the following: six pegs about 5 inches long, six shorter pegs, six animals—two eels and two different pairs of lizards—a man, a woman, a penis, and a log (ga'ōnda). These are evenly divided among the players. If the patient is a woman, her moiety has the woman and log, and if a man, his moiety has the man and penis. The Wolves always draw the short pegs. Although inquiry was made of three of the scorekeepers, a coherent set of rules could not be ascertained, and all three versions were different. Even when the writer participated in the game, the scoring seemed completely random and there was an obvious amount of indecision and variation between each move.

Finally, there are at Six Nations other methods of working witchcraft than by the use of hunting charms or bundles; for example, sticking a doll with a sharp object in the place where harm is intended to the victim, strewing graveyard dirt in the path of the victim, and contaminating his food with a magical powder. These are immediately directed and are typically motivated by jealousy. These techniques are not directly related to the medicinal complex, but since Iroquois witchcraft is supposed to cause derangement, physical sickness, maiming, and ultimately death (but not such metaphysical debilities as soul loss), witching is never far removed from the area of health.

It is an ironic fact that although helpfulness is a central idea of the Iroquois medical complex, there is nevertheless, in the real culture at Six Nations, a tremendous amount of anxiety and suspicion below the surface.

CONCLUSIONS

THE foregoing survey has been an attempt to understand the composition and *Gestalt* of the conservative culture at Six Nations Reserve and to explain, as far as possible, its endurance. However, before summarizing, it may be worthwhile to point out that raising the question of the endurance of the culture suggests somewhat that the culture is in a state of siege. Such a suggestion is partly true and partly misleading. The members of the Reserve are undoubtedly subjected to much acculturative pressure, ranging from missionizing to the corrosive influence of comic books. Furthermore, the Dominion government directly controls many of the internal affairs of the Reserve, maintains a contingent of Mounted Police, and has installed an elective legislative system in place of the traditional council of hereditary chiefs. Consequently, one finds much bitterness among the conservative group against the white man, resentment against those factions on the Reserve which cooperate with the Canadian Indian Office, and chauvinistic revivals which tend to make the members "consciously Indian." On the other hand, all the Indians of the Reserve, including the conservative group, are protected by such legal provisions as the inalienability of Reserve land and the exemption of Reserve members from Canadian military service. Furthermore, there is official toleration, however condescending, of the Longhouse religion and of many private aspects of the Indian way of life. It is therefore possible to a large extent for the conservative members to participate naturally in the traditional activities. In this sense they can be "unconsciously Indian," without a feeling of making a last-ditch defense. However, if full Canadian citizenship were forced upon the Indians, with concomitant permission to alienate Reserve land (and these are not merely theoretical possibilities), there would indeed be a crisis in the traditional culture of the Reserve.

In spite of the difficult external circumstances of the conservative culture at Six Nations, its internal structure is remarkably coherent. This does not mean that the conservative culture is free from ideological inconsistencies, or that the real and ideal cultures coincide, or that it is highly conducive to the happiness of its participants. It means rather that there are certain central themes which are found in most of the areas of the culture, and that the different institutions of the culture are interlocked and reinforce each other.

The most pervasive theme in the ideology of the conservative group is probably the theme of *being an Indian*. The antithesis of being an Indian is understood to be conformance to the ways of the white man, and therefore this theme is not so much a survival of aboriginal Iroquois ethnocentrism as a response to acculturative pressure. It is not surprising to find that a theme of *collectiveness* is important today, especially since the aboriginal Iroquois culture was very sophisticated in matters of social and political organization. One of the first sentiments of the Thanksgiving Address, which is recited at the beginning and end of almost all formal gatherings of Longhouse members, is that "we now unite our minds to greet each other and rejoice that we have come together." In any activity the participants should have "united minds," and it is always pretended that the decisions of conferences are unanimous (though ironically the real culture contains much bitter factionalism). Related to the theme of collectiveness is that of *reciprocity and helpfulness*. The rules of reciprocal obligations between moieties in the Longhouse and in the League, and the feasting and hospitality patterns are formal expressions of these conceptions. Furthermore, the individual member helps at the "doings" of others in expectation of reciprocal services, and even the characteristic behavior toward the spirit forces—supplication, offering Indian tobacco, performing "pass dances," and thanksgiving—is an instance of reciprocity. In the ideal culture, a corollary of the theme of helpfulness is an injunction against jealousy, suspicion, and gossip; but the condemnation of these things is actually a reflection of their ubiquity in the real culture. Several somewhat metaphysical themes are exhibited in many areas of the conservative culture. One of these is the conception of *hierarchy*. It is demonstrated most completely in the ordering of the spirit forces in the Thanksgiving Address, but there are also a hierarchy of offices in the Longhouse and a hierarchy of medicines arranged according to power. Finally, there is a theme of *mind* in the Iroquois conception of man. For example, chiefs especially ought to have "straight minds," mourners are conceived as being "deranged in mind," and their comforters are "clear minded." It is thought that the qualities of mind are largely independent of material circumstances, and in fact this is sometimes offered as a rationalization for accepting the white man's technology and even using artifacts of the white man in ceremonials.

It is characteristic of a coherent culture that an explanation of the function of one of its institutions is bound to be somewhat circular: an institution works because it interlocks with other institutions, which in turn can be explained only by reference to the one initially considered. With certain qualifications, the conservative culture at Six Nations Reserve is coherent in this sense. Its major institutions are the Longhouse, the medical complex, the institutions of the life cycle, the social system, and the traditional political system. The Longhouse and the medical complex are by far the most important of these, and they depend upon each other and reinforce each other in intricate ways. In the first place, "Indian" cures make considerable use of Longhouse paraphernalia and often are copies of Longhouse rituals. More important, however, the Longhouse inculcates an ideology—specifically, a doctrine of the superiority of everything Indian and a metaphysics of spirit forces inherent in natural objects—which is highly conducive to belief in the efficacy of Indian medicine. Conversely, the intense concern with medical matters is a major cause for adherence to the Longhouse, since, for example, the recurrent obligations incurred by joining a medicine society must be fulfilled on Pass Dance Day in the Longhouse. Similarly, the Longhouse and such institutions of the life cycle as naming, ritual friendship, and mortuary practices mutually support each other. Similarly, also, the medical complex reinforces the institutions of the life cycle, especially because the fortunetellers like to point to neglected dead feasts or friendship obligations as the causes of disease. The traditional social system is intimately linked with the Longhouse and the institutions of the life cycle, for in both the calendric and the mortuary ceremonies there are ritual obligations between two moieties, and moiety affiliation is determined by clan affiliation. Although considerable laxity and confusion in the moiety division are tolerated as long as the basic pattern of reciprocity is maintained, the traditional social system continues to be kept relatively intact for ceremonial purposes. The least interlocked of the institutions of the conservative culture is the traditional political organization, the council of hereditary chiefs, and there is no doubt that it has atrophied since the Canadian government deprived it of official political functions. It is interesting, however, that many of the chiefs have tried to maintain the importance of the council and their own prerogatives by claiming that chiefs are essential for the functioning of the Longhouse. If their maneuvers succeed, the probability of survival of the hereditary council will increase, though its functions will be radically changed.

Most of the factors which explain the endurance of the conservative culture at Six Nations Reserve are implicit in what has been said about the coherence of the culture. Thus, the fact that there are a few simple themes which occur in all areas of the culture and which are repeatedly preached in the same phrases makes the conservative way of life seem familiar and reasonable. The themes of collectiveness and of being an Indian have the further effect of stimulating in-group sentiment and mutual defense against white encroachment. The interlocking of various cultural institutions is perhaps the most important factor in the perpetuation of the culture. In the first place, it has the effect of relating the area of most intense personal concern—that of health and good fortune—to every other area of the culture. And secondly, it tends to make conservatism an all-or-nothing commitment, which psychologically encloses many individuals in the old patterns, since it is usually more painful to discard a way of life in one step than piecemeal. (However, the tendency to enforce all-or-nothing commitment is an imperfect mechanism, for in fact one finds members of the Reserve in very many stages of acculturation.) The glorification of the Indian way of life and the integration of the various institutions seem to imply cultural intransigence. Actually, however, there is a remarkable amount of flexibility; and this helps to preserve the culture, because it prevents demoralization and allows the central patterns to remain intact whenever, either on account of forgetting or due to external pressure, peripheral traits are lost. For example, there is a rationalization for adopting the technology of the white man, which is considered to be a peripheral matter, for "our religion is not one of paint or feathers; it is a thing of the heart." And even within the central areas of the culture, simplification and substitution are condoned, for the spirit forces and the Great Creator appreciate devout intentions, even when part of a ritual speech is forgotten or when a speaker has to be borrowed from the opposite moiety. Finally, one should note two factors which are always involved in cultural survival. One is simply the momentum of a going concern, which is expressed by the sentiment: "We have always done it this way." The other is the existence of individuals with special prerogatives or special devotion—at Six Nations these are the chiefs, the speakers and deacons of the Longhouse, and the ritualists and fortunetellers—who actively perpetuate the traditional practices and may even revitalize them.

APPENDIX

BIBLIOGRAPHY

INDEX

APPENDIX

IN SEARCH OF FLUENT NATIVE SPEAKERS

Cayuga

1. Alice Bomberry
2. Arnold Bomberry
3. Beatrice Bomberry
4. Clara Bomberry
5. Ethel Bomberry
6. Evelyn Bomberry
7. Hilton Bomberry
8. Leona Bomberry
9. Palsey Bomberry
10. Peter Bomberry
11. Sadie Bomberry
12. W. Allen Bomberry
13. Casey Buck
14. Gordon Buck
15. Grace Buck
16. Joyce Buck
17. Levina Buck
18. Stanley Buck
19. Vera Buck
20. Burnita Burnham
    (or Audrey Benita)
21. Joyce Burnham
22. Muriel Burnham
23. A. Joan Crawford
24. Bert Crawford
25. Elliott Crawford
26. Bernice (General) Davis
27. Cora Belle Davis
28. Alta Doxtator
29. Mrs. Tom (Florie) Elliot
30. Susan Fraser
31. Frances Froman
32. Arnold General
33. Cleveland General
34. Sidney General
35. Alice (Hill) Gibson
36. Dorothy Green
37. Eva Green
38. Ariel (Johnson) Harris
39. Esther Harris
40. Harrison Harris
41. Vera Harris
42. Irwina (Harris) Henhawk
43. Lloyd Henry
44. Marge Henry
45. Marion Henry
46. Maybelle Henry
47. Reuben Henry
48. Cassie (Gussie) Hess
49. Delos Hill
50. Doris (Tootsie) Hill
51. Josie Hill
52. Lorna Hill
53. Louise Hill
54. Raymond (Wheels) Hill
55. Ronald Hill
56. Scott Hill
57. Hulsie Isaac

This appendix lists Six Nations speakers as of January 1994. It was compiled by the Sweetgrass First Nations Language Council Inc.

58. Carmen Jacobs
59. Cassie Jacobs
60. Evelyn Jacobs
61. Freeman Jacobs, Jr.
62. Nelles Jacobs
63. Norman Jacobs
64. Oliver Jacobs
65. Pete Jacobs
66. Alva Jamieson
67. Daisy Jamieson
68. Hannah (General) Jamieson
69. Art Johnson
70. Carl Johnson
71. Eileen (Hill) Johnson
72. Eileen (Skye) Johnson
73. Elizabeth Johnson
74. George Johnson
75. Lena Johnson
76. Manual Johnson
77. Murray Johnson
78. Pearl Johnson
79. Georgina Jonathan
80. Alfred Keye
81. Austin Keye
82. Lottie Keye
83. Robert Logan
84. Wilfred Logan
85. Barry Longboat
86. Cleveland Longboat
87. Harvey Longboat
88. Irene Longboat
89. Janet Longboat
90. Ruth Longboat
91. Wilma (Babes) Martin
92. Carmen Manuel Miller
93. Dolly Miller
94. Elizabeth Isabel
    (Juk Juk) Miller

95. Elizabeth Miller
96. Rachel (Warner) Miller
97. Clara Powless
98. Elizabeth Sandy
99. Joyce Sandy
100. Mitchell Sandy
101. Pat Sandy
102. Vincent Sandy
103. Annie Silversmith
104. Elizabeth (Smoke) Silversmith
105. Seymour Silversmith
106. Bruce Sky
107. David Sky
108. Eleanor (Bomberry) Sky
109. Flora Sky
110. Gloria Sky
111. H. Harold Sky
112. James Sky
113. Marvin Sky
114. Rosemond Sky
115. Donald Skye
116. Hubert Skye
118. Rena (Bomberry) Skye
119. Olive Smoke
120. Lorne Sprague
121. Raymond Sprague
122. James Styres
123. Ronald Styres
124. Garnnet Thomas
125. James Thomas
126. Rita VanEvery
127. Bernard Williams
128. Elwood Williams
129. Faye Dell Williams
130. Fred Williams
131. Joyce Williams
132. Laura Eleanor (Williams)
     Porter

133. Roberta Williams
134. Ruby Williams
135. Phyllis Winnie

136. Rose Winnie
137. Greta (Greet) Wright

Mohawk

1. Rose Anderson
2. Daniel Butler
3. Mabel Butler
4. Thomas Deer (from Kahnawake)
5. Birdie Doctor
6. Louella Elliot
7. Mary Elliot
8. Robert Elliot
9. Adeline Elliot-Isaacs
10. Martin Froman
11. Francis Garlow
12. Greta Garlow
13. Sylvanus General
14. Albert (Bones) Green
15. Albert (Bull Dog) Green
16. Carrie Green
17. Ervin Green
18. Harry Green
19. Ruby Green
20. Albert Harris
21. Cecil Harris
22. Irvin Harris
23. Murray Henhawk
24. Elma Hill
25. Frances Hill
26. Freda Hill
27. Harry Hill
28. James Hill
29. Melinda Hill
30. Merle Hill
31. Minnie Hill
32. Norman Hill
33. Sandra Hill
34. Truman Hill
35. Wesley Hill
36. Ruth Isaac
37. Peter Isaacs
38. Marjorie Jacobs
39. Mary (Wally) Jacobs
40. Minnie Jacobs
41. Robert (Bob) Jamieson
42. Virginia Jamieson
43. Ima Johnson
44. Maisie Jonathan
45. Edna Lickers
46. Gary Loft
47. Kenneth Loft
48. Peter Loft
49. Sandra Loft
50. Vina Loft
51. Janet Longboat
52. Katherine Longboat
53. Lee Longboat
54. Stanley Longboat
55. Leone MacNaughton
56. Vernon MacNaughton
57. Isabel Maracle
58. John Maracle
59. Richard Maracle
60. Stanley Maracle
61. Betty Martin
62. Charles Martin
63. Donald Martin
64. George Martin
65. John Martin

66. Mike Martin
67. Frank Miller
68. Garnette Miller
69. Raymond Miller
70. Ruth Miller
71. Thomas Miller
72. Muriel Montour
73. Louella Porter
74. Calvin Powless
75. Maynard Powless
76. M. Wilma Powless

77. Ross Powless
78. Theda Powless
79. Alice Sero
80. Christine Skye
81. Myrtle Smith
82. Joe Squires
83. Inez Staats
84. Mel Staats
85. Beatrice Thomas
86. Pauline White
87. Hazel Whitlow

ONONDAGA

1. Yvonne Beddard
2. Archie Bomberry
3. Cassie Bomberry
4. Charles (Jackie) Bomberry
5. George Bomberry
6. Larry (Dutch) Bomberry
7. Helen Burning
8. Isabelle (Henry) Burning
9. Nora Carrier
10. Betty Henry
11. Daisy (Lavina) Henry
12. Maria Henry
13. Wilbert Henry
14. Bernice Johnson
15. Maggie (Green) Johnson
16. Seafort (Bob) Keye
17. Claudia (Bomberry) Longboat
18. Huron Miller
19. Anthony Wayne Nanticoke
20. Beulah (Skye) Nanticoke
21. David Jeffrey Nanticoke
22. Harry Nanticoke

23. Jennifer Nanticoke
24. Lawrence Naticoke
25. Steven Craig Nanticoke
26. Verna (Nanticoke) Logan
27. Geraldine Sandy
28. Isabelle Skye
29. Joe Skye
30. Peter Sky
31. Abby Smoke
32. Harry Smoke
33. Peter Smoke
34. Jake Thomas, Sr.
35. Rita (Skye) Vyse
36. Daisy Warner
37. Cecil Williams
38. Gladys (Thomas) Williams
39. Gloria Williams
40. Hilda Williams
41. Jack (Thomas) Williams
42. Lester Williams
43. Reta Williams

SENECA

1. Teresa (John) Mitten

BIBLIOGRAPHY

ACKERKNECHT, ERWIN H.
  1942. *Primitive Medicine and Culture Pattern* (Bulletin of the History of Medicine, vol. 12, pp. 545–574, Baltimore).
BARBEAU, M.
  1917. *Iroquoian Clans and Phratries* (American Anthropologist, n.s., vol. 19, pp. 392–405, Lancaster).
BEAUCHAMP, W. M.
  1879. *Wampum Belts of the Six Nations* (Annual Report of the Board of Regents of the Smithsonian Institution, pp. 389–390, Washington).
  1885. *Permanence of Early Iroquois Clans and Sachemships* (Proceedings of the American Association for the Advancement of Science, vol. 34, pp. 381–392, Salem, Massachusetts).
  1885a. *The Iroquois White Dog Feast* (American Antiquarian and Oriental Journal, vol. 7, pp. 235–239, Chicago).
  1886. *Permanency of Iroquois Clans and Sachemships* (American Antiquarian and Oriental Journal, vol. 8, pp. 82–91, Chicago).
  1888. *Onondaga Customs* (Journal of American Folk-lore, vol. 1, pp. 195–203, Boston and New York).
  1890. *Wampum and Shell Articles Used by the New York Indians* (New York State Museum Bulletin, no. 41, Albany).
  1891. *Iroquois Notes* (Journal of American Folk-Lore, vol. 4, pp. 39–46, Boston and New York).
  1895. *An Iroquois Condolence* (Journal of American Folk-Lore, vol. 8, pp. 313–316, Boston and New York).
  1895a. *Onondaga Notes* (Journal of American Folk-Lore, vol. 8, pp. 209–216, Boston and New York).
  1896. *Iroquois Games* (Journal of American Folk-Lore, vol. 9, pp. 269–277, Boston and New York).
  1897. *The New Religion of the Iroquois* (Journal of American Folk-Lore, vol. 10, pp. 169–180, Boston and New York).
  1902. *Horn and Bone Implements of the New York Indians* (New York State Museum Bulletin, no. 50, Albany).
  1905. *A History of the New York Iroquois* (New York State Museum Bulletin, no. 78, Albany).
  1907. *Civil, Religious and Mourning Councils and Ceremonies of Adoption of the New York Indians* (New York State Museum Bulletin, no. 113, Albany).
  1921. *The Founders of the New York Iroquois League and Its Probable Date* (Researches and Transactions of the New York State Archaeological Association, no. 3, Rochester).
  1922. *Iroquois Folk Lore* (Syracuse: Onondaga Historical Association).
BENEDICT, RUTH
  1923. *The Concept of the Guardian Spirit in North America* (Memoirs of the American Anthropological Association, no. 29, Menasha).

299

BOYLE, DAVID
    1898.   *Society of the False Faces* (Annual Archaeological Report, being Part of Appendix to the Report of the Minister of Education, Ontario, pp. 157–160, Toronto).
    1899.   *Iroquois Medicine Man's Mask* (Annual Archaeological Report, pp. 27–29, Toronto).
    1905.   *The Making of a Cayuga Chief* (Annual Archaeological Report, pp. 56–59, Toronto).

CANFIELD, W. W.
    1902.   *The Legends of the Iroquois* (New York: A. Wessels Company).

CASWELL, HARRIET S.
    1892.   *Our Life among the Iroquois Indians* (Boston: Congregational Sunday-School and Publishing Society).

CHADWICK, EDWARD M.
    1897.   *The People of the Longhouse* (Toronto: Church of England Publishing Company Limited).

CLEMENTS, F. E.
    1932.   *Primitive Concepts of Disease* (University of California Publications in American Archaeology and Ethnology, vol. 32, pp. 185–252, Berkeley).

COLDEN, CADWALLADER
    1866.   *The History of the Five Indian Nations of Canada which are dependent on the Province of New York* (2 vols. New York: New Amsterdam Book Company).

CONKLIN, H. C., AND W. C. STURTEVANT
    1953.   *Seneca Indian Singing Tools at Coldspring Longhouse: Musical Instruments of the Modern Iroquois* (Proceedings of the American Philosophical Society, vol. 97, pp. 262–290, Philadelphia).

CONVERSE, HARRIET MAXWELL
    1908.   *Myths and Legends of the New York State Iroquois* (A. C. Parker, editor, New York State Museum Bulletin, no. 125, Albany).
    1930.   *The Seneca New-Year Ceremony and Other Customs* (Indian Notes, Museum of the American Indian, Heye Foundation, vol. 7, pp. 69–84, New York).

CORNPLANTER, JESSE J.
    1938.   *Legends of the Longhouse* (Philadelphia: J. B. Lippincott Company).

CURTIN, JEREMIAH
    1918.   *Seneca Fiction, Legends, and Myths* (J. N. B. Hewitt, editor, Thirty-second Annual Report of the American Bureau of Ethnology, Washington).

CUSICK, DAVID
    1848.   *Sketches of Ancient History of the Six Nations* (Lockport, New York: Turner and McCollum, Printers).

DEARDORFF, MERLE H.
    1951.   *The Religion of Handsome Lake: Its Origin and Development* (in "Symposium on Local Diversity in Iroquois Culture," W. F. Fenton, editor, Bureau of American Ethnology Bulletin, no. 149, Washington).

DODGE, ERNEST S.
    1945.   *Notes from the Six Nations of the Hunting and Trapping of Wild Turkeys and Passenger Pigeons* (Journal of the Washington Academy of Sciences, vol. 35, pp. 342–343, Menasha).

FELLER, WILLIAM

1950. *An Introduction to Probability Theory and Its Applications* (New York: John Wiley and Sons).

FENTON, WILLIAM N.

1936. *An Outline of Seneca Ceremonies at Coldspring Longhouse* (Yale University Publications in Anthropology, no. 9, New Haven).

1937. *The Seneca Society of Faces* (The Scientific Monthly, vol. 44, pp. 215–238, New York).

1937a. *The Seneca Eagle Dance: A Study of Personality Expression in Ritual* (Ph.D. Dissertation, Yale University, New Haven).

1939. *A Further Quest for Iroquois Medicines* (Explorations and Field-Work of the Smithsonian Institution, Publication no. 3586, pp. 93–96, Washington).

1940. *Problems Arising from the Historic Northeastern Position of the Iroquois* (Smithsonian Institution Miscellaneous Collections, vol. 100, pp. 159–251, Washington).

1940a. *Masked Medicine Societies of the Iroquois* (Annual Reports of the Board of Regents of the Smithsonian Institution, Publication 3624, pp. 397–430, Washington).

1941. *Tonawanda Longhouse Ceremonies: Ninety Years After Henry Lewis Morgan* (Bulletin of the Bureau of American Ethnology, vol. 128, pp. 140–166, Washington).

1941a. *Contacts between Iroquois Herbalism and Colonial Medicine* (Annual Reports of the Board of Regents of the Smithsonian Institution, pp. 503–526, Washington).

1941b. *Iroquois Suicide: A Study in the Stability of a Culture Pattern* (Bulletin of the Bureau of American Ethnology, vol. 128, pp. 80–137, Washington).

1942. *Songs from the Iroquois Longhouse: Program Notes for an Album of American Indian Music from the Eastern Woodlands* (from records in "The Archive of American Folk Song," The Library of Congress, Washington: The Smithsonian Institution).

1944. *Simeon Gibson: Iroquois Informant, 1889–1943* (American Anthropologist, n.s., vol. 46, pp. 231–234, Menasha).

1946. *An Iroquois Condolence Council for Installing Cayuga Chiefs in 1945* (Journal of the Washington Academy of Sciences, vol. 36, pp. 110–129, Menasha).

1947. *Iroquois Indian Folklore* (Journal of American Folk-Lore, vol. 40, pp. 383–397, Boston and New York).

1949. *Seth Newhouse's Traditional History and Constitution of the Iroquois Confederacy* (Proceedings of the American Philosophical Society, vol. 93, pp. 141–158, Philadelphia).

1949a. *Collecting Materials for a Political History of the Six Nations* (Proceedings of the American Philosophical Society, vol. 93, pp. 233–238, Philadelphia).

1950. *The Roll Call of the Iroquois Chiefs: A Study of a Mnemonic Cane from the Six Nations Reserve* (Smithsonian Miscellaneous Collections, vol. 111, no. 15, Washington).

1951. *Iroquois Studies at the Mid-Century* (Proceedings of the American Philosophical Society, vol. 95, pp. 296–310, Philadelphia).

1951a. *The Concept of Locality and the Program of Iroquois Research* (in "Symposium on Local Diversity in Iroquois Culture," W. F. Fenton, editor, Bureau of American Ethnology Bulletin, no. 149, pp. 1–12, Washington).

1951b. *Locality as a Basic Factor in the Development of Iroquois Social Structure* (in "Symposium on Local Diversity in Iroquois Culture," W. F. Fenton, editor, Bureau of American Ethnology Bulletin, no. 149, pp. 35–54, Washington).

1953. *The Iroquois Eagle Dance: An Offshoot of the Calumet Dance* (Bureau of American Ethnology Bulletin, no. 156, Washington).

1961. *Symposium on Cherokee and Iroquois Culture* (Bureau of American Ethnology Bulletin, no. 180, Washington).

FENTON, WILLIAM H., AND MERLE H. DEARDORFF
1943. *The Last Passenger Pigeon Hunts of the Cornplanter Senecas* (Journal of the Washington Academy of Sciences, vol. 33, pp. 289–315, Menasha).

FENTON, WILLIAM H., AND GERTRUDE P. KURATH
1951. *The Feast of the Dead, or Ghost Dance at Six Nations Reserve, Canada* (in "Symposium on Local Diversity in Iroquois Culture," W. F. Fenton, editor, Bureau of American Ethnology Bulletin, no. 149, pp. 139–165, Washington).

FLANNERY, REGINA
1939. *An Analysis of Coastal Algonquian Culture* (Washington: Catholic University of America Press).

FRAZER, J. G.
1943. *The Golden Bough: A Study in Magic and Religion* (abridged edition, New York: The Macmillan Company).

GILBERT, WILLIAM H.
1937. *Eastern Cherokee Social Organization* (in "Social Anthropology of North American Tribes," F. Eggan, editor, pp. 283–338, Chicago: The University of Chicago Press).

GOLDENWEISER, A. A.
1912. *The Death of Chief John A. Gibson* (American Anthropologist, n.s., vol. 14, pp. 692–694, Lancaster).

1913. *The Clan and Maternal Family of the Iroquois League* (American Anthropologist, n.s., vol. 15, pp. 696–697, Lancaster).

1914. *On Iroquois Work, 1912* (Summary Reports of the Geological Survey of Canada, 1912, pp. 464–475, Ottawa).

1914a. *On Iroquois Work, 1913* (Summary Reports of the Geological Survey of Canada, 1913, pp. 365–372, Ottawa).

1916. *Review of Parker's The Constitution of the Five Nations* (American Anthropologist, n.s., vol. 18, pp. 431–436, Lancaster).

GOODENOUGH, W. H.
1941. *Basic Economy and the Community* (unpublished article, undertaken in the files of the Cross-Cultural Survey).

HALE, HORATIO
1881. *A Lawgiver of the Stone Age* (Proceedings of the American Association for the Advancement of Science, vol. 30, pp. 324–341, Salem).

1883. *The Iroquois Book of Rites* (Brinton's Library of Aboriginal American Literature, no. 2, Philadelphia: D. G. Brinton).

1885. *The Iroquois Sacrifice of the White Dog* (American Antiquarian and Oriental Journal, vol. 7, pp. 7–14, Chicago).

1895. *An Iroquois Condoling Council* (Proceedings and Transactions of the Royal Society of Canada, series 2, vol. 1, ii, pp. 45–65, Ottawa).

HALLOWELL, A. IRVING
  1941.   *The Social Function of Anxiety in a Primitive Society* (American Sociological Review, vol. 6, pp. 869–881, Menasha).
  1945.   *Sociopsychological Aspects of Acculturation* (in "The Science of Man in the World Crisis," Ralph Linton, editor, pp. 171–200, New York: Columbia University Press).
  1946.   *Some Psychological Characteristics of the Northeastern Indians* (in "Man in Northeastern America," Frederick Johnson, editor, Andover, Massachusetts: The Foundation of Phillips Academy).
HARRINGTON, M. R.
  1908.   *Some Seneca Corn-foods and Their Preparation* (American Anthropologist, n.s., vol. 10, pp. 575–590, Lancaster).
HERSKOVITS, MELVILLE J.
  1938.   *Acculturation: The Study of Culture Contact* (New York: J. J. Augustin).
HEWITT, J. N. B.
  1895.   *The Cosmogonic Gods of the Iroquois* (Proceedings of the American Association for the Advancement of Science, vol. 44, pp. 241–250, Salem).
  1895a. *The Iroquoian Concept of the Soul* (Journal of American Folk-Lore, vol. 8, pp. 107–116, Boston and New York).
  1903.   *Iroquoian Cosmology* (Annual Reports of the Bureau of Ethnology, vol. 21, pp. 127–339, Washington).
  1916.   *The Requickening Address of the League of the Iroquois* (in "W. H. Holmes Anniversary Volume," Washington).
  1916a. Account of His Field Studies (in "Explorations and Field-Work of the Smithsonian Institution in 1916," Smithsonian Miscellaneous Collections, vol. 66, pp. 121–129, Washington).
  1917.   *Review of Parker's The Constitution of the Five Nations* (American Anthropologist, n.s., vol. 19, pp. 429–438, Lancaster).
  1920.   *A Constitutional League of Peace in the Stone Age of America* (Annual Report of the Board of Regents of the Smithsonian Institution for 1918, pp. 527–545, Washington).
  1928.   *Iroquoian Cosmology* (Annual Reports of the Bureau of Ethnology, vol. 43, pp. 449–819, Washington).
  1932.   *Field Studies among the Iroquois Tribes* (Explorations and Field-Work of the Smithsonian Institution in 1931, pp. 175–178, Washington).
  1944.   *The Requickening Address of the Iroquois Condolence Council* (William N. Fenton, editor, Journal of the Washington Academy of Sciences, vol. 34, pp. 65–85, Menasha).
HEWITT, J. N. B., AND WILLIAM N. FENTON
  1945.   *Some Mnemonic Pictographs Relating to the Iroquois Condolence Council* (Journal of the Washington Academy of Sciences, vol. 35, pp. 301–315, Menasha).
HUNT, GEORGE T.
  1940.   *The Wars of the Iroquois: A Study in Intertribal Trade Relations* (Madison: The University of Wisconsin Press).
HUOT, M. C.
  1948.   *Some Mohawk Words of Acculturation* (International Journal of American Linguistics, vol. 14, pp. 150–154, Baltimore).

JACKSON, HALLIDAY
  1830.   *Civilization of the Indian Natives* (Philadelphia and New York).
KLUCKHOHN, CLYDE
  1941.   *Patterning as Exemplified in Navaho Culture* (in "Language, Culture, and
          Personality: Essays in Memory of Edward Sapir," L. Spier, A. I. Hallowell,
          and S. S. Newman, editors, Menasha: Sapir Memorial Publication Fund).
  1944.   *Navaho Witchcraft* (Papers of the Peabody Museum of American Archaeology
          and Ethnology, vol. 22, pp. 1–149, Cambridge).
KROEBER, ALFRED L.
  1939.   *Cultural and Natural Areas of Native North America* (University of California
          Publications in American Archaeology and Ethnology, vol. 38, Berkeley).
KURATH, GERTRUDE P.
  1951.   *Local Diversity in Iroquois Music and Dance* (in "Symposium on Local Diver-
          sity in Iroquois Culture," W. F. Fenton, editor, Bureau of American Ethnology
          Bulletin, no. 149, pp. 35–54, Washington).
  1953.   *An Analysis of the Iroquois Eagle Dance and Songs* (Bureau of American Eth-
          nology Bulletin, no. 156, pp. 223–306, Washington).
  1953a. *The Tutelo Harvest Rites: A Musical and Choreographical Analysis* (The Scien-
          tific Monthly, vol. 76, pp. 153–162, Lancaster).
LABARRE, WESTON
  1947.   *Primitive Psychotherapy in Native American Cultures: Peyotism and Confession*
          (Journal of Abnormal and Social Psychology, vol. 47, pp. 301–307, Boston).
LAFITAU, J. F.
  1729.   *Moeurs des Sauvages amériquains* (2 vols., Paris).
LEIGHTON, A. H., AND D. C. LEIGHTON
  1942.   *Some Types of Uneasiness and Fear in a Navaho Indian Community* (American
          Anthropologist, n.s., vol. 44, pp. 194–209, Menasha).
LINTON, RALPH
  1936.   *The Study of Man* (New York: D. Appleton-Century Company).
  1943.   *Nativistic Movements* (American Anthropologist, n.s., vol. 45, pp. 230–240,
          Menasha).
LOWIE, ROBERT H.
  1937.   *The History of Ethnological Theory* (New York: Rinehart and Company, Inc.).
  1948.   *Primitive Religion* (New York: Liveright Publishing Corporation).
MALINOWSKI, B.
  1944.   *A Scientific Theory of Culture and Other Essays* (Chapel Hill: The University
          of North Carolina Press).
MORGAN, LEWIS H.
  1871.   *Systems of Consanguinity and Affinity* (Washington: Smithsonian Institution).
  1877.   *Ancient Society* (New York: Henry Holt and Company).
  1901.   *League of the Ho-Dé-No-Sau-Nee or Iroquois* (H. M. Lloyd, editor, 2 vols.,
          New York; reprint, Behavior Science Reprints, New Haven: Human Relations
          Area Files, 1954).
MURDOCK, G. P.
  1934.   *Our Primitive Contemporaries* (New York: The Macmillan Company).
  1949.   *Social Structure* (New York: The Macmillan Company).
  1953.   *Ethnographic Bibliography of North America* (second edition, New Haven:
          Human Relations Area Files).

MURDOCK, G. P., C. S. FORD, ET AL.
1950. *Outline of Cultural Materials* (third edition, revised, New Haven: Human Relations Area Files).

NOON, J. A.
1949. *Law and Government of the Grand River Iroquios* (New York: The Viking Fund, Inc.).

PARKER, A. C.
1909. *Secret Medicine Societies of the Seneca* (American Anthropologist, n.s., vol. 11, pp. 161–185, Lancaster).
1909a. *Snow-Snake as Played by the Seneca-Iroquois* (American Anthropologist, n.s., vol. 11, pp. 250–256, Lancaster).
1910. *Iroquois Uses of Maize and Other Food Plants* (New York State Museum Bulletin, no. 144, Albany).
1912. *Certain Iroquois Tree Myths and Symbols* (American Anthropologist, n.s., vol. 14, pp. 608–620, Lancaster).
1913. *The Code of Handsome Lake, the Seneca Prophet* (New York State Museum Bulletin, no. 163, Albany).
1916. *The Constitution of the Five Nations* (New York State Museum Bulletin, no. 184, Albany).
1918. *The Constitution of the Five Nations: A Reply* (American Anthropologist, n.s., vol. 20, pp. 120–124, Lancaster).
1919. *The Life of General Ely S. Parker* (Publications of the Buffalo Historical Society, vol. 23, Buffalo).
1923. *Seneca Myths and Folk-Tales* (Publications of the Buffalo Historical Society, vol. 27, Buffalo).

PARKMAN, F.
1867. *The Jesuits in North America* (part 2 of "France and England in North America," Boston: Little, Brown and Company).

QUAIN, B. H.
1937. *The Iroquois* (in "Cooperation and Competition among Primitive Peoples," Margaret Mead, editor, New York: McGraw-Hill Book Company).

RANDLE, MARTHA CHAMPION
1951. *Iroquois Women, Then and Now* (in "Symposium on Local Diversity in Iroquois Culture," W. F. Fenton, editor, Bureau of American Ethnology Bulletin, no. 149, 167–180, Washington).
1953. *The Waugh Collection of Iroquois Folktales* (Proceedings of the American Philosophical Society, vol. 97, pp. 611–633, Philadelphia).

REDFIELD, R., R. LINTON, AND M. J. HERSKOVITS
1936. *Memorandum on the Study of Acculturation* (American Anthropologist, n.s., vol. 38, pp. 149–152, Menasha).

RIOUX, M.
1951. *Medicine and Magic among the Iroquois* (Journal of the Washington Academy of Sciences, vol. 41, pp. 152–158, Menasha).
1952. *Relations between Religion and Government among the Longhouse Iroquois of Grand River, Ontario* (Annual Report of the National Museum of Canada, Bulletin no. 126, pp. 94–98, Ottawa).

RITZENTHALER, R. E.

306

1941. *The Wisconsin Oneida Wake* (Wisconsin Archaeologist, n.s., vol. 22, pp. 1–2, Milwaukee).

1950. *The Oneida Indians of Wisconsin* (Bulletin of the Public Museum of the City of Milwaukee, vol. 19, pp. 1–52, Milwaukee).

1953. *Chippewa Preoccupation with Health* (Bulletin of the Public Museum of the City of Milwaukee, vol. 19, no. 4, Milwaukee).

SAPIR, EDWARD

1916. *Time Perspective in Aboriginal American Culture* (Canada, Department of Mines, Geological Survey, Memoir 90, Anthropological Series, no. 13, Ottawa).

1917. *Do We Need a "Superorganic"?* (American Anthropologist, n.s., vol. 19, pp. 441–447, Lancaster).

1921. *Language: An Introduction to the Study of Speech* (New York: Harcourt, Brace, and Company).

1924. *Culture, Genuine and Spurious* (American Journal of Sociology, vol. 29, pp. 401–430, Menasha).

1927. *The Unconscious Patterning of Behavior in Society* (in "The Unconscious: A Symposium," S. Dummer, editor, New York: Knopf).

SCHOOLCRAFT, H. H.

1847. *Notes on the Iroquois* (Albany: Erastus H. Pease and Company).

SCOTT, DUNCAN C.

1912. *Traditional History of the Confederacy of the Six Nations* (Proceedings and Transactions of the Royal Society of Canada, third series, vol. 5, pp. 195–246, Ottawa).

SEAVER, JAMES EVERETT

1932. *A Narrative of the Life of Mary Jamison, the White Woman of the Genesee* (New York: American Scenic and Historical Preservation Society).

SNYDERMAN, GEORGE S.

1948. *Behind the Tree of Peace, A Sociological Analysis of Iroquois Warfare* (Bulletin of the Society for Pennsylvania Archaeology, vol. 18, nos. 3–4, Philadelphia).

1951. *Concepts of Land Ownership among the Iroquois and Their Neighbors* (in "Symposium on Local Diversity in Iroquois Culture," W. F. Fenton, editor, Bureau of American Ethnology Bulletin, no. 149, Washington).

SPECK, F. G.

1915. *The Family Hunting Band as the Basis of Algonkian Social Organization* (American Anthropologist, n.s., vol. 17, pp. 289–305, Lancaster).

1915a. *The Eastern Algonkian Wabanaki Confederacy* (American Anthropologist, n.s., vol. 17, pp. 492–508, Lancaster).

1918. *Kinship Terms and the Family Band among the Northeastern Algonkian* (American Anthropologist, n.s., vol. 20, pp. 143–161, Lancaster).

1923. *Algonkian Influence upon Iroquois Social Organization* (American Anthropologist, n.s. vol. 25, pp. 219–227, Menasha).

1931. *A Study of the Delaware Big House Ceremony* (Publications of the Pennsylvania Historical Commission, vol. 2, Harrisburg).

1935. *Naskapi* (Norman, Oklahoma: University of Oklahoma Press).

1940. *Penobscot Man* (Philadelphia: University of Pennsylvania Press).

1942. *The Tutelo Spirit Adoption Ceremony, Reclothing the Living in the Name of the Dead* (Publications of the Pennsylvania Historical Commission, Philadelphia).

1945. *The Iroquois, A Study on Cultural Evolution* (Bulletin of the Cranbrook Institute of Science, no. 23, Bloomfield Hills, Michigan).

1949. *Midwinter Rites of the Cayuga Long House* (Philadelphia: University of Pennsylvania Press).

1949a. *How the Dew Eagle Society of the Allegany Seneca Cured Gahehdagowa (F. G. S.)* (Primitive Man, vol. 22, pp. 39–59, Washington).

SPIER, LESLIE

1935. *The Prophet Dance of the Northwest and Its Derivatives: The Sources of the Ghost Dance* (General Series in Anthropology, no. 1, pp. 1–74, Menasha).

STITES, SARA HENY

1905. *Economics of the Iroquois* (Lancaster, Pennsylvania: New Era Printing Company).

STONE, W. L.

1838. *Life of Joseph Brant* (2 vols., New York: Alexander V. Blake).

THWAITES, REUBEN GOLD, EDITOR

1896–1901. *The Jesuit Relations and Allied Documents. Travels and Explorations of the Jesuit Missionaries in New France, 1610–1791* (73 vols., Cleveland: The Burrows Brothers Company).

TITIEV, MISCHA

1944. *Old Oraibi: A Study of the Hopi Indians of Third Mesa* (Papers of the Peabody Museum of American Archaeology and Ethnology, vol. 22, Cambridge).

VOGET, FRED

1951. *Acculturation at Caughnawaga: A Note on the Native-modified Group* (American Anthropologist, n.s., vol. 53, pp. 220–231, Menasha).

1953. *Kinship Changes at Caughnawaga* (American Anthropologist, n.s., vol. 55, pp. 385–394, Menasha).

WALLACE, A. F. C.

1949. *The Tuscaroras: Sixth Nation of the Iroquois Confederation* (Proceedings of the American Philosophical Society, vol. 93, pp. 159–165, Philadelphia).

1951. *Some Psychological Determinants of Culture Change in an Iroquoian Community* (in "Symposium on Local Diversity in Iroquois Culture," W. F. Fenton, editor, Bureau of American Ethnology Bulletin, no. 149, pp. 55–76, Washington).

1956. *Revitalization Movements* (American Anthropologist, n.s., vol. 58, pp. 264–281, Menasha).

WALLACE, PAUL

1946. *The White Roots of Peace* (Philadelphia: University of Pennsylvania Press).

WAUGH, F. W.

1913. *On Work in Material Culture of the Iroquois* (Summary Report of the Canadian Geological Survey, Department of Mines, no. 26, pp. 476–480, Ottawa).

1916. *Iroquois Foods and Food Preparation* (Canada, Department of Mines, Geological Survey, Memoir no. 86, Anthropological Series, no. 12, Ottawa).

WILSON, EDMUND

1959, 1960. *Apologies to the Iroquois* (New York: Farrar, Strauss and Cadahy).

WITTHOFT, J.

1946. *Cayuga Midwinter Festival* (New York Folklore Quarterly, vol. 2, pp. 24–39, Ithaca).

1951. *Iroquois Archaeology at the Mid-Century* (Proceedings of the American Philosophical Society, vol. 95, pp. 311–321, Philadelphia).

WITTHOFT, J., AND W. S. HADLOCK

1946. *Cherokee-Iroquois Little People* (Journal of American Folk-Lore, vol. 59, pp. 413–422, Boston and New York).

WRAXALL, PETER

1915. *An Abridgement of the Indian Affairs . . . in the Colony of New York, 1678–1751* (edited, with an introduction, by C. H. McIlwain, Cambridge: Harvard University Press).

INDEX

I would like to thank Ms. Sheila Staats of the Woodland Cultural Centre for suggesting the addition of an index and for generously permitting me to incorporate her index into mine.